BUILDERS
of the
AMERICAN
DREAM

BUILDERS
of the
AMERICAN
DREAM

James K. Fitzpatrick

SH PRESS
HARRISON, NEW YORK

To my mother,
MARGARET BURKE FITZPATRICK,
and to the memory of my father,
CORNELIUS MICHAEL FITZPATRICK,
for a childhood open to
the best of American dreams

Contents

Introduction

Myth." To most Americans it is a term of criticism, an allegation of fraud, deceit, and sham. When used in reference to an individual, it usually implies unsubstantiated claims of talent and worth. Certainly no athlete or entertainer would relish hearing his reputation called a "myth" by an American newsman.

This interpretation of the word, however, is of recent origin as history measures time. In a way it is an American phenomenon, although like most experiences in our modern world of instant global communications, it has spread to Europe as well. But in Europe myth still has another meaning, familiar even to those who have been given only the bare bones of a formal education. Indeed, those who have not gone on to higher education tend to cherish the old myths most of all—men and women who have learned the history of their people from the tall tales of their elders in the shady alcoves of Mediterranean piazzas, or round the fires in Scandinavian villages, or in the fields of British and Irish farms, rather than from film spectaculars prepared in New York, Los Angeles, or London. These

9

people think of Hercules, Galahad, El Cid, Cuchulainn, Thor, Jason, and Ulysses, not of con men, schemers, and ignorant superstition, when they hear the word myth.

Why the more skeptical American reaction? On one level the answer is obvious. We do not "need" myths the way the Europeans did. The great myths were , to a large extent, an attempt to explain to society its origins and historical growth—events shrouded in the mists of time. It is difficult for us who live in the so-called historical period—the time since written records have been kept and preserved—to imagine what it must have been like for young Greeks, Romans, or Northern tribesmen coming of age in the centuries before the birth of Christ. These young people knew that they were members of a society with a way of life separate and distinct from that of "other" peoples (the enemy in most cases); that there was a music, language, poetry, and architecture all their own, unlike that of the outsiders; that the magnificent temples and arenas or intricately carved stone and wooden religious shrines that adorned their cities and villages had been built by their forefathers. But who were their forefathers? When and where did it all start? This Rome? This Troy? This Sparta? Did their people always live on these hills or in these forests? Why did outsiders behave so strangely and crudely in comparison to their own people? (We must imagine that there were also some who began to ask that question the other way round.) What is life? And death? There were no libraries with history books that answered these questions. They could not read of a Boston Tea Party or a Battle of Bunker Hill, a Patrick Henry, a Declaration of Independence, a George Washington.

Myths took the place of the history books. The exact moment when a myth was born is of course buried in the same mists as the historical occurrence the myth was designed to explain. But myths *were* of ancient origin—the Greek and Roman youths knew that. And if they contained elements difficult to accept as fact, at least they brought one's mind back through time for a closer look at "how it all began." Europeans (and recall, most Americans are of European origin if they trace their lineage far enough back) today have not lost that need. Archaeologists and anthropologists and our modern scientific approach to learning have pushed the frontiers of knowledge far enough back to make us doubt mythology. But if they make it hard for us any longer to believe that Atlas holds the earth on his shoulders or

10

that there are islands in the Aegean populated by one-eyed giants called Cyclops, they have not, alternatively, given us a genuinely clear picture of the early history (before the fifth century B.C.) of the people of Europe. How did we go from those apelike cavemen we see pictured in our history books to the people who built temples and arenas? If there was no Jason or Odin at the beginning—what was there? We do not know.

But myths did more than explain historical origins. They served as teaching agents too, a means by which early societies established, and then extended to the young, notions of right and wrong, honor and shame. Behavior for which the mythological heroes received the favor of the gods provided a model for the citizens of the social order; that for which they met with catastrophe gave warning. Far beyond the years when the advances of history and science (and common sense) destroyed the believability of myths they were retold for this purpose. An Englishman reading to his young son the legends of Camelot cares little if they ever find the remains of the Round Table somewhere in Wales. If his curious child, astounded by the bravery of Lancelot or Galahad, asks: "Are these stories true, Father?" he will answer confidently and uncompromisingly: "Some people say so."

In a sense, then, whether the myths are true is irrelevant. They are "truer" than mere factual accounts, since they represent the high principles and moral convictions of an entire culture—the ultimate realities held by the society down through the ages—the eternal truths. The yearning to do great deeds like those of the heroes is the important point; the fact that the people who held the myths wanted such actions to be practiced and imitated by their fellow citizens, most especially their young.

Examples abound. They are the essence of myth. They do not endure by accident, but rather because they express—they are —the moral imagination of the societies and cultures that hold them dear. Everyone knows the names, but to those who preserved the memories it was the lesson—the moral—of the stories that was the key.

Prometheus. One of the Titans, a race of giants said by the Greeks to have inhabited the world before the creation of man. Not only did Prometheus make man from the stuff of the earth, kneading the dust with water and fashioning it into a shape comparable to his own, but he was determined to make this

11

creature different from the animals that inhabited the earth. He would make man a creature like the gods. Prometheus rode his chariot into the domain of the gods themselves, where he touched his torch to the sun; and then he brought this creative and destructive power back to earth to be used by man. With it, man could become an innovative godlike creature, able to fashion tools for warfare and for cultivating the soil, to build homes, to light the night, to warm himself in protection against the killing winters. The spark of the divine gave man the potential to refashion his existence in an approximation of the gods. It also gave him the power to create incalculable horror. Whatever man would be from that day forward, he would not be just an animal. He could be a creature in the image and likeness of the gods or a creature wicked and perverse beyond the instinctive level of animals. Since Prometheus, man has never again been merely an animal striving for food, shelter, and warmth, seeking a place to sleep for the night. Human history, for good or for evil, has been high drama. Those raised on the story of Prometheus would never forget that.

Hercules. Americans know this name in good part through the splashy Hollywood versions of his adventures (and the script writers certainly let poetic license get the better of them in these epics). But even before Hercules (the son of Jupiter and a human mother) received the Hollywood treatment, his name was familiar to many as a synonym for stupendous accomplishments. And Americans far in the future will be talking, too, of "Herculean tasks" and athletes with the "strength of Hercules" long after the movies have been relegated to the dusty back shelves in the studio warehouses. The Twelve Labors of Hercules, ordained as a test by the gods, have captured readers' imaginations since they first were recorded in ancient Greece: his battle against the ferocious Nemean lion; his sword-slashing attack against the giant nine-headed reptile, the Hydra; his diverting of the rivers Alpheus and Peneus to clean the stables of King Augeas (the proverbial Augean stables); his battles with dragons and giants; his willingness to take the place of Atlas (who had been condemned by the gods to bear the weight of the pillars of the heavens on his shoulders) while Atlas sought the golden apples of the Hesperides—these are but a few of the most memorable adventures. Why so memorable? Because they make such great yarns; but also because they give to all who hear them a great hero to admire: the knight; the cowboy;

the brave, undaunted, persevering, upright, bold man of action who proves that the great and honorable deed can—and must —be attempted in the face of overwhelming odds.

Pandora. Of course the Greeks warned of foolhardy behavior too, of prideful refusal to comply with the directives present in the order of the universe. Pandora was the first woman, according to myth. Lovingly endowed by the gods with the best of their attributes—from Venus, beauty; from Apollo, an ability with music, etc.—she was intended to live a life of fulfillment and contentment. But irresponsible curiosity led her to violate the secret chambers of her host Epimetheus, the Titan, and to open the box that loosed the scourges of human existence— sickness, envy, spite, jealousy, hatred, plagues. By acting against divine law she reaped divine retribution. Those are the stakes in life. One's behavior matters.

Not surprisingly, Norse mythology too created dramatic heroes like those of Greece and Rome. Societies around the globe have generally agreed that man, theoretically, should be honorable, creative, and true. But the Eddas, the Norse myths, added an element that some, in recent years, have branded as cruel and savage. The case has been pressed, in fact, that the Norse gods created an atmosphere in Germany that led to Hitlerism, the glorification of combat and the splendor of the clash of arms—the adulation of the violent and destructive warrior found in the legends of Odin, Thor, and Siegfried. The adventures of Thor, especially, are chock full of encounters with giants, whose skulls Thor usually smashes to pieces with his mighty hammer, a hammer that returns of its own accord after he has thrown it. Indeed Valhalla, the place of highest honor in Asgard, the heaven of the Norse gods, is reserved for those who die with sword in hand. In Valhalla, Odin's own castle, those slain in combat—and those alone—feast heartily on succulent roast boar and staggering draughts of the finest wine.

It is not too far-fetched to conclude that children raised with such gods as storybook heroes could develop, as adults, the militarist vigor that rocked the world in this century's two great World Wars (a fact that not even Germany's greatest apologists have ever denied). It is easy to blame German and Norse folklore for German militarism; too easy. That same military vigor, when displayed by our own soldiers or those of our allies in pursuit of causes we hold dear, wins our highest awards and admiration. American soldiers at the Battle of the Bulge; the

13

French resistance to Hitler; Winston Churchill standing before the British Parliament, summoning up the memory of those who had fallen in defense of the British Empire, in order to fire the British defense against the coming German invasion; Israeli soldiers laughing and singing atop captured Arab tanks on their victorious march home from the firing lines—these we hold in high esteem. The lessons taught through the tales of Odin and Thor are not a Norse idiosyncrasy. Enshrined in those Germanic gods are emotions shared by all who feel that war is going to remain part of the world's future—like it or not.

Similar messages shine as clearly from such stories as the French legends of Charlemagne and his gallant knight Roland, the Spanish warrior El Cid who led the wars against Moslem rule in Spain, the Slavic epics of Michael Strogoff, Irish tales of Finn McCumhail, and the time-worn English yarns of King Arthur, Robin Hood, and Richard the Lion-Hearted on the Third Crusade.

Americans, because of heir European roots, share much of this literary heritage. Or, at least we used to when educational institutions in America made a more conscious effort to maintain such memories from the Old World. Nowadays, even America's native myths are given little time or attention because of the newer objective of "educating for modern living."

America's native myths? But there aren't any, and isn't that the whole point? That America's origins lie within a historical period clearly recorded for posterity. That we need no tall tales to explain it.

True—our curiosity about our past does not require a mythological explanation. But Americans have not been freed from that other social need satisfied by myth: the national character is built and transmitted from one generation to the next by tall tales, legends, and folklore.

There have grown up in America certain fictitious characters so beyond belief that, at first glance, they appear to be the American counterparts of Hercules and Prometheus. Paul Bunyan and his blue ox Babe; Pecos Bill riding cyclones across Texas; John Henry, the steel-driving man; Johnny Appleseed. But reflection on these characters makes clear that they are closer to fairy tale than myth; they are more American versions of the steadfast tin soldier or Hansel and Gretel than Achilles. They do not embody the moral imagination of our people; certainly not as much as do the stories of the careers of certain

14

revered real-life heroes. Which is not unique. While there probably was no Hercules, certainly not one capable of the Twelve Labors, there *was* a King Richard, a Robin Hood, a Charlemagne. What is different about the American versions is a greater concern for differentiating the tall tales from the realm of historical occurrence. This is not because of our greater honesty, but because our heroes became heroes within the historical period when the scientific attitude made tales of magical powers and superhuman strength largely unacceptable to the audience.

But the requirements of accuracy little hindered the development of an American "mythology." The birth and growth of a new nation with a wild and open frontier, the experience of wars both civil and foreign, the dazzling breakthrough of science in an industrial age, provided a setting in which men of daring and genius assumed heroic proportions. They were the winners, the champions, those who succeeded at the tasks Americans agreed had to be done; and with a style, often a nobility and grace, that Americans wished was their own. More important for our theme, they did it in a way Americans would have their children emulate. Their names became part of the vocabulary of our people. Fathers told and retold the stories around the hearth, school systems included their exploits as part of the curriculum, and the writers of popular literature and the creators of mass entertainment frequently found in their careers themes that touched the nerve endings of our people. In the mid-years of the twentieth century Americans found themselves deluged with books and movies that celebrated the lives of these giants of the past.

Interestingly, one can see this process—in reverse—in recent years. We are all aware that the 1960s and early 1970s were troubled times for America. Americans undertook a deep and thorough reconsideration of their identity and place in the world. It continues to this day. Many Americans developed grave doubts about our economic system, our Christian religious roots, the treatment of minorities within our borders, and the values we strove to secure through our foreign policy and the application of military force. For many, the result was a deep disillusionment. Some even took to movements that preached a revolutionary Marxism.

During these years a new kind of movie and popular fiction became evident, with a new breed of hero (called an antihero)

15

reflecting the new, lower opinion of the American historical development. Historical figures once revered and idealized by Hollywood became objects of cutting satire in an exposé format. Buffalo Bill was portrayed by Paul Newman as a charlatan and self-centered rogue. Gore Vidal wrote historical fiction—*Burr* and *1876*—designed to show a seamy underside to America's political past. *Serpico* informed us that metropolitan police departments were riddled with corruption from the top down. Radio and television talk shows discussed calmly the possibility that the FBI and the CIA had conspired to kill President Kennedy. Television offered its viewers a steady diet of sadistic saddle-tramp cowboys, maniacal generals, bribe-taking politicians, hypocritical priests and ministers, lecherous small-town merchants, and racist suburbanites. More recently, a spate of books and movies and television shows—*The Way We Were* starring Barbra Streisand, *Scoundrel Time* by Lillian Hellman, *Tailgunner Joe, The Front* starring Woody Allen—have tried to turn the complex and difficult "McCarthy Era" into a clear-cut morality play. The great question of that period—whether or not there were Communist sympathizers working to help Russia expand its world influence after World War II—is treated as melodrama. The anti-Communists searching out spies are inevitably portrayed as sneering, narrow-minded, hate-filled enemies of democracy. Those involved with groups sympathetic to Communism invariably are cast as idealistic and sensitive humanists. In fact, that idealism and sensitivity is pictured as the *cause* of the anti-Communist suspicion. No effort is made to recreate in a dramatic context the reasons why some suspected an unhealthy pro-Communist presence in the United States in those years. No effort is made to inform modern readers or viewers of the fact that there *were* people in America then, filled with a contempt for our country and its political, religious, and economic systems, who *were* acting in sympathy for the Soviet Union and its global ambitions. These books and movies do admit, however, that there were people in our country attracted to Soviet policies (something that was not admitted at the time—back then anti-Communists were attacked for seeing Communists "under every bed" when there were none); but they seek to show us that pro-Communist leanings or excesses are the result of idealism. But is any excuse made for possible anti-Communist excesses? No. We are told that anti-Communism is hateful and ugly. These are morality plays, in

16

other words, where the message takes precedence over a concern for truth.

The point is not whether these images reflect the truth more accurately than the brave and virtuous Gary Cooper, Robert Young, and Tyrone Power-type heroes of old. Probably the truth lies somewhere in between. What is of primary interest is the motivation behind the contrasting media presentations. John Ford, perhaps the best known of the Hollywood image makers of old, a director who turned out dozens of westerns and cavalry adventures, was once asked if he expended great efforts to insure historical accuracy in his films. His answer?

"I'm more interested in the way it *should* have been."

Ford was an unabashed patriot. He loved the America he knew in the middle years of the twentieth century, and sought to enshrine the character traits and virtues of his people in his films; to show the behavior that made America what it was when America was at her best (from an American viewpoint). Moderns, fearful and condemnatory of the America they dwell in—what they call the post-Vietnam and post-Watergate atmosphere—seek to condemn in a dramatic context the lives and times of the people who made America what it was. They hope that by doing so they will be able to change America's view of herself—to make us different in the future. In fact, the villains of the past—Bonnie and Clyde, for example—have become the heroes. Conmen, hustlers, hookers, desperadoes, dope pushers, marauding Indians become the "victims" of a corrupt and vicious society. It is still a myth-making process, but with different values championed.

In the chapters that follow, Americans from different times and different fields who have risen in the esteem of their fellow countrymen will be examined—to find out *why*. The cast of characters is neither complete nor is it based on an individual's true contribution to America's national growth. Some very good and important people—scientists, members of minority groups, clergymen, women, etc.—have not been included. That should not be considered a slight. The topic is who *has* become an American "myth"—not who *should* have. Certainly it could be argued that George Washington Carver and Susan B. Anthony, to take two obvious examples, did far more for America than Daniel Boone and Babe Ruth. But they did not capture the public imagination in quite the same dramatic way. We seek to find out why.

17

It is hoped this book may demonstrate that the American historical experience is a noble and good one, one that can be projected into a just and virtuous future. Those already convinced will see anew in these giants what the Romans called their *pietas:* the national vision of the good man and the good life. It is hoped as well that those who demand a radically new vision of life for America will profit from a re-examination of exactly what it was that made America the kind of country it is today; that they will be able to find what it is that they want changed.

Are all the stories included in this volume true? Well, none that is known to be false or exaggerated or of doubtful authenticity has been included, but it just could be that legend has taken over from fact in certain cases. Has the bad as well as the good been told? Not in most cases.

But if the reader has grasped the point so far, it should be clear that these qualifications are not really of crucial importance. Americans have told and retold these stories, making them part of our common consciousness, blotting out through a kind of collective amnesia much of what they didn't want themselves or their children to know. Yet we are still interested in the *why* if we would get some insight into the American mind at work. The way we respond to what we see in our past may very well determine how we will act in the last quarter of this century.

Daniel Boone

1

Daniel Boone
Frontier Hero

I t is not immediately obvious why Daniel Boone should be a name known to almost all Americans. He certainly was not the only frontiersman to live through hair-raising close calls with death or to endure successfully the hardships of frontier life. Those who know the history of the American frontier often argue—and convincingly—that George Rogers Clark (memorialized in Kenneth Roberts' beloved saga of early America, *Northwest Passage*) did more to quell the Indian opposition to white settlement in the lands between the Ohio and the Mississippi; that Simon Kenton had even more bone-chilling adventures and displayed a taste that Boone never did for hand-to-hand battle with the Shawnee, Cherokee, and Wyandot; and that it was, after all, a man called John Finley who first dared to enter the "dark and bloody ground" of Kentucky, not Boone. Why, then, was it Boone whose body was brought back from the place where he died in Missouri, by Kentucky state officials, for a funeral in which the hearse was drawn by four white stallions, the oration was delivered by the state attorney general, and the Kentucky militia served as an honor guard while taps was being played by an army bugler? All this after a cast had been made of his skull? What was it about this man that led Stewart Edward White, his biographer, to describe Boone as he did in the 1920s:

> He was one of the many great Indian fighters of his time: lived for years with his rifle and tomahawk next his hand: lost brothers and sons under the scalping knife. He was a master of woodcraft, able to find his way hundreds of miles through unbroken forests, able to maintain himself alone not merely for a day or a week but for a year or more without other resources than his rifle, his tomahawk, and his knife; and this in the face of the most wily of foes. He was muscular and strong and enduring; victor in many a hand-to-hand combat, conqueror of farms cut from the forest; performer of long journeys afoot at speed that would seem incredible to a college athlete. He was a dead shot with the rifle, an expert hunter of game . . . reverent in the belief that he was ordained by God to open the wilderness. He was brave with a courage remarkable for its calmness and serenity . . . Boone never cherished rancour against the Indian so that as honourable antagonists they always met, both in peace and war. He was trustworthy, so that when wilderness missions of great responsibility were undertaken, he was almost invariably the one called. He was loyal to the last drop of his blood . . . ever ready to help others . . . Gentle, kindly, modest, peace-loving, absolutely fearless, a master of Indian warfare, a mighty hunter, strong as a bear and active as a panther . . .

Such praise came Boone's way, for one thing, simply because Boone had more, and more attentive, biographers than other men of the time. He had become a legend by the time he reached old age, and more than a few writers made the journey to Missouri to get first-hand accounts of his fabulous career—which they then brought back East and turned into bestselling books. But that begs the question. Why was it Boone that they pursued with such determination and enthusiasm, and not others? The East Coast publishers in search of profit certainly helped spread the Boone legends, but they did not invent them.

His looks might have had something to do with it. People like their folk heroes to look the part. Modern athletes often complain that fame and fortune come only to those who look "right" in the glossy commercials in the sports magazines. The pictures we have of Boone were painted when he was rather elderly, but they show a lean and muscular man with clean and regular features—"aristocratic lines" as the saying goes—and a headful of gently curling hair. Contemporary accounts tell us he was about six feet tall and blessed with a well-proportioned, graceful, athletic body. But the pictures do not show a man with the face of a movie star. No, it was not his looks alone that led some to call him "striking" and "bold" in appearance. His reputation had more to do with it. And that reputation, as White's account makes clear, was based on a sense of fairness and justice as well as bravery; on compassion as well as consummate skill with the knife, tomahawk, and Kentucky long rifle; on understanding and genuine respect for the Indian and his way of life (and a willingness to co-exist with it) as well as on ferocity and ingenuity in battle in the Indian wars. Boone had a sense of responsibility and a love of family as well as a yearning for adventure; an understanding of the need for justice and civil standards of behavior as well as a longing for the ultimate unchecked individualism of a woodsman's life.

Boyhood on the Frontier

The times in which Boone lived and blazed his way into the national consciousness were dramatically unlike our own. As you drive the interstate highways into Louisville and Knoxville today, seeing the tall glass buildings, the smokestacks, telephone poles, gas stations, and roadside restaurants, it is difficult to believe that the land beneath the asphalt is the land that the Indians called the "dark and bloody ground" because of the fierce battles fought by one tribe against the other within its borders. It was a land of mystery known to the colonial whites only through tales told by friendly Indians living along the Atlantic seacoast. Moderns know more about the surface of the moon or Mars than the residents of the 13 colonies did about that wilderness in the mid-1700s. As Judge Marshall phrased it so well at the time: "The country beyond the Cumberland mountains still appeared to the people of Virginia almost as obscure and doubtful as America itself to the people of Europe before the voyage of Columbus. A country there was—of this

23

none could doubt; but whether land or water, mountain or plain, fertility or barrenness predominated; whether inhabited by men or beasts, or both, or neither, they knew not."

But the colonials, so far, had found the new world rich with fertile lands and abundant with game and there was no reason to believe that it would be any different farther West. The West was a constant lure, especially to the hardy and adventurous like Boone, a chance for the penniless and obscure to hew from the forests a life not unlike that lived by the nobility of Europe. And it was there for the taking. If a man was willing to endure hardships and danger and pour his sweat and skill into the soil, a life of plenty (although not usually a life of ease) could be his. There was no excuse for failure.

It should be noted in passing that this frontier experience and our shared memory of it explain much of the American resistance to the idea of socialism, the welfare state, and large government and business bureaucracies in general. The legacy of a society where individual hard work, inventiveness, and a wise husbanding of resources would pay off proportionately in material well-being—a way of life that promises its rewards to those who earn them rather than to those who play the system, those with connections in high places, schemers, wheeler-dealers, and bureaucratic meddlers—is one that Americans, understandably, show a reluctance to leave behind (even if our modern industrialized world demands a more managed and collectivized way of life, which is, of course, an open question).

Boone's early years were spent in a typical settlement on the border of the Kentucky wilderness, the valley of the Yadkin River in the colony of North Carolina. We have little record of these years, but if the boy was the father of the man, the yearning to see what lay beyond the next mountain, so pronounced in the adult Boone, was if anything even stronger in the boy. The forests and streams around the Yadkin must have offered excitement enough for a few years, though. Life in those cabins near the dark forests was arduous and filled with danger. Roving bands of Indians frequented the wooded areas near the settlements and, although during Boone's boyhood peace treaties had been secured with neighboring tribes, sporadic attacks by hunting parties were not unheard-of. True tales of Indian cruelty were plentiful: of cabins burned to the ground; men killed and scalped; babies grabbed by their feet, their heads bashed against trees; women carried away and tortured. Even

24

today, many people find the dark stretches of forest in modern state parks menacing and eerie as they gather round their electrically lit campers. It is easy to imagine the vast and unexplored expanse of woodland mysteriously stretching, for all the colonials knew, all the way to the Pacific, populated by unknown tribes of Indians and wild beasts unlike any seen elsewhere in the world.

Of course Boone could not spend all his time hunting, fishing, trapping, and exploring the neighboring forests. Like other boys of the area he had to assist in the family chores: driving teams of oxen through the fields, felling trees, cutting timber, searching out berries and nuts, tapping maple trees and boiling down the sap into syrup. But there was more time for hunting and developing the skills of a woodsman than a modern might think. Hunting was not a sport to the men of the time (although certainly most of them seemed to love it as much as modern sportsmen), but a skill that required mastering. Without it, life on the frontier would be near to impossible. Hunters provided the meat for the family table. The days when beef would be raised in huge quantities on Western ranches, butchered in the Middle West, and distributed by refrigerated car throughout the country were still far in the future.

As soon as a boy could manage to handle the long single-shot rifles of the time, he was taught how to move quietly over the thick carpet of browned leaves on the forest floor in search of game: deer, grouse, squirrel, and wild turkey. He learned how to position himself upwind along deer trails or at salt licks, and to follow a trail deep into the wilderness (and to find his way back of course!). He learned to differentiate among the sounds of the forest, the routine noises from those that signaled danger: the brushing of branches in the wind; the soft, padded step of the lynx (an animal all but unknown on most of the East Coast these days); the quick step of Indian moccasins trotting briskly and gracefully along forest trails; the boisterous crash of a black bear through the underbrush. The wild nuts—hickory, beechnuts, butternuts, walnuts—and berries that a man can live on for months on end became as familiar as streetlights to a modern citydweller.

But the rifle was not just for food—and everyone knew that. It was as much for defense against Indians, and against the white outlaws and brigands who thrived in the lawless atmosphere of frontier America (whose cruel behavior toward the

Indians did much to make the Indian an enemy of the white settler). A boy had to learn to load his rifle quickly as well as to shoot accurately, for if there would be time for another shot later in the day if you missed a buck, a two-legged target would not likely give you a second chance. And handling those muzzle-loaders was no easy chore.

Powder had to be measured, usually half the weight of the bullet, while being poured from the shaved and shaped animal's horn where it was stored; then poured down the long barrel. A bullet wrapped in a greased linen patch was dropped on top of the powder and "rammed" down with a long rod until it sat gently but firmly and fully on the powder. Then more powder was placed as a primer on a small pan next to the flintlock, where it would be ignited as the hammer struck the flint, igniting in turn the charge of powder at the end of the barrel and sending the patched ball on its way. The greased patch protected the barrel of the rifle, made a seal that prevented gas from seeping into the barrel ahead of the bullet and also took the "rifling" of the barrel, giving the ball a spin to keep it on course. The weapon was primitive by comparison with modern firearms, obviously, but in the hands of a skilled and practiced marksman it was a deadly weapon.

Boone, like most people of the time, married young and set upon the task of building a homestead with his new wife, Rebecca, in the same Yadkin valley where he was raised. To support himself he hunted and scouted, as well as raising crops on his modest farm. But the land beyond the Cumberland Gap beckoned, where the Shawnee from the north and the Cherokee from the south followed the famed Warriors' Path to hunt and trap. A man could carve out his future in that "Kaintuck," and when a peddler named Finley drew up to the Boones' cabin door in 1769 and told stories of a land he had seen with deer clustered thick at every salt lick, buffalo herds so dense and numerous that they made the ground thunder as they passed, ducks and geese abundant enough for a man to catch them by hand, Daniel's imagination was fired. Success for men of Boone's stripe came to those willing to reach out for it—even into the wilderness of Kentucky—not to those who sat back and waited. And even if the expedition Finley proposed failed to turn a profit, there would be a chance to explore and hunt in a new land, Boone's greatest loves.

It is not certain whether Boone had anything in mind like the later settlement that came to be called Boonesborough, or just a hunting and trapping trip for profit, but an excursion into Kentucky was planned, and with it the stage was set for the years of remarkable wilderness adventures that captured America's attention.

Indian Fighter

As we know, most of Boone's adventures center on his life as an Indian fighter—a role that many find distasteful to defend today when so many books, movies, and television shows seek to expose the exploitation and abuse of the American Indian; presumably by men like Boone. It is, of course, right and just for America to face up to the distortion of the character of the Indian in some movies and popular mass fiction of a few decades back. To be honest, though, a review of the films of the 1940s and 50s, for example, does not at all confirm the charge that is leveled so often of late: that Americans were trained to think that "the only good Indian is a dead Indian." Quite the contrary. But the attention given to the Indians in the late 1960s and early 1970s has forced Americans to think more deeply than was their custom about the tragedy—and perhaps the deliberate injustice—that befell the American Indian upon the opening of the American frontier. Some of the attention, undoubtedly, has been motivated more by an ideological desire to point out another blemish on the American record than by a concern for the Indian. There are those, for instance, who go so far as to argue that if America had been socialist the Indian wars would never have occurred. But the overall effect of the spate of books and movies that could be labeled "pro-Indian" has been to awaken an American sensitivity to the way of life lost by the Indian as a result of the westward march of industrialized America.

However, a curious reversal of the narrow-minded "the only good Indian is a dead Indian" point of view has developed. It could be called "the only good frontiersman is a dead frontiersman" school of thought. And it is that frame of mind that has led to the discomfort many feel at the memory of men like Boone: a view of early American history that imagines a gentle and generous race living in harmony with God and each other on lands bequeathed to them by the Creator at the beginning

27

of time, until a white race of wild-eyed, greedy cutthroats crossed the Atlantic for the express purpose of taking their lands and committing genocide upon them. Such a view, if it needs be said, is distortion.

For one thing, the Indians were hardly a gentle and introspective pastoral people. Most of the eastern tribes known to Boone were fierce and cruel. That is not said in criticism. The male Indian was proud—and trained to be proud from infancy—of his role as warrior and hunter. The capacity to endure hardship and pain and artfully to inflict them on the enemy was taught to Indian boys in preparation for the wilderness life they lived; a life that would include frequent warfare with neighboring tribes. It was the Indians, remember, who gave the name "dark and bloody ground" to Kentucky in recognition of the amount of blood they had spilled there. Torture was used against their captives with a cold and deliberate precision. The tribes expected it of each other, and those capable of enduring it stoically were held in high esteem. One of the Indian folk tales favored by the Ohio Valley tribes, repeated in all the white settlements at the time, tells of the warrior who, after hours of torture, scoffed at his captors' skills. He took their instruments of torture to show them some new methods, demonstrating the superior techniques on his own body. Some of the mentionable tortures commonly used at the time? Tearing fingernails from their sockets, biting off fingers at the knuckle joints, slicing the skin with countless knife strokes, among others.

Captives were usually greeted at an Indian village with the "gauntlet." Sometimes even friends and guests of honor were expected to make a run through it. (Remember the point of all this is not that the Indians were an especially evil people, but that they viewed pain and the ability to endure it in a near-religious sense. It was the test of manhood.) For those unfamiliar with the gauntlet, picture two lines of people facing each other, about six feet apart, stretching for a hundred feet or more. Along these parallel lines were the inhabitants of the village, armed with sticks, rocks, thorned branches, deer antlers, and clubs of various shapes and sizes. The captive would be forced to run through these two lines while the Indians pelted and beat him with enthusiasm. Only the strong and the brave would make it still standing on their own two feet, running as fast as possible straight down the middle, never stopping for the pain, shielding their faces with their upturned forearms.

28

And that was the purpose of the ordeal. Those who made it would be greeted with honors and, often, invited to become adoptive members of the tribe; while those who faltered and fell would—if they survived the beating—be treated to even harsher punishment for their disgrace.

Burning at the stake was not a Hollywood producer's brain-child to add an element of horror to cowboy-and-Indian movies. After the famous "Braddock's Defeat," when the British forces under Major General Edward Braddock were defeated by an army of French and Indians in the French and Indian War, some of Braddock's men surrendered, thinking no doubt that they would be taken to French army headquarters and treated as prisoners of war. Instead they were brought to the Indian camp, tortured, and then tied to poles while the brush and branches piled round their feet were fired with a torch. Eyewitnesses told of the slow and agonizing death, and the frightful cries of pain that filled the forest near the Indian camp. Boone used to tell the story of Colonel William Crawford, who was captured by the Shawnees on the Sandusky River in Ohio. He was at the stake for over two hours, succumbing only after he had been scalped alive and hot coals poured on top of his head.

Boone had a brother Edward whom he found beheaded by the Indians, and a son James who was methodically sliced to death after being taken in an ambush.

These stories are related not to blemish the Indian historical record or to renew a white hatred for the Indian. As many tales and worse could be told about white settlers, and training in the use of torture was not a part of their culture. They had no excuse, in other words, except the blind hatred that can build up in people seeking vengeance for the torture and death of their loved ones.

Who killed and tortured whom first? It is an unanswerable question. And in any event, it would be an irrelevant one. Would it really make a difference if someone could show that a few days after Columbus landed in the Caribbean the first death was caused by a white—or vice versa? Would that absolve the French or British colonials who killed North American Indians—and vice versa?

Isn't it true that if the whites had stayed in Europe there would have been no interracial warfare? Yes—while if the Indians had stayed in that part of Asia whence they are said to have emigrated thousands of years earlier, there would have been no

29

white-Indian wars either. That kind of historical retrospection can go on forever.

The facts we must deal with are these: European whites came to a wilderness vast beyond their imagination, and *unpopulated* as such. The widely scattered Indian tribes never claimed the land mass in its entirety—much to their credit and honor. They claimed as private—i.e., tribal—property only small portions around their villages. The rest of the land belonged to the Creator. Kentucky, once again, was open to all tribes for hunting purposes. When the first white settlers arrived, they were so few in number, in relation to the enormous reaches of the continent, that the Indians willingly "sold" land rights to them. The Indians, in many cases, did not really think it "theirs." Scholars now feel that the purchase of Manhattan was more an Indian "con job"—getting $24 worth of trinkets for something they didn't have the right to sell in the first place. And when the whites moved into other lands, in Boone's time, treaties were usually made with the Indians in the area to ensure legal rights, such as they were, to the settlement areas.

And the arrangement could have worked—at the time. There was room for a hundred Boonesboroughs in those Shawnee and Cherokee hunting grounds—at first. The corn fields and wooden stockades threatened the Indian way of life not at all—at first. We know now what happened as a result of industrialization and increased immigration into North America. But the original deal between the Indian and the white settlers was a sincere attempt at accommodation between two nations—one white, the other red—trying to live together in peace. It didn't work; as so often in history, neighboring peoples feuded over border lands, struck out in retribution for acts of violence that often were acts of retribution on the enemy's part that were acts of retribution for . . . etc., etc.

Modernity and the growth of industrialization made the Indian way of life impossible, not the avarice of men like Boone.

Interestingly, the Indian tribes near the Kentucky earned the hatred of many of Boone's contemporaries, a hatred that made a peaceful sharing of land on the frontier much less likely, for the murders committted by them as part of an alliance they had made with the British army during the American Revolution. Some of the bloodiest battles around Boonesborough, in fact, were fought between the colonials and Indian tribes fighting with British financial support and military advisors. The British had hoped to make the area around Kentucky safe by knocking out this rebel stronghold in the West.

In time, though, the Indians in the East started warring against the white settlers on their own, a systematic, deliberate warfare that they later continued to wage in the West. They came to see that the Long Knives were not going to remain a small rival tribe in scattered villages in the forest. When they understood that the white way of life meant the end of their own they committed themselves to an offensive war in the strictest sense of the term. They knew that the ever-growing farms and settlements would end the open forests and plains upon which their hunter's life depended. Two irreconcilable ways of life were staring each other in the face, and the Indians decided to wage a war to eliminate the white presence. It could be called attempted genocide. Who was right? If the whites in the states bordering the frontier had been willing to live like Indians, and if immigration into the New World could have been stopped, war might have been avoided. If the Indians had been willing then, as many are now, to live within the political and economic system of the whites, peace would have been possible. Who came first? Whites had been in North America at that time for more than two hundred years. Most could not return to England or France. They were Americans. We cannot —or should not—drain this great historical question of its drama and tragedy (in the strictest use of that word in the ancient Greek context). Should all immigration from Europe have been outlawed to keep the white population low? Often those who are convinced that America's finest moments were during the time our doors were opened to the poor and oppressed of Europe also express shame over the white man's inroads against the Indian way of life. One cannot have it both ways.

Whatever answers students of ethics work out for these questions, the fact remains that for a white settler or an Indian in the late 1700s the other side was the enemy, hellbent upon taking your land from you and killing you and your family. And there were enough bloodthirsty men on both sides to give credence to such a thought. This context must be kept in mind. When Boone threw a tomahawk or fired his rifle at an Indian, he was living in a total war environment, an omnipresent combat zone where those slow on the trigger usually had a short life.

Those who fail to take into account the grim reality of the times, the "kill or be killed" situation that existed in many

31

frontier areas (and remember, blame is not being assigned, now, to either Indian or white), and insist on picturing the Indian as a victim only, sound very much like the man who became the arch villian of the Boone legends: the infamous Simon Girty. In one early movie about Boone's life, Girty was played by John Carradine as a bedraggled, wild-eyed fanatic who joined the Indians against the pioneers from a deranged and irrational hate for whites. There is one scene where he smacks his lips and leers in anticipatory glee from under his matted coonskin hat at the horrors that will be visited upon a white woman and her children being carried off into the woods by their scalp-laden captors.

One gets a more accurate reflection of Girty's mind, though, from a speech he is alleged to have delivered before an Indian war party at the Shawnee town of Old Chillicothe. Even if the speech is an invention of the whites of the time, it offers revealing insight into Girty's mind. If it were not genuine, but contrived by frontiersmen who hated and feared Girty, the tone and content would be such as to cast what was known of Girty's thinking into the worst possible light. Therefore, Girty either said things like this—or things *even more highminded:*

> Brothers: The fertile region of Kentucky is the land of cane and clover spontaneously growing to feed the buffalo, the elk, and the deer. There the bear and the beaver are always fat. Indians from all the tribes have had a right from time immemorial to hunt and kill these wild animals unmolested.

> Brothers: The Long Knives have overrun your country and usurped your hunting grounds. They have destroyed the cane, trodden down the clover, killed the deer and buffalo, the beaver, the raccoon . . .

> The intruders on your land exult in the success that has crowned their flagitious acts. They are planting fruit trees and plowing the lands where, not long since, were the canebrake and the clover field. Was there a voice in the tree of forest, or articulate sounds in the gurgling waters, every part of this country would call on you to chase away these ruthless invaders, who are laying it waste. Unless you rise in the majesty of your might and exterminate their whole race, you may bid adieu to the hunting grounds of

your fathers—to the delicious flesh of the animals
with which they once abounded . . .

These complaints are hardly deranged or maniacal. In fact,
they sound very much like the progressive view of the plight
of the Indian encouraged in recent years. It would not be unfair
to say that most moderns who express sympathy for the Indian
would not display reservations until Girty calls for the extermi-
nation of whites. (Although if the Indians were determined to
maintain their way of life it is difficult to see an alternative to
an all-out war.) The difference, of course, is that moderns who
say such things are dealing with a historical question in the
abstract, one that can be debated idealistically and quietly in
living rooms and classrooms. Girty's words, however, were a
call to slaughter the whites, and whatever the complexities of
the white-Indian confrontation on the frontier, one cannot
imagine a white settler seeing them in any other way.

But we are moving ahead of ourselves. Boone's earliest adventures occurred during the time when a peaceful accommodation between Indian and white seemed possible. During
Boone's first stay in Kentucky, for example, he fought more
than his share of Indians, but always in chance encounters between rival hunters from different though not warring nations
—much as Indians from different tribes would fight each other
in Kentucky. Or against Indians determined to discourage further white encroachments upon the land beyond that point
which the Indians were willing to concede to them.

Entering Kentucky

Boone first entered Kentucky with the now-forgotten peddler Finley and a party of four other men. They journeyed from
North Carolina through the Cumberland Gap and along the
Warriors' Path, at times sleeping in rough lean-tos, but more
often on the ground. They dressed in buckskins and carried
their tomahawks in their belts. A shot pouch was slung over the
left shoulder so that it hung on the right side, with the powder
horn slung directly above it. The hunting knife was carried in
a buckskin sheath suspended from the belt. They had none of
the food or bedding that moderns take with them when they
"rough it." The wilderness was their home, and they had to
squeeze from it the means of their survival.

33

One month and seven days after the start of their journey they struggled atop mountainous terrain overlooking one of the headwaters of the Kentucky River. Below them stretched the panorama of unspoiled Kentucky, the hardwood forests, sparkling waterways, bluegrass prairies, and miles of lush canebrake. The sight must have been breathtaking even for men accustomed to the grandeurs of nature on the North American continent.

After entering Kentucky, Boone and his companions hunted and trapped. But Boone often went off by himself on scouting trips as well. It might have been at this time that the possibility of bringing a settlement into the area firmed in his mind. He sought gently sloping areas where pawpaw, canes, and clover flourished, indicating good soil; where trees were abundant enough to provide building material, but sparse enough to be cleared with a reasonable effort; where sugar maples and salt licks and fresh water were nearby. The ideal site would contain fresh water within the area where the fort would be built, but an area with all the other desirable features and fresh water as well was a rare find. A fortress without a water supply on site might seem intolerable to a thoughtful modern reader. After all, during a raid the Indians could just sit back and wait for thirst to force a surrender. But the settlers had learned from past experience that Indian raids rarely lasted more than a day or two.

It was during the early weeks in Kentucky that Boone had his first encounter with buffalo. Until then he had little knowledge of their ways. It must have been a horrifying moment when he and his companions found themselves staring at a stampeding, dust-billowing wave of the beasts, dark brown, muscular, and immense. Fortunately Finley had seen the animals before and had learned something of their habits from Indian hunters. He raised his rifle and dropped the leader with a shot between the eyes. Into the wedge of space in front of the bulky mass of the fallen bull darted the men as the herd separated to avoid the body of its dead leader and then swept together again like waters around a rock. The men lay still in the cloud of dust, the ground beneath them vibrating wildly from the thousands of hoofbeats.

By mid-December the pelts were piling high in their makeshift cabin, and there had been no sign of Indians. The men decided to cover more ground with their traps by separating into smaller groups.

Boone and a man called Stuart were moving through buffalo "traces" in the canebrake, matted passages cut through the high sea of cane by the weight of thousands of hooves. As they mounted a small hill, a large party of Indians rushed them and disarmed them without a shot; Boone and his companion had seen that they were surrounded and vulnerable. But Boone displayed a way with the Indian hunters that was to stand him in good stead all through his life. He began to talk and joke with them (they did speak some English after living on the same continent with the whites now for two centuries), even dancing in white man's style for their amusement. He was, of course, playing a role, bargaining for his life to be exact, but his ease with the Indians revealed a side of him noted by many of his contemporaries. To his last days he insisted that he never hated the red man, and that he never killed with glee. But his behavior showed more than that: a genuine affection for them, a reverence for their ways, and a relish for the experience of "shooting the breeze" and learning and living their customs. The Indians seemed to sense this. He was released by them many times when other men probably would have been killed. Even those determined to kill him spoke of him with a grudging respect, and admitted to the high honor that would be theirs if they killed "Old Boone."

His pleasantries worked. Boone and Stuart were not killed, and managed to make their escape a few nights later under the cover of darkness. When they returned to their cabin they saw that their companions had not been so lucky. The cabin was ransacked; the pelts and the other men, including Finley, gone, never to be seen again.

It was a different expedition from then on. Boone and Stuart felt they had no choice but to stay in Kentucky and to continue setting their traps in an attempt to recover some of their losses. When they were joined, as planned, by Boone's brother Squire and a companion, the increase in numbers gave little extra protection against the larger hunting parties of Indians they were likely to encounter and, in fact, made it more difficult for them to keep themselves undetected. But they worked at it diligently and with all the woodsmen's skills they possessed. They built their cabin in a more secluded location. All of their cooking was done under the cover of darkness, with the flames carefully concealed. The approach to their hiding place was through a stream, over rocks and fallen logs to minimize footprints. Often they doubled back upon their tracks, or brushed them away with leaves, or crossed open areas by swinging from the sturdy vines of the wild grapes in the area.

Even with all these precautions, Stuart disappeared. Five years later Boone found his skeleton in a hollow tree—he recognized it by the initialed rifle and powder horn. Boone could only guess that Stuart had been wounded and had crawled into the hollow to hide. His disappearance so unnerved Neely, the man who had come to Kentucky with Squire Boone, that Neely decided to try to make it back to the Yadkin on his own. He was never heard from again either.

By spring the Boones decided that Squire would return home with the pelts they had accumulated thus far, and assure the Boone families that Daniel and Squire were alive and well. Squire would return with supplies as soon as possible while Daniel continued to hunt and trap. By that time, too, Daniel's dream of a future settlement was stronger than ever. He was determined to find the best location possible for the future Boonesborough.

It is a question which of the two men chose the more perilous task: journeying back to the Yadkin along trails frequented by Indian hunters, or staying alone for months in the thick wilderness forests—completely alone in an area that had already swallowed up four of their companions.

Boone admitted to missing his family sorely. He was to say later that "I never before was under greater necessity of exercising philosophy and fortitude . . . The idea of a beloved wife and family, and their anxiety upon the account of my absence and exposed situation made a sensible impression on my heart." But there is no doubt that his life in the wilds satisfied as well a deep yearning for adventure. He wandered wide, his diaries tell us, over the myriad watercourses, hills, and valleys. He marveled at the vegetation: the sugar maples, honey locusts, catalpas. He found the now well-known Kentucky salt licks, where the salt deposits from millions of years ago, when the oceans covered even Kentucky, seep up from deep beneath the earth's crust, providing salt for man and animal. These licks are among the best hunting spots in the world for men in search of those animals: Big Lick, Blue Lick, and Big Bone Lick (so called because of the fossil remains of ancient mastodons scattered about. The frontiersmen, however, took them in stride and used the bones for hatracks, seats in their cabins, and braces for their pots over the fire. They destroyed many archaeological treasures in their ignorance of the scholarly importance of these remains.)

During his solitary months the body-hardening rigors of frontier life paid off for Boone on numerous occasions. Once, while traveling along the edge of a cliff with a sharp drop of more than 60 feet, somewhere between his base camp and the Ohio River, he turned to find himself surrounded by warriors on three sides. The fourth side was the thin air where the land ended. The Indians moved forward menacingly, their tomahawks raised. Without hesitation, Boone leaped from the precipice onto the upper reaches of a maple tree below, scampered through the branches that saved him from his death, and slid down the trunk to safety, leaving the Indians staring in amazement on the edge above. He managed to bring his rifle with him—even though "Tick Licker" weighed more than 11 pounds.

Boone stayed two more winters in Kentucky, Squire returning twice during that time. When he finally returned to the Yadkin, he had become a legend in his own time. Here was the man who had seen what was beyond the mountains. He had survived in the land of mystery to the west; he had known the wonders and dared the perils. He had shown the colonials that a new and better life in the west was possible—for those who dared.

Boonesborough

Before returning with settlers, however, the Indian menace had to be handled, a treaty of safe-conduct secured. There would be a degree of misrepresentation involved in any treaty granting settlement rights to Kentucky since, as mentioned previously, no tribe claimed ownership of that land. The tribes to the south, the Cherokees and the Algonquin Confederation, had granted settlement rights in an earlier treaty. The main problem was with the Shawnee to the north. Business associates of Boone managed to put together a package worth some $50,-000, however, that secured their assent as well. Agreement was not as hard to come by as one might imagine, since the Indians

37

were signing away something they did not claim to own—and $50,000 worth of weaponry, tools, jewelry, and rum piled in one location was a most impressive display in those days. In reality, the treaty was more for other whites than it was for the Indians, a means of demonstrating to possible future claimants that property rights had been purchased in accordance with accepted legal standards from a rightful owner.

Boone then gathered a team of the finest woodsmen in the area and began the laborious chore of carving out a trail wide enough for wagons, packhorses, and oxen. Following the Warriors' Path in places, buffalo traces, and his own hunting paths, he blazed the trail that was used by thousands of later settlers as they poured through the Cumberland Gap into the West: The Wilderness Road. This accomplishment in itself would have earned Boone some passing mention in the history books.

The wagon trains followed and in short order the trees were felled, their ends shaped and notched for cabins, "shakes" cut to serve as roofing material, deep trenches dug for the logs that would form the stockade wall. Cabins were built in the area around the fort on individual homestead sites, but also inside the perimeter of the stockade, with the stockade wall serving as the back wall of the cabin. The settlers would have to live in the stockade in time of siege. The roofs of these cabins were pitched away from the back walls so that a man could lie concealed on the roof and fire over the top of the stockade, and also to insure that flaming arrows and torches could be brushed from the roof with a minimum of exposure. There was no wishful thinking, in other words, that they would live free from Indian attack.

And, indeed, within a few months two boys named McQuinney and Saunders, who had been climbing the hills opposite the fort in play and boyish curiosity, never returned. McQuinney's body was found later about three miles away in a cornfield; Saunders was never seen again.

But months passed without similar incident; the fear that gripped the settlement faded. It was about seven months after the abduction, on a summer day, when Boone's daughter Jemima and her friends Elizabeth and Frances Callaway decided to take one of the bark-covered canoes and paddle just a short distance down the river that flowed past the fort. Jemima, who like most girls and women on the frontier went barefoot in the summer, had injured her foot and was bathing it over the side of the canoe in the cool river currents. The beauty and calm of the day must have led the girls to daydream, for the canoe drifted downstream and ran aground on a sandbar just beyond a bend in the river, out of sight of the fort. It was not a serious problem, though; the girls could push themselves free in short order. Or so they thought, until a band of Shawnees, who must have been lying in wait observing the fort, sprang from the thick canebrake along the river edge brandishing their tomahawks. They hauled the canoe to shore by its "buffalo tug" at the prow. The girls were ordered to make no sound on the threat of their lives, and were taken, terror-stricken, with the Indians into the forest. (Although it is recorded that one of the Calloway girls, "Miss Betsy," managed to thump a few Indian heads soundly with her canoe paddle before surrendering.)

It was several hours before the girls were missed and a search party organized by Boone. By that time the Indians had taken the girls miles into the wilderness. Fortunately, frontier life had bred into the girls self-reliance and level-headedness. They kept their wits about them, and realized that the most urgent task facing them was to leave a trail for the search party that they knew their fathers and fiances would organize. (The girls were only fourteen and fifteen, but that was the marrying age at the time.) They ripped off small pieces of their clothing and left them on branches, broke twigs on surrounding bushes and shrubs, explaining to the Indians that they were merely grabbing for support from the branches when they stumbled. One of the Calloway girls who had worn shoes with a heel that day went to great efforts (and took the great risk) to dig her heel into any soft ground along the way. The print would be immediately distinguishable from the soft track of an Indian moccasin. When the Indians allowed them to ride a stray pony they had captured in order to make better time (the girls explained that they were too tired to walk as fast as the braves demanded), the girls pretended to be inexperienced riders and fell repeatedly into the brush along the trail, making a mass of crushed twigs and branches their rescuers could not fail to see. They also screamed in great pain at each "fall" in the hope that the men from the fort would hear them if they were anywhere in the vicinity.

The combination of these signs so ingeniously left and Boone's remarkable skills as a tracker brought the search party within striking distance a few days later. They found a freshly killed buffalo and the still-warm remains of a campfire where the Indians had stopped to cook a meal. Up ahead was a still-wriggling snake they had killed. Boone surmised that they must be within hearing range.

The element of surprise was essential. If the Indians knew they were about to be attacked, they could kill or threaten to kill the girls. But if they could be found and overrun without any warning, the chances were good that, in their haste to save their own lives, they would ignore the girls. Modern military and police rescue teams are faced with the same dilemma. Can they strike suddenly enough to force the kidnappers or terrorists into confused self-defense? It can be done, but it is ticklish business.

Boone and his men crawled on their bellies through the rough brush around the small clearing where the Indians had stopped to rest. It was, Boone's account tells us, "up a little creek that puts into Licky [River] just above Parker's Ferry." From their vantage point they could see the girls: Betsy Calloway sat leaning against a tree, the other girls lying on their backs with their heads in her lap. Only one Indian stood guard and he had propped his rifle against a tree. Boone and his men had followed the trail at such an unbelievable rate of speed that the Indians—although they had learned that one of the girls was Boone's daughter and knew he was a remarkable woodsman—felt confident that help could be nowhere near.

Betsy Calloway later told how she was watching the Indian nearest to them skewering some buffalo meat with his broiling stick when suddenly she saw blood burst from his chest and heard the cracking report of rifles. Jemima Boone cried: "That's Daddy!"

Boone's men swept into the camp after the first round of fire. There were a few minutes of savage hand-to-hand fighting with those Indians who had not been killed or had not escaped into the surrounding wilds. One threw a tomahawk at the girls, just missing Betsy Calloway, and others threw knives before scampering for cover. The girls were taken back to Boonesborough and greeted with jubilation by their relieved families and friends, and within a year all three were married in Boonesborough weddings.

Even the most workaday chores could lead to adventure in Boonesborough. One of Boone's most exotic adventures took place during salt-boiling time at the Blue Licks, the salt springs in the forest traces of the Licking River, a tributary flowing into

40

the Ohio River in northeast Kentucky. Salt boiling was not a complex chore, but it took time. The boilers had to boil down 800 and more gallons of the salty water to get one bushel of salt residue. But salt was essential as a preservative in those days before refrigeration, so it was a job that had to be done—and if saved for the depths of winter, not a bad one.

Men from the fort had been boiling for weeks without a hint of trouble. Not that they expected any. Indians usually preferred to stay near their tribal lodges in the worst of the winter months, even now that the Revolution had broken out and they were being paid by the British to attack the western "rebel" centers of population. Boone was on a hunting trip when the trouble began, a not unusual way for him to be spending a day even during salt boiling. The boilers needed meat, and who better to send for it than Boone? As he was leading his horse through the knee-high snow along the bank of a stream after killing and skinning a buffalo, he turned to see a party of Shawnee coming over a small bank to his rear. His first thought was to slash free the thongs which held the buffalo meat to the saddle and make a run for it, but he could not free his knife from its sheath. The hilt was still slimy with the grease and fat of the buffalo, and the blade, streaked with blood, was frozen to the sheath. He surrendered without a fight against the overwhelming odds. He had not lived to be a legend by fighting battles foredoomed to failure. He went with the Indians to the salt-boiling camp and convinced the other men to surrender as well.

It looked at first as if Boone and his men were to be killed, for when they were led to the Indian camp as prisoners they found a burning log around which had gathered a party of more than a hundred Shawnee, fully armed and painted in the black and white colors of war. The famous chief Blackfish was personally in charge of the campaign; Boonesborough was the only possible objective.

Knowing that the fortifications at Boonesborough would be inadequate to hold off an attack, especially without his leadership, Boone did some of the quick thinking for which he became famous. He played on the discomforts of winter, hoping that the Indians would be tempted by the idea of coming home to their village with "Old Boone" in tow—enjoy the glory now and take the fort in the spring! It was not every day that a man could parade before his women and children with the most famous of the Long Knives as captive. "Old Boone" promised that he

41

would go in the spring to persuade the other Long Knives at the fort to surrender without bloodshed.

Boone even managed to convince his captors that he and his family would be willing to become adopted children of the Shawnee. He was so convincing (and, of course, such a prize captive) that the Indians refused to turn Boone over to the British authorities in Detroit with the rest of the men as a prisoner of war.

Boone became a Shawnee. His hair was pulled from his scalp a piece at a time and his head shaved—except for the narrow scalplock down the middle, which was tufted, divided into three parts, and adorned with ribbons, feathers, and silver brooches. His clothes were taken and burned, and he was dressed in breech clout and moccasins after he had been bathed, naked, in a nearby river and scrubbed by the women of the village "to take all his white blood out." Then his body was painted in bright ceremonial colors. "Sheltowee," or Big Turtle, became his Indian name, and he was presented with a pipe, a tomahawk, flint and steel, and a tobacco pouch. He became a member of the household—an adopted son—of chief Blackfish, a high honor indeed, indicating the esteem in which he was held by the Indians.

He soon came to be trusted. In his own words: "I was exceedingly friendly and familiar with them, always appearing as cheerful and satisfied as possible, and they put great confidence in me . . . often entrusting me to hunt at my liberty." But they did count the bullets and weigh the powder they gave him and made sure that all that had not been fired were returned. Boone's skills as a hunter, however, gave him a way around these restrictions. He found that he could get near enough to his prey to make a kill with only half a bullet and load of powder (something that could not be done with modern cartridges)— and hide the rest for his escape.

In the meanwhile he lived as an Indian, taking part in the tribal dances—the calumet dance, the dead dance, the marriage dance, among others. He participated in their athletic contests, always being careful to lose often enough to leave the Indian pride undamaged—except in rifle contests where the greatest of the Long Knives was expected to excel. He is said to have enjoyed and to have taught to his own children *atergain*, a game played with a handful of beans in a bowl. The contestants try to get a marked bean to hop out of the bowl with a loss of as few as possible of the other beans. It takes considerable skill and is a pleasant way to while away a few winter evening hours. All in all, one gets the impression that Boone enjoyed his captivity, living a life far more agreeable to him than town life.

But in the late spring he made his escape. He learned at that time of the planned attack on Boonesborough and knew that, without forewarning, the settlers would be doomed. So, after receiving his bullet allotment for the day, he struck out boldly across 160 miles of wilderness—over forests, swamps, mountains, and swollen rivers, with the fleetest of the Shawnee runners on his trail. At times he was forced to crawl through the underbrush or hide in trees as they surrounded him. But five days later he made it—160 miles of wilderness travel on foot in five days!

To his great disappointment he found that his wife, Rebecca, had taken the children back to the Yadkin, presuming him dead. He wrote of the great anguish he felt at the moment; but knowing the imminent danger facing Boonesborough he volunteered to stay and lead the defense against Blackfish rather than go to the Yadkin himself. Duty was a word with a special meaning to him.

Having shored up the defenses and prepared the arms for the coming siege, one would think that Boone, after his journey, would have wanted to rest as much as possible before the attack. Instead he decided to give the advancing Indians something to worry about. With the daring, death-defying, and battle-loving Simon Kenton and 19 other men from the fort, he set out back into Indian country, where they met and defeated in a fierce ambush a party of 30 of Blackfish's men. The battle made their presence in the forest known, of course, so they were compelled to rush back in the direction of the fort and safety. All except the indomitable Kenton, who decided that this was a fine chance to steal a few horses and to "get a shot or two" behind the Indian lines. Consequently, he missed the early stages of the attack on the fort—much to his disappointment.

The Siege

When the attack finally came, it came in a frenzy. Assisted by British advisors and the mysterious renegade Girty, Blackfish's Shawnee warriors staked out positions in a full circle in the forest around the compound. Hundreds of Hollywood movies have used it as a model. Behind the walls of the stockade the settlers peered through the apertures between the angle-cut logs and through the circular rifle loopholes. Women dressed as men, and men's hats were placed on poles level with the top of the stockade to give the impression that the defenders were more numerous than they were.

Either a fear of the losses they would suffer in a direct attack, or a basic humanitarianism, or a combination of both led the Indians to first attempt to negotiate a surrender. A delegation from the fort met with an Indian council—although Boone had no intention of surrendering. He was using a delaying tactic. He had good reason to believe that there was a detachment of militia from Virginia on its way to relieve the settlers. The calumet, or peace pipe, was passed by Blackfish; the peace wampum was displayed; ceremonial fans of eagle feathers were slowly waved by the braves. They parted at nightfall with the promise to meet again for further discussion.

Morning arrived and Boone, against the advice of some of his fellow Kentuckians, decided to meet with Blackfish again. The longer the delay the better, was Boone's thinking. Boone and eight representatives of the Boonesborough community moved out into a brightly sunlit clearing directly in front of the gates of the stockade. Watchful eyes, pressed to the sights of long guns, followed their every step toward the advancing Shawnee.

Boone realized almost at once that something was in the air. The warriors with Blackfish were not those of the day before, but the youngest and strongest of the war party—18 of them, two to each white man. But they came in the white stripes of peace and stepped forward to shake hands in a friendly gesture. Each brave took one arm of a pioneer—and then gripped it with all his strength and tried to pull him into their midst! What followed was a donnybrook of the highest order. The settlers kicked, punched, bit, butted, and wrestled themselves free, and raced for their lives back toward the stockade. Rifle fire from behind the wall barked over their heads, covering their retreat.

The cards were on the table. The siege was on.

Bullets poured from the Indian positions, puffs of smoke rising to a gauzelike canopy over the green woods. The settlers answered in kind from every loophole and crack in the stockade, women and children loading and passing the rifles to their men with assembly-line precision. Later the Indians used firebrands, torches made from bundles of splay ended strips of shell-bark hickory that burned fiercely. They would loft the torches onto the roofs of the cabins inside the stockade walls. Flaming arrows tipped with the same material did even more damage, since the Indians could fire them from a greater distance and from under cover. The settlers labored furiously trying to douse the numerous small fires on the sloped cabin roofs. When they could not reach the flames with buckets of water they tried to sweep out the fire or knock off the blazing shingles by poking at them from inside the cabin with a broom handle. But the fires seemed everywhere and the task of quenching them impossible. Flames leaped high over the fortress. It seemed only a matter of time before Boonesborough would fall. The Indians must have been watching with great satisfaction— probably unaware at first of the sudden breeze that brought up storm clouds and a couple of hours of driving rain!

When the fire attacks failed, the British advisors convinced Blackfish to try a tactic highly irregular for an Indian siege. A lookout high on the stockade wall noticed a muddy streak in the river current, and when Boone went aloft to look he noticed what he thought were men shoveling near the river. They were digging a tunnel from their lines in the direction of the walls of the fort. Through it they could bring explosives or the brush for a huge inferno of a fire, or march a line of warriors to a point within the walls of the stockade itself, where they could break through and attack.

For days the work went on, with Boone's men able to do little more than take pot shots at Indian snipers who were trying to pick off the settlers or the cows herded together in the center of the compound. The Indians were biding their time until the tunnel was completed. One brave, perched high in a tree, was proving especially dangerous, firing from his elevated angle until Boone, with what many consider his finest shot (there was undoubtedly an element of luck involved here, as in much of his career), managed to hit the only portion of his body that was exposed. Boone placed a shot in his forehead, just above the

45

right eye, as the brave leaned from behind the tree to take another shot.

But the work on the tunnel proceeded. The Indians broke through at the base of the front wall of the fort, and from their protected position inside the tunnel piled brush and logs high alongside its face. Boonesborough seemed doomed; all that was needed was the torch. Except that it rained again! The Indians were unable to get a flicker out of the water-soaked wood. And it continued to rain, until the earth above the tunnel became so heavy and soft that it caved in and collapsed, taking with it the Indians' entire plan. The spirits seemed to have blessed this Boone.

Blackfish, apparently deciding that enough was enough, withdrew and Boonesborough survived its most serious challenge. Never again would a war party of that size invade the area. Other settlers poured into the settlement after the worst of the Indian threat had passed, and converted the primeval forest into a patchwork of homesteads, villages, and small frontier towns. Other settlements sprang up in other areas of Kentucky. Boone had pushed the frontier west.

At which point, typically, Boone moved further west. He often spoke of the need for "elbow room," and for him that meant not being able to see the smoke from his nearest neighbor's chimney. He spent his last days in the Missouri Territory, hunting and exploring (some say far into the Pacific Northwest), remaining a living symbol of the early American determination to build a nation on the American continent in the face of the harshest challenges of the wilderness. He died in 1820 at the age of 86, after a short illness of three days.

George Washington

2

George Washington
Founding Father

Although the life of a scout and Indian fighter like Daniel Boone is exciting and attractive to our people (especially young people), there are missing elements. Another kind of hero was needed to satisfy the mythological picture of Founding Father, a figure who grew up in the developed parts of early America, one more at home in civilization than in blazing its trails. Exploring the forests, narrowly escaping death by tomahawk, knife, and gun: these things are quite romantic, certainly, but as adventure, not as a way of life. The career soldier, explorer, and adventurer are exceptions to the rule. Most of us are just not cut from that cloth, and do not really wish we were. The military services often complain that some of their best men regularly leave the service because—as daring and imaginative as they are as soldiers—other rhythms tempt their soul: home, hearth, family; a well-established career in business or the professions, in service to the community as well as self; access to fine music and good books, museums, and the theater on a regular basis; the enjoyment of attentively prepared food, occasionally in the comfort of tastefully appointed restaurants; a

49

pewter, brass, and cut-glass life, rather than one of flint, raw-hide, and steel.

Probably most of us, when we reflect on what life must have been like in colonial America, think not of the wilderness but of small villages, winding shop-lined streets, lead-mullioned windows, neatly painted cupolas, filigreed weather vanes, and the fine wrought-iron farm tools in front of a blacksmith's shop. Or of open stretches of corn or cotton on a well-contoured farm, livestock roaming a fenced pasture, horse-drawn carriages, carefully maintained barns, and a large and comfortable manor house possibly designed and constructed with one's own hands. The appeal of America was rooted in the promise that such a life could come even to the debtors of the stinkhole prisons of Europe. In 1782, Hector St. John de Crevecoeur, the trans-planted French farmer and writer, in his widely read (at the time) *Letters from an American Farmer,* expressed the dream: "From involuntary idleness, servile dependence, penury, and useless labor, he [the American] has passed to traits of a very different nature rewarded by ample subsistence." The homage paid to men like Boone was due to the role they played in opening the wilderness so that this dream could come alive. So while we need men like Boone, and admire them greatly, few, when the chips are down, really want to live like Boone. The Indian scout falls into the same category as astronauts, military commandos, foreign missionaries, and undercover police.

The longing for a founding father of heroic proportions, the American King Arthur, then, could not be satisfied by a fron-tiersman like Boone, so different in taste and temperament from the ordinary folk of his time (and ours). But George Wash-ington was made to order; at least until fairly recently, when his reputation seemed to do an about-face.

We have a picture of Washington in America today that is quite curious. Historians and students of political development in this country often complained that, in the past, there was an excessive glorification of Washington and an exaggeration of both his personal virtue and his importance to the development of the early republic. Mention Washington now to a 14-year-old, who has read nothing about the man at all—not even the brief blurbs in his social studies textbook—and chances are you will get a confident and disdainful smirk. "Yeah, he's the one with the cherry tree, right? And who threw the quarter across the Hudson? And people used to believe all that stuff? Man even the

50

best arm in baseball couldn't make that throw. Good thing we're more with it these days . . . know where it's at." Everyone, in other words, has somehow learned that Washington's reputation is fraudulent, a deliberate attempt to make America "look good," to invest our revolutionary experience with a sense of dignity and worth where there should be none.

The fact of the matter, however, is that recent scholarship gives some credence even to the cherry tree story. That story, as well as most of the others familiar to Americans in the past, was spread by an early biographer, Parson Weems. His accounts of Washington's life were designed to serve as illustrations of high principle to the youth of the mid-1800s. He prepared a sequence of pamphlets with Washington as the hero, pamphlets that centered on desirable moral attributes. As he explained it, his goal was to bring out "his Great Virtues. 1 His Veneration for the Diety [sic], or Religious Principles. 2 His Patriotism. 3 His Magninimity [sic]. 4 his Industry. 5 his Temperence and Sobriety. 6 his Justice, &c, &c." The pamphlets, or copybooks as they were called, unfolded with all the well-known anecdotes: Washington chopping down a cherry tree, but answering his father's angry questions with complete honesty in spite of the likely punishment he would meet ("I can't tell a lie, Pa; you know I can't tell a lie. I did cut it with my hatchet!" "Run to my arms, you dearest boy," cried his father . . .); Washington scolding his friends for fighting; throwing that coin across the river near his boyhood home; riding fearlessly in the front lines at Braddock's Defeat, apparently invulnerable, through God's intercession, to the Indian bullets; his discovery, by a man named Potts, while praying on bended knee in the snow at Valley Forge for the safety of his soldiers and the success of the war effort ("As he approached the spot whom should he behold but the commander in chief of the American armies on his knees at prayer!").

Weems' "history" had impact wider than it would have otherwise had when portions of it were included within the famous McGuffey's Readers—the reading texts used by almost all American children during the late nineteenth and first quarter of the twentieth centuries.

Now certainly none of these Weems stories has been proven true. That is not the point. What some have suggested is that Weems' research was not as irresponsible as was presumed in the last 50 years or so, and that he did, at the very least, use stories that were told by contemporaries of Washington. So while the accounts may have been exaggerated, even false, Weems did not invent them. He used an approach—consulting primary sources—that historians do not usually dismiss out of hand.

What catches one's interest, then, is the reason why Washington's legends have so easily been found unbelievable in our own time. Why? Well, the derogation of him just could be rooted more in a refusal to believe good things about American leaders of the past than in an objective evaluation of his shortcomings *on the actual evidence.* Perhaps a cynicism created by the impact of political scandals has led to a reflexive and unthinking contempt for all of the American past. Perhaps, too, an outright ideological bias has entered into the evaluation of his career; those convinced that our "system" is corrupt work to disparage its founders in the hope of building a case against the current political order. It is no easy task to make radicals of those who cherish the history of their country and the memory of its heroes. Not that such a bias is always worthy of criticism. It would be hard to find fault with a subject of a totalitarian government who reacted with disbelief to stories of heroic accomplishments by the ruling dictator and his circle of strongmen: Chinese who doubt the stories told about Mao perhaps, or Germans who doubted some of the Führer's adventures. The question is whether there is as much reason for Americans to be suspicious about American history in general and, for our purposes, about the career of George Washington.

First, it should be said that none of the "legends" mentioned so far is beyond belief. (There are others that are—Washington talking to angels, for example. But these were never greeted with serious acceptance; hardly an American has even heard of them in the last 50 years.) The cherry tree? Let's say that someone tells the story of a young boy he knows, who, out of curiosity, took his friends for a joyride in his father's car while his parents were out for the night. Would people find it totally unbelievable if, after he lost control and dented the fender on a tree, the young man decided to tell his father how it all happened rather than pretend that a passing motorist hit the car while it was parked along the curb? "Look, Dad, I don't want to lie to you. I thought I could get it back in one piece and you would never know I took it. I'm sorry." It would take an honorable and upstanding young person to say such a thing, but certainly not an angel. There are such people. Most of us know a few. Should we assume that the first President of the United States could not have been such a young man?

The coin across the Hudson? Or was it the Potomac? Weems' story has it neither. It was the Rappahannock River—the only one of the three that flowed anywhere near Washington's boyhood home. And it was a dollar. The silver dollars of the time were heavy enough for a very good modern high school athlete to stand a chance of making the throw at certain spots on the river. To believe that Washington did it requires that we believe no more than that he was a fine physical specimen—which he was.

Kneeling in prayer at Valley Forge? That moderns find such a scene beyond belief tells us more about those moderns than it does about Washington. Washington, although not a regular nor an especially devout churchgoer, never in his career showed the slightest indication of doubting the existence of the Creator. His writings—letters, diaries, etc.—are filled with mention of God, God's will, and Providence. To picture such a man praying to that God during the most trying period (as we shall soon see) of the Revolutionary War effort against Great Britain—a war effort for which he could end up on the gallows —does not take vivid imagination.

But even if one puts aside these doubtful legends, the remaining stories, those that meet all the tests of historical accuracy, paint a picture of a man worthy of the affection given his name. And in case anyone doubts that affection was given:

In 1799, while he was still alive, his contemporaries, even political rivals, agreed that the new capital of the United States, being built near the Potomac on the Maryland and Virginia border, should be named after him. The monument built to his honor in that city is more than 555 feet high—higher even than the tallest of the pyramids.

One state, seven mountains, eight streams, ten lakes, thirty-three counties, nine colleges, one hundred twenty-one towns and villages were named after him.

His birthday is a national holiday.

His face is on the quarter and on the dollar bill.

His portrait hangs in banks, post offices, and government buildings all over America.

His face is carved—60 feet from top to bottom—on the face of Mount Rushmore.

Within his lifetime—in 1783 to be exact—a minister could be heard extolling his virtues at Sunday services: "O Washington! How I do love thy name! How have I often adored thee the great ornament of human kind . . . our very enemies stop the madness of their fire in full volley, stop the illiberality of their slander at thy name, as if rebuked from heaven with a—'Touch not mine Anointed, and do my Hero no harm!' Thy fame is of sweeter perfume than Arabian spices. Listening angels shall catch the odor, waft it to heaven, and perfume the universe." Apparently the saying "First in war, first in peace, and first in the hearts of his countrymen" was a not inappropriate estimate of his place in early America.

Clearly, then, in the eyes of his contemporaries Washington was a very special man. Weems popularized his reputation, but did not invent it. One angry reviewer of a Thackeray novel *The Virginians*—a novel that was certainly not harsh or unfair in its treatment of Washington—wrote that the book's depiction of him was "the very essence of falsehood. Washington was not like other men; and to bring his lofty character down to the level of the vulgar passions of common life, is to give the lie to the grandest chapter in the uninspired annals of the human race." Another wrote: "Washington's character has come to us spotless, and if you impute to him the little follies that have belonged to other great men, the majestic apparition you have called up may visit you, pure and white as you see him in Houdon's statue, and freeze you into silence with his calm, reproachful gaze."

Even those less given to emotion, who felt such high praise dangerous in a republican system of government, nevertheless were compelled to defend Washington against those, especially foreigners, who treated his reputation with less than respect. John Adams is a case in point.

Is this strange? Not when you remember that Washington, to the early Americans, was a symbol of their new republic. He was a living representative of the Revolution: the Commander-in-Chief of the American forces. He would have been one of the first men executed if the Revolution failed. He was born in America; operated a farm for a living. He never set foot in Europe; he wore American-made clothes on most occasions. He was an Indian fighter; a frontier surveyor; a soldier cited for bravery in combat; a dutiful husband; a self-disciplined and diligent businessman; a lover of sports, cards, horses, and the feel of a fine gun. He was seen as the embodiment of the national character, of our customs, manners, and beliefs. His success and his honors were America's. His defeats would be the new nation's.

The Career

It is almost as if fate chose this man to become a living legend. From his early adult years, he found himself in the right spot to build the kind of track record that would bring him to the fore in the national consciousness, lead to his eventual appointment as General in command of the army in the Revolutionary War, and his election as first President of the new republic.

Washington's family was not especially wealthy, a fact no longer particularly noted these days. In fact, many imagine that his was a rich and spoiled childhood—the opposite of Lincoln's hardy life in the famous log cabin. The affection given Lincoln is due in large part to his humble beginnings; he climbed to the top from the depths of poverty, supposedly in contrast to Presidents like Washington who had their way greased with expensive educations and monied connections in high places. Nothing could be further from the truth.

Washington's father died when he was 11. By the time he was 17 he was making his living as a surveyor in some of the least explored regions of the frontier. For five years he lived the life of Indian fighter and soldier. Andrew Jackson, "the President of the common man," had more formal education than Washington, who never went beyond what we know as the elementary school level. His was hardly, to be blunt, the life of a pampered aristocratic plantation owner, as we are sometimes led to believe. By the time he reached his middle years, certainly, Washington was a man of substance with a large and prosperous Virginia plantation, but it was the kind of wealth Americans to this day have admired rather than resented—wealth flowing from industriousness and a careful management of resources, not from unearned privilege.

Between his surveying and the careful and innovative management of his farmlands, Washington achieved a position of prominence and respectability in Fairfax County, Virginia by 1753. He was not an absentee farmer. He worked the land himself, took a keen interest in experimental agriculture and animal husbandry. He was to write often in his diaries of the joys of managing a large and well-coordinated plantation, everything from soil preparation to shipping techniques in the Tidewater colonies (so called because at high tide ocean-going vessels could sail inland to river ports along the East coast). He had also earned the rank of adjutant in the local militia.

The road seemed marked to a quiet life as a gentleman farmer in the British colony of Virginia. There was no trace of revolutionary dissatisfaction or ideological anger in him. On the contrary—Washington first established himself as a man of some note fighting for the Crown in the French and Indian War.

That war was long in coming—and probably inevitable. In the 1750s the 13 English colonies lay in a narrow strip along the seacoast; the French were to the north in Canada and in a crescent-shaped swath of western land down to New Orleans along the Mississippi River. (We were later to acquire this land from the French in the famed Louisiana Purchase.) The English colonies, to be brief, were surrounded, cut off from any frontier expansion. A disinterested observer at the time would, in all likelihood, have concluded that the future of the American continent belonged to the French, as soon as they squeezed tighter their encirclement of the British holdings.

In the 1750s the threat became imminent. The French began constructing a series of forts from the shores of Lake Erie southward to the Ohio River, forts that, when completed, would close the western waterways to the British and effectively stake out a claim to all the land to the west. The keystone to the plan was Fort Duquesne, near modern Pittsburgh. The issue was clear: either the French or the British would achieve dominance in the North American continent. War broke out unofficially at first in a series of border skirmishes and later, officially, at the French centers of population in Canada. The famous English assault on Quebec in which the British general Wolfe led an attack against the French forces of General Montcalm was the most decisive battle of the war. Washington's exploits in the Ohio Valley were not in the same league, but they did prove to be sufficiently harrowing to spread his name throughout Virginia. .

The most dramatic moment for Washington was at Braddock's Defeat. The battle was, of course, a disaster for the British. Colonel Edward Braddock, fresh from the experience of warfare on the open fields of Europe, arrived in Virginia in 1755 with two battalions of British Army regulars that had the same training and background. His task was to clear the French from the area around Duquesne. In May he set out with his men and an additional force of colonial regulars and militia—a total of more than 2,000 men—from Fort Cumberland. It would be a march of 160 miles. Washington, a leader of the Virginia militia, was an unpaid aide-de-camp. When the battle came, it signaled that a new day had dawned in warfare—and not entirely a better one.

The story has been told often. Braddock's men, in their bright red coats and shining brass buttons, marched in the straight battle lines regularly used in Europe. They fired in three lines —one on bended knee, one upright, and one reloading. Drums beat, perhaps a piper piped, echoing through the forests and announcing the British presence as they neared Duquesne. Warfare was meant to be like that—open, straightforward, with full panoply and grandeur—or so thought the moral guardians of Christian Europe. Armies were to announce their presence, wait until the enemy was prepared for a fair fight; and then launch frontal attacks in which bravery, perseverence, and *élan* (a style and grace under fire, in this instance) were to determine the victor. May the best man win! God's blessing would come to the virtuous in pursuit of a just cause, and men had to demonstrate their virtue in combat in order to earn it. A victory achieved through stealth and cunning was a victory to be scorned. The presumption was that, in combat, one was meeting a fellow Christian from a nation with which honorable and friendly relations would be resumed once the differences that had led to war were settled. The thought of a victory at *any* cost was a reprehensible one to the military men of such a tradition.

Braddock's soldiers marching towards Duquesne apparently expected such an encounter with the French and their Indian allies. Instead, they met an ambush of well-conceived dimensions. From behind trees and rocks, the Indians and French fired furiously, fighting "Indian-style," encircling an enemy standing like tenpins in a forest clearing. The British fired blindly at the unseen foe, unable to meet the attack in any way other than by regrouping into their tight firing-line formations. That clearing became a slaughtering ground, the bodies of the redcoats piling up one atop the other. Close to 900 fell that day before the order to retreat was given and the Indians advanced with their scalping knives drawn to take their prizes. "The terrific sound" of their war cries "will haunt me till the hour of my dissolution" said an officer who witnessed the carnage.

It was hardly the kind of action in which Washington's reputation would soar, one would think. But he fought valiantly in the front lines, earning the admiration of the men under him. He helped organize the retreat, dashing on horseback from column to column, pointing the way through the forest, rallying the rearguard to cover the escape, until the demoralized troops could reach relative safety.

During the war years Washington discovered a side of himself he had not known as a Virginia planter. The glamor and excitement of warfare appealed to him more than he had expected. "I heard the bullets whistle," he later said, "and, believe me, there is something charming in the sound." Like other great military men in history, he felt the drama of war, in so many ways the ultimate human endeavor. The flash of muskets, the roll of cannonry, the pounding hoofbeats of a cavalry charge, awe-inspiring infantry dashes into the enemy lines, the knowledge that life and death are the issues at hand—war may be frightening and gruesome in so many ways, but there is little doubt that it is in such an arena that a man discovers the qualities that lie in the deepest recesses of his mind and heart. After combat, say many, the rest of life seems a preoccupation with matters of secondary importance. Such a thought seemed to tempt Washington.

But without a war, Washington could not be a warrior; when the war ended, he returned to his farmlands and the task of rebuilding his neglected plantation. It was not a difficult choice. Managing his fields; country dances; riding to hounds; overseeing the sale of his cotton and tobacco downriver in Williamsburg, Annapolis, and Fredericksburg proved to be a more than satisfactory way of life.

The Rebel

Often moderns seem to forget, as the English writer G.K. Chesterton noted, that the verb "revolt" is a verb that requires an object. One revolts *against* something. There must be a recognizable evil before a (sane) revolution becomes an acceptable activity for moral men.

This point must be kept in mind when observing Washington's career in the American Revolution. It is not sound logic to argue, as certain modern political radicals do, that revolutionary activity against the "establishment" in our modern world is defensible—almost by definition—since America was founded by revolution and revolutionaries; that modern political radicals—by definition—are in the tradition of Washington, Jefferson, Adams, and Patrick Henry, and therefore noble men and women. That *might* be the case. But the point is that such an association must be demonstrated; it is not self-evident. Washington revolted against a limited and specific series of what he was convinced were tyrannical abuses of the political rights of the American people. After the revolution succeeded, however, and the new republic was established, he ceased—*immediately*—being a revolutionary. He became instead a defender of the new government, and proved willing to defend the new government against its potentially revolutionary opponents (Shays' Rebellion and the Whiskey Rebellion are cases in point) with as much vigor and force as he used when a revolutionary to establish it. He became, simply, an antirevolutionary. It was a system of government, a quite specific idea of political liberty, that he fought for, not the right to revolution as a general principle. Modern revolutionaries argue that men like Washington would be in favor of their activities because Washington *et al.* also were revolutionaries. But the fact that the moderns are proposing a system of government radically different from the one established by the revolutionaries of 1776 gives them a most difficult, if not impossible, task to convince us.

An examination of Washington's life in the years just before Bunker Hill and the Declaration of Independence gives little indication of a revolutionary in the making. As a successful colonial planter and businessman, Washington had every reason to want to preserve the political framework within which he had done so well. Until the outbreak of the war effort itself, men of Washington's stripe went to great pains to make clear that their primary interest was in securing their legitimate rights as citizens of the English crown. It was not until they became convinced that they would have to live forever in a second-class-citizen status that the revolutionary decision was made to sever political bonds with the mother country.

The incidents leading to that fateful decision are familiar: The

Stamp Acts, Townshend Acts, and various other measures designed for the express purpose of making the economies of the 13 colonies serve England's financial interests rather than those of their own citizens. The English government at the time was led by men who accepted the so-called "mercantilist" theory of economics; that a country should export more than it imports, thereby continually increasing its gold supply. And what better way to insure that "favorable balance of trade" than by using the colonies as forced markets for English goods, as political and economic entities that existed specifically for the good of the mother country.

These economic policies brought into clearer vision a situation that was blurred in more peaceful times: that the colonies were not, after all, self-governing political bodies. They were more like overseas corporations instituted for the financial gain of Great Britain, and under the ultimate control of the British Parliament—or so claimed the Crown and the Parliament. Colonial legislatures could debate and pass laws, but only when their decisions were acceptable to Parliament could they make them stick. When they were not, Parliament overrode them, no matter how much those decisions were in line with the thinking of the vast majority of the citizens of the colonies. This, as one might expect, was a position clearly intolerable to the justifiably proud leaders of the colonies, who had demonstrated their ability to live virtuous and successful lives quite well without Parliament's aid, thank you.

By 1774 the unrest in the colonies reached the stage of formal organization and protest. The First Continental Congress was summoned to Philadelphia. It was to be a meeting of delegates from each of the colonies for the purpose of presenting their demands to the King. Washington was one of seven delegates from Virginia. Once in assembly, Washington proved to be a minor and scarcely noticeable figure by comparison to the more vocal and radical types such as Patrick Henry. He never, even after becoming President, was comfortable in the role of speechmaker before a large group. Nevertheless, by the time the decision was made to elect a commanding officer for the American forces in the spring of 1775, the Congress selected him as their unanimous choice. Washington tells us he was surprised and flustered. He was younger than the other candidates: Charles Lee, Horatio Gates, and Artemis Ward. But his reputation had preceded him. He was already known by his peers as a man who would stand by the colonies, to the bitter end if need be, but not a rabble-rouser who would force the coming crisis. Even at this point, 1775, there was hope that a show of determination might convince the English Parliament to make the desired concessions to the colonies.

Almost at once the curious Parson Weems-type yearning to make a godlike figure of Washington became evident. A story, without foundation, began to circulate: that Washington had offered to pay the salaries of his Virginia regiment of more than a thousand men entirely out of his own pocket. But, typically, a grain of truth was present. Washington *had* agreed to serve as commander of the Continental Army without pay.

By the summer of 1776, as we know, the confrontation reached the crisis stage. Hopes for accommodation died. Jefferson's Declaration of Independence proclaimed the beginning of a war against the forces of the crown. The die was cast. For men like Washington, now, the question was either independence or the hangman's noose.

The task awaiting him was a staggering one. There was no standing army—only the loosely organized colonial militias. There were no staff, artillery, food, blankets, reservoirs of powder and shot. And there was no procedure for raising the money to pay for any of these things; or for soldiers' pay.

By August, however, an army was put in the field and, one year later, after a year of maneuver, countermaneuver, and minor skirmishes in the area between Virginia and Massachusetts, Washington faced his first major battle: Brooklyn Heights. It was a setback for which many blamed Washington. The British, under General Howe, landed on the tip of Long Island and moved westward in the direction of the American troops, under General Putnam, stationed in strong fortifications at Brooklyn Heights. Howe had spotted a serious gap—the left flank was inadequately fortified—so he moved his troops through it after launching a diversionary move against the right and center. The Americans found themselves trapped against the East River, sitting ducks as the British forces moved forward. Two thousand rebels were killed or captured.

But then Howe delayed. In addition, a sudden storm swept across the river. This combination of fortunate events allowed Washington to move a rescue operation into place and evacuate Putnam's men.

Most military experts now feel that Washington cannot es-

61

cape some of the blame for the disaster. For one thing, at first he tried to fight it out in a hopeless situation. Lives could have been saved if he had evacuated Putnam sooner, instead of trying, as he did, to reinforce him with combat troops. But Washington learned from his errors in situations like this, and, as the war progressed, his decisions became increasingly clever and farsighted and were praised even by his opponents.

After Brooklyn Heights, though, victory seemed assured to the redcoats. Washington retreated further, down through New Jersey. The British moved into Manhattan and made short work of the armies Washington had left in position on the northern end of the island: the area now known as Washington Heights. Lord Cornwallis, one of Howe's commanders, moved across into New Jersey in pursuit of the retreating Washington.

By early December Washington was forced to flee across the Delaware, giving Cornwallis an apparently uncontested route straight to Philadelphia, the capital of the newly independent country. It was at this point that Washington made the military move that has been memorialized in the painting more familiar to Americans than any other—except perhaps the *Mona Lisa*. He "crossed the Delaware" and launched a surprise attack on the British forces at Trenton.

Near Trenton were garrisoned some two to three thousand Hessians, German soldiers fighting for pay and because of dynastic ties with King George (who was of German origin, the House of Hanover). Washington's plan was to strike on Christmas Day, hoping to catch the Hessians by surprise, perhaps in a holiday hangover. His strategy was aided by a storm that arose on the day of the attack. Even when the first reports of an advancing column of Americans were received at the Hessian base, they could not believe that anyone would choose to fight on such a day, and decided not to arm themselves in preparation. Apparently Washington had learned a lot from the Indian wars about the element of surprise. Some have even suggested that he could be called one of history's first "guerrilla war generals" (although that word—"little war" in Spanish—was not used until the Spanish opposed Napoleon's armies with ambush, hit-and-run, and sniper attacks after he had captured and occupied their country).

Washington launched his boats under the cover of darkness. Make no mistake, it was a hazardous venture. The flat-bottomed boats were propelled by long thin poles pushed against the river bottom. On the partially frozen surface of the river floated chunks of ice large enough, and moving rapidly enough in the swirling currents, to crush or capsize the heavily loaded vessels. The storm increased in velocity. Sleet and freezing rain at first, then a layer of snow—the most hazardous footing of all. Horses slid wildly around the decks, lurching and slipping dangerously as the boats rolled with the river.

By the time they disembarked, still nine miles from Trenton, Washington was aware that the storm had severely delayed them. The plan to strike before dawn had to be scrapped. But the snow served as a partial cover, still swirling as it fell from the gray skies. The Hessians were caught so completely off guard that Washington lost not a single man in the attack. When he led his men back across the river later in the day, after the storm had abated considerably, his men were elated by the more than 900 prisoners they brought with them. And so were the rest of the citizens of the ex-colonies. The battle was of more value symbolically than strategically, but that was the point. From the depths of despair, on the verge of a possible total collapse of the Revolution, the Americans were given a ray of hope. The British could be beaten. Washington had done it.

On the face of it, though, the British still had all the advantages on their side. Better supplied and trained, aided by a navy the Americans could not match, they seemed to have the upper hand. But only on the face of it. The war was costly, and growing unpopular back in England. Other wars were being fought by England at the same time, and the British Army was scattered across the globe. From Ireland to India there was talk of revolution. There were 3,000 miles between England and the battlefronts in America, making communications slow and irregular. And Washington knew all that. If the Americans could persevere they could win. They did not have to drive the British into the sea; only inflict casualties sufficient to drain them of the will to resist. The British could not occupy every East Coast city at the same time, and, even if they could, Washington's men could vanish into the wilderness in small bands to regroup for continued resistance. If the Americans could only maintain their will to struggle on, even in the face of adversity, victory could be secured. And if the money held out.

By mid-1777 the British war choices became clear: either invade in force from Canada, or move from the sea, probably at Philadelphia; or both. General Clinton's army in northern

New York was assigned the task of defending against a Canadian invasion; Washington took it upon himself to prepare for an attack by Howe somewhere along the coast. In late July Howe did the expected. His armada set sail from New York, and one month later he disembarked at Head of Elk on the Chesapeake Bay. From there the march on Philadelphia began.

Washington was outnumbered—11,000 to 15,000—but he had to resist. The loss of Philadelphia might be endurable from a military standpoint, but the loss of the capital would "strike a damp" to the Revolution. And he would be able to choose the sites of the battles to come.

The first was in September at Brandywine, a creek a few miles from Wilmington. Howe tried to duplicate his success at Brooklyn—using the right flank this time instead of the left. And it worked again. After the first day of fighting the Americans were in flight. But they were not defeated. They were able to regroup and continue their hit-and-run—"Indian style"—attacks, retreating again and again, but only after inflicting serious casualties on their pursuers.

Howe plodded on through the fall, until Washington decided to meet him again in full-scale battle formation, this time at Germantown, Pennsylvania. The battle was fierce and, once again, before it was over, the Americans were disorganized and in flight. American casualties were higher than the British; but the British losses were high. It was a method to be used 35 years later by the Russians in their defense against Napoleon, and in 1941 against Hitler: meet the enemy; inflict casualties and retreat to fight again (and to inflict more casualties) until the enemy force is depleted, far from reinforcements and supplies. Rather than oblige Washington, Howe decided to spend the winter in quarters. (Despite Washington's efforts, Howe had earlier taken Philadelphia, and he made it his winter quarters.)

From Disaster to Triumph

While Howe hibernated, Washington experienced his most trying hours of the Revolution. It was easy to see why.

Washington had not been beaten decisively. His army was still in the field. But neither had he secured a great victory, aside from his daring but largely inconsequential escapade at Trenton. And while it may have been unfair to ask more of him, considering the circumstances, some did. There was a move afoot to replace him with another commander. In addition, his men were beginning to grumble; the Congress was finding it difficult to meet the payroll and supply them regularly and adequately. The long, cold winter in the log huts of Valley Forge brought talk of mutiny and desertion. Washington's skills as a leader of men were put to the test. Could he convince his men that they were not putting their lives and farms (largely neglected during the war) on the line in a cause foredoomed to failure? Could those seeking to remove him from his command do so? Whether a man called Potts ever came across him in prayer in the snow at Valley Forge might be questionable, but not that Washington prayed sincerely, and often, in such a time. The Revolution, and possibly his life, could be near its end.

But the crises never reached a head. Ben Franklin, negotiating for the colonies in Europe, put together an alliance with the "most Christian kings" of France and Spain "to make a common cause with the United States" to secure and guarantee "their liberty, sovereignty, and independence, absolute and unlimited." France and Spain declared war on England. The successes of Washington's armies, limited as they were, were sufficient to convince the European enemies of England that their national interests could be assisted by a vigorous and successful "second front"—as it were—in North America. Money and military leaders crossed from Europe (Thaddeus Kosciusko, the Marquis de Lafayette, Baron von Steuben) to assist in the American war effort. Washington echoed the sentiments of most of his countrymen when he exclaimed, "I believe no event was ever received with more heartfelt joy."

But Washington had little time to rejoice. By June of 1778 the redcoats, under General Clinton now, moved out of Pennsylvania and to the east. They were going to solidify the British position around New York. Holding Philadelphia, they had learned, was not going to force a surrender. Washington was determined, however, now that French assistance had been secured, to make a decisive move. As Clinton's armies moved out of Monmouth, New Jersey on a steamy summer day, he gave orders to attack. This encounter again proved inconsequential, but the British realized that they were on the defensive now. In the coming months Washington would move his forces around them to the north to White Plains, from which he pressed south and to final victory. Other battles followed through 1781, until finally, in October of that year, General Cornwallis found himself facing a combined French and American army at Yorktown in Virginia. Seventeen thousand troops under Washington's leadership (8,000 were French) pressed forward, preceded by a heavy artillery barrage upon the British lines. For days the artillery exchange continued furiously, until, on October 17, Cornwallis surrendered. The British and Hessians marched out, battalion after battalion, to lay down their arms before Washington.

The years of military reversals and fears of defeat were over. The war was over. Washington's will and perseverance, his refusals to concede defeat in the darkest hours, his daring and resourceful military tactics had earned him the day against all odds.

Gentleman Farmer Again

Once Britain was out of the 13 colonies, Washington, like most Americans, felt that life could go on as before. The colonies had allied themselves against the common enemy, and now would stay together in a loose confederation, getting down to the business of building a prosperous life for themselves in this land of opportunity and abundance. He returned to Mount Vernon and—he hoped—a life away from politics except on the local level. The Articles of Confederation provided a framework within which Virginians and New Yorkers and Pennsylvanians could work out their separate and distinct destinies. The war had been fought against the central authority of the British crown, for the independence of the 13 colonies, and they had no intention of surrendering that independence to a central authority *in* America. The ex-colonies saw themselves as 13 new and sovereign (self-ruling) states—new countries, so to speak—aligned with each other for certain common interests.

Few persons, and certainly not Washington, saw anything wrong with that. Not at all. It is one of mankind's oldest aspirations to experience the degree of freedom possible under a government of neighbors, elected officials with needs and wants, beliefs and convictions, near-to-identical to your own. But, like the Greeks earlier in history in their city-states, Ameri-

66

cans came to see that there are difficulties in such a political bond as well.

In foreign affairs their vulnerability was obvious. The new Congress found itself without authority and power to negotiate with Spain over the question of access to the lower Mississippi, or with Britain over the question of her continued occupation of forts on American soil south of the Canadian border. The peace treaty that ended the Revolutionary War called for the British to vacate these bases, but the new American legislature had no army to enforce it. The Congress could raise an army only when (and if) the separate states decided to volunteer their militias for a central war effort. Pirates from North Africa, with the not-too-silent encouragement of the British, preyed upon American vessels or forced them to pay tribute to guarantee safe passage.

At home there was a financial crisis. The states taxed each other's trade in what amounted to commercial warfare. They issued paper money on their own: debtor states in large quantities to inflate the currency and make repayment easier. Rhode Island's money became notoriously undesirable and creditors went to great lengths to avoid being repaid with it.

In 1784 came the straw that broke the camel's back—Shays' Rebellion. Daniel Shays and his followers were, for the most part, small Massachusetts farmers. During a period of economic depression, which Shays' men blamed on East Coast bankers and money managers, they found it impossible to secure the cash with which to pay their debts, and were being dispossessed of their property. Theirs was a situation that could elicit the support and sympathy of many of us. Banks were foreclosing on the farms needed by these farmers to raise the crops to pay off their debts. When, however, mobs gathered, threatening judges and court buildings, and when a well-organized group under Shays made plans to capture the national arsenal (where there were "ten to fifteen thousand stands of arms in excellent condition," as a report at the time read), it became another issue entirely. As justifiable as were many of the complaints of these farmers, what would be the consequence if the government, under the Articles of Confederation, proved unable to preserve an orderly process of law? Without that process—"law and order" if you will—there would be no systematic way of redressing their grievances (if one assumes that Shays' followers were unquestionably in the right). If this angry mob was not stopped from taking the law into its own hands, what would stop other mobs, acting on less righteous, less understandable complaints, from doing the same? Did the Confederation have the means to defend itself against a willful mob of disgruntled farmers, to say nothing of foreign powers? The question arose that troubled many observers of the political life of the late eighteenth century (and a question that has not been settled completely, even today): Will democracy and political liberties *inevitably* lead to chaos and anarchy as human beings, most of whom are incapable of self-discipline and self-restraint and are scarred by envy (so the theory goes), prove unable to live without an authority above them? Even those Americans most confident in the feasibility of a government with extensive personal freedoms became alarmed. If the great majority of men could live as free men, what could the legislature, under the Articles of Confederation, do in extraordinary cases to restrain an outlaw mob? (Even if one did not think that Shays' followers fit this description, future rioters might.)

Fortunately for the new republic, Shays' Rebellion petered out. A combination of the threat of force by a small Massachusetts militia and the realization that the ballot box could be used to relieve their difficulties led them to surrender their arms.

But leaders all through the states, convinced now that a stronger government was needed, agreed to meet in Philadelphia in the summer of 1787 to lay the groundwork. Washington expressed the general sentiments: "I feel," he wrote to a friend, "infinitely more than I can express to you, for the disorders which have arisen in these States. Who, besides a Tory, could have foreseen, or a Briton predicted it?"

The rest, as they say, is history. The Constitutional Convention was convened and George Washington was there, chosen to represent his fellow Virginians. In the great debates, recorded in part for posterity by James Madison, contrasting views of the nascent nation-state came to the fore, questions of the power of the President, states' rights, representation for large and small states and slave populations. As the smoke cleared, it became apparent that two visions of the future political order were at loggerheads. They could be called the Hamiltonian and the Jeffersonian views, in recognition of their most noted champions.

The Hamiltonians argued for a strong central government

68

with powers clearly superior to and corrective of the States. Their major concern was to form a national union with a centralized leadership sufficiently powerful to deal on an equal basis with the established nation-states of Europe. They were determined, as well, to set up an economic authority to supervise the growth of an expanding industrialized society. They were convinced that anything less would leave the new country a disorganized second-class nation, a spectator of European development of the areas adjacent to the 13 ex-colonies. Their opponents described such talk as a call for a new monarchy and a new aristocracy, this time with American personnel.

The Jeffersonians stressed instead the need for vigilantly maintaining the political liberties fought for in the revolution. They wanted states' rights rather than a highly efficient central government. For them, the nation would be healthy and free (in line with the goals and achievements of the Revolution) only so long as political power was retained as much as possible on the local level—in the hands of independent and responsible citizens, or their local representatives. They envisioned a nation of virtuous, responsible, and intelligent independent landowners, providing for their own needs for the most part, without any use for Hamilton's national banks and economic overlords. Only in such a future could political freedom be preserved, they argued.

A man was needed as President who could hold these disparate segments within the same political bond—a man who could convince the opposing factions that his primary interest as leader would be the health and survival of the new nation, not the dominance of Hamiltonians over Jeffersonians or vice versa. In spite of some Jeffersonian skepticism (not so much from Jefferson as from some followers of his school of thought), Washington became the choice of the Convention. He was elected the first President of the new political system to be governed by the Constitution they drew up and ratified—and was elected by a unanimous vote in the Electoral College, the only man ever to be so honored.

Washington accepted the position with great hesitation. He came to the Convention out of patriotic duty, with no ambition except to solve the problems of the republic and then return home to his happy and prospering plantation at Mount Vernon. He wrote of the prospects awaiting him: "I should consider myself as entering upon an unexplored field, enveloped on every side with clouds and darkness." And, "My movements to the chair of Government will be accomplished by feelings not unlike those of a culprit who is going to the place of his execution: so unwilling am I, in the evening of a life nearly consumed in public cares, to quit a peaceful abode for an Ocean of difficulties, without that competency of political skill, abilities and inclination which is necessary to manage the Helm. I am sensible, that I am embarking the voice of my Countrymen and a good name of my own, on this voyage, but what returns will be made for them, Heaven alone can foretell."

During his two terms as President, Washington demonstrated that the country had been wise to choose him. He proved remarkably highminded, able to rise above interest-group squabbles to make decisions in the interest of the nation as a whole (the role that supposedly is played by kings in the European tradition). And the problems were numerous and trying.

The struggle between Hamiltonians and Jeffersonians went on. Reluctantly Washington agreed to run for a second term, primarily because he feared that without his unifying presence the two factions would tear the country apart.

Foreign issues came to the fore as well. Revolution broke out in France. The monarchies of Europe banded together in a war against the new French republic, especially after the revolutionaries executed the French king, his queen and family, and thousands of clergy and supporters of the monarchy. Americans, understandably, had mixed emotions about the turmoil on the Continent. France had aided us during our Revolution. And, emotionally, the idea of a new republic was attractive, since the French made the point that their revolution was patterned after our own; that they were opposed to the same monarchical system we had fought. On the other hand, most Americans were still of English stock and had lived a history in which the enemy was always France. A change in regime, however radical, could not erase all the memories—of the French and Indian War, for example. The bulk of our overseas commerce continued to be with England. And there was a growing recognition, even then, that the French Revolution was somehow different and decidedly more radical than the American. The thought of king and clergy being executed to the applause of the mob sent shivers through America.

Washington urged neutrality in the wars in Europe, but was

opposed by those who felt that America had a role to play in the service of French democracy. A representative of the French revolutionary government, the so-called "Citizen Genet," was greeted with thunderous applause when he arrived in America to solicit support, perhaps for an invasion of Canada. When Washington, instead of negotiating with Genet, went so far as to send John Jay to England to settle the outstanding differences between England and the United States (their continued presence in Western forts and their encouragement of Indian raids along the frontier, among other things), Jay was burned in effigy and Washington was accused of being a "political hypocrite" and the "Stepfather of His Country" by the pro-French faction. But Washington held fast to his course, putting the interests of the nation above ideological and factional concerns. War with England was avoided (at least until 1812, by which time Washington was no longer in office).

Undivided loyalty to the American nation-state, duty, honor, country were the watchwords of his two terms of office. And Washington's memory went on to serve these same lofty goals. We would become a nation of immigrants in time. The words of Washington's Farewell Address, a summary of his lifetime dedication, have been a model of what it means to become a responsible American patriot. We are Americans, members of a new nation, but a nation that demands and deserves our undivided allegiance as much as any of the older nations of Europe. Our concerns for the lands of our forebears can be real, our support of ideological causes fervent, but we are Americans first—this was the lesson of Washington's presidency. To be a country worthy of our undivided allegiance, America needs the undivided support of its people; the nation cannot be all it is capable of being without the loving service of its citizens, even if that service requires sacrifice on our part as it did for Washington. The words of the Farewell Address ring as movingly now as then. We must keep uppermost in our minds "the true and permanent interests of our country, without regard to local considerations—to individuals, to parties, or to nations." We must never forget that without the healthy survival of the nation-state, there will be no social order to guarantee our liberties and rights. They will be defined, instead, by the strongest, the most cunning and treacherous of our own people, or by dominant foreign powers. It is not that we should despise the rest of the world in a fit of superpatriotism and xenophobia—

71

not at all. We should, he said, "observe good faith and justice towards all nations; cultivate peace and harmony with all . . . The Nation which indulges towards another an habitual hatred or an habitual fondness is in some degree a slave." But, America first. "Europe has a set of primary interests, which to us have none, or a very remote relation. Hence she must be engaged in frequent controversies, the causes of which are essentially foreign to our concerns . . . Our detached and distant situation invites us to pursue a different course . . . 'Tis our true policy to steer clear of permanent alliances, with any portion of the foreign world . . . Taking care always to keep ourselves, by suitable establishments, in a respectable defensive posture, we may safely trust to temporary alliances for extraordinary emergencies."

It is true that modern transportation, weaponry, and communications have made events and developments that take place halfway around the world important to us. It is not likely that a Washington of today, for example, would suggest that America ignore Europe. But his point stands. We are a people separate and distinct from the other nations of the world, members of a nation-state with a claim on our loyalty and affection comparable to a human family's. We share a commonweal, a common past, a common future. Washington could see that more clearly than other men of his time. We cannot easily talk of being "just people" or of having loyalties to "mankind" in a world of competing, and often warring, nations. When one says his loyalties are to "mankind in general," the course of duty can be vague and subjective. Duty does not make its presence felt. We follow our preferences, instead of sacrificing them. Loyalty to the nation—patriotism—on the other hand, makes demands upon us. The call is to responsibility, sacrifice, heroism, and subordination of personal choice to the good of the national brotherhood. Washington earned the title of Father of His Country because his life was a living lesson of how exceptional men answer such a call.

Robert E. Lee

3

Robert E. Lee
Gentleman Soldier

It is likely that young men and women living in the Old South, the states that fought on the side of the Confederacy in the American Civil War, need little introduction to the career of Robert E. Lee. Informal education in the South—tall tales from parents, grandparents, and village raconteurs, for example— still makes for a distinct "rebel" heritage, but as the mass media and centralized education proceed to standardize us all, that reservoir is bound to recede and to weaken the South's collective memory even of Robert E. Lee.

Admittedly, the revered memory of Lee is part of the white Southern experience, not the black. That is understandable, but in many ways unfortunate. Racial harmony and understanding require cultural growth on the part of blacks as well as whites. All too often Southern blacks view Lee in caricature, solely as the leader of the slaveholding forces, a man who pledged his life to the defense of a social order that held their forefathers in bondage. To ask a Southern black (or a black who has emigrated to the northern urban centers) to look at Lee's good points can seem like an insult; comparable to asking a Jew to remember that Hitler, after all, did build some good roads in Germany and get people off the unemployment lines.

But since Lee remains such a revered historical figure to so many decent and cultured Southerners, the question has to be asked: Why? Perhaps the time is not yet right to ask a black to consider such a problem. Perhaps it is bad manners. But such reluctance can be patronizing, too, a not-too-hidden suggestion that blacks, for some reason, cannot handle the full story in this instance. So the question is a valid one: Why?

Is it that Southerners who find Lee a hero are totally debased as human beings, without a shred of honor? Is there nothing good at all to be said about the Confederate cause in the Civil War? Have we finally found an exception to what we have been told is the "progressive" insight into the nature of armed conflict: that rarely do all the forces of evil line up against the forces of virtue; that most wars are complex events with mixed motives and aspirations on both sides. There is no school of modern scholarship that views the Civil War in such a simplistic way— left or right, conservative or liberal. Modern leftist historians argue that the war was fought more for the purpose of furthering the interests of northern manufacturers than to free the slaves (curiously coming around to a position held by the South at the time of the struggle). Modern Southerners, and blacks, often point to the troubled race relations in the North at this time to demonstrate the unlikelihood that Northerners by the hundreds of thousands marched south to free their enslaved black brothers. Much has been made of late of the statements of Lincoln just before the war—statements that quite explicitly demonstrate his willingness to allow slavery to continue for the foreseeable future in those areas of the South where it was a well-established institution, as long as the South stayed in the Union without insisting on the right to expand slavery into the new states being carved out of the Western territories. We have come to see, in other words, that the story of the war just cannot be told as a morality play.

There is a need, then, for blacks and whites to look at Lee's career with an open mind. Blacks can profit from such an undertaking if for no other reason than that it will help them to come to grips with Confederate mentality. There is no reason to presume that a black will end up "liking" Lee after he reads about him—or the people who held him in such high esteem. A valid reason for studying him and the events of his time might be, simply, to uncover more fully what was "wrong" with him and his admirers, the way a Jew would study Nazism or a policeman criminology.

Of course the result is likely to be something else: a broader and more tolerant view of Lee and the Confederate cause; a greater sympathy for the historical circumstances that made good and decent men seem to fight for the evils of slavery. And that would be a good thing. Anyone who understands the suggestion that we look at the childhood environment and the problems of a ghetto youth involved in a life of crime before we become too harsh in our criticisms of him should understand as well the suggestion that we must look at the United States in the 1850s and 1860s before condemning Lee for leading the pro-slavery forces in the Civil War.

Many whites in the North, too, encounter an obstacle in reaching an honest evaluation of Lee. They often are victims of what must be called a one-sided view of the war, yet that is not necessarily to say that it is an inaccurate view. But it is one-sided, and denies the Northerner important insight into the mind of men like Lee. Lee might have been on the wrong side of the Civil War, and his rationale for waging so determined a resistance to the North may seem unsound when judged with the advantage of hindsight. But he *did* have a rationale, which did not resemble in the least the caricature of it one often hears derided outside the South: that he was a wealthy, slaveholding plantation owner fighting a war to protect all wealthy slave-owning plantation owners from liberty-loving Northerners who were determined to give their lives, if need be, to end slavery. From the point of view of Lee (who was a slaveowner only for a brief period in his life and then only through his wife's inheritance) and the hundreds of thousands of non-slave-owning Southerners who made up the bulk of the Confederate armies (and they were the foot soldiers who fought the bloodiest battles), there were other far more important issues at stake.

Even the northern scholars who concede that there was more at issue for the North in the war than the question of slavery— that there were "other things"—fail to develop a full understanding of the Confederate position. They seem reluctant to take the next step: an examination of the "other things" for which the South fought. There is a school of thought known as the New Left, for example, that argues that Northern industrialists were fearful that the extension of slavery from the South into the West would threaten their plans for an industrialized America in which large-scale employers with a mass of potential employes could hire and fire according to the dictates of supply and demand. But they leave it at that, without even an attempt to examine what the Confederates wanted for the America of the future as an alternative, giving the impression that it was nothing except flourishing black chattel slavery. (There were wealthy slaveowners and their defenders for whom that was the most urgent question at stake, but they were a small portion of the southern population.)

Other Things

Richard M. Weaver, the late professor of history at the University of Chicago, a highly respected philosopher, critic, and rhetorician, as well as historian, spent a good portion of his academic career trying to demonstrate to Northerners, and to Southerners who had lost contact with their heritage, the nature of the way of life for which Southerners fought. In his *The Southern Tradition at Bay*, especially, he argued convincingly that there was a vision of the "good life" and the "good man" that Southerners felt was being threatened by continued inclusion within the Union.

Weaver reviewed the writings of spokesmen for the South just before and after the War to make the case that it was a defense of certain ideals, and not slavery *per se*, that inspired the valiant Confederate war effort: ideals such as chivalry, constitutionalism, states' rights, individualism, and an agrarian way of life. His book is one that all who are genuinely interested in understanding the Civil War owe it to themselves to read. Weaver, a Southerner himself, had a firm hold on the point of view of the South and, more than that, expressed it clearly. (Much of what follows is highly colored by Weaver's work—although it is not a summary.)

The difficulty with the explanation of the war as a Southern effort to perpetuate slavery is the fact that most Southerners had come to realize that slavery was an evil long before the war broke out. Lee, for example, had stated quite explicitly in a letter to his wife that he had no doubts on the issue:

"In this enlightened age, there are few I believe, but what

will acknowledge, that slavery as an institution is a moral and political evil in any Country."

The main question for men like Lee was what should be done with the hundreds of thousands of black Africans that had been brought, rightly or wrongly, into the United States as slaves? Likewise, how to achieve justice in a realistic and workable manner that would do good for both slave and freeman, not just wound the freeman? The abolitionists, those who demanded an immediate and unconditional emancipation of the slaves, lacked good judgement, thought Lee, and, more importantly, displayed a disturbing and callous indifference to the entire social order of the South. Lee would speak angrily of those who dealt with the issue only in the abstract, who called for an immediate emancipation but would accept no responsibility for the consequences of it; saying in effect that the slaves must be freed and if that meant bloodshed and severe economic disloca- tion, well, that was the South's problem.

Lee wanted to end slavery. In fact he was an active member of an organization that set up procedures by which slaves could be freed and assisted in returning to Africa. But not all slave owners would free their slaves. More important, not all slaves wanted to be sent back to Africa. What was the next step? Free all the slaves by force? Then what? Send them all back to Africa by force, dumping them on the coast of some European colony? If not, where would they find work? Where would they live once they left their plantations? The problems seemed so insur- mountable, totally beyond instant solution, that Lee saw only one way out. First the slaves had to reach a level of develop- ment that would enable them to handle life as free men in the American political and economic order. When, and only when, they were able to live as self-disciplined and self-supporting members of society could emancipation come. Such talk does not imply racism. To give independence to a white somehow transported into an African jungle village in the 1860s would be to give him a death sentence. He would not be able to survive on his own. He could live as an African only after he had learned the habitat, the skills as hunter and artisan needed in that part of the world, the nature of neighboring tribes, what wildlife was dangerous, what was edible, etc., etc., and the only way he could learn these things would be from benevolent African tribesmen. If the white was foolish enough to demand the right

79

to set out on his own in the jungle, the Africans would be cruel to grant him his wish for freedom; they would be humanitarian to restrain him even against his will.

The South in the 1850s and 1860s was not filled with slave owners dedicating their lives to the education and enlightenment of their slaves. There *were* cruel and inhuman slave owners—that was not a fantasy of Harriet Beecher Stowe. But there were many more, such as Lee, who wanted an eventual emancipation. But how? He could see only one answer:

> ... emancipation will sooner result from the mild and mellowing influence of Christianity, than the storms and tempests of fiery Controversy. This influence though slow, is sure.
>
> The doctrines and miracles of our Savior have required nearly two thousand years, to Convert but a small part of the human race, and even among Christian nations, what gross errors still exist! While we see the Course of the final abolition of human Slavery is onward, and we give it the aid of our prayers and all justifiable means in our power, we must leave the progress as well as the result in his hands who sees the end; who Chooses to work by slow influence; and with whom two thousand years are but as a Single day.

The abolitionist, the Confederates insisted, showed more a contempt for the white Southerner in demanding immediate emancipation, by force if necessary, than a love for the black, since his call would result in a social upheaval unlikely to improve the lot of the blacks in any way. But it *would* wreak havoc on the lives of most whites. The rebellion of Nat Turner, in which Turner and his slave followers set out upon an indiscriminate slaughter of whites, seemed to Southerners an omen of the state of affairs that would follow upon sudden and forced abolition. Far better for the white slaveowner to maintain responsibility for the black slaves on his plantation or farm than to free them to seek their way in a fluctuating and unsure industrial job market.

In fact, after emancipation an accommodation was reached between many ex-slaves and ex-masters that could be described as slavery operating under another name: farmhands working for food and lodging and a small salary—just enough to pay for the clothing and odds and ends formerly given to them as slaves.

(It must be noted in passing that many modern movements for social and economic reform make this same point: that employers in the capitalist system of today—free to hire and fire workers, who are free to take the job or reject it—should be made more responsible for the lives of their employees and not be allowed to fire them at will in times of low profits, as if the workers were worn out pieces of machinery. This call for worker security, or a government-guaranteed job or income, is an admission that there are many who are unable to take care of themselves in a genuinely free and competitive job market. The promises of those who urge the creation of a welfare state, such as is found in certain European countries, are, in many ways, reminiscent of slavemaster paternalism. The money comes anonymously, it is true, from the taxpayers through the government, but nevertheless it is money provided for those unable to provide for themselves as freemen in a competitive world.)

The slavery issue, then, was, for Southerners, part of a larger picture: the question of whether continued membership in the Union implied that the North would have the right to transform the South's agrarian system into an industrialized order. Southerners were eager to preserve a social order more to their taste: a society of independent landowning farmers, self-employed craftsmen, and small businessmen co-existing around villages and towns, with cities existing mainly as centers of shipping and international trade. And they feared what they thought was developing in the North: large, congested, dirty, uniformly ugly cities populated by a faceless mass of strangers, a proletariat—industrialized workers sometimes in the employ, and sometimes not, of powerful capitalists who neither knew nor cared for them; cities without identity, without neighborhood ties or local pieties, without church and familial disciplines, without a heritage, without soul. The Northerners were concerned not just with freeing the slaves but with building that future for the South, thought the Southerners. Better to be a slave in the Confederacy.

It was not that all citizens would be equals in this agrarian scheme, of course. (Nor, for that matter, did the North claim that owners and managers and manual laborers would be social

81

equals in its system.) But the defenders of the South argued that with property ownership spread out among many planters and artisans (and the opportunity to achieve property ownership thereby increased) rather than concentrated in the hands of a few wealthy industrialists, an agrarian society faced a far more desirable prospect for the future. Southerners did not claim to have achieved anything like this ideal in 1860, of course. They knew that the slaves certainly were not allowed any significant ownership of property. But the argument of Southerners like Lee, who wanted the slaves freed when they and the white Southerners could bring about the change in peace, was that when the slaves were freed, the South's plan would provide them with an opportunity for genuine self-sufficiency and dignity, while the North's offered only the prospect of joining the faceless, impersonal mass of urbanized factory workers.

Moreover, the South argued that even if the North's scheme for life in the United States were better for the South, to impose it by force would violate the Constitution of the United States, the original "deal" through which the separate states joined the Union. The South raised a troublesome question about the nature of the union of the states that scholars tell us is still alive to this day. It is only a scholarly and academic issue now; the Civil War settled the political controversy, at least for the foreseeable future. But it is still an argument that most Americans find perplexing on first hearing, and usually long after.

The Confederacy insisted that the Constitution, as originally constructed, was a pact or agreement between *separate* and *individual* (sovereign) states. In that pact, local issues were to be left to the local governments of the states; the Federal government was to have authority only in those areas specifically stipulated in the Constitution. Hence the separate states that joined the pact could also withdraw—or secede—if they felt that the original "deal" was being violated by the Federal government. The Southern states, when they seceded, argued that they did so because the Federal government was overstepping its legal bounds, moving into areas not within its jurisdiction, assuming the right to impose a Northern solution upon a Southern problem: slavery. As the number of free, as opposed to slave, states increased in the new western areas of the country, the North would achieve political power to dominate the South. If the states were free to join a political association to further their individual interests, why not secede if they felt those interests threatened by increasingly powerful interests in the North?

(Certainly there are compelling arguments against such a line of reasoning. They will be examined in the next chapter through a study of the career of Abraham Lincoln.)

One does not have to be a legal scholar to see that the Confederates had an argument about the nature of the relationship among the states that cannot be dismissed out of hand. Whether or not slavery was wrong, did the North have any *legal* right to work for its abolition in the South? Was the North violating the Constitutional rights of the Southern states—the rights to manage their local affairs and solve the problems of slavery as they saw fit? By what authority did one section of the country move into another to effect such social reform?

Lincoln, before the official secession of the Confederacy, had promised not to interfere in the matter of slavery in areas where it had existed for a considerable period of time. But John Brown's siege of the Federal arsenal at Harper's Ferry convinced Southerners that there was an abolitionist mentality in the North that would brook no gradualism. Brown, who had killed a number of people a few years earlier in the "Pottawotami massacre" in Kansas, was a radical supported by Northern abolitionist money. His plan was to lead an army of ex-slaves in a war effort against the South for the purpose of carving out a republic for fugitive slaves. At Harper's Ferry he lead a troop of 13 white men and five blacks. They captured the arsenal, killed the mayor of the town, and imprisoned people from the area until they were overrun by the Virginia militia (under Lee's command). The attack was disturbing enough for Southerners, but not as much as the heroes' eulogies delivered by prominent northern abolitionists to the memory of Brown's campaign.

At stake, too, for the South was its understanding of the good man and the good life—its *pietas,* to use the Roman term. Southerners had developed a distaste and a contempt for a type of individual they felt was becoming all too common in the industrial centers of the North. They feared that Northern domination of the country would mean a new style of life for the South too, in which such men would become leaders and models for the young.

The South was alarmed that its vision of the good man—the gentleman planter, the horseman, gallant soldier, God-fearing family man, the man of letters and manners, the gambler, adventurer, gay blade (in short, the chivalrous knight of the Sir Walter Scott romances so popular in the South at the time)— would be replaced by something else in its children's affections if their way of life were altered to fit Northern designs. That "something else" was a money man, shyster, huckster, con man, wheeler-dealer, a Yankee peddler with a change purse, doling out his life the way he doled out his coins—selfishly, timidly, fretfully, without daring, imagination, or style.

An unfair caricature? Possibly—even probably. Remember, though, the point is not that history has proven that the fears of the Confederates were well grounded, but that they did fear a new and foreign way of life that seemed to threaten their ways, their local liberties, their freedom. As one impassioned man of the Confederacy, Daniel C. De Journette, a Congressman from Virginia, phrased it, the South had built a civilization of "good and gentle people." That civilization included a serious imperfection: slavery. But to exchange it for the dehumanizing alternative found in the North—never!

> There is more humanity, there is more unalloyed contentment and happiness among the slaves of the South, than any laboring population of the globe.

> For every master who cruelly treats his slaves, there are two white men at the North who torture and murder their wives.

"Hogwash!" many would say, especially blacks and Northerners. We will never know for sure whether slave life was better represented by the idyllic images of Joel Chandler Harris' Uncle Remus stories or by the savagery of Simon Legree in *Uncle Tom's Cabin.* Scholars of the antebellum South, using the best of modern research techniques, fight the question out to this day, and in a manner convincing on both sides. But, there is no question that the Southerners who fought so valiantly in the war, and who viewed Lee as their champion, were inspired by the notion—right or wrong—that they were fighting for an older and finer civilization against the challenge of a barbarous modernity. Men just do not fight and die for somebody else's right to enslave and brutalize blacks. (Once again it must be stressed that the vast majority of Confederate soldiers did not own slaves.) Furthermore, mean-spirited and base-minded men and women do not turn to a man like Lee to represent them and their cause. Enemies of the Confederacy have searched widely for a scrap of evidence to besmirch the reputation of

"Marse Robert," but have come up with empty hands. They almost always end up sounding like the Pennsylvania lady who jeered the Confederate troops as they passed on their way to Gettysburg, waving the stars and stripes to infuriate them. A soldier reported the scene as Lee approached on his fabled giant gray charger, Traveller:

"At that moment General Lee rode up. His noble face and quiet reproving look met her eye and the waving flag was lowered. For a moment she looked at him, and then, throwing down the miniature banner, exclaimed audibly as she clasped her white hands together, 'Oh, I wish he was ours!' "

It was not an unusual reaction. Throughout his career Lee's behavior was nothing short of exemplary, an inspiration to friend and foe alike. The most laudatory comments come from opposing generals—Grant, McClellan, Scott—exceeded only by those recorded from his own soldiers. He had a special mystique, perhaps unique in the annals of warfare. Other generals have been respected by their opponents, but mostly because they were feared. Lee was respected for his military skills, certainly, but also because he was a good, honorable, decent man.

In Defense of My Native State

Like so many of history's heroes, Lee was blessed with the appearance of greatness. He "looked like" a great man, especially in his later years when he assumed command of the Confederate armies. He was tall and stately, with an impressively powerful upper body. His full beard was nearly white, and he combed his hair in a gentle full sweep back over his ears. As a rider he was unsurpassed, and his Traveller was a horseman's dream. The poet Stephen Vincent Benet, a supporter of the Union, echoes the sentiments of many who had seen the noble steed:

> —an iron-gray, sixteen hands high,
> Short back, deep chest, strong haunch, flat legs, small head,
> Delicate ear, quick eye, black mane and tail,
> Wise brain, obedient mouth.

From Samuel Eliot Morison:

> ... Robert E. Lee—and what a leader! Fifty-five years old, tall, handsome, with graying hair and deep, ex-

pressive brown eyes which could convey with a glance a stronger reproof than any other general's oath-laden castigation; kind at heart and courteous even to those who failed him, he inspired and deserved confidence. No military leader since Napoleon has aroused such enthusiastic devotion among troops as did Lee when he reviewed them on his horse Traveller. And what a horse!

Lee was as concerned with his personal grooming as with his horseflesh. Always conscious that in his tradition, a general was to be a gentleman as well, Lee strove even in the heat of battle to wear finely tailored and neatly laundered Confederate "grays." His boots were always polished to a high lustre. Not that he was gaudy or a dandy. There is a story often repeated in books written in the North about Lee's surrender at Appomattox: how he came dressed in elegant finery, while Grant, the victor, appeared in his battle-worn blue trousers and sweat-stained, open-necked shirt. The inference, of course, is that Grant represented the cause of the common man while Lee stood for the wealthy and aristocratic South of the plantation owner. Well, the pictures taken on that day do not show Lee in frills and satin, like a character out of an operetta about life in the court of a nineteenth-century baron—all feathers and braided epaulets. He was neat and clean, a picture of elegant reserve and taste, as would befit an American gentleman.

Frequently the diaries of Southern soldiers make note of the inspiring effect of Lee's appearance on battle-scarred troops. We call it charisma now: that certain something that fortunate entertainers and politicians possess—the ability to generate awe, excitement, and an enthusiastic willingness-to-follow in a crowd. It is present in different people for different reasons. Lee's charisma stemmed from a rare combination of untarnished honor and unquestionable courage.

Early in the war, before he had demonstrated the military prowess that earned him the title "The Gray Fox," Lee's associates noticed that "something special." Major Robert Stiles, a Confederate officer who kept a diary of his campaigns, talks of seeing Lee before the worst of the fighting in the first campaigns in Virginia:

"A magnificent staff approached . . . and riding at its head, superbly mounted, a born king among men. At that time General Lee was one of the handsomest of men, especially on horseback, and that morning every detail of the dress and equipment . . . was absolute perfection."

As one would expect, while the tide flowed in favor of the Confederates, the affection shown Lee was effusive and warm. But even after Gettysburg, when the tide had turned and the Southern forces suffered great casualties, it continued—if anything, increasing in intensity. General Alexander, one of Lee's officers, reports the scene when the troops were reviewed at Gordonsville, just after Gettysburg, when one would expect morale to be at its lowest level:

"Lee . . . bares his good gray head and looks at us and we give the 'rebel yell' and shout and cry and wave our flags and look at him once more."

But when the review commenced an absolute silence fell over the campground, what Alexander called "a wave of sentiment . . . the effect was as of a military sacrament."

A South Carolina private recorded the moment as well:

"The men hung around him and seemed satisfied to lay their hands on his gray horse or to touch the bridle, or the stirrup, or the old general's leg—anything that Lee had was sacred to us fellows who had just come back. And the General—he could not help from breaking down . . . tears raced down his cheeks, and he felt that we were again to do his bidding."

The affection was not one-sided. Lee was not acting out a role merely to get his troops to follow him into long and bloody combat. Often he would write to relatives and friends, urging them to pray for his soldiers. One such letter was directed to Margaret Stuart, a young cousin:

". . . cast your thoughts on the Army of Northern Virginia, and never forget it in your prayers. It is preparing for a great struggle, but I pray and trust that the great God, mighty to deliver, will spread over it His almighty arms, and drive its enemies before it." (Once again, it is obvious that to the finest men of the South the war was for a noble and virtuous cause—which they expected God to favor—and not for the cruel and perpetual enslavement of blacks.)

Another Southern impression of Lee at yet another review:

"The General was mounted on Traveller, looking very proud of his master, who had on a sash and sword, which he very rarely wore, a pair of new cavalry gauntlets, and, I think, a new hat . . . The infantry was drawn up in column by divisions . . . their bands playing, awaiting the inspection . . . General Hill and staff

87

rode up to General Lee, and the two generals with their respective staffs, galloped around front and rear of each of their divisions . . . Traveller started with a long lope, and never changed his stride. His rider sat erect and calm, not noticing anything but the gray lines of men he knew so well. The pace was very fast, as there were nine good miles to go . . . When the General drew up . . . flushed with exercise . . . he raised his hat and saluted. Then arose a shout of applause and admiration from the entire assemblage . . . the corps was passed in review at a quick step."

It was not just the striking figure that Lee cut in his dress grays, however, that drew applause. Stonewall Jackson, hardly a mushy sentimentalist, once stated emphatically that "I would follow him blindfolded." He did not say that because he admired Lee's wardrobe. Not Stonewall Jackson. It was the record that made the legend.

Since Lee fought so bravely and determinedly in building that legend, it is often assumed, mistakenly, that he was an enthusiastic secessionist for much of his life. On the contrary, until the very last moment, until Lincoln made the decision to march Federal troops into Virginia, Lee remained firmly opposed to the idea of secession. Lincoln felt compelled to send in the troops since Confederate forces had occupied Federal military installations, most notably Fort Sumter. It was an understandable decision but, Lee felt, a mistaken one. Better to continue to work for a peaceful understanding of the relation between the central government and the individual states. Even after the Federal troops were in place, Lee argued that he took up arms out of necessity, only in defense of his native state of Virginia, his friends, family, and home. He had written to one of his sons not long before the outbreak of the war that:

"Secession is nothing but revolution. The framers of our Constitution never exhausted so much labour, wisdom and forbearance in its formation, and surrounded it with so many guards and securities, if it was intended to be broken by any member of the Confederacy at will . . . In 1808, when the New England States resisted Mr. Jefferson's Embargo law, and the Hartford Convention assembled, secession was termed treason by Virginia statesmen; what can it be now? Still, a Union that can only be maintained by swords and bayonets, and in which strife and civil war are to take the place of brotherly love and kindness, has no charm for me. If the Union is dissolved, the government disrupted, I shall return to my native state and share the miseries of my people. Save in her defense, I will draw my sword no more."

At first blush, Lee's words here and his unreserved commitment to a Southern military victory appear dramatically inconsistent. Indeed, to other generals from the South who remained loyal to their oath to the Union, they were. On further examination, however, Lee's position becomes understandable, perhaps even admirable. For him the Southern states, in seceding and seizing Federal forts, were acting to secure for themselves a stronger bargaining position in the ongoing debate with the North about the nature of the political union forged by the Constitution. The term "confederacy" must be kept in mind when considering Southern motives. The implication is that the Southern states had "confederated" with each other in a political association that provided for local control over local decisions: states' rights. If the Northern states were willing to join in such a political union with the South and the new Western states, thereby reestablishing (from the Southern point of view) the original Constitutional "deal," there would be no need for armed conflict.

Lincoln's decision to send in the troops foreclosed further debate. Lee felt he was forced into a corner. With Federal troops moving South to enforce *their* definition of the Constitutional bond—rather than seeking a compromise—it became a clear-cut issue. Would Lee, as a soldier of the United States, join in that assault, or would he instead pledge his military skills to the defense of his family and neighbors—and Virginia?

"The whole South is in a state of revolution, into which Virginia, after a long struggle, has been drawn, and though I recognize no necessity for this state of things, and would have forborne and pleaded to the end for a redress of grievances, real or supposed, yet in my own person I had to meet the question whether I should take part against my native state. With all my devotion to the Union and the feeling of loyalty and duty as an American citizen, I have not been able to make up my mind to raise my hand against relatives, my children, my home."

He accepted first a commission to lead a portion of the armies of Virginia. But in short order, Jefferson Davis, the new President of the Confederate States of America, gave him command of the entire army of the Confederacy.

And from that point, through the next four years, one of

history's most dazzling military careers unfolded. The sites of the fierce and bloody battles are legendary where Lee, outnumbered and lacking the finances and supplies of his Northern foes, nearly carried the day. For most Americans the very names strike responsive chords deep in our hearts, even if we are unable to recall any factual information about the battles. They reverberate in our collective memory, instilled in us through poetry, folk songs, schoolbooks, *Gone with the Wind:* Bull Run, Manassas, Sharpsburg, Fredericksburg, Chancellorsville, the Wilderness Campaign, Richmond, Antietam, Gettysburg, Seminary Ridge, Pickett's Charge, Spotsylvania, Cold Harbor.

The immediate problem facing Lee at the outset of the war was how to stop the Northern troops from moving South across the Virginia border. The Union strategy, what General Winfield Scott labeled "the anaconda," called for military movements into the three segments of the South divided by the Mississippi River and the Appalachians. If the west could be secured—the area between the Mississippi and the Appalachians—and if the union armies could secure strongholds along the Atlantic coast to block European trade with the Confederates, a "squeeze" could be applied effectively on Lee in Virginia, the Carolinas, and Georgia east of the Blue Ridge Mountains. Lee understood the strategy perfectly—and knew that it would work. His plans centered on a quick strike up into Pennsylvania to sever rail-supply connections between the Eastern industrial centers and the armies in the west, and then a move against Washington itself to deliver a quick and decisive knockout punch. Readers often express surprise that Lee contemplated an offensive against the North, that he in fact moved into parts of Pennsylvania during the war. After all, did he think that he could conquer the North? Needless to say, he did not, and he did not want to. His objective was to demoralize the North, to persuade Lincoln to cease his war efforts in the South; to get agreement from the North that if there was to be a union between North and South in the future it would not be on Northern terms. Lee had no intention of holding the North under Confederate control for any length of time.

But his first necessity was to defend Richmond against the Northern thrust, to hold on until a Southern army could be built to the necessary level of manpower. And to delay until Lee's right-hand man could be moved into position with his cavalry:

General T. J. "Stonewall" Jackson. This holding action became known as the "Seven Days." It could hardly be called a stunning victory for Lee; still it was not a defeat. The Federal troops did not take Richmond, yet the South endured greater losses than the North.

But once Jackson was in place things were different—"pure gold for the Confederacy" is the way one historian sympathetic to the North puts it. In the months that followed, Lee was nothing short of brilliant, stunning the Northern generals with a virtuoso display of military ingenuity. His artillery would pound away at the Union lines, while Jackson's light mobile cavalry would swoop in like hawks from the flanks. No one, not even Lee's aides, could predict when or where. His infantry would charge forward to pierce the enemy lines, apparently without fear, willing to die for "Marse Robert" and the Cause, howling their stirring rebel yell right up until the moment Northern bullets pierced their lungs. He would retreat and then deftly encircle the Union troops, with Jackson, as usual, closing up the ring around the befuddled opposition. He would launch frontal cavalry attacks designed to thrust the enemy into the open or high onto a ridge—where his artillery and riflemen would bombard them furiously and relentlessly. When the Union forces charged in an offensive of their own, Lee would be there, riding behind his lines at breakneck speed, urging his men to stand firm until the Northern charge was spent, an onrushing wave splattered on shoreline boulders.

Lincoln's problem became manifest. He had the manpower, especially now that the population of the North was swelling from European immigration. He had the industrial centers to turn out matériel far in excess of Southern supplies. The Northern navy controlled the Mississippi and was blockading the Atlantic Coast ports. No longer did it seem likely that European nations would intercede in any way for the South. But where to get generals to match Lee? The North *was* losing the war.

And the Gray Fox was coming north. Lee had won Davis' consent to begin an invasion of the Union through Maryland and Pennsylvania. But Fredericksburg preceded his crossing the border.

General Ambrose E. Burnside (whose habit of letting his hair grow in a wide swath straight down past his ears gave us the word "sideburns") was now in charge of the Union armies. Burnside's plan was to deflect Lee's offensive by forcing him onto the defensive—to mass Union troops on the south side of the Rappahannock and move directly against the city of Fredericksburg and from there on to Richmond. Lee and Jackson, he correctly surmised, would have to postpone their plans to strike north in order to defend the capital. A smashing victory against Lee, then, would not only put an end to his plans to invade the North, but could force a Confederate surrender as well. It was a bold move.

Burnside moved his forces across the river. Lee took his position on the wooded heights just above Fredericksburg on December 13, 1862. Lee had 75,000 men; Burnside, 113,000. Military historians have criticized Burnside severely for what followed: he ordered a direct frontal attack. Then another, and another—six in all. They all failed. If he had succeeded it would have been one of history's most daring military moves, the swift and mammoth stroke that broke the back of the Confederacy. But he did not. The Union troops moved forward, guns blazing, flags unfurled, swords drawn, bayonets gleaming in the afternoon sun. The gunsmoke rose high above their heads, a thick, undulating mist at the base of the Fredericksburg heights. Men shouted their war calls as they charged; the Confederates gave their rebel yell; the wounded groaned and screamed for assistance. Six times the blue lines moved forward, then retreated, only to move forward again, stepping gingerly around their fallen comrades literally heaped upon one another. Lee rode his charger behind the lines, coaxing, encouraging, pleading, scolding when necessary. They can't keep coming forever! Hold firm! But they came again, and again.

On December 15 Lee agreed to a brief truce to bury the dead. Randolph A. Shotwell witnessed the carnage:

Eleven hundred dead bodies—perfectly naked—swollen to twice the natural size—black as Negroes in most cases—lying in every conceivable posture—some on their backs with gaping jaws—some with eyes large as walnuts, protruding with glassy stare—some doubled up like a contortionist—here one without a head—there one without legs—yonder a head and legs without a trunk—everywhere horrible expressions—fear, rage, agony, madness, torture—lying in pools of blood—lying with heads halfburied in mud—with fragments of shell sticking in the oozing brain—with bullet holes all over the puffed limbs.

Total losses were 12,653 for the Union, 5,309 for the Confederacy. In most European conflicts of the time the war would have been over. No political conflict between the Christian nations across the Atlantic would have been viewed, at that time, as critical enough to justify such a loss of life. By the previous standards of warfare, Lee had won his victory. But Lincoln refused to admit defeat. For him it would have been an immoral compromise with slavery and the dissolution of his country, a price too great to pay even to end killing at the level of Fredericksburg. (A position the Confederates thought irrational, conceived from an unbalanced zealotry. The Union could go on if Lincoln agreed to a peace; slavery would eventually be ended—although not in the manner demanded by the North. Why wouldn't the President deal with the South as with fellow Americans also interested in justice?)

Burnside was replaced after Fredericksburg by General Joseph Hooker, who met with as little success against Lee. To his later embarrassment, Hooker boasted at first how he would rout Lee. (Although Hooker did not leave himself as open to ridicule as General Pope, who boasted that his tireless leadership would overwhelm the South. "My headquarters are in the saddle," he said. To which Stonewall Jackson responded with a twinkle in his eyes: "I can whip any man who doesn't know his headquarters from his hindquarters.") "What Lee did to him is history," Samuel Eliot Morison phrased it—at Chancellorsville.

Chancellorsville became the subject of one of the most widely read of American novels, by Stephen Crane: *The Red Badge of Courage*. It was fought in wooded terrain just a few miles west of Fredericksburg. Hooker's plan was to encircle Lee and overwhelm him with the superior numbers at his disposal. But, once again, Lee's armies rose to the occasion. Hooker was driven back. And, then, while Hooker paused to reconsider an alternative offensive, Lee did the unexpected: he went on the offensive, catching Hooker by surprise. Lee divided his army, inferior to Hooker's in size as it was, and sent Stonewall Jackson with half of it, by backwoods roads and roundabout ways, to attack the Union left flank. It took a full day for Jackson's troops, trudging over hot and dusty roads, to get into position; their movements were easily spotted by Northern observation balloons. Hooker surmised that it must be a retreat. Well, it wasn't. One of Jackson's legendary cavalry charges swept down on Hooker's camp while his men were cooking, washing, and playing cards. So total was the surprise that it is said that Hooker's armies first knew they were being attacked when they saw deer, rabbits, and foxes scampering in panic from the woods. Hooker's army, demoralized and in disarray, fled across the Rappahannock.

But Chancellorsville was a Pyrrhic victory. The incomparable Jackson was wounded during the siege and later died. The South's devastating one-two punch was gone.

It would be difficult, to say the least, to carry on without Jackson. Lee knew that. But he must strike. Time was of the essence. The longer the war dragged on, the more likely that the North's numerical superiority, greater wealth, and industrial power would become decisive. Lee's troops were now positioned in a right-curving crescent from Richmond up and across the Pennsylvania border, where the tip of the crescent ended near the central Pennsylvania town of Gettysburg. Gettysburg was the key. Either the Confederate forces would be stopped there, and the crescent would retreat back down into the Confederacy, or it would be extended until it formed a nearly complete circle at Washington, D.C. The Union troops dug in along Cemetery Ridge, a limestone outcropping shaped like a fishhook with its cutting edge turned west and north against the Confederate positions.

Lee struck the following day at the tip of the hook, inflicting serious casualties on the Union forces under General Meade. But Meade held his ground, forcing Lee to regroup for another charge the following day. That assault has become legendary in military annals: Pickett's Charge. Fifteen thousand Confederate soldiers roared across the open ground for a head-to-head encounter with Meade's men. Halfway across, they were met with the thunderous reception of artillery and musketry. The thunderstorm ripped through Pickett's forces, decimating them. This time a carpet of gray-clad youth covered the plain.

Had Lee forgotten the lessons of Burnside's mistake at Chancellorsville? Had he assumed that his Southern warriors could do what the men of the North could not? Probably there is an element of truth in both questions—especially the latter. But there is more to his apparent error. He had planned a supportive attack from the flank for Pickett's assault, an attack that one of his generals failed to launch. It could have made the difference.

Lee's forces were beaten but not destroyed. They regrouped

and retreated out of Pennsylvania. Lee knew the significance of the loss at Gettysburg—that little hope for Southern victory remained. With Southern momentum stopped, the North could begin pressing toward Richmond once again, slowly but surely growing in size and power, like a snowball rolling downhill.

Lee showed his colors when asked about the failure at Gettysburg. Rather than blame the general who failed to carry out orders or call into question the determination and valor of his men, he wrote to President Davis:

"No blame can be attached to the army for its failure to accomplish what was projected by me, nor should it be censured for the unreasonable expectations of the public. I am alone to blame."

It was this side of Lee that earned the love of his contemporaries. It was the same highmindedness he had displayed as his men marched through Pennsylvania. There had been reports of looting:

"There have, however, been instances of forgetfulness on the part of some that they have in keeping the yet unsullied reputation of this army, and that the duties exacted of us by civilization and Christianity are not less obligatory in the country of our enemy than in our own."

Such concerns for honor and decency can be seen as well in Lee's refusal to retain a supply of molasses, which he enjoyed immensely on his morning cornbread, when he learned that there would not be enough to go around for the men in his regiment. "Then I direct, Colonel," he said, "that you immediately return every drop you have, and send an order that no molasses shall be issued to officers or men, except the sick in hospital."

Nonetheless, it was for military valor above all that he is remembered. He could be gentle and charitable, but he demanded courage and steadfastness in combat as well. And he needed those qualities in abundance from his troops after Gettysburg, as the Northern forces pressed into the South, eventually under the leadership of General Ulysses S. Grant.

The Test of Will

An offensive against the North was no longer feasible. Now the South's hopes were pinned on an effort to wear down the opposition, to force them to slog their way inch by inch through enemy terrain until they, and Northern politicians, despaired of achieving a Southern surrender. Lee was confident such a strategy could work—a Southern version of the tactics the Russians used against Napoleon's invasion. He might be unable to drive Grant from the South, but Grant would be unable to force a Confederate surrender. Lee's soldiers could fight forever, from the mountains in a guerrilla war if need be.

The goal, then, was to make the North feel the pain, to meet the enemy's every step and inflict casualties. Hold the line. Northern troops could not stay in the South forever. In pursuit of this strategy, Lee rose to the heights as a leader of men.

At Spotsylvania, one of the last battles before he finally felt he had no alternative but to surrender (for reasons we will examine shortly), Confederate troops were in disorganized flight from an army under General Hancock. Robert Stiles, who was one of those in retreat, tells the story:

"We passed General Lee on horseback . . . His face was more serious than I had ever seen it, but showed no trace of excitement or alarm. Numbers of demoralized men were streaming past him, and his voice was deep as the growl of a tempest as he said:

" 'Shame on you men, shame on you! Go back to your regiments; go back to your regiments!' "

The Confederates fleeing in panic pleaded with Lee. The Union forces had broken through their lines in a bold strike. They had to be driven back or it would spell doom for the Confederates, but the soldiers did not think it could be done.

Lee, rather than heeding their excuses, turned Traveller's head in the direction of the advancing bluecoats. General Gordon, an officer from the fleeing ranks, reported what followed:

"As he rode majestically in front of my line of battle, with uncovered head . . . Lee looked a very god of war . . . evidently resolved to lead in person the desperate charge and drive Hancock back or perish in the effort . . .

"Instantly I spurred my horse across Old Traveller's front, and grasping his bridle in my hand, I checked him. Then, in a voice which I hoped might reach the ears of my men, I called out,

" 'General Lee, you shall not lead my men in a charge. No man can do that, sir. Another is here for that purpose. These men behind you are Georgians, Virginians, and Carolinians.

They have never failed you on any field. They will not fail you here. Will you, boys?'

"The response came like a mighty anthem . . . 'No, no, no; we'll not fail him . . .'

"I shouted to General Lee, 'You must go to the rear!'

"The echo, 'General Lee to the rear, General Lee to the rear!' rolled back . . . from the throats of my men, and they gathered around him, turned his horse in the opposite direction, some clutching his bridle, some his stirrups, while others pressed close to Old Traveller's hips, ready to shove him by main force to the rear."

General Gibson, another Southern witness to this remarkable event, narrates further in a separate account:

". . . amid redoubled shouts of 'Lee, Lee, Lee to the rear! Lee to the rear!' the soldiers led him . . . and they passed through in single file, and the field of coming carnage resounded with wild shouts of 'Lee, Lee, Lee!' "

Finally Lee halted Traveller, rose in his stirrups and shouted above the uproar: "If you will promise to drive those people from our works, I will go back!" The rebel yells reverberated through the clearing.

Some of the fiercest fighting of the war followed. The inspired Southern troops pushed back the Union forces, re-established their lines, and then in frenzied and tireless perseverence stood their ground against the North's muskets.

Of course, as we all know, despite such determined resistance, the South eventually was worn down. And Lee was forced to surrender to Grant in the famous courthouse at Appomattox. Why? Where did Lee's belief that the South could outlast the North go wrong? First, the industrial might of the North and its increasing supply of manpower (immigration to the North from Europe continued all through the war) proved to be more of a factor than he foresaw. The numbers of Union soldiers killed would have led, in ordinary circumstances, to a Confederate victory. (Which, remember, did not require a conquest of the North. The South never dreamed of being able to do that. Victory for the South required only a Northern withdrawal from Southern territory and a concession that the South would not have to stay in the Union on Northern terms.) But the reservoir of men and supplies in the North seemed inexhaustible.

More important than all that, however, argue many Southerners, was the North's decision to fight the war in a new way —General William Tecumseh Sherman's way. As Samuel Eliot Morison puts it, "Robert E. Lee was the finest general of a Napoleonic Age that was passing; Sherman was the first general of an age that was coming, and whose end we have not yet seen."

Sherman's mission was to launch a drive from his base camp at Chattanooga, Tennessee to Atlanta, and thence "to the sea," to break Confederate supply lines, establish a Union base of operations deep within Confederate territory, and begin the encirclement of the still spirited armies of Lee in Virginia, which were being pressed by Grant from the northwest. Sherman undertook his task with a vengeance. He initiated an approach to warfare that we now call "total war." He burned houses, farms, crops, workshops, factories, and the city of Atlanta; he stole livestock—in short, made war upon the civilian populations of the South as well as on her fighting men. "War is hell," he said, and set about to prove it: to secure victory at any price. The people of the South were shocked, terrified, and infuriated. Sherman was violating one of the most basic standards of warfare for a Christian people. "If the people raise a howl against my barbarity and cruelty, I will answer that war is war, and not popularity-seeking," he said self-assuredly, but in recognition, nevertheless, of his startling new ethic of warfare.

All of Lee's plans were thrown out of kilter by the new considerations brought to the conflict by Sherman's tactics. He could win a war fought by his older standards of warfare—the chivalrous standards of soldiering that had been made part of the Christian consciousness during the Middle Ages in Europe— but "total war"? The general who had taken such care to thwart looting by his troops while they were in the North, who instructed his men to rest their horses in areas where they would not disturb Northern crops, was unprepared for a situation in which his enemy burned entire towns and cities to the ground and systematically ravaged civilians as a matter of policy. As Richard Weaver puts it:

". . . it seemed to the South that one of the fundamental supports of civilization was being knocked out, and that warfare was being thrown back to the naked savagery from which religion and the spirit of chivalry had painfully raised it."

Lee surrendered in the famous scene at Appomattox on Palm

Sunday, April 9, 1865, after getting a written guarantee from Grant that his men would be permitted to keep their horses to work their small farms once they returned home. He mounted Traveller and with a look of grim resignation in his eyes returned to his field headquarters.

Many of Lee's biographers have recorded from original sources the scene of Lee's farewell to his troops. Solid walls of men met him as he approached on Traveller. His eyes brimmed with tears. His soldiers cried and sobbed, and waved their hats for the last time to "Marse Robert." One held his arms wide above the crowd and called "I love you just as well as ever, General Lee." General Longstreet was present:

"Those who could speak said goodbye, those who could not speak, and were near, passed their hands gently over the sides of Traveller. Lee had sufficient control to fix his eyes on a line between the ears of Traveller and look neither to right nor left until he reached a large white oak tree."

Lee turned and spoke his last words to his command:

"Boys, I have done the best I could for you. Go home now, and if you make as good citizens as you have soldiers, you will do well, and I shall always be proud of you. Goodbye and God bless you all."

It is this curious and ambiguous ending to the Civil War that accounts for the longevity and sturdiness of the Rebel spirit in the South. The Southern troops had plenty of fight left in them. As a Carolina private put it: "Every man fully armed, cartridge boxes full, and the men well rested . . . we did not lag or sulk. Had General Lee then and there ridden out and said, 'Boys, there are the enemy. Go for them,' there would have been no man to question the odds."

Undoubtedly, however, Lee was correct. In the long run the Grant-Sherman tactics would have brought about an unbearable defeat for the South to which no leader with a conscience would knowingly subject his people, especially in view of the promises of a benevolent peace that were extended by Lincoln through Grant (a peace that never followed after Lincoln's assassination).

But Southerners (as Northern tourists discover to their astonishment) often act as if they believe that the South *won* the war —the war that was a war of civilized Christian gentlemen: that is, the first war, the one before Southern victories forced Sherman and Grant to resort in despair to their unprincipled pursuit of victory at any cost. Only that dishonorable betrayal of military propriety forced Robert E. Lee, a Southern gentleman, to lay down his arms. That is the conviction, usually unspoken, that leads Southerners to bittersweet satisfaction when they think back on the struggle between Gray and Blue.

Abraham Lincoln

4

Abraham Lincoln
One Nation, Under God, Indivisible

I s it possible to write in praise of Abraham Lincoln after singing the praises of Robert E. Lee? Many would argue "No"—and
point to the fact that most Americans who lionize Lee show an
enduring contempt for Lincoln, and vice versa. Well, there is
no denying that there are Southerners who refuse to open
themselves to the Lincoln mystique, just as some Northerners
and blacks refuse to open themselves to Lee. Not infrequently
there appear articles by Southern intellectual spokesmen who
insist on picturing Lincoln as a tyrant of sorts, obsessed with a
religious extremism and a dictator's complex, jealously determined to impose his own drab and unimaginative way of life on
the higher civilization of the South. There is a wisecrack (a
clever and perceptive one in fact) that circulates in these anti-
Lincoln quarters: "Abraham Lincoln? He's a nineteenth-century politician often confused with an imaginary character of
unrealistically high virtue by the same name found in the fiction
of Carl Sandburg." The barb is pointed at the tendency of historians like Sandburg to paint a picture of Lincoln as a godlike
figure without fault or moral weakness; and, as such, it is on

target. There is sometimes a syrupy sentimentality found in the Lincoln literature, and Hollywood's version of it, that can be unrealistic, even offensive.

But much more so than in the case of Lee? That is an open question, some would argue. Can it not be said that Southerners who sneer, almost reflexively, at the memory of Lincoln make the same closed-minded error that blacks and Northerners make when they deride the memory of Lee? Are they not refusing to consider the complexities of the issues that compelled Lincoln (made him *feel* compelled at any rate) to act as he did in the crises that precipitated the Civil War? Often one gets the impression that certain Southern writers refuse to read about Lincoln's career for fear that they will end up liking him, that it is a point of honor. There might be some logic in this: it is hard to read about him, especially to read his words, and still detest him.

Admittedly, it must be trying for Southerners who recall the blood spilled by their familial and cultural forefathers in the Civil War to look with an open mind on Lincoln's career. Probably it is just about as trying for blacks to reconsider Lee. But in this instance, too, historical accuracy and racial reconciliation demand it. It is possible to admire *both* Lincoln and Lee. The large percentage of Americans whose families were not in the United States in the 1860s (at least those who have taken the time to think about these things) know that. It can be done—when one's main concern is to recognize that good men fought on both sides in that terrible civil conflict rather than to prove which side was right—when one looks at the Civil War as an American, not as a Southerner, Northerner, black, or white.

The point is that Lincoln and Lee represent *contrasting* visions and aspirations for America, but not conflicting ones. They contrast in the way the brass section swells against the strings within the flow of a moving symphony. We want and need both. Lee represents the dream of a nation of individual local freedoms, where regional differences are admitted and cultivated, where sectional and cultural pieties prevail over an intruding, standardizing, and materialistic central government of "experts" and "planners." Lincoln, well—something else. Let us approach that "something else" cautiously and with all due care and thoroughness. But before we do, it is necessary to look at one of the minor streams of praise that continues to refresh the nation's love of Lincoln: Lincoln as the poor boy who made

104

good, proof that anyone can grow up to be President in this land of opportunity, even a child born and raised in a log cabin. Surely there would not be as much attention paid to this part of Lincoln's life if he had been President during a noneventful period in the country's history. What is truly remarkable is that a loved and respected President, who guided the ship of state through the stormiest of seas, came from such a humble background. (It matters much less what kind of boyhood Calvin Coolidge or Warren G. Harding lived, for example.) But even on its own merits, Lincoln's climb up the ladder of life is genuinely worthy of praise.

Kentucky Boy Makes Good

There is an irony in the continued Southern resistance to Lincoln. In so many ways he exemplifies a kind of man near and dear to the heart of the South: a good old boy (yes, even a "redneck") who meets the city dudes on their own ground, beats them and outsmarts them without becoming like them; the country kid who succeeds but retains with pride the simple and unaffected ways of the frontier. And Lincoln was a Southern boy—a Kentucky boy. (Kentucky did not join the Confederacy, although there was considerable sympathy for such a move. But it certainly is considered a Southern state, and lies south of the Mason-Dixon line.)

Some of the accounts of Lincoln's boyhood (even some of the best known) may be less than 100 percent factual, although to say so is to accuse Lincoln of knowingly encouraging falsehoods, since these stories were circulated during his lifetime. Most of them, in fact, are found in his own autobiographical writing. And to *presume* that Lincoln was a conscious liar is irresponsible by scholarly standards alone. The usual critical charge given some credence is just the reverse—that he was a moralist without patience or understanding, a fanatic who would fight a civil war rather than compromise on a problematical social evil. But all this takes us (slightly) afield. The main concern of our study is the reason why men like Lincoln have been remembered by Americans; why stories about them have been told and retold by one generation after another; what it is Americans *wanted* to be true about them.

The log cabin? There is no doubt about that. Lincoln's boyhood was that of a frontier boy, first in Kentucky, then, from the age of eight on, in Indiana. His formal schooling amounted to less than a year in one of the one-room schoolhouses of the time where the educational objective was, as the saying went, "readin', writin', and cipherin' to the rule of three." But rather than brood and feel sorry about his culturally deprived background, and make excuses for himself because of it, Lincoln strove to overcome its limitations. He wanted to be more than an "average guy" of his time and place—even if that required self-deprivation and sacrifice. Somehow the young Lincoln managed to get his hands on a sampling of the classics. It could not be called a library, but near the loft bed in the log cabin Lincoln had copies of *Aesop's Fables, Robinson Crusoe, The Pilgrim's Progress,* a *History of the United States,* and Parson Weems' *Life of Washington.* (This last book Lincoln, later in life, called a great and healthy influence on his development as a man.) He read and reread these books, most often by the light of a candle after the day's work was through. He would copy down favorite passages on scraps of paper or on a board if he had no paper. (One cannot help but contrast the effect of these few books on Lincoln with that of modern education on today's students. After being exposed to an abundance of textbooks, pamphlets, study guides, films, tapes, records, etc., etc., the complaint is often heard that students are "bored" by school. Lincoln developed a love of learning from exposure to a handful of the uplifting classics.)

He would memorize stirring passages, and recite them over and over to develop his speaking style. Neighbors and friends, in fact, would joke about this boy who would get up and give a recitation at the drop of a hat at social gatherings.

Later in life, after he had made the decision to become an attorney, this early self-discipline stood him in good stead. It was no easy task for even the best-educated men of the time to pass the examinations required to earn the right to practice law. For a young man without any schooling to speak of, it might have seemed impossible. But not to Lincoln: "The more I read [Blackstone's *Commentaries*—the text used by almost all student lawyers at the time] the more intensely interested I became. Never in my whole life was my mind so thoroughly absorbed. I read until I devoured them." During breaks from his chores, on days off, nights, lunch periods, wherever and whenever the opportunity arose, Lincoln pursued his goal, even if friends and acquaintances scoffed at him for chasing unreachable dreams. But Lincoln would not permit himself to be limited by the standards of those who would settle for a comfortable mediocrity.

A man named Russel Godby who once employed Lincoln to do some farmwork tells of a revealing incident with his hired hand. He found the long and lanky young man at the top of a woodpile reading a book:

"This being an unusual thing for farm hands in that early day to do, I asked him what he was reading. 'I'm not reading,' he answered. 'I am studying.' 'Studying what,' I inquired. 'Law, sir' was the emphatic response. It was really too much for me, as I looked at him sitting there proud as Cicero. 'Great God Almighty!' I exclaimed and passed on."

Another neighbor commented:

"He dwelt altogether in the land of thought. His deep meditation and abstraction easily induced the belief among his horny handed companions that he was lazy . . . His chief delight during the day if unmolested was to lie down under the shade of some inviting tree and read and study . . . No one had a more retentive memory. If he read or heard a good thing it never escaped him. His power of concentration was intense, and in the ability through analysis to strip bare a proposition he was unexcelled. His thoughtful and investigating mind dug down after ideas and never stopped until bottom facts were reached."

Another says:

"Wherever he was and whenever he could do so the book was brought into use. He carried it with him in his rambles through the woods and his walks to the river. When night came he read it by the aid of any friendly light he could find. Frequently he went down to the cooper's shop and kindled a fire out of the waste material lying about, and by the light it afforded read until far into the night."

One of his boyhood companions added:

"He never appeared to be a hard student, as he seemed to master his studies with little effort, until he commenced the study of the law. In that he became wholly engrossed, and began for the first time to avoid the society of men, in order that he might have more time for study."

He came to realize, simply, that enjoying the pleasures and comforts (such as they were on the frontier) of being "just one of the boys" would stunt his growth as a man.

107

But Lincoln's desire to excel did not result in an arrogant disdain and contempt for people and their ways. He wanted to develop all of his own potential as a man in order to serve his fellow men (as well as to advance himself, of course), not to deride them in the name of the superior sensitivities of the well-educated. He did not, in other words, become what people (often unfairly) call an "egghead" or a member of the "intelligentsia." He never affected a speech pattern different from his neighbors', nor a superior air. He retained the colloquial expressions and frontier wit he learned in the crossroads and towns of his youth. He continued to participate in wrestling matches and rail-splitting contests at neighborhood picnics. There is an oft-repeated story of one such wrestling match in which he became so angered at the unfair tactics of his opponent that he "fairly lifted the great bully by the throat and shook him like a rag," as one biographer phrases it.

On another occasion, while he was working as a clerk in a general store, a loud and obscene border tough, probably under the influence of some frontier moonshine, began taunting several women making purchases. Lincoln ordered him to stop, at which point the man laughed uproariously, saying that he had not yet met the man who could tell him to shut up and that he didn't think this clerk selling fabric to women would be the first. Seeing that the man would not be satisfied with anything less than a fight, Lincoln stated calmly, "Well, if you must be whipped, I suppose I may as well whip you as any other man," and went outside with him. Doctor Holland, one of Lincoln's biographers, described what happened next. Lincoln "threw him upon the ground, held him there as if he had been a child, and gathering some 'smart weed' which grew upon the spot, rubbed it into his face and eyes, until the fellow bellowed with pain. Lincoln did all this without a particle of anger, and when the job was finished, went immediately for water, washed his victim's face, and did everything he could to alleviate his distress."

It is said that he excelled in village weight-lifting contests, too, especially drinking from the spigot of a full whiskey barrel by holding it at eye level. Lincoln was one of the few who could do it, although he never took a swallow of the whiskey.

But it was more for honesty and kindness than for strength and fighting prowess that he became known. There are so many stories that can be used to demonstrate why he was nicknamed

"Honest Abe" that it is difficult to know where to begin. Lincoln biographies abound with tales of him rescuing drunks and animals, coming to the aid of threatened children, protecting Indians from angry and drunken mobs. There are two, however, that have become the most famous. Thirty or so years ago every student who attended an American school (in the North) was as familiar with them as with the alphabet.

The first revolves around a copy of the Parson Weems book on Washington. It seems that Lincoln as a young boy first encountered the book in the home of a neighbor, Josiah Crawford. Crawford was known in the area as a tight-fisted pennypincher of the first order. Only with much persuasion was Lincoln able to convince Crawford to let him borrow the book. One night, after Lincoln had read by his candle, he placed the book near his bed in a chink between the logs in the wall of the cabin. He had done this many times before when he read late into the night, rather than climb down the ladder in the darkness to return a book to the shelf. This night, however, it rained so heavily that the water seeped between the logs and ruined the book. When the boy awoke he was hurt and frightened. Not only was the book he loved waterlogged and stained, but the skinflint Crawford would be proved right. He should never have trusted his fine book to a neighborhood roughneck! Of course Lincoln could have begged off. He did not have the money to pay for the book. Neither did his father. It was an accident—no one could question that. He had exercised reasonable care. Anyone who has spent any time in an American school today knows how much longer the list of excuses would be if such a thing happened to a modern student after he borrowed a book from the school library. But Lincoln was not average. He was different. He worked for three full days for the farmer to pay for the damaged biography.

On another occasion, while he was working as a clerk, he sold a woman a bill of goods amounting to two dollars and six and a quarter cents, not a small amount of money in those days. Upon checking his addition at the end of the day, long after the woman had left for home, he noticed that he had overcharged her by six and a quarter cents. Night had already fallen. We know what the reaction to such a situation would be from most people. The best of us would probably put the money aside to give to the woman when she returned; some of us might take advantage of the opportunity to make a little extra money for ourselves: "finders keepers," so to speak. Lincoln, though, realizing that even such a small amount of money could make a big difference to a tight frontier budget, walked two or three miles through the night to the woman's home to return it.

Any Lincoln biography would give dozens more episodes in the same vein. Are they all true? Well, they cannot all be false. The two above are repeated too often to be seriously doubted, if the usual standards for judging such things are maintained. Whatever one wants to make of the Lincoln legends, he *was* known to his contemporaries as an exceptionally honest man.

Attorney at Law

The long years of arduous study, as we know, paid off. Lincoln became a trial lawyer of note in Illinois (where he had moved after leaving his father's home; he had decided that he would not be able to pursue his dream of practicing law unless he left the homestead). His judgement, coolness under stress, rhetorical skills, and deep concern for justice made him a reputation in legal and political circles. The man could be a crowd-pleaser.

In this western atmosphere, where family ties and connections counted less than energy and ability, men like Lincoln were able to rise to the top. Lincoln was aware and appreciative of the opportunities afforded him in such a world. His career, in a decided sense, was committed to preserving and advancing this frontier ideal of offering opportunity to all (including blacks), not just to a privileged few. It was not an eastern industrialist America that he championed, but an America with a frontier commitment to advancement based on merit: government of, by, and for the people rather than for an elite (whether from industrial centers or plantations). If there was substance to the Southern fear that Lincoln's Presidency meant an increase in power for the industrial "robber barons," there is little to the claim that Lincoln planned it that way.

Probably his most famous case as an Illinois lawyer was his defense of William "Duff" Armstrong, the son of a boyhood friend. Armstrong was accused of killing a man at a religious camp meeting. Lincoln was convinced that the boy had been charged wrongfully. At the trial, all of Lincoln's diligently acquired skills were brought to bear in his defense. He was eloquent, precise, and thorough in his handling of the early pro-

110

ceedings of the trial—obviously a man who knew the law and how to present it to a jury. But his success was due, as well, to the reservoir of common sense he had acquired on the frontier.

The state's star witness was one Charles A. Allen, a man who had testified previously at the trial of another man alleged to have been involved in the murder. That man had been found guilty based on Allen's testimony, and the strong presumption was that Lincoln's client would meet with the same fate. Allen had testified that Armstrong and his companion hit the deceased on the back of the head with clubs and slingshots. He stated that he had been able to see the assault clearly from his vantage point 150 feet away since there was a full moon that night.

"Lincoln sat with his head thrown back, his steady gaze apparently fixed upon one spot of the blank ceiling, entirely oblivious to what was happening before him, and without a single variation of feature or noticeable movement of any muscle of his face," reported Judge Abram Berger, then a young lawyer present in the courtroom. To some it appeared that Lincoln had conceded the case and had lost interest. Until he began his cross-examination.

One biographer paraphrases it thus:

"Did you actually see the fight. Yes. Well, where were you standing at the time? About a hundred and fifty feet from the combatants. Describe the weapon again. The slingshot was pictured in detail. And what time did you say all this occurred? Eleven o'clock at night. The moon was shining real bright. A full moon? Yes, a full moon, and as high in the heavens as the sun would be at ten o'clock in the morning. He was positive about that.

"Then with dramatic suddenness Lincoln requested the sheriff to bring him an almanac for the year 1857. Turning to the date of August 29, the night of the murder, he pointed a long forefinger to the page and bade Allen to read."

The almanac stated clearly that there was no full moon that evening. It was a quarter moon—which had disappeared entirely from the heavens by eleven o'clock. Allen's credibility as a witness destroyed, Lincoln moved into his summary speech. Duff Armstrong was acquitted.

Lincoln's career as an attorney was interrupted by a tour of duty as a state legislator. It was a position he held only briefly, failing at re-election. Hardly an auspicious beginning in politics!

At first Lincoln considered forgetting political life altogether. And he just might have, if it had not been for the furor, and his keen interest in it, aroused by the Kansas-Nebraska Bill. During the time the bill was being debated, Lincoln moved back into the public arena, campaigning for the re-election of Richard Yates, a Congressman from Illinois who was a staunch opponent of it.

Why such a to-do about a proposed piece of legislation? For Lincoln, this bill, if passed, would bring about a base desertion of the principles upon which America was founded. It was a historical fork in the road; America would either move forward to perfect the union established by our Founding Fathers, or select instead a road that would lead to tyranny. How could one bill evoke such fears in him?

In order to get a handle on that question it is necessary to understand what Lincoln thought were the implications of the Kansas-Nebraska Bill, and the Missouri Compromise of 1820, which it would override if enacted. From the very beginning of the union established by the Constitution of 1787, there was a conflict between slaveholding Southern states and the free states in the North. The question arose: Would slavery be allowed in the new states? If it were forbidden in the entire west, as it had been in the territories of the Northwest Ordinance of 1787 (which began the process of adding new states to the original 13), the Southern slave states would, eventually, become subject to the directive control of the North. Such a prospect led to serious protests, and even the threat of secession from the Union. In 1820 a compromise was reached—the Missouri Compromise (since the territory then in question was the Missouri Territory). In return for allowing Missouri to enter the Union as a slaveholding state, the North got Maine admitted as a free state. From then on, however, slavery would not be permitted within the territory secured by the Louisiana Purchase, north of 36°30'. This scheme, worked out in the main by Henry Clay, "The Great Compromiser" as he became known, solved the problem only temporarily, however. What about the rest of the west? Would the new states be slave, free, some slave, some free—what?

In 1854 the Kansas-Nebraska Bill was proposed as an answer, introduced by Senator Stephen A. Douglas. It called for, in sum, the principle of "popular sovereignty" or "squatter sovereignty" in the new territories. Slavery would not be banned beforehand in the territories, but instead would be put before the settlers ("squatters") for a vote. The voters in each state would decide for themselves whether their state would be free or slave.

Lincoln's speeches on behalf of Yates and against Douglas's proposal brought him once again into the spotlight. One observer said that his eloquence surpassed Daniel Webster's on this issue. Webster had enhanced his reputation as an opponent of increased states' rights in his famed debates with Senator Robert Y. Hayne of South Carolina.

Lincoln's efforts, as impressive as they were, were hardly enough in themselves to stop the bill. It was passed in 1854. That did not resolve the question, however—not by a long shot. For one thing the "right to decide" on this question turned the western territories into veritable battlegrounds as the pro-slavery and anti-slavery factions fought out the issue with gunfire as well as speeches and the ballot box. Kansas became known as "Bleeding Kansas," so vicious was the struggle. Pressure mounted in Congress to reverse the act; to outlaw slavery in the new states as a national policy, or, at least, to restore the Missouri Compromise prohibitions north of 36°30'. Lincoln moved to the forefront in the debate in Illinois; so much so that when Douglas came up for re-election to the Senate in 1858, Lincoln was chosen by the Republican Party to run against him.

The famed Lincoln-Douglas debates followed. In them, Lincoln began to work out a coherent public policy statement giving his "answer" to the question of slavery in America. It could be said that he spent the rest of his life bringing that answer to the nation.

Why was Lincoln so opposed to the call for popular sovereignty, as found in the Kansas-Nebraska Act—the idea that the people of each state should decide for themselves whether their state should permit slavery or not? Was it because he feared that the entire country would vote for slavery? No, all the political pundits of the time were aware that slavery stood little chance of being voted in in the West (the northeastern states had already expressed disfavor), except for, perhaps, New Mexico. The people of the Western states, who had journeyed to these new areas to find opportunities for themselves as farmers or as paid employes, were not likely to vote for a slaveholding economy within which they could not compete. A man looking for a job, or a farmer trying to market his crops, just could not

113

beat the price of slave labor. It is true that the Dred Scott decision increased the likelihood that slavery might spread into areas where it had been voted down. But was this a real threat?

Dred Scott was a slave who, brought by his master into free territory, refused to remain a slave after being brought back to the South. Arguing that he was a free man once he entered free territory, Scott claimed he had been illegally transported back into slave territory. The Supreme Court, however, found against Scott. The decision stated, in brief, that slaves were the "property" of their owner. An owner, consequently, could bring them wherever he wanted in the United States. Moreover, a slave who had fled from his master to a free state would have to be returned by the free state. The slave owners were declared entitled to the protection that the Constitution gives to property. It appeared that this decision in one fell swoop negated the provisions of both the Missouri Compromise and the Kansas-Nebraska Act. Now slavery would have to be permitted wherever a slaveowner wanted to go—or so many thought at first. In reality, slavery could not possibly prosper in a state that refused to set up the police procedures to return escaped or liberated (by the owner or others) blacks, and states that had voted against slavery were not likely to initiate such police agencies. Slavery was not likely to spread in any appreciable degree beyond the South.

Was it that Lincoln was an abolitionist, a man committed to an immediate and complete emancipation of slaves everywhere, and that a defeat of the Kansas-Nebraska Act was part of that strategy? Hardly. Lincoln was not an abolitionist. His statements on slavery up to his fateful Emancipation Proclamation in 1863 surprise many modern readers. He was willing to tolerate slavery for the foreseeable future, as long as it remained strictly in those areas of the South where it had become an entrenched institution. He made the point on numerous occasions. As early as his debates with Douglas, for example, he argued that he had no desire to force the South to change the entire way of life that had grown up around slavery. Not right away, in any event. But, the South must not demand the right to *spread* slavery. This was the key (for reasons we will examine shortly).

> I surely will not blame them [slave owners] for not
> doing what I should not know how to do myself [free
> the slaves in a way just and fair and without creating

114

absolute chaos in the process]. If all earthly power were given me, I should not know what to do as to the existing situation . . . When they remind us of their constitutional rights, I acknowledge them, not grudgingly, but fully, and fairly; and I would give them any legislation for the reclaiming of their fugitives, which should not, in its stringency, be more likely to carry a free man into slavery, than our ordinary criminal laws are to hang an innocent one . . . But all this, to my judgement, furnishes no more excuse for permitting slavery to go into our free territory, than it would for reviving the African slave trade by law.

Slavery is founded in the selfishness of man's nature—opposition to it, in his love of justice. These principles are an eternal antagonism, and when brought into collision so freely, as slavery extension brings them, shocks, and throes, and convulsions must ceaselessly follow.

His words must be read carefully here, as elsewhere on this topic. He is taking the same position, at this stage in his career —the years just before he became President—as that taken by Robert E. Lee. That is: Slavery is an evil. America must work to end it; but patiently and without demanding social upheaval as the price. His only unconditional demand is for Americans *to point themselves in the direction of eventual emancipation;* to make that an aim and goal of our political life:

We are now into the fifth year, since a policy was initiated [Kansas-Nebraska Act] with the avowed object, and *confident* promise of putting an end to slavery agitation.

Under the operation of that policy, that agitation has not only, not ceased, but has constantly augmented.

In my opinion, it will not cease, until a crisis shall have been reached, and passed.

A house divided against itself cannot stand.

I believe this government cannot endure, permanently half slave and half free . . .

It will become *all* one thing, or *all* the other.

Either the opponents of slavery, will arrest further spread of it and place it where the public mind shall

115

rest in the belief that it is in the course of ultimate extinction; or its *advocates* will push it forward, till it shall become alike lawful in *all* the States, old as well as new—North as well as South.

The last three paragraphs should be read most attentively, and reread. He does not demand that the South free every slave by the next day at high noon. There is no warning; no threat. He is saying, in effect, that he wants to believe that the South is committed to the vision of Robert E. Lee! Will the South pledge itself to the eventual abolition of slavery, by going on record now that it has no intention of spreading its "peculiar institution" into new areas? Will the South accept the responsibility of viewing slavery as "peculiar"—an evil brought about by historical circumstance in the American South, but one that Southerners are pledged to end in due course? Will they agree to keep it "where the public mind shall rest in the belief that it is in the course of ultimate extinction"? Or will they desert the idealism of Lee, and instead proclaim slavery to be *a good* that they intend to perpetuate and extend?

Lincoln lost that election to Douglas. Douglas returned to the Senate and Lincoln to his law practice. He admitted, however, that he enjoyed the intellectual combat of campaigning for public office on the national level; that "the taste is in my mouth a little." But his chances for going further in party politics seemed slight, to say nothing of being nominated for the Presidency. He had failed to win re-election to Congress once; he had campaigned well against Douglas, but lost. Political parties in search of Presidential candidates do not usually seek to give a man a chance to become a three-time loser.

But in the unstable political atmosphere of the time, Lincoln got his chance. He became what we now would call a "compromise candidate" of the Republican party in 1860—not one of the top two favorites, but the man supporters of the top two accepted when they despaired of placing their own man in the winner's circle (but still refused to go along with the other leading contender).

And he won the general election, too, largely as a result of a split vote and unusual circumstances. The tension between North and South became so intense that Southern slave states refused to back the candidate of the Democratic party, thereby splitting the Democratic vote. Lincoln received 1,866,452 pop-

116

ular votes. His opponents polled 2,915,617. But Lincoln won a majority in the Electoral College and was elected President.

President Lincoln

There are some historians who speculate now that the election of Lincoln may have been a bad thing for the country, coming when it did. The theory is that moderates in the South, like Lee, were still dominant before the election, and would have been able to keep in line those eager to break with the Union—if it had not been for the election of Lincoln, who (unfairly) had the reputation of being a radical abolitionist.

Sensing the increasing tension that followed upon his election, Lincoln expended great effort in his inaugural address in 1861 to convince the South that he had no scheme in mind for moving into their section of the country for abolitionist purposes:

"I have no purpose . . . to interfere with the institution of slavery in the States where it exists. I believe I have no lawful right to do so, and I have no inclination to do so."

But he was as emphatic about what he was convinced was the larger, dominant issue. He would not tolerate a dissolution of the Union over the question. He would not preside over the destruction of the country established by our Founding Fathers.

"In your hands, my dissatisfied fellow countrymen, and not in mine, is the momentous issue of civil war . . . You have no oath registered in heaven to destroy the government, while I shall have the most solemn one to 'preserve, protect, and defend' it."

His closing words were a moving plea. Let us Americans work together in the spirit of the Founding Fathers to build the kind of country to which they dedicated their lives:

We are not enemies, but friends. We must not be
enemies. Though passion may have strained, it must
not break, our bonds of affection. The mystic chords
of memory, stretching from every battle-field and
patriot grave to every living heart and hearthstone
all over this broad land, will yet swell the chorus of
the Union when again touched, as surely they will be,
by the better angels of our nature.

117

But, Southerners might object, if Lincoln had such a generous disposition toward the South, and was confident that men like Lee would one day prevail, and abolish slavery, why not compromise with the South in the 1860s? The South was fearful of a Northern-sponsored, irresponsible, and radical abolitionist drive against the South. Why not guarantee the South at least a chance to prevent Northern domination, a chance to maintain a balance between slave and free states in the union by permitting the residents of the new states—especially those in the Southwest—to vote for slaveholder status if they so desired? Why not give the Southerners he professed to respect the time to make the reforms on slavery free from Northern interference—interference they feared would be inevitable if all new states were to be, by definition, free states?

Lincoln's position cannot easily be summarized. But it can be understood with some effort, and Lincoln was as diligent as any man ever in public life in explaining his position clearly. It centered upon an understanding of the relation between the Declaration of Independence and the Constitution.

Lincoln took the Declaration of Independence quite seriously. He did not see it, as some do, as merely a dramatic statement designed to give respectability to the colonies' rebellious break with England. To him it was a clear and well-thought-out, deliberate and precise statement of the kind of country we were to become: a piece of political philosophy. It defined a new country in which all men were to be treated as individuals, created equal by God, possessors of certain inalienable rights. Their government was defined as a human institution deriving its just powers from the consent of the governed—the people, *all* the people.

But if that truly was the sincere intention of the Founding Fathers—if the Declaration was not just flowery rhetoric—how could those same individuals establish or consent to a Constitution for their new country that provided for the continuation of black chattel slavery? Lincoln argued that there was no inconsistency. The Declaration, he argued, was a pledge to work for a country in which all men would be treated as equals before the law; it established a national ideal, *an aspiration.* It outlined the kind of society that the Founding Fathers hoped would one day be established in the new country. The Constitution on the other hand was a working instrument with which to organize the American society *as it existed* in the late eighteenth century. The Constitution made compromises. It allowed for the imperfections of man, but left the door open to "form a more perfect union" in the future (as stated in its Preamble). One of the most glaring imperfections was the institution of slavery. The Founding Fathers knew that, but knew as well that it was unrealistic to demand that the Southern states abolish it immediately. They knew, too, that such a demand would not be heeded, and would only lead the Southern states to refuse to join the Union. Hence the compromise. Slavery would be allowed—but as an unavoidable *temporary evil* that would one day be ended. No laws restricting the slave trade (Art. V Sec. 8) would be allowed until 1808, implying that after that *they would be*. And the first Congress did forbid slavery outright and completely in the new states created by the Northwest Ordinance. The South, because of the deeply entrenched nature of its "peculiar institution," would be given time to abolish slavery —as much time as it needed, in fact. But the country *as a whole* was going on record as a free republic. That, argued Lincoln (and by implication, at least, Lee), was the original "deal" between the states.

As long as the South remained faithful to that "deal," by not insisting upon elevating slavery into a *new* national ideal, thereby destroying the original understanding, he would apply no presidential pressure against them. He would initiate no crisis, unless the South threatened to destroy the Republic or to replace its democratic idealism with a slaveholder's notion of government by a chosen few. And he feared that just such a sentiment was growing:

> When you have succeeded in dehumanizing the Negro: when you have put him down and made it impossible for him to be but as the beasts of the field; when you have extinguished his soul in this world and placed him where the ray of hope is blown out as in the darkness of the damned, are you quite sure that the demon you have roused will not turn and rend you: What constitutes the bulwark of our liberty and independence? It is not our frowning battlements, our bristling sea coasts, our army and our navy. These are not our reliance against tyranny. All of those may be turned against us without making us weaker for the struggle. Our reliance is in the love of liberty which God has planted in us. Our defense is

119

in the spirit which prized liberty as the heritage of all men, in all lands everywhere. Destroy this spirit and you have planted the seeds of despotism at your own doors. Familiarize yourselves with the chains of bondage and you prepare your own hands to wear them. Accustomed to trample on the rights of others, you have lost the genius of your own independence and become the fit subjects of the first cunning tyrant who rises among you.

Lincoln feared, in other words, that a new breed of leader was coming to the fore in the South, men who would willingly deny the validity of the original "deal," men with a new vision —of slavery as the wave of the future. John C. Calhoun, one of the most respected intellects in the South, seemed to have succumbed to the allure of such a view. Would his replace the outlook of Lee?

"Many in the South once believed that slavery was a moral and political evil. That folly and delusion are gone. We now see it in its true light, and regard it as the most safe and stable basis for free institutions in the world."

Lincoln saw the issue clearly (mistakenly or not). America in time would be either all slave or all free. If the South was determined to make it all slave, he would resist, not only to thwart the extension of slavery, but to end an attack on the American attempt to maintain a government by the people.

In another speech, at Independence Hall, Philadelphia, itself, he developed further his fears that popular government was the issue at stake:

I have often pondered over the dangers which were incurred by the men who assembled here and framed and adopted that Declaration of Independence. I have pondered over the toils that were endured by the officers and soldiers of the army who achieved that independence . . . It was not the mere matter of a separation of the Colonies from the Motherland, but that sentiment in the Declaration of Independence which gave liberty not alone to the people of this country, but I hope to the world for all future time. It was that which gave promise that in due time the weight would be lifted from the shoulders of all men. This is the sentiment embodied in

120

the Declaration of Independence. Now, my friends, can this country be saved on this basis? If it can I will consider myself one of the happiest men in the world if I can help to save it. If it cannot be saved upon that principle, it will be truly awful.

Secession

Unfortunately, the debate over the question of slavery in the Western territories became moot. Not long after Lincoln's election the Southern states began the process of secession and the formation of the Confederate States of America, thereby shifting the ground of the argument. Now one question above all others came to the fore. Did Lincoln have the authority—and the power to back it up—to preserve the Union *against* the wishes of the Southern states? Was the Union a permanent bond or a "confederation," as the South would have it, that could be broken at will? The text of Lincoln's speeches indicates the new priority. He had agreed not to interfere with slavery in the South; he had promised to enforce a reasonable fugitive slave law; he would continue to explain his case for outlawing the extension of slavery, confident that he could make his point with the large majority of nonslaveholders in the South. But he would brook no talk of secession:

"I hold that, in contemplation of the universal law and of the Constitution, the union of these States is perpetual . . . No state upon its own mere motion, can lawfully get out of the Union . . . I shall take care, as the Constitution expressly enjoins upon me, that the laws of the Union be faithfully executed in all the States . . . The power confided to me to hold, occupy, and possess the property and places belonging to the government, and to collect duties and imports . . ."

Once the Southern states had seceded (which, in fact, the first of them did while Lincoln's predecessor, James Buchanan, was still in office), the question in the minds of responsible statesmen, North and South, was how to heal the breach. The hope endured that some compromise plan could be constructed that would persuade the Confederates to return without the need to resort to force. Even after Federal forts in the South had been seized, Buchanan threatened no military action. But Buchanan knew he would soon be leaving office; he could bequeath the problem to the new President—Lincoln.

Lincoln did not immediately send troops to take back Federal property and end the secession. He understood all too well that such an action could result in civil war. It was not until he felt his hand forced at Fort Sumter that he made his momentous decision.

By March of Lincoln's first year in office the Confederates, who had surrounded Fort Sumter in the harbor at Charleston, South Carolina, refusing to admit food, supplies, or reinforcements, were close to forcing a surrender. Major Robert Anderson, the officer in charge of the fort, notified Lincoln that he would be unable to hold out much longer without supplies. Lincoln's problem was obvious. If he moved troops to supply and reinforce the fort, they would be fired upon by Southern soldiers, bringing on war. If, however, he allowed the Confederacy to force a surrender in his first months in office, he would encourage similar attacks all over the South and give other Southern states, which had not yet seceded, the confidence that they could do so without fear of Federal resistance. He could, in other words, give the impression that he had resigned himself to a breakup of the Union. Several of his advisors pleaded with him to take no action—to continue negotiating with the Confederates to reach an accommodation along the reasonable lines he had been suggesting all along. To send in troops would end all hope for a reasonable compromise and put the most radical secessionists in the driver's seat. It would look like an attack on the South, to which even moderates might respond with armed resistance (as did Lee). Others argued that he had to take a stand someday or see the dissolution of the country, and that the longer he waited the more difficult it would be; that a decisive show of force at this stage could crush the rebellion, and avert large-scale civil war.

We all know what followed. Lincoln did decide to send in the troops—and the South responded, taking Sumter by siege. The larger war was not averted. A mammoth four-year struggle ensued, a long and bloody war, the scars of which remain to this day. Lincoln insisted to his death that he had no intention of initiating the conflict; that the Confederates fired first, in response to his intention only to bring food to the besieged force at Sumter; that he was willing to reach a compromise—until the first shot had been fired by Southern troops. But the South failed to see the logic in such talk. Lincoln sent troops onto Southern soil—an act it held tantamount to a declaration of war and invasion.

After hostilities broke out, Lincoln continued to hold out the olive branch. His proposal was not very different from the one he had offered before the war. Time and again, he insisted that he envisioned a peace that demanded no Federal conquest or occupation of the South. If the Confederates would pledge allegiance to the Union and promise to abide by laws made by the legally elected officials of the Federal government in respect to the extension of slavery, he would not interfere with the way they handled the slavery question within their own borders. He was not on a moralistic crusade to abolish slavery at once. He continued to press the arguments he had made earlier, such as in his famous speech at Cooper Union, a college in New York. (It is a brilliantly analytical and insightful speech that should be read in its entirely by all who claim to be students of the Civil War—Northerners and Southerners alike.)

> . . . you make these declarations [that] you have a specific and well-understood allusion to an assumed constitutional right of yours to take slaves into the Federal Territories, and to hold them there as property [he is addressing himself to the arguments of Confederate spokesmen, of course]. But no such right is specifically written in the Constitution. That instrument is literally silent about any such right. We, on the contrary, deny that such a right has any evidence in the Constitution, even by implication.

But, the main point . . .

> Your purpose, then, plainly stated, is that you will destroy the government, unless you be allowed to construe and force the Constitution as you please, on all points in dispute between you and us. You will rule, or ruin, in all events . . .

> . . . do you really feel yourselves justified to break up this government unless such a court decision as yours is shall be at once submitted to as a conclusive and final rule of political action? But you will not abide the election of a Republican president! In that event, you say, you will destroy the Union; and then, you say, the great crime of having destroyed it will

123

be upon us . . . A highwayman holds a pistol to my ear,
and mutters through his teeth, 'Stand and deliver, or
I shall kill you, and then you will be a murderer!'

If he has promised not to interfere in the South's handling of the slave question, and the South continues to demand the right to secede, where can he turn next, he asks.

"The question recurs, What will satisfy them? Simply this: we must not only let them alone, but we must somehow convince them that we do let them alone. This we know by experience, is no easy task. We have been so trying to convince them . . . but with no success."

Then why, later in the war (1863), did he issue the Emancipation Proclamation? The motivation for this presidential edict remains a matter of some discussion. It did not really free the slaves. It took the Thirteenth Amendment to do that. The Proclamation applied only to the States that had seceded—but since they had seceded they declared it invalid and paid no attention. It freed no slaves in the rest of the Union. Some argue that it was a war tactic designed to pressure the South into a surrender. In fact, in the first draft of the text, Lincoln ordered the slaves freed only for the duration of his administration, implying that the slaves could be returned to their masters if a satisfactory peace treaty were arranged. Others argue that it was more an attempt to gain sympathy from the European nations —to make the North the side of justice and humanity—in order to forestall Confederate hopes for support from abroad in their war effort. But it is as likely that Lincoln, after leading the nation through two long years of civil war, had come to see that slavery, after all the bloodshed, simply could not be brought back as usual. The crisis had arrived for the Union; *the price had been paid* by men-at-arms. What he feared slavery could bring about *had come.* He had been willing to compromise on slavery to avoid war, but *war had come.* The issue had to be settled. To allow slavery to return to the South would be to permit a re-creation of the conditions that led to the deadly conflict in the first place. The Union could not be placed in jeopardy again. The bloody sacrifice could not be allowed to go for naught. The Union must be made secure. As Lincoln once wrote to newspaper editor Horace Greeley:

"My paramount objective in this struggle is to save the union, and is not either to save or destroy slavery. If I could save the union without freeing any slave, I would do it; and if I could do it by freeing all the slaves, I would do it; and if I could save it by freeing some and leaving others alone I would also do that."

One must, of course, read these words in light of Lincoln's other comments on slavery. He is *not* saying that slavery is not an evil. He had spoken often and clearly on that point before this letter to Greeley. Again—he was willing to tolerate it *for a time* so that the Union, which was pledged to ending it when the time was right, could survive to accomplish that goal of "a more perfect union."

Lincoln had an opportunity, after the Battle of Gettysburg, to put these thoughts into words he hoped the public would be able to understand. Almost everyone has heard the speech before. Read it now to see how clearly Lincoln makes the point that the overriding objective of the struggle was the preservation of a Union *pledged* to a future condition of political equality. Notice how often the word "dedicate," or words that stand in its place, appear in the text. Only an unquestioned defeat of the Confederacy could guarantee that government by the people "would not perish from the earth"—and the abolition of slavery was a necessary part of that defeat. To allow it to return would create the impression that the very nature of the Union had been compromised.

LINCOLN'S GETTYSBURG ADDRESS
(AN ANALYSIS)

Fourscore and seven (eighty-seven) years ago (1776, not 1789) our fathers brought forth upon this continent a new nation conceived in liberty and DEDICATED to the proposition that all men are created equal.

Now we are engaged in a great civil war testing whether that nation or any nation so conceived, and so DEDICATED can long endure.

We are met on a great BATTLEFIELD (where life is dedicated) of that war.

We have come to DEDICATE a portion of that field as a final resting-place for those who here gave their lives that that nation might live.

It is altogether fitting and proper that we should do THIS.

But in a larger sense we cannot DEDICATE, we cannot consecrate, we cannot hallow this ground.

The brave men living and dead who struggled here have CONSECRATED it far above our poor power to add or detract.

125

The world will little note nor long remember what we may say here, but it can never forget WHAT THEY DID HERE. (Dedication of human life.)

It is for us the living rather to be DEDICATED here to the unfinished work which they who fought here have thus far so nobly advanced.

It is rather for us to be here DEDICATED to the great tasks remaining before us, that from these honored dead we take increased devotion to that cause for which they gave the last full measure of devotion; that we here highly resolve that these dead shall not have died in vain; that this nation under God shall have a new birth of freedom, and that government of the people, by the people and for the people shall not perish from the earth.

From R.M. Wanamaker, *The Voice of Lincoln* (New York: Scribner's, 1918), p. 225.

The Lincoln who had been willing to compromise before the war was faced with a new moral imperative: ". . . that these dead shall not have died in vain."

The Peace

Even after the Emancipation Proclamation, Lincoln maintained a posture of reconciliation. The continuation of slavery was no longer an open question, of course, making his offers less attractive to the South. At a meeting between a group of Southern politicians and himself in the last year of the war—a meeting held to seek common ground for a mutually-agreed-to peace—he stated:

> . . . if I were in Georgia . . . I'll tell you what I would do, if I were in your place: I would go home and get the Governor of the State to call the Legislature together, and get them to recall all the State troops from the war; elect Senators and Members to Congress, and ratify this Constitutional Amendment [the one which would abolish slavery] *prospectively,* so as to take effect—say in five years [implying that it could be more, if necessary]. Such a ratification would be valid in my opinion. Whatever may have

126

been the views of your people before the war, they
must be convinced now, that slavery is doomed. It
cannot last long in any event, and the best course, it
seems to me, for your public men to pursue, would
be to adopt such a policy as will avoid, as far as possible, the evils of immediate emancipation.

Still tolerant, still forgiving—if the South would only agree to
the continued existence of the United States with its original
principles intact. In his second Inaugural Address, he repeated
the theme—and continued to implore his fellow countrymen to
return to the Union. He would seek no revenge; he would not
seek to punish the South:

With malice toward none; with charity for all; with
firmness in the right, as God gives us to see the right,
[once again, at the risk of seeming excessively repeti-
tive, we note that Lincoln is speaking of the "right"
that men like Lee had seen: that slavery was wrong],
let us strive on to finish the work we are in; to bind
up the nation's wounds; to care for him who shall
have borne the battle, and for his widow, and his
orphan—to do all which may achieve and cherish a
just and lasting peace among ourselves, and with all
nations.

We all know that the South never got the just and lasting
peace promised by Lincoln; that politicians after Lincoln's
death were concerned more with punishing the South than
with binding wounds. The term "Reconstruction politics" has
become a term of criticism in both the North and South, along
with "carpetbaggers" and "scallawags." But surely Lincoln cannot be blamed for the reversal of his policies after his death.
There is not an inkling anywhere in his behavior or words
before his assassination that he intended, or would have gone
along with, punitive measures. He had said many times that he
considered Northern merchants as guilty of the slave trade as
the Southerners who bought the slaves from them. When the
Confederate states had returned, in Lincoln's scheme, they
were once again to be given the responsibility for their local
affairs under the Constitutional arrangement. As soon as they
accepted the authority of Federal law, especially on the question of slavery, they would be brothers again, and as such, entrusted with the responsibility for conducting their affairs in a

responsible way. He made no threats of martial law or Federal takeovers of the legislative process.

Lincoln—the Symbol

At the beginning of this chapter it was stated that Lincoln stands in the memories of Americans for ideals that are different from, but not opposed to, those that Robert E. Lee represents. By now those ideals should be obvious. Ironically they seem more alive, at our time in history, in the South than anywhere else in the country. The South continues to provide the lion's share of career military officers for the American armed forces. The Union must be preserved. If we are to survive as a free, responsibly strong, and moderately prosperous people—the Union must be preserved. If we are determined to withstand the forces that threaten us in the world—the Union must be preserved. If the Union had been dissolved in Lincoln's time into northern and southern sections, what would have prevented it from dissolving further later on? Rather than helping to perfect our national brotherhood, the Civil War would have proved conclusively that Americans could not overcome their regional and ideological differences. Where would that have left us in the twentieth century, as the powerful nation-states of the world feuded for territory, natural resources, and empire—where in the face of the surging twentieth-century "isms," Communism and Nazism? We can be free only as long as we are strong enough to protect our legitimate national interests—and we are strong only as long as we are united. Lincoln stands for a united America—one nation, under God, aspiring for liberty and justice for all.

William Jennings Bryan

5

William Jennings Bryan
The Great Commoner

The Great Commoner"—the man who made a career of representing the beliefs and hopes of the "average guy," the "common man," the "little people," the "masses"; the "silent majority" might be the way his constituency would be described in our time. But his followers were quite different from the common man of today. Bryan represented the small-town, God-fearing, agricultural America of the nineteenth century and defended it, its way of life, and its values against the changes being ushered in by modern science, large-scale industry, and the progressive social theorists. It could be said, then, that he lost the battle: Bryan's America has declined in numbers and influence. We are now largely an urban people. Certainly our tastes and attitudes are shaped in urban centers; the television shows and movies we watch, the books and newspapers we read, the attitudes and lifestyles that seem to dominate, all originate in the great metropolitan complexes. Nevertheless, questions continue to pop up—often unexpectedly—when modern Americans study seriously the career of this midwestern politician, orator, and newspaperman; enduring questions that lead many who expect to dislike Bryan and the "backward" forces he represented to entertain second thoughts. In recent years thinkers of widely differing political persuasions have found elements in his career that they consider worthy of praise. Those who lean to the Left have applauded his understanding of the threat posed to democracy by enormous concentrations of wealth and power in the hands of a relatively small number of industrialists. New Left revisionist historians, in fact, now point to the election of 1896—when Bryan was defeated by William McKinley—as a watershed in our history. They assert that the question whether private wealth (capitalism) was going to be forced to operate under strict public control was—perhaps for the only time in American political history—truly up for grabs that year. Only a massive and dishonest application of power by wealthy industrialists and their political supporters, the New Left historians continue, stopped Bryan from putting America on the path toward socialism. (This is a controversial argument, to say the least, since Bryan argued against socialism throughout his career. The New Left revisionists insist, however, that the kind of control over private ownership Bryan proposed would have led to a socialist economy.) Those who tend to be called "right-wingers," on the other hand, find encouragement and wisdom in Bryan's defense of a religious foundation for society and the right of parents to control educational policies in their children's schools. Others praise his attacks on imperialism, his arguments against American intervention in World War I, and his call for a well-thought-out American policy of neutrality in foreign wars. Even the term "populism," which was commonly used to describe Bryan's political posture, has increased in favor of late, with politicians for high national office freely describing themselves as "populists."

In certain scholarly circles, however, there is a deep and abiding contempt both for the political causes Bryan championed and for the caliber of his mind. Some, indeed, seem to imply that only an outright fool would have been attracted to the ideas Bryan espoused. Below is only a sampling of the criticism that is commonplace in books about either him or the social movements associated with his name:

On Bryan's belief in the Bible as the Word of God:

"Obviously, a person who accepts literally all parts of the often self-contradictory scriptures will parade many inconsistencies in his own beliefs. So with Bryan, who was hardly a logical thinker and who felt no compulsion to develop his powers of reasoning."

And:

"The President of the United States may be an ass, but he at least doesn't believe that the earth is square, and that witches should be put to death, and that Jonah swallowed the whale." Bryan is a "peasant," a "zany without sense or dignity," a "poor clod." (All this from H.L. Mencken.)

On his ability as a leader:

" . . . in desires and in intelligence he was undistinguished. His indifference to facts was matched by his ignorance of them. He was meagerly equipped to cope with the nation's problems, but hordes of voters wanted to entrust them to him."

On his argument against the right of school teachers to promote an acceptance of Darwin's theories of evolution against the wishes of parents and taxpayers:

"From the mystical notion that all men are equal in the eyes of God, he lapsed into the absurdity that all men are equal in their ability to set up courses in biology."

On his belief in woman's suffrage:

"Bryan's softheadedness about women brought him in 1919 to a declaration that female votes could cure the worst problems of the age."

On the values of a life on a farm:

" 'Given a young man with a thorough education, good habits, willingness to work, and a desire to make himself useful, where can he fare better than on a farm?' [asked Bryan.] The answer was simple: In any city, but Bryan could not hear it."

It will be left for the reader to decide, after reading a sampling of Bryan's words, whether his analysis of these and other questions was soft-headed, absurd, and without sense or dignity. The adulation heaped upon him by so many millions of Americans (including millions who voted against him when he ran for the Presidency) indicates that much of the country thought not. They argued that those who found him "stupid" did so because he disagreed with them, as if that in itself were a proof of stupidity. (Curious that followers of his would vote against him? We will soon examine some of the reasons for this apparent inconsistency.)

133

Two Americas

It is possible, in other words, that those who find Bryan impossibly "stupid" do so largely because they have accepted one of the radical world views that have taken root in America since the end of the nineteenth century, especially in the growing cities of the East. These new philosophies have been given many labels—secularist, pragmatist, naturalistic, positivist, Darwinian, empiricist, subjectivist, among others—but they hold as common ground a rejection of the Bible-influenced, small-town morality of rural America that Bryan retained to his death. Those who accepted this new thinking denied, for the most part, that Scripture really is the Word of God (many denied that there is a personal God), and therefore that legitimate standards for living our lives can be learned from its pages. Much of the "wisdom" of the average American then—religious beliefs, morality, social standards, political convictions—they called into question. They demanded that Americans re-examine their accepted thinking; encourage freedom of discussion; tolerate those who refused to abide by the older, Bible-based beliefs, since the older beliefs were likely to be mere opinions about life developed by custom and prejudice down through time.

But not all Americans followed this advice. Many clung determinedly to the older views and saw the new theories as dangerous attacks on the very foundations of their lives, as heresy, even treason. They held fast to their religious beliefs, and the moral and political positions deduced from them, in the face of the challenge, insisting that the Bible did not have to meet the standards of modern scientists and philosophers; that it is above such scrutiny, unique, since it is the word of God. And they remained confident, as well, that people who read and lived their lives by the Bible could make the decisions required to run a country.

Two Americas, competing and conflicting Americas, could be seen. One, more interested in experimentation and change in morality and politics—to see what "worked," what made people happy, what increased material wealth. The other, determined to preserve the beliefs and convictions of its forefathers, to protect religious faith and public morality, and to promote a just distribution of material wealth in the land. The first group tended to be found in the cities and urban universities; the other in small towns and on the farms. The first tended to distrust the beliefs of the common man (since they were formed under the influence of unreliable religious authority) and to extol the wisdom of the freethinker, the innovator, the expert, the nonconformist whose new insights would encourage the ferment from which healthy social change would grow. The other championed the average man, the majority, the good citizens of Christian America who had been reared in a healthy religious environment and were able, as a result, to tell a villain from a man of virtue, a wrongful idea from a righteous one. Bryan, of course, was the hero of the agrarian, religious, small-town side of the equation.

Bryan entered the political arena fairly early in life. When he was only 30 he was elected to the U.S. House of Representatives from Nebraska. The year was 1890. Before that he had been a moderately successful lawyer in Illinois, where he was born. He moved to Nebraska to take advantage of the greater opportunities afforded a young man in the less-developed state to the west. It was not unexpected that Bryan would move into politics, since his father, Silas Bryan, had been a member of the Illinois state senate and had served as a circuit judge. As a boy, Bryan became accustomed to the atmosphere of discontent in the farm states, the complaints against "Eastern money men" and "manipulators." Farmers' associations, the Grange, and other agrarian movements for reform became part of his everyday life: "I lived in the very center of the country out of which the reforms grew, and was quite naturally drawn to the people's side," was the way he told it to historian Mark Sullivan.

It was over these economic issues, rather than a directly moral or religious question, that he first made his mark on national politics. But even economic questions for Bryan fit into the overall question of whether the country was going to be ruled by the "old" or the "new" faith. In 1893 a financial panic hit the country. Banks closed, unable to make good on their depositors' demands for their savings. Prices dropped on farm goods. Farmers had their mortgages foreclosed. Unemployment climbed rapidly. Midwestern farm groups began to seek the root cause of the economic dislocation, the villain. They asked, *Why?* What happened? They had grown their crops and were willing to sell them, but the prices dropped so low that they could not turn a profit. Why should something like that happen?

135

In simpler times such questions did not have to be asked—and many of the older farmers of Bryan's era remembered the simpler times. Before the railroad networks linked the farms with city markets, farmers operated by a fairly simple version of the laws of supply and demand. They would grow the food crops required for their own family needs, and then specialize in whatever market crops they thought would sell at the best price in nearby towns. If a farmer worked his soil diligently and if the weather was good, he could sell his crops at a fair price. What was fair? Whatever the laws of supply and demand dictated. If his corn or wheat was healthier looking than the farmer's down the road, he could get a higher price. If it was not, he would get a lower price. If too many farmers grew wheat, there be an overabundance at the markets and the price would go down. And the farmer could see why. Too much of the stuff. So the next year he might try corn or potatoes—try to raise a crop that would bring a profit. The harder he worked and the more knowledgeable he was in forecasting demand, the more profit he would make. There was a seemingly direct and simple connection between effort and reward, talent and reward, even virtue and reward. The better man won. One's standard of living was dependent upon forces under an individual's control. Profits could be used to purchase tools, clothing, and even occasional luxury items. Or maybe a man could cut down on some luxury items this year and put the money into seed or equipment to turn an even greater profit next year. Intelligence, effort, industriousness, planning could make a difference.

The price a man paid for tools and clothing and other necessities? It was set by the same process. Village craftsmen turned out their wares. The better craftsman got the better business. If he raised his prices excessively, people would go elsewhere, make do with a homemade product, or do without.

The railroads and the factories ended that simple way of life. And at first the burgeoning growth of industry looked good. There were a lot more mouths to feed and the farmer made a lot more profit. But he sold his crops to "agents" now. He had no idea any longer who it was that bought his crops. He himself bought his equipment and clothing and household incidentals from merchants who "carried a line" of products manufactured in a far-off factory in a city somewhere, not from a local artisan.

Prices? They were still set by the laws of supply and demand —he was told. But he could no longer see how or why. The agents would tell him the price of wheat was "down" in Chicago. "The market was down." And that was that. People were out of work and were not buying the way they used to. Why? Who knows? Vast and impersonal economic forces were at work: the price of gold on foreign markets; inflation; deflation; recession; depression. The farmer saw his fields filled with grain. He heard the people in the cities needed it. He had taken out a loan from the bank to buy the equipment to plant his crop to supply that need. He did everything he was supposed to. He watched the land, tended it lovingly; the weather was good. But the price was "down," they told him. Who were "they"? The dealers in Chicago and St. Louis. *They* said the market was down. There would be no profit this year. But that didn't mean he would not have to pay back his loan to the bank.

And meanwhile the farmer would read in the newspapers about rich industrialists—millionaires and tycoons they called them. The market didn't seem down for them. Especially the ones who owned the railroads. The price of shipping grain to market continued to be "up." And the big bankers—they didn't seem bothered by that market. As a matter of fact it appeared to help them. They were foreclosing on farmers who couldn't pay back the loans they had made—taking their farms from them. Something was rotten somewhere. The farmers were convinced of that. Something was wrong with a system so complex and intricate that a good man, or a group of good men, could not work through their elected representatives to right its wrongs. A government of, by, and for the people shouldn't work that way.

Was there a villain? To this day the experts argue about whether the economy of the time was actually being manipulated and controlled by wealthy bankers and industrialists— "robber barons" they were called—for their own profit, at the expense of the average working man. But what was clear to Bryan and his followers was that there was something mixed up when a privileged few could amass fortunes for themselves, while others—the workers, the producers—lost their farms and jobs.

The Gold Bugs

The forces in society that Bryan represented developed a theory about the source of their economic troubles—*gold* was the villain. They argued that a dangerous degree of control over the American economy had been reached by a small group of wealthy bankers and industrialists because the United States government printed currency in accordance with the *gold standard*. Simply put, the gold standard meant that for every dollar printed there had to be a proportionate value in gold on deposit in the U.S. Treasury. The government had to buy a dollar's worth of gold for every dollar it printed. Consequently, if enormously wealthy industrial and financial giants with control over large amounts of gold refused to sell their gold to the government—or worse, bought up much of the gold being sold on the international and domestic markets—they could force the United States Treasury to cut back on the number of dollars put into circulation.

Why do that? The law of supply and demand again. If the amount of money in circulation is low, prices should go down. If people have little purchasing power because they have little cash (which will be the case if the government is not printing it), there will be little demand for products of any kind. Since buyers are few, prices will go down as manufacturers and farmers seek to get rid of their product, almost at any price. The less money there is in circulation the lower the prices will go. (Inflation is the opposite. When there is a great deal of money in circulation, for whatever reason, prices are likely to rise as producers realize that people can pay more and as buyers increase the demand for the product. People have money and are willing to spend it. The problem with inflation, however—as we know—is that the rising prices can actually lower the standard of living. People have more money in their pockets, but it buys less than smaller amounts did before. They have less purchasing power.)

But why would wealthy bankers and industrialists want to create such a situation? Suppose a farmer borrows $1,000 from a bank or wealthy moneylender. Let us say his obligation, then, in five years, is to pay back $1,000 plus a reasonable amount of interest. If, however, during those five years prices have dropped considerably because of the shortage of money being printed on the gold standard, that $1000 will buy considerably more than it did previously. If prices, say, on corn have dropped from $200 to $100 a ton, that $1000 will buy twice as much corn as it did at the time the loan was made. The farmer then has to pay back an amount of cash twice the value in purchasing power of the amount he borrowed. *And* he is, at the same time, getting less—one-half in fact—than he used to get from those who buy corn from him. As Bryan explained it:

"The mortgage remains nominally the same, though the debt has actually become twice as great. If he should loan a Nebraska neighbor a hog weighing 100 pounds and the next spring demand in return a hog weighing 200 pounds he would be called dishonest, even though he contended that he was only demanding one hog—just the number he loaned. Society has become accustomed to some very nice distinctions. The poor man is called a socialist if he believes that the wealth of the rich should be divided among the poor, but the rich man is called a financier if he devises a plan by which the pittance of the poor can be converted to his use.

"The poor who takes property by force is called a thief, but the creditor who can by legislation [the gold standard] make a debtor pay twice as large as he borrowed is lauded as the friend of a sound currency. The man who wants the people to destroy the Government is an anarchist, but the man who wants the Government to destroy the people is a patriot."

The remedy proposed by Bryan became known as "bimetallism"—the use of silver as well as gold as backing for the American money supply. The government would, under this proposal, buy silver at a fixed ratio to gold. This would mean additional amounts of metal in the Treasury, and, therefore, more dollars in circulation in the country. And more dollars would mean higher prices for the farmer and merchant, higher profits that could be used to repay loans to banks and creditors. The control that the "gold bugs" held over the economy would be loosened.

At the Democratic convention in 1896, Bryan, as a delegate from Nebraska (he was no longer a Congressman, having been defeated in his bid for re-election in 1894, largely because of his position on gold), decided to take his fight for bimetallism to the floor, in hopes of getting the Democrats to include a provision for the coinage of silver as part of their platform in the upcoming campaign. It was one of history's most eventful speeches. It transformed an obscure ex-Congressman from Nebraska into a dynamic national figure, in the limelight at center stage.

Bryan, still young and robust with dark flowing hair falling down over his stiff, white winged collar, moved confidently to the platform in the noisy convention hall. The delegates milled and rustled about, as delegates tend to do, and proceeded with their private discussions. Another speech—they had heard too many already and would hear too many more. The big question was who would be the party's candidate for the Presidency, not what some hick ex-Congressman had to say about the complex relation between gold and silver as backing for our currency. But when the deep and sonorous voice began to echo through the rafters, each word resonant with a bell-like purity, an attentive silence settled over the auditorium. People tapped each other on the shoulder and pointed toward the podium, hushed their neighbors and craned their necks to see the dark-suited figure gesturing emphatically on the flag-draped platform. It was one of those moments of genius when a talented individual rises to almost superhuman heights—an opera singer hitting an uncharted note, a runner breaking from the pack with a burst of energy from some unknown reservoir, a soldier darting unexpectedly to brave a staccato burst of machine gun fire on his way to rescue a fallen comrade. Bryan had the crowd hanging on his every word, holding their breaths at each dramatic pause in his oration, ready to rise from their seats in uproarious approval as his sentences mounted to their exclamatory endings. Time and again the crowd was brought to its feet. There was a new hero in American politics:

> We say to you that you [the spokesmen for the gold standard] have made the definition of businessman too limited in its application . . . the farmer who goes forth in the morning and toils all day—who begins in the spring and toils all summer—and who by the application of brain and muscle to the natural resources of the country creates wealth, is as much a business man as the man who goes upon the board of trade and bets upon the price of grain; the miners who go down a thousand feet into the earth, or climb two thousand feet upon cliffs, and bring forth from their hiding places the precious metals to be poured into the channels of trade are as much business men as the few financial magnates who, in a back room,

corner the money of the world. We come to speak for this broader class of business men . . .

What we need is an Andrew Jackson to stand, as Jackson stood, against the encroachments of organized wealth . . .

Upon which side will the Democratic party fight; upon the side of the idle holders of idle capital or upon the side of the struggling masses? . . .

You come to us and tell us that the great cities are in favor of the gold standard; we reply that the great cities rest upon our broad and fertile prairies. Burn down your cities and leave our farms, and your cities will spring up again as if by magic; but destroy our farms and the grass will grow in the streets of every city in the country . . .

Having behind us the producing masses of this nation and the world, supported by the commercial interests, the laboring interests, and the toilers everywhere, we will answer their demand for a gold standard by saying to them: *You shall not press down upon the brow of labor this crown of thorns, you shall not crucify mankind upon a cross of gold.*

That did it. A hooting, howling demonstration shook the arena to its foundations. The unknown Nebraskan's name was shouted in unison to the heavens: "Bryan! Bryan! Bryan! We'll shoot the gold bugs everyone!" And most surprising of all, in the vote taken the following day, on the fifth ballot, the unknown speaker—the "boy orator of the Platte"—at the age of 36 became the Democratic Party's candidate for the Presidency, to run against the Republicans' William McKinley.

He lost. His defeat in 1896 brings up a question perplexing to most who study his career. He seemed to have the momentum. He was the up-and-coming new star, the people's choice. Yet he lost. Why? Well, for one thing, he carried more counties in the nation than McKinley: 1551 to 1163. But McKinley won the vote in the densely populated city areas of the East and carried the popular vote 7,098,474 to 6,379,830. Bryan did not carry a single county in New England. But one would think that Bryan's appeal would have been strong with the working classes of the East. He was from a farm state but his pitch was directed at the working classes everywhere, and certainly factory workers in the East had as much to complain about as the

141

Midwestern farmers. Why was he unable to capitalize on that discontent?

Some historians argue that Bryan put too much stress on bimetallism, ignoring the broader reform movements that might have appealed to the Eastern workers. After all, bimetallism meant higher prices, and unless the big picture was painted—and very clearly—to explain how that would benefit the average worker, those who pushed for it were not likely to get a factory worker's vote. Some say the voters, after an initial bout of enthusiasm for the "boy wonder," had fears that their man might not be able to handle the complex responsibilities of the Presidency, and opted for a mature and experienced-looking McKinley. Some say the support he received from certain Southern and Midwestern Know-Nothing and Ku Klux Klan-type groups offended many urban Catholic voters, even though Bryan himself did not hold anti-Catholic views. Some say he was too clearly a regional candidate without understanding or sympathy for the city worker.

But everyone says that money played a large part in his defeat, too. Bryan had to run not only against McKinley but against wealthy industrialists led by a Cleveland businessman named Mark Hanna. McKinley's supporters admitted to spending about $16 million in their campaign, while Bryan's people could raise only $500,000. But it was not just the money—although that certainly was important. What has to be called a propaganda campaign was launched against him by large segments of upper-class America, which feared that a wave of potentially revolutionary sentiment had been set loose by the fiery young speaker. It might even sweep *them* from their life of ease and affluence. The then influential magazine *The Nation* said in an editorial that the election was a contest between "the great civilizing forces of the republic [McKinley's supporters] and "the still surviving barbarism bred by slavery in the South and the reckless spirit of adventure in the mining camps of the Far West." Theodore Roosevelt referred to "Bryanism" as "ugly," "criminal," "vicious," "a genuine and dangerous fanaticism," "a semi-socialistic, agrarian movement," "a revolt aimed foolishly at those who are better off merely because they are better off; it is the blind man blinding the one-eyed." John Hay called Bryan "a half-baked, glib little briefless jack-leg lawyer . . . grasping with anxiety at that $50,000 salary, promising the millennium to everybody with a hole in his pants and destruction to everybody with a clean shirt."

But more important and effective than these scatter-shot accusations was the threat that, if he were elected, the economic system would come apart at the seams. Not because of anything Bryan would do. Bankers and industrialists threatened that *they* would bring the economy to a halt before they would submit to the reforms of a Bryan administration. And where would that leave the common man? Maybe he was living in a slum, unemployed part of the year. But he probably had some kind of a roof over his head and food on his dinner table most days. Could Bryan provide even that if he were elected and the industrialists closed down their operations? Could he provide jobs? Could he raise capital? He said that he could—after he put all his reforms into operation. How long would that take? Three years? Five? Longer? What would people do in the meanwhile? Factory owners on the East Coast made it clear to their workers: If that man was elected there would be no jobs for them in the morning.

Mark Hanna offered a more direct threat in Kansas: "Do you think that we'd let that damned lunatic get into the White House? Never! You know you can hire half of the people of the United States to shoot down the other half if necessary, and we've got the money to hire them."

One of the most perceptive evaluations of the campaign came from a McKinley backer, Mrs. Henry Cabot Lodge, the wife of a wealthy New Englander, in a letter to the ambassador from Great Britain:

"The great fight is won and a fight conducted by trained and experienced and organized forces, with both hands full of money, with the full power of the press—and of prestige—on the one side; on the other, a disorganized mob at first, out of which there burst into sight, hearing and force—one man, but such a man! Alone, penniless, without backing, without money, without scarce a paper, without speakers, that man fought such a fight that even those in the East can call him a Crusader, an inspired fanatic—a prophet! It has been marvelous. Hampered by such a following, such a platform . . . he almost won . . . We had during the last week of the campaign 18,000 speakers on the stump. He alone spoke for his party, but speeches which spoke to the intelligence and hearts of the people, with a capital P."

Considering the lengths to which men like Hanna admitted they were willing to go to defeat Bryan, one is left to guess at the unknown illegal activity that went on—bribes, blackmail, fraud, miscounted votes, threats of violence, etc. It may have been quite substantial.

It seems safe to say, at the very least, that in an election where expenditures were more nearly equal, Bryan would have won.

Crusader As Private Citizen

Bryan's defeat did not deaden his verve and determination to eliminate the abuses of power and wealth in society. If anything it gave him new fire. That there were people with enough power to determine the outcome of an election—able to use their position as directors of the economy to force their employees either to vote against their own interests or starve—was proof to him that America was moving, as he had charged, from a democratic system of government to one that he called a "plutocracy": rule by a wealthy and powerful few.

Now that he was out of public office, he founded a newspaper called *The Commoner*, and toured the country as well, making speeches designed to expose the undesirable influence of these men of privilege. He constantly referred to them as the possessors of "unearned wealth." And he found a new enemy to attack, along with the gold standard: the trusts.

Trusts were business enterprises that controlled every step in the production of a particular good, from the harvesting and shipping of raw materials and related products to the advertising posters that went into store windows. Some oil companies, for example, built the drilling equipment, pumped the oil, built the ships that carried it, refined it, packaged it, distributed it, and leased out the stations where the product was sold to the consumer. By dominating the industry, they could ruin the competition. The trust could set the rates *it* thought appropriate for raw materials, market prices, wages, etc.

Bryan feared that such industrial giants were the beginning of an economic system in which the people of the country would be put entirely at the mercy of a relative handful of owners and managers. He saw it as his mission to place the "plutocrats" under the people's control; to force them to be responsible for the overall economic health of the country, not just for increased profit for themselves. When the owners argued that their increased size would mean increased efficiency and a better life for all—more jobs and higher pay—Bryan responded that he had seen in the past no reason to trust them with such power; and that even if they could increase material prosperity as much as they promised, the accompanying price, a loss of individual independence, was too great to pay:

> No; I tell you that I would not give up the blessings of home life for all the economy hotel life could promise. I believe in the family; I believe in its sacred associations and I would not be willing to barter the home life of this nation for any economy that might be shown to result from any other kind of living; and so no economy that a private monopoly can promise will compensate for the destruction of individual independence, of the citizen's right to think as he pleases, to act as he pleases, and to be his own master.

Bryan's goal was to keep the economy *decentralized;* to break up and make illegal domination of our economic—and thus political—life by a wealthy few; to increase individual freedom by keeping us free from the kind of control over our lives that the wealthy industrialists had displayed over their employes when they coerced them to vote against Bryan in 1896. A man whose economic needs were under his own control, provided for by his own labors or through trade with neighboring (and competing) tradesmen, could not be subjected to the political intimidation of the power brokers. What about industries that could not operate efficiently except on a large scale (e.g., railroads)? He proposed government regulation of the prices they charged, the wages they paid, and close and constant scrutiny of their political activities. He also became one of the pioneers in the fight for a progressive income tax, on the theory that the wealthy, who required large-scale government protection and services for their large-scale business activities, should be forced to pay the bill.

It is Bryan's continued stress upon a decentralized economy that makes so curious the charge often leveled against him, in his time and and ours: that he was a socialist. Actually, he was as opposed to socialism as to plutocracy. Both systems shared the same fault: excessive concentrated power. Socialism, he

145

argued, would only aggravate the dangers of a concentration of power, since government ownership would do nothing more than place the excessive power in the hands of politicians instead of tycoons. The socialists of Bryan's time never doubted his opposition to them. They directed some of their harshest attacks against his theories. It is true that his recommendation of government regulation of business does seem like a step toward socialism—more and more control until it becomes total. But to attribute such a goal to Bryan is to misread him. His hope was that the government would intervene to decentralize, not to substitute itself as the monopoly power:

"Will socialism purge the individual of selfishness or bring a nearer approach to justice?" he asked. "Under individualism [which is what he called his preference for decentralized economic power] a man's reward is determined in the open market, and where competition is free [free from the government as well as the trusts] he can hope to sell his services for what they are worth. Will his chance for reward be as good when he must do the work on the terms fixed by those who are in control of the government?" Furthermore: "What outlet will there be for discontent if the government owns and operates all the means of production and distribution?"

His approach, in fact, was what modern Americans call "free market" economics—laissez-faire capitalism. *But,* he insisted, it must be kept genuinely free and competitive, even if to do so required government-directed limitations on the businessmen who considered themselves free-market capitalists; and even if they found such limitations offensive. To make his point, Bryan went to great effort to analyze the nature and purpose of society in a little-known essay far different in style from his campaign oratory. It is an essay that does much to support the view of those who argue that the detractors of Bryan's intelligence were (and are) motivated by a prejudice against him. Below are just a few samples from "Individualism versus Socialism."

The words "individualism" and "socialism" define tendencies rather than concrete systems; for, as extreme individualism is not to be found under any form of government, so there is [or was in his time] no example of socialism in full operation. All government being more or less socialistic, the contention, so far as the subject is concerned, is between those who regard individualism as an ideal to be approached as

146

nearly as circumstances will permit, and those who regard a socialist state as ideal, to be established as far and as fast as public opinion will allow.

The individualist believes that competition is not only a helpful but a necessary force in society, to be guarded and protected; the socialist regards competition as a hurtful force, to be entirely exterminated. It is not necessary to consider those who consciously take either side for reasons purely selfish; it is sufficient to know that on both sides there are those who with great earnestness and sincerity present their theories, convinced of their correctness and sure of the necessity for their application to human society . . .

Assuming that the highest aim of society is the harmonious development of the human race, physically, mentally, and morally, the first question to decide is whether individualism or socialism furnishes the best means of securing that harmonious development. For the purpose of this discussion, individualism will be defined as the private ownership of the means of production and distribution where competition is possible, leaving to public ownership those means of production and distribution in which competition is practically impossible; and socialism will be defined as the collective ownership, through the state, of all the means of production and distribution.

One advocate of socialism defines it as "common ownership of natural resources and public utilities and the common operation of all industries for the public good." It will be seen that the definitions of socialism commonly in use include some things which cannot fairly be described as socialistic, and some of the definitions (like the last one, for instance) beg the question by assuming that the public operation of all industries will necessarily be for the general good. As the socialists agree in hostility to competition as a controlling force, and as individualists agree that competition is necessary for the well-being of society, the fairest and most accurate line between the two schools can be drawn at the point where competition begins to be possible, both

147

schools favoring public ownership where competition is impossible, but differing as to the wisdom of public ownership where competition can have free play . . .

Then, too, some of the strength of socialism is due to its condemnation of abuses which, while existing under individualism, are not at all necessary to individualism—abuses which the individualists are as anxious as the socialists to remedy. It is not only consistent with individualism, but is a necessary implication of it, that the competing parties should be placed upon substantially equal footing; for competition is not worthy of the name if one party is able arbitrarily to fix the terms of the agreement, leaving the other with no choice but to submit to the terms prescribed. Individualists, for instance, can consistently advocate usury laws which fix the rate of interest to be charged, these laws being justified on the ground that the borrower and the lender do not stand upon an equal footing. Where the money-lender is left free to take advantage of the necessities of the borrower, the so-called freedom of contract is really freedom to extort. Upon the same ground, society can justify legislation against child labor and legislation limiting the hours of adult labor. One can believe in competition and still favor such limitations and restrictions as will make the competition real and effective. To advocate individualism it is no more necessary to excuse the abuses to which competition may lead than it is to defend the burning of a city because fire is essential to human comfort, or to praise a tempest because air is necessary to human life . . .

Probably the nearest approach we have to the socialistic state today is to be found in the civil service. If the civil service develops more unselfishness and more altruistic devotion to the general welfare than private employment does, the fact is yet to be discovered. This is not offered as a criticism of civil service in so far as civil service may require examinations to ascertain fitness for office, but it is simply a reference to a well-known fact—viz., that a life position in the government service, which separates one from the

148

lot of the average producer of wealth, has given no extraordinary stimulus to higher development . . .

There should be no unfriendliness between the honest individualist and the honest socialist; both seek that which they believe to be best for society. The socialist, by pointing out the abuses of individualism, will assist in their correction. At present private monopoly is putting upon individualism an undeserved odium, and it behooves the individualist to address himself energetically to this problem in order that the advantages of competition may be restored to industry. And the duty of immediate action is made more imperative by the fact that the socialist is inclined to support the monopoly, in the belief that it will be easier to induce the government to take over an industry after it has passed into the hands of a few men . . . The individualist, on the contrary, contends that the consolidation of industries ceases to be an economic advantage when competition is eliminated; and he believes, further, that no economic advantage which could come from the monopolization of all the industries in the hands of the government could compensate for the stifling of individual initiative and independence. And the individualists who thus believe stand for a morality and for a system of ethics which they are willing to measure against the ethics and morality of socialism.

Whatever one's reaction to this analysis, it is not exactly the thought of a man who "felt no compulsion to develop his powers of reasoning."

A Free and Virtuous People

Bryan's attacks against the trusts, however, were not based merely on economics. He was convinced that the country would not only enjoy a more just distribution of wealth if the power of the money men was reduced, but society would become more virtuous, too. The healthiest society would be one where decision-making power was kept in the hands of the majority of the population. He did not want an economy or a government of "planners" and "experts." The common man

149

knew what was best for him and America. For Bryan it was a
reflex action: if the masses wanted something it was right almost
by definition. "The voice of the people is the voice of God"—
he never went that far. The majority can be wrong. Everyone
admits to that. But for Bryan, the American people of his time
and area and class could be trusted, in most cases, to come up
with virtuous social and political decisions. It is said that when
he was first asked why he favored bimetallism his response was:
"I'm for it because the people want it. I'll look up the reasons
later."

Naturally, a position like this can be difficult to justify. It has
earned Bryan much of the scorn directed at him by scholars and
educated groups in general. It does seem to be what people call
"demagoguery"—an unscrupulous flattering of the masses in
order to get their support and to win political office.

Was Bryan a demagogue? A clever orator, without principle,
who fed the crowd what it wanted to hear? It is a serious charge.
Responsible leadership often entails a willingness to educate
your followers, to lift them to a level of understanding they
might not reach on their own because of a lack of awareness or
information on a particular issue; to challenge them when they
are wrong, to *lead* them to greater perception of all the ramifi-
cations of the issue. If good government means nothing more
than transforming popular opinion into law, government could
be run best by pollsters and computers.

The question, simply put, is this: Why did Bryan see the
masses as such depositories of virtue and wisdom? Does it make
any sense?

It is on this point that Bryan's great stress on the need for a
strong religious foundation for society becomes most relevant.
Often Bryan's stout and unreserved belief in the Bible as the
Word of God is treated as an eccentricity in his thought, un-
related to his political positions. Quite the contrary—there is a
remarkable degree of overlap. Bryan's faith in democracy in
America, in the masses, was not a blind and unquestioning faith.
He was confident in the American people *because* they were a
moral people. And they were a moral people because they were
a God-fearing people; because they lived their lives by the
Bible. They were a self-disciplined, virtuous people—the majority anyway—and could be trusted with freedom. They would
not abuse it. They would be able to pick the best man for
political office. The necessary implication, of course, is that if

that religious faith were diluted or destroyed, the very basis for democratic government would be undermined as well. Only as long as the people were good, should they be free. What kind of government should take democracy's place if they ceased to be good? It was a question he did not consider at any length in public. The point was that the small-town, rural Americans he knew *were* virtuous (by his Christian standards) and therefore should have control over the political life of the country; not the "new Americans"—the other Americans of the secularized, cosmopolitan, and impersonal business and academic worlds. His mission: to preserve the "old time" religion so that the American democratic way of life could go on as envisioned by the Founding Fathers. (All of this, by the way, brings up problems seldom analyzed in America, where words like "liberty," "freedom," "independence," and "rights" are tossed around as if they describe unqualifiedly desirable political conditions. But no sane person would want to live by majority rule on an island with a population of psychopathic murderers, rapists, thieves, and convicted felons; or in a jail. We are *for* freedom only when we are convinced that our fellow citizens are a pretty decent lot who will not use their freedom to molest us.)

The Scopes Trial

Bryan's longtime concern for maintaining an obvious and strong religious presence in American life was faced with its most serious challenge late in his life, as the ideas of Charles Darwin began to to spread, especially in the urban and university centers of the country. The growing acceptance, in those circles, of the theory that man evolved from lower forms of animal life made clear to all the split between the two Americas: Bryan's Bible-centered America, and the new scientific and secular America.

There were several issues for Bryan involved in this struggle. His aforementioned fear that a weakening of religious faith would symbolize the eventual end of a government by the people was one:

> Evolutionists are leading their followers away from
> the Creator, away from the word of God, and away
> from the Son of God. They teach that man is the
> lineal descendant of the lower animals—that he has

151

in him, not the breath of the Almighty but the blood of the brute. They tear out of the Old Testament the first chapter of Genesis, and then, having discarded the miracle, they tear out the first chapter of Matthew and deny the Virgin birth of the Savior. They would, in effect, dethrone Jehovah, strip the Bible of its claim to inspiration and libel the Master, by branding him as the illegitimate son of an immoral woman. Their creed denudes life of its spiritual elements and makes man a brother of the beast.

". . . denudes life of its spiritual elements and makes man a brother of the beast." These are the key words.

If we are animals, he is asking, by what warrant do we expect people not to behave like beasts? If we are a true democracy, we have no king or emperor to force people to behave virtuously. The people live by their own standards, not by rules made by their superiors, not by the "noble" men. But the Darwinists tell us that we are animals; they give us a "Godless philosophy—a philosophy which led the world into its bloodiest wars—and it is bringing chaos to the industrialized world." The problem facing modern man: "What can be done to combat it and to save church and civilization from its benumbing influence?"

His constituents, the farmers and small-town folk of America, were not yet under the influence of these secular philosophies —which was why he was determined to keep his constituents in control over as much of the country's life as possible. They did not think of themselves as animals. They felt a responsibility to live a moral life, to save their souls by rising above animal instincts. They could be trusted with political power. On farms, especially, men and women would never forget their dependence upon God:

"Those who toil the soil are brought near to nature, and their contact with the earth and its marvelous activities breeds reverence and respect for the Creator of all things. The farmer lives amid miracles and feels each year his dependence upon the unseen Hand that directs the seasons and sends refreshing showers."

But it must be stressed that this defense of religion as necessary for a free society was not what made the masses love Bryan. At issue for his followers was a much more personal matter— in many ways more important to them than any long-run danger to democracy posed by a decline of religion. The common man's own religious beliefs were coming under attack. The "other America" seemed to be reaching into the strongholds of the Bible-belt, right into their children's schools.

The problem was inevitable. Biology teachers in high schools all over the country were being educated in universities where Darwinism had become the accepted—near official—school of thought. The high school biology teachers, quite naturally, came to share the view, and to teach it in their high school classes, even if they were teaching in an area where the vast majority of the parents clung to the Biblical account of Creation found in Genesis, the first book of the Bible. For a while the issue seemed to lie dormant, either because the students did not realize the incompatibility (apparent or real) of what they learned about evolution in school and what they were taught by their parents and preachers; or, more likely, because the biology teachers soft-pedaled their own position on evolution, teaching it as a theory that some experts accepted and some did not. But such a tightrope act was a difficult feat. Many states had laws on the books that explicitly forebade teaching an explanation for the origins of man contrary to that found in Genesis.

A group operating out of New York City, known as the American Civil Liberties Union, decided to make a test case of these anti-Darwin laws in the state of Tennessee. Their argument centered on the claim that such laws were a violation of the freedom of speech. They demanded that the courts "establish that a teacher may tell the truth without being sent to jail." A biology teacher named Scopes, who taught the theory of evolution, admitted to doing so in public at the ACLU's prodding, in order to initiate the court proceedings.

Famed criminal lawyer Clarence Darrow, an admitted agnostic himself, came to Tennessee to assist in Scopes' defense. Bryan was asked by Tennessee authorities to appear as a witness in favor of that state's right to prevent attacks on the Biblical account of man's origins. The stage was set for one of American history's most dramatic courtroom confrontations: Darrow versus Bryan, 1925.

Bryan had established his position on this question long before the trial:

> . . . those who preach and teach should be called
> upon to announce their views so that their positions
> may be clearly understood. Every citizen has a right

153

to think as he pleases—to worship God according to the dictates of his conscience, or to refuse to worship him. That is an unalienable right that should not under any circumstances be interfered with, but those who employ a minister for themselves or an instructor for their children have a right to know what the preacher is to preach and what teachers are to teach.

In the case of Scopes, then, since the vast majority of the people in the district where he taught accepted the Biblical accounts of the Creation, Bryan argued that Scopes had no business undermining that faith: "Christian taxpayers should insist upon a *real* neutrality in religion wherever neutrality is necessary. The Bible should not be attacked where it cannot be defended."

His position, in other words, is far more sophisticated than many of us have been led to believe. He did not demand that Scopes teach Genesis in the public schools against his will—only a *"real* neutrality." He would have been satisfied if the Bible was treated as sympathetically and intelligently as Darwin's theories. Both must be treated as theories in the eyes of a disinterested scientific observer. There are no *proofs,* or empirical demonstrations, for Darwin's theories. They remain speculation, hypotheses that cannot be demonstrated. To most with a scientific mind they seem highly probable, but, even so, deep and perplexing questions sturdily endure. So, since Darwinism cannot be called fact, Bryan argued, by what right can a teacher choose to present this theory as fact over the objections of his employers, the parents of the children he teaches? Bryan, to the applause of his followers, argued that teachers had no such right.

But did Bryan, himself, really take everything in the Bible literally? Not actually. Earlier in his career he had stated clearly —disappointing many fundamentalists—that he was willing to accept that God, for example, might have used a slow evolutionary process to create the world and that the "days" mentioned in Genesis might actually have been periods of time, even lengthy periods. This position, for those who are unaware of it, is taken by many sophisticated and well-educated Christians in our day and age. (Many other intelligent Christians still stand by the literal Genesis account, of course.) What Bryan objected

154

to was the attitude demonstrated by many of those who rejected Genesis: their refusal to accept it because, *and only because*, it demanded that one be willing to accept the possibility of miraculous interventions by a personal God in the workings of the universe. The premise that the miraculous must be held suspect was a manifestation of a tendency he found menacing. If God could not create the world in seven days, make man from the slime of the earth, or divide the Red Sea, how could Christ heal or raise himself from the dead? The foundations of the Christian religion could be undermined by such a premise, and with them American democracy: "Eliminate the miracles and Christ becomes merely a human being and His gospel is stripped of divine authority." "Christ can not be separated from the miraculous; His birth, His ministrations, and His resurrection, all involve the miraculous, and the change which His religion works in the human heart is a continuing miracle."

In his confrontation with Darrow, Bryan worked under this premise. Miracles are possible for Christians. Christians hold that at the core of their faith. A miracle is an event that cannot be explained by the laws of science; that is what makes it a miracle. It is an event that supersedes those laws through divine power. When Darrow sought to demonstrate that the events in the Bible that Bryan was willing to accept as true were unbelievable by all laws of scientific reason, he was setting up a straw man. Christians agree with him!

We get the impression from many modern commentators that Darrow made a fool of Bryan at the trial. Many of us have seen at some time the play or motion picture *Inherit the Wind,* the fictionalized account of the trial. In the movie production, a maniacally wild-eyed, sweating Fredric March, playing a character that is supposed to represent Bryan, is left dumbfounded and on the verge of death by the artful and incisive questioning of a secure and wise Darrow, played by Spencer Tracy. Below are some revealing lines of dialogue—not from the movie, but from the actual trial. Who really gets the best of whom from the standpoint of the great majority of Americans who believe that there is a personal Creator God? (Deny the existence of God and, of course, Darrow destroys Bryan.) In point of fact, the laws against teaching evolution stayed on the books in Tennessee, so in a narrow legal sense Bryan won. But

155

that is not the question at issue now. *Logically,* who is making the better case?

"Q.—(Darrow)—Do you claim that everything in the Bible should be literally interpreted?

A.—(Bryan)—I believe everything in the Bible should be accepted as it is given there; some of the Bible is given illustratively. For instance: 'Ye are the salt of the earth.' I would not insist that man was actually salt, or that he had flesh of salt, but it is used in the sense of salt as saving God's people . . .

Q.—But when you read that Jonah swallowed the whale—or that the whale swallowed Jonah—how do you literally interpret that?

A.—I read that a big fish swallowed Jonah—it does not say whale.

Q.—Doesn't it? Are you sure?

A.—That is my recollection of it. A big fish, and I believe it, and I believe in a God who can make a whale and can make a man and make both do what He pleases . . .

Q.—But you believe He made them—that He made such a fish and that it was big enough to swallow Jonah?

A.—Yes, sir. Let me add: One miracle is just as easy to believe as another . . . A miracle is a thing performed beyond what man can perform. When you get beyond what man can do, you get within the realm of miracles; and it is just as easy to believe the miracle of Jonah as any other miracle in the Bible . . .

Q.—Then, when the Bible said, for instance, 'and God called the firmament heaven. And the evening and morning were the second day,' that does not necessarily mean twenty-four hours?

A.—I do not think it necessarily does.

Q.—Do you think it does or does not?

A.—I know a great many think so.

Q.—What do you think?

A.—I do not think it does.

Q.—You think those were not literal days?

A.—I do not think they were twenty-four-hour days. . . . I think it would be just as easy for the kind of God we believe in to make the earth in six days as in six years or in six million or in six billion years. I do not think it important whether we believe one or the other."

156

Dead Issues?

The controversies discussed above by no means exhaust the list of Bryan's causes. He was in the thick of American political life for more than 30 years. But always he argued from the same standpoint: that the conscience of the American people, formed by the inheritance of almost 2,000 years of Christianity, was basically sound; that Christianity was the religion of the vast majority of the American people and therefore a legitimate ingredient in public debate (by democratic standards); that a society shaped by citizens operating upon Christian convictions would be healthy, just, and durable; that the coming twentieth century would be scarred with wars, economic disasters, racial strife, the breakdown of the family, rising crime rates, and a general breakdown of public morality if the religious roots of American life were damaged—if the typical American became a self-centered, pleasure-seeking materialist. He was beloved by his contemporaries for fighting that fight. And echoes of his words haunt those of us who read him now. He just might have been right.

Thomas Alva Edison

6

Thomas Alva Edison
The Wizard of Menlo Park

There is a kind of American who, rather than watch television or sit in traffic waiting to get into the parking lot for a ball game, prefers to run a router along the edge of an unblemished plank of fine oak, or listen to the responsive roar of his engine as he turns his distributor with a deft rotation of the wrist. He is the kind of guy who goes to a party and ends up in the host's garage trying out some new tools. Sometimes he builds a shed or installs new brakes for a friend—for fun. It is something to look forward to on a weekend; a nice way to spend a day. Invite him to a cookout and he invites himself back the next weekend—to nail up the new back porch you told him you wanted. He might even live in a house he built himself; or, at the very least, he is planning to build one someday on some land he has out in the country. He builds radios and radio-controlled model planes. Sawdust and graphite are his favorite smells. And the black smoke from an engine with a sloppily adjusted carburetor is one of his pet peeves. Chances are, his first car was a beat-up Ford or Chevy that sat in his driveway for two years before he was old enough to drive it on the streets—the two years he spent rebuilding the engine, dropping the old transmission, and applying seven or eight hand-rubbed coats of metallic paint. He loves gadgets, too—calculators, CB radios—but he has ruined a lot of them taking them apart "to see how they work."

He might have been thought a little bit "slow" by his teachers during his schooldays. But probably more than a few of those teachers were rescued on cold and rainy afternoons in the faculty parking lot when our boy started their cars for them with a quick flick of his finger on the choke linkage and a warning to spray some solvent around the choke and the high-speed idle cam. Perhaps those teachers were no more able to find the choke linkage than the fountain of youth, and couldn't take his advice. But they developed a new respect for our boy that day. Maybe they would not want to spend the years it took to get to know a car that way, working grease around ball-joint fittings or adjusting oily valve lifters. But they learned to respect his knowledge. People who can fix things, who can make machinery go; who understand generators and resistors and gear ratios; who have a feel for the power and potential of the "stuff" of the universe, for minerals and chemical reactions, batteries, combustion, induction—you can't live without them. Certainly not the way we *want* to live. Where would we be today without the granddaddy of the tinkerers and workshop dreamers, Thomas Alva Edison?

There may have been other men in history with the inventive genius of Edison, but we will never know. If he had lived 50 years earlier, the scientific equipment and expertise needed in his experiments would have been unavailable. Fifty years later other men probably (but only probably) would have come up with many of his inventions. It might have taken 50 of them, but they could have done it. Probably. The genius of Edison is seen not so much in any one of his inventions as in the range and variety of them. If he had invented only the light bulb he would have made it into some American history books. But he has a place in them all because, in addition to the light bulb, he invented the phonograph and motion pictures; he improved storage batteries, generators, and ore-milling machinery; and he helped perfect the telephone, typewriter, and megaphone, as well as fruit preservers, electric locomotives, poured concrete, and compressed-air apparatus. That's for starters.

Edison was fortunate to be born at the moment in history when a revolutionary idea was just beginning to rumble around in the back of a few minds—that the mysterious force in the universe known as electricity could actually be put to work in the service of mankind. That strange property in lightning that made Benjamin Franklin's key glow in the jar; the property that permitted village jokesters to sprinkle sparks in the dark when they stroked a stray cat's hair, had been used to turn an iron bar into a magnet—an "electromagnet" that would draw other iron and steel objects to it. And an English inventor, Michael Faraday, had even demonstrated that a copper disk rotating between the arms of a horseshoe magnet could "generate" a flow of electric current into wires wrapped around those arms—a generator, or dynamo. There was a new force available to man. The power of lightning had been harnessed. But now—how to put it to work? More than anyone else, Edison answered that question.

Edison was born in 1847 in Milan, Ohio. When he was only seven, the family moved to Port Huron, Michigan, where young Tom attended school for the first time. His academic career was hardly a success. Edison was a flop as a schoolboy. Public school systems, after all, are set up to provide the best possible education for the average student. It is not really surprising that the exceptional individual often cannot fit in. But Edison's first teacher must have been an extraordinarily short-sighted individual. He complained to Edison's parents that their boy "asked too many stupid questions," that he was "weak in the head," and that his brains were "addled." One can only wonder what some of those stupid questions were—probably some of the "unanswerable" ones Edison spent a lifetime answering in his laboratories, to the wonderment of the world.

In any event, Edison spent less than three months in a classroom. Though his mother had little formal education, she knew that her quiet boy was anything but stupid, and would not allow him to be subjected to any more abuse. She took him out of school, resolved to give him all the education he would need at home. This treatment could not have hurt him too much. By the time he was nine he was reading voraciously—especially a weather-beaten book he had picked up somewhere on electricity.

Electricity! The word fascinated the boy. A source of power in the universe that could split the mightiest of oaks or strike a man dead in his tracks. Just one touch of it could do that. If man could learn to tame its power the way he once learned to

161

domesticate horses and oxen . . . Before he reached his teens Edison committed himself to that task. (Would it not be fascinating to have a recording of his thoughts at this stage in his life? Were there vague outlines for all the brilliant later inventions? Did he picture the possibility of making machines that talk and that light the highways of the nation and that project the images of people in motion? But, alas, there was no Edison before Edison.)

To become an inventor required money, and Edison had little of that. So by the time he was 12 he was working full time. He would leave his Port Huron home each morning at seven o'clock and report to the Detroit express railroad, where he sold apples, candy, peanuts, and newspapers to the commuters. He would not return home until long after dark.

Most of his earnings went toward helping out at home. But there was some left, and he spent that for a single purpose— buying the wires, chemicals, and minerals he needed to stock his home laboratory, a small room in his father's house. He even printed his own newspaper, while still in his early teens, in order to get extra cash. He bought an old printing press, fixed it up, and installed it in a quiet corner of the baggage car on the railroad. He called it *The Weekly Herald.* It sold fairly well on the train, and before long he was able to outfit a respectable amateur lab.

There was a problem, however. By the time young Edison returned home in the evening it was too late for him to work on his experiments. Later in life he displayed a marked capacity to go for days on end without sleep when he was hot on the trail of a discovery. But his mother was not about to allow all-night sessions for her teen-age son, so Edison came up with an answer —as one would expect. He moved his entire laboratory into the baggage car, next to his printing press. It might have been history's first moving laboratory. When he was not hawking his wares, he would settle down in that quiet, cramped corner of the dark, bouncing railroad car, and follow his dream.

It was while working on the railroad that Edison suffered the kind of unfortunate accident that might have discouraged lesser men. One day, while running to catch a train pulling away from the station, he leaped for the handrail on the caboose. He managed to get a hold on it, but not a secure one. His grip loosened while the train gathered speed, dragging him along. He might have fallen to his death if it had not been for a man on the train, who grabbed at him. Unfortunately, all the man could reach was Edison's head. He had to pull on his ears to get the boy up onto the train.

Tom said that he heard something "snap" inside his head. He lost his hearing; the inventor of the phonograph was almost completely deaf. He could hear only loud sounds—and those only faintly. Edison struggled for a few years, but once he mastered lip reading, the handicap no longer impeded his progress. Yet, as he was to admit sadly later in life: "I haven't heard a bird sing since I was twelve years old."

Working the Line

Like most young people of his time, Edison early in life broke the strings that tied him to home. He was living on his own at 15, working as a telegraph operator, and he became one of the best. It is not certain whether there was a connection between his interest in the properties of electricity and his skill at tapping out a message in Morse Code at a blistering pace. They seem to be separate and distinct attributes. But Edison was a marvel, known in communications centers all along the East Coast. Nor is it likely that there was a connection between his scientific genius and his daring rescue of Jimmie Mackenzie. Edison is remembered for his inventive genius, not his bravery; but apparently he was exceptionally brave.

Jimmie Mackenzie was the young son of one of the other telegraph operators at an Ohio railroad station where Edison worked. One quiet afternoon Edison looked out the station window to see the boy playing on the tracks as a train came barreling in. The boy was too young to understand the danger. He looked up calmly at the smoking, whistling locomotive that would soon cut him to pieces. Edison flew through the door, took the steps in one wild leap, and hurled his body between the boy and the onrushing train. He grabbed the boy's upper body and tumbled forward with him across the tracks. Edison's heel was flicked by the heavy spinning wheels of the locomotive, it was that close.

Edison spent the next five years wandering from station to station, partly because he was able to get work wherever he wanted, since his skills as an operator were so widely recognized, but also because—as unlikely as it seems—he often turned out to be a poor employe. While working the night shift he fell asleep on the job, missing important messages. It sounds like irresponsible behavior. And it was. But not for the usual reasons; Edison was not tired out from partying the night before. He was spending too many hours in his lab. In his eyes, his job as a telegraph operator was a means of raising the money to conduct his experiments. The experiments were his main interest, his first responsibility. He did not intend to cheat his employers out of an honest night's work. He did not fall asleep on purpose. It was just that he could not allow the job to get in the way of his vocation. He had to follow his star. There were ideas in his mind, ready to explode.

During these wandering years Edison saved his money, pored over his books on electrical theory and experimented constantly with electromagnets and induction coils. These were the years of preparation—nothing brilliant, but occasional flashes of the genius to come. Sometimes they were comical flashes, it is true—his electric cockroach killer for example. One of the stations where he worked for a while was plagued by a thriving population of roaches. The men complained that the bugs would get into their lunchpails, and that they would often carry them home in their cuffs and pockets. These were like complaints about the weather, though. There was little you could do about bugs in those days except hit them with your shoe. Edison's remedy was not much better—it got more laughs than cockroaches. He ran a wire from a dry-cell battery along the top of one particularly infested desk—just a fraction of an inch away from a long, thin strip of metal. When the unsuspecting insect crossed the desk, touching the wire with its front legs and the metal strip with its hind legs, it completed a circuit and shocked itself with a bolt of electricity. Every morning scores of rigid bugs could be found scattered along the desktop.

When he was 21, Edison decided that the time had come to make his move. He did not want to be a telegraph operator all his life. He followed the road taken by many men from the small towns of America in those years; he went to New York City. There he struggled at first, but finally he was able to demonstrate his unique scientific capabilities to the owners and managers of the many new factories sprouting up in the area. He began to make money—big money in fact.

He had something to offer—a skill of demonstrable value. He did not have to ask for a salary, because he was able to demand compensation for contributions no employer could deny. He would take creaking, sputtering machinery and make it work efficiently. Often he was asked to fix machines that would not work at all, or would turn out inferior or damaged products. By sticking a larger gear here, a clean brush there, a trip lever, a tightened contact spring—he soon got them running like clockwork. One invention, an improved "stock ticker," a kind of telegraph used to record stock prices in Wall Street brokerage houses, brought him a check for $40,000 (quite a sum in those days) from the delighted owner of the firm. Edison used most of these commissions to build his famed laboratory in Menlo Park, New Jersey: the home of the "Wizard of Menlo Park."

Edison did much work during these years for his old employer, the telegraph company—Western Union. He worked for them now, however, as a private contractor, a provider of inventions. Western Union was one of the most logical markets for what Edison had to offer. Their operation was still in its primitive stage and plagued with "bugs." The telegraph was based on one of the well-known properties of electricity—its ability to convert a bar of iron or steel into a temporary magnet, an electromagnet. Electricity was run through wire coiled around the metal bar. A strip of metal on a spring, placed near the electromagnet, would be pulled toward the magnet's surface when the telegraph operator pushed a key and closed the circuit. If another piece of metal was placed between the electromagnet and the metal on the spring, the two pieces would strike, "click," metal against metal, when an operator hit the switch that closed the circuit. When the circuit is closed the pieces of metal "click." When the circuit is opened, the magnetism ceases and the spring pulls the strip up again. When the switch is closed again, it clicks again; and on, and on, in whatever pattern the operator, opening and closing the circuit, desires. Once a code was agreed to—the Morse Code for example—messages could be forwarded by spelling out words. Three clicks, or "dots" as the operators called them, would be an "S". Three "dashes" (holding the circuit closed and allowing the metal strips to vibrate against each other for a longer interval) would be an "O."

String your wires along poles all over the map and—there you have it! A country united as never before by a communications network.

But Western Union had a problem. If the telegraph was to

become practical, a money-making operation, some way was needed to send a message to many different locations without having to get an individual operator to tap it out over and over again. Could a news service, for example, send the same message to a hundred different newspapers without having to tap it out a hundred times? Could it be tapped out once and then sent to the different locations? Was that possible? Edison's solution sounds amazingly simple—as do most great ideas once someone thinks them up.

He perforated a strip of tape so that it would force the arm of the telegraph up and down—to open and close the circuit—as the tape was pulled through beneath it. If the holes were arranged in the right sequence and at the right intervals, the arm would tap out a message. That tape then could be whipped at high speeds through a telegraph, over and over again. Seven thousand words per minute were possible. You could hardly see the arm, it was vibrating so fast, but it was sending exactly the message it was prepared to send.

There was another problem. If the telegraph was to gain acceptance in the United States, a way had to be found to send more than one message through a wire at the same time. Imagine the sea of poles and wires if there had to be a separate wire for every telegraph receiver in a city like New York or Chicago! But sending more than one message at a time over one wire sounded impossible—like fitting two cars into a one-car garage.

Edison's answer was ingenious. Through persistent research and experimentation, he discovered that electric currents transmitted at varying strengths would find their own channels or "paths" in a wire—as many as two sending and two receiving operators could work the same wire at the same time if they agreed beforehand to transmit at different strengths. Eight operators, in other words, could work the same wire, with receivers set up to handle currents of differing strength. Where Western Union once thought 400,000 miles of wire were necessary, 100,000 now would do the job. Edison's "quadruplex wire" earned him another $30,000.

When we think of the telephone we usually think of Alexander Graham Bell. That is not inaccurate. Bell did work out the problems involved in getting the vibrations made by the human voice to set off electrical impulses through a wire, and then picking them up on a receiver a considerable distance away. But Bell's messages were a tinny and buzzing cacophony.

If one spoke slowly and precisely, and if the listener on the other end concentrated determinedly, he could just about—just about—make out what was being said. It would have made an interesting toy that would hold a child's attention until the novelty wore off; Bell's telephone would not have made an effective means of communication for serious purposes. It took an application of Edison's genius to get the working telephone.

Edison worked with Bell's basic system. He added to it an induction coil and a carbon button. They made a crucial difference. He attached the carbon button to a spring and inserted it against the diaphragm in the phone's mouthpiece. When the diaphragm was vibrated by a human voice passing over it— sound waves—a constantly varying pressure was applied to the sensitive carbon button, altering its electrical resistance in unison with the volume and pitch of the human voice. That in turn produced an identically patterned series of variations in the current running through the primary coil, and identical changes were induced—but amplified—in the secondary. These induced currents were then transmitted across the phone line. At the other end, in the receiver, the electrical impulses patterned by a human voice were registered in a receiver that made sounds like that voice. Someone listening to it would actually think he was hearing the voice. Instead of using electric current to make "dots" and "dashes," as in the telegraph, Edison found the way for current to carry accurately the sound of a voice.

Though still only in his early thirties, Edison became the talk of the town. He put on demonstrations in auditoriums and concert halls all over the East Coast. People lined up in disbelief to see if the "nutty inventor" from Menlo Park was a hoax or not. Could he really transmit a human voice? They went away convinced. The voice came across clear and distinct as Edison read into his speaker from a distant room in the building.

Edison's telephone was a remarkable step forward. He eventually sold his improved apparatus to Bell, rather than trying to set up a rival system. Bell went ahead to launch the immense telephone network we now know as The Bell System. Measured in dollars and cents, Edison's decision to sell out was an unwise one. Bell's company became one of America's most profitable corporations. But Edison was an independently wealthy man as a result of his inventions—not a millionaire yet, but very comfortable. More important, he had little interest in establishing and administering a business. He was a scientist and inventor, not a businessman. There were still too many projects waiting to be finished in his workshop.

The telephone, for example, had one serious limitation. Its messages could not be retained or replayed. Would it be possible, Edison wondered, to preserve a spoken message so that it could be repeated again and again? Could he, in other words, do for the telephone what he had done for the telegraph? His perforated tape could be used to transmit a message in Morse Code. If telephone messages could be "put on a tape" too—why, the prospects were staggering. The voices of famous political leaders could be preserved for posterity. Renowned actors, opera stars, perhaps even performances by symphony orchestras, could be captured in New York or Paris and played at some later date in small towns in Texas or Alaska. Civilization's finest moments could be made available to all. We take phonographs and tape cassettes for granted now—turn a switch and hear a London-based Shakespearean company perform *Hamlet,* a German orchestra play Wagner, an inauguration speech by Franklin Delano Roosevelt originally delivered in the 1930s. We hear them right in our living room, as if they were talking to us over the telephone, as if a message had been recorded just for us. No big deal.

But it is. It has changed mankind. Just five years before Edison invented the phonograph, people would have laughed at the idea of such a development. They would have reacted the way we would to a neighbor, fiddling around in his garage workshop, who informed us that the contraption he was nailing together was a machine that would transport us bodily, in an instant, to any place on the globe by making us dematerialize in one spot and reassemble in another. Impossible? Right!

But Edison thought that sound could be captured. His work with the telephone showed him that the vibrations made by a spoken word could be transmitted across a wire to a distant receiver. Could they be placed as dents or ridges or undulations on some material? On wax or tin maybe? If they could, perhaps a wire could be run across them to pick up the voice of the original speaker. Could the sound vibrations of the human voice, or of instrumental music be reproduced? Perhaps a fine-tipped needle could be made to vibrate as the undulated material was moved across it. And if that needle was attached to a wire, perhaps those impulses could be sent through the wire—

168

not to a distant phone receiver, but to a receiver located in the same room—and reproduced as sound.

Edison had one of his workmen turn out a tin cylinder on a crank. As the handle was turned the cylinder revolved and scraped against a rigid needle. He invited his workmen into his room after his experiments with the strange machine were completed.

"What is it?" they asked.

"It is a machine that will talk," he answered. Most of the workmen had been with Edison for some time, so it took a pretty wild claim to make them skeptical. They had seen other impossible ideas take shape in that workshop. But a talking machine? There were a few doubting faces in the group. Edison leaned over and talked into the machine.

"Mary had a little lamb, little lamb . . ."

Then he turned the crank. And back came his voice:

"Mary had a little lamb . . ." It was the first phonograph record in history.

From there he went on to experiment with different recording surfaces, types of needles, and improved amplification systems until he came out with a product that began to pop up in homes all over America: the black box with the big megaphone speaker on which flat records made of a sensitive and long-lasting material were "played." The apparatus was primitive in comparison with a modern stereo set, but nevertheless it enabled people to hear—to "witness"—with a clarity they found remarkable, things they thought they would never hear in their lives. (The system was refined enough for Edison to put on demonstrations in which the audience was asked to try to tell the difference between a live and a recorded voice saying the same lines. They could not with any regularity.)

It must be remembered that the old records we think so poor in quality, compared with what we have now, *are* old. But think how different we are from generations of the past. We can hear the voices of Churchill, Hitler, Caruso. (We cannot hear the voices of Julius Caesar or Robespierre, or an original performance of a play by Shakespeare or Aeschylus. How fascinating it would be if we could.) The sounds of historic events and performances that have occurred since Edison's time are now available for all generations. He was a turning point in the history of the human race. Oh yes—we will be able to see the sights too; Edison invented the motion picture as well. But let us hold off

169

on that. He had to invent the electric light first.

It was not that there were no lighting systems operating by electric current before Edison invented his light. There were —the so-called "arc lights." But they were huge affairs, taking so much current and shining so brightly that they were suitable only for lighting streets or large stores. And they flickered and sputtered. One certainly would never dream of trying to read by one of those balloon-like contrivances in the comfort of his home. The light was actually a fire created within a bulb, an electric fire that fed on carbon rods for fuel. A spark was "jumped" across a small gap between the carbon rods—much as the spark jumps in a spark plug—creating a bright "arc" of light. The arc lamp was invented by Sir Humphrey Davy, an English scientist, in 1800.

Edison's plan was to make a smaller light suitable for use in private homes, a light with about the same brilliance as the gas lamps used at the time. He knew from his own experience that an electric current passing through a wire created heat. His problem: how to find a wire with enough resistance to provide a luminous glow (incandescence) without dissolving from the high heat? It sounded easy, but it was not. Every metal he tried quickly burned out, breaking the circuit, as soon as enough current was applied to get it to glow brightly. Platinum seemed to work best. It would glow with white heat when current passed through it. But it melted too quickly to be of any use. A light bulb that would have to be changed every few minutes was not practical. He tried other metals, as well as alloys, but there was little improvement. For 13 months he tried with no success, often going for days on end when he thought he was closing in on an answer. Edison could do that: work through night and day when he had to, and then sleep for 18 or so hours straight to recuperate.

He tried everything. Curiously, lampblack and tar rolled into thin wires seemed to work pretty well, especially when it was mixed with carbon. It burned longer than his other alloys, but still not long enough. Finally he tried a scheme most of us would think was in the wrong direction.

He had been experimenting with costly metals. The problem seemed to be to find the most durable one. But he was tempted by the idea that plentiful carbon, in the right form, might be the answer. He sent for a spool of cotton thread, bent a piece into a loop like a hairpin, and baked it until it was carbonized. Then

170

came a painstaking and nerve-racking job: keeping the carbonized strand in one piece while sealing it inside a glass bulb. We all know what a burnt wooden match is like—a chalky black powder. The cotton thread had to be made into carbon, but kept from crumbling. It took Edison and his crew two and a half days without sleep to get a loop—a filament—of it inside a bulb, and connected to an electric current.

It was worth it. The bulb, when connected to a battery, burned for 45 hours straight. There still were problems, but Edison was on his way. One problem was to insure a perfect vacuum inside the bulb so that there would be no oxygen present. As soon as oxygen entered the bulb, the filament burned out in a flash. We know now that even the advanced filaments of today will burn out instantly if there is so much as a pin prick in the surface of the glass bulb. Edison later discovered that slivers of bamboo would last longer and could be handled more easily when carbonized than cotton thread. So the earliest light bulbs manufactured had a filament made from the wood of a bamboo tree!

A very big problem remained. Edison had a bulb he was confident he could market; for home lighting it was vastly preferable to gas or kerosene: cleaner, safer, and easier to handle. But how would he provide the current? A separate battery for every lamp would be clumsy and expensive. It would not be practical for every family to have a dynamo of its own. Could a dynamo be built in a central location, powerful enough to provide electric power for millions of families?

Edison did not invent the dynamo. But he made it work—he made it more than a classroom demonstration of the nature of electricity. Michael Faraday had shown that a copper disc revolving through the poles of a magnet would create electric current—the reverse of the process by which an electric current creates an electromagnet. Now, Edison wondered: could a dynamo powerful enough to light bulbs all over a city be constructed, using Faraday's basic idea? Could a powerful gas or steam engine revolve a core of metal inside immense coils of wire, transforming the horsepower of the engine into electrical power? Could wires be stretched from that dynamo, or generator, to every home in a city? We are used to the sight of telephone poles with their top strand of high-voltage electrical wire. We take it for granted. But imagine the reaction when Edison first started to play with the idea. Wooden poles carrying

171

deadly electrical current down every street in the town! Are you crazy?

Well it was not the first time someone thought Edison was crazy. He took his scheme with him to New York in 1880. The density of housing was sufficient there to make a beginning. One wire could feed electricity into dozens of apartments over a hundred-foot span. He built his power plant; rounded up subscribers; hired people to install and service the delivery system; designed all the necessary hardware: sockets, switches, plugs, cutoffs, fuses, voltage- and ampere-measuring devices, conductors, and fixtures.

Within 20 years of the invention of the light bulb, the investment in lighting plants in the United States was $750 million. The idea caught on, and it was not long before everyone wanted to be in on the Wizard's scheme. The Edison Light Company was established and grew into the giant Consolidated Edison Company of today, one of New York's largest corporations. Soon people took it for granted: you somehow got the power to light and heat the house, and run countless gadgets, from little outlets along the walls. Just stick a plug in—that's all. Not bad for a small rural workshop in New Jersey in the 1880s.

Naturally Edison made a tidy profit once the power company got rolling. But even the enormous financial stakes in this undertaking could not coax him out of his workshop. For a few years he didn't produce anything as spectacular as the light bulb. Some "lesser" inventions took up his time: a magnetic ore separator to lower the cost of extracting the impurities from iron ore; an electric pen with a vibrating needle that enabled the user to pierce paper and "write" a stencil; even a vocal engine—a device that used vibrations of the human voice to turn a flywheel with enough drive to drill a hole through wood.

Lights, Action, Camera!

A major breakthrough came again in 1889. Edison had been working on the idea for some time in a locked room in his lab. A few of his inventions had been pirated by false inventors who sold products based on his groundwork. Edison's associates knew that he must be on to something big this time if he thought it was important enough to work in such secrecy. They talked about the "secret of Room 5."

One day that summer he burst through the door into the main workshop, shouting, "We've got it! Here's your work!" He distributed plans to the mechanics. Then he set off to Europe for a vacation with his family.

When he returned, a big machine was sitting in the back of his room. He had one of his men bring in a phonograph. Someone else lowered the shades. Edison turned a switch. On a white wall facing the small group—Edison and his most trusted workers—was a picture of a man. In motion! He tipped his hat, bowed slightly, and from the phonograph his voice came in a rough synchronization with the movement of his lips. "Good morning, Mr. Edison, good to see you back." The movies were born.

Edison had worked out the details of a process that many other inventors thought possible for some time, but were unable to complete. Photography had been around for more than 30 years and was a near-perfected process. They did not have color photography or speedy development of pictures. But they were able to take a picture and reproduce it clearly. Some of the photos we have of Abraham Lincoln and Robert E. Lee, for example, are as good as any you will find of modern Presidents. But could they be made to move, to appear "live" right in front of you?

It seemed possible. Cartoonists had known for many years that if a series of their drawings, each slightly altered from the last, was flicked quickly past the eye, the illusion of movement could be sustained. If a way could be found to take photographs of moving objects in rapid succession, and then project them in sequence, the same illusion might be created.

There were many problems. A film sensitive enough to receive an image after an extremely brief exposure was the first need. For the moving pictures to seem lifelike when projected, they would have to be taken in quick succession—40 to 50 per second in fact. An earlier experimenter had come up with the idea of photographing a horse in motion by placing a number of cameras in a row. The shutters of these cameras were opened by strings attached to them and to the horse's saddle. As the horse raced by, the strings would pull open the shutters in sequence, taking pictures of the horse. When flashed past the eye in rapid succession, the pictures did give a rough impression of a horse in motion. But it was a gimmick people would quickly grow tired of. Edison wanted lifelike imagery. One camera, with a spinning roll of film, would have to snap hundreds— thousands—of pictures as the operator followed the motion of people, animals, cars, ships, railroads—anything the eye could see.

Although Edison knew little about photography before he started his search, he soon became an expert. He developed the chemistry to produce the quality of film he wanted.

But how to project the images onto a surface large enough to be viewed comfortably and enjoyably by a large number of people? The sequential photos could be flashed by a small hand-cranked, bulb-lighted viewer held up to the eyes. But the kind of pictures Edison wanted would require huge expenditures. The only way it could be done economically would be if the resulting "movies" could be shown before a large paying audience.

Edison's knowledge of the electric light enabled him to devise the high-intensity lighting needed to project the pictures through magnifying lenses. With help, he was able to perfect a film—celluloid—pliable enough to be whirred rapidly in front of the bulb. The magnifying lenses did the rest. His machinists built electric-powered reels to spin the pictures at a speed that would give them lifelike movement. Hollywood took it from there. The pioneers of the motion picture industry knew how much they owed to Thomas Alva Edison. On his seventy-seventh birthday, in 1924, the leaders of the film industry sponsored a dinner in New York. Six hundred producers, directors, actors, screenwriters, cameramen, film manufacturers, newspapermen, and critics came to pay homage to the persistent workshop tinkerer who started one of America's great industries.

Did Edison ever fail? Or come up with something less than earthshaking in importance? Certainly. He experimented constantly. You have to fail often in order to learn how to succeed —to see why what does not work does not work. But even when he "failed" he often displayed an inventive genius, a remarkable understanding of the "nature" of nature; what the world we live in is like, and how it can be used by men to improve life.

During World War I, for example, U.S. military leaders called upon Edison to apply his genius to the war effort. One of the major problems of the time was the effectiveness of German submarines—the notorious U-boats. From their undersea positions they were able to strike with impunity, launching torpedos against American ships in the Atlantic. Edison came up with a diaphragm that could be carried on a rod protruding about 10 to 20 feet ahead of the vessel. A torpedo slicing through the water would send out sound vibrations that could be picked up by the diaphragm from as much as 4,000 yards away. His next step called for fastening four huge anchors, each about nine feet in diameter, on ropes four inches thick, to the bow of the ship. As soon as a torpedo in motion was "heard" by the diaphragm, the anchors would be dropped and the helm thrown hard over, bringing the ship to a standstill and turning her at right angles to the original course. In a test on a loaded vessel 325 feet in length, the ship was turned 90 degrees in two minutes ten seconds, with an advance of only 200 feet. Not fast enough to be worth the expense and effort, old Navy salts agreed—the torpedo, in all likelihood, would hit in that amount of time—but, yessir, that was some way to turn a battleship. The military did make use of his sensing diaphragms, however, to pick up the position of hidden guns. By measuring the intervals between the time it took the sound ("report") of the firing to reach certain known points, the hidden gun position could be plotted. Under the right weather conditions, Edison was able to come within 2 percent, plus or minus, of any gun's location.

There is no Menlo Park laboratory anymore. After Edison's death in 1931, the building stood empty for years. Finally a pig farmer moved in and used it as a barn. Not long after that it burned to the ground. But there is an Edison museum at the site of one of his other laboratories, in West Orange, New Jersey. Visitors can see his first electric light, movie camera, phonograph, and dozens of other inventions. Pictures of Edison at work cover the walls. There are early storage batteries, electric trains, and more than 3,000 of his notebooks, as well as the drawings for his experiments. (Those who would like to visit, by the way, can write for more information: The Edison National Historical Site, Box 126, Orange, New Jersey.) But the most appropriate Edison "museum" is the world around us. That is where we see him at his best. His genius is a daily part of most of our lives. He has transformed the texture and rhythm of life on the planet, from the most barren of deserts to the densest of jungles.

But, was it worth it? Does having a television and an electric hair dryer compensate for all the pollution and the threat of mechanized warfare? Was not Edison the first of the ecology's "destroyers"—the first to "tamper" with God's creation, the

175

first of the breed of men who, in the name of progress and prosperity, would dehumanize life, create faceless cities, ugly industrial hells? Was he not one of the first afflicted with the fateful disease that makes men feel themselves "conquerors" and "masters" of the universe rather than participants in God's creation? Would we not be better off, more human, without the gadgets, the noise, the glitter and glare of an electrified neon life? These can be perplexing questions when considered calmly.

There are those who would have us believe Edison began a process that has done more harm than good. Not that there are anti-Edison societies, as such, in operation. No one is pushing things to that extreme. There are those, however, who favor the proposition that we must withdraw from Edison's vision of the future and return to a simpler life, closer to the earth; that we can no longer depend on the vast quantities of electrical power needed to maintain the life of ease and comfort we now enjoy, especially since the fossil fuels required to operate the huge generators are running out. They feel it was a false hope in the first place—that we will be happier and more fulfilled when we once again return to a more "natural" way of life; that it will be no great loss to cross out, as a mistake, the whole idea of a life filled with electronic marvels.

Probably most of us are attracted by at least some portion of this critique. Environmental groups, ecology activists, back-to-earth societies abound. Strip mining is condemned by bird-watchers and hunters. We are warned of pollution from factories and automobiles. Peasant blouses, brown rice, home-baked bread, jeans, back-packing, and wheat germ have become symbolic preferences for a substantial segment of Americans who nurture in themselves a reaction against what they call the "impersonal" and "computerized" life of modern America.

It is not hard to be against what industrialization has done to American life when driving through a sooty, grimy factory town, or paddling through the slimy refuse on the surface of a river that runs alongside a chemical plant. If we asked any of the bathers at Jones Beach or Malibu what they thought of industrialized life in the 1970s as they sat sadly watching the globules of oily sludge deposited in thick wedges along the sparkling sand, there is little doubt what their answer would be.

But the question that demands to be asked is whether the

176

villains are mechanization, electrification, and industry themselves—or the abuses of them. Can the use of electricity be
included within nature—seen as part of our life? Or did Edison
somehow stumble across something man was never meant to
possess—a version of the Biblical forbidden fruit? Is it impossible to enjoy the benefits of a life that includes industry and
electric power without destroying ourselves in the process? Or
must there be a censorship of sorts over the ideas that men like
Edison uncovered?

Only time will tell for sure. But there is little doubt that up
to now Edison has remained an admired figure in American
history because most of us are confident that the conveniences
and leisure time (which we can use for painting pictures, writing poetry, reading fine literature, family recreation, among
other things) brought to us by men following his lead are a
blessing not a curse. We cling determinedly to the conviction
that our survival does not depend upon a return to a frontier
way of life. Most moderns, in short, reject the idea that the
application of human inventiveness to the material substance of
the planet is "unnatural"—including the harnessing of electricity.

Americans in their middle years or older usually intuit this a
bit easier than do younger folk. Those who were teenagers
before World War II, especially, grew up in an America where
science and technology did not seem incomprehensible or
menacing powers. Boy Scouts earned merit badges in electricity. Boys' radio clubs were not uncommon. Comic-book heroes
often were skilled pilots, mechanics, and electronics experts.
Machinery, electrified or not, was no more "sinister" than a
hammer or screwdriver. It was a tool, a better way of using
metal in the service of mankind. Boys built ham radios in the
basement, strung telegraph wires from the bedroom window to
the apple trees and beyond to a friend's window down the
street. They tore apart toasters and rebuilt the straight-six engines on old "bombs" in their backyards. Electricity was the
fascinating new presence in the universe, an advanced way of
getting things done. Atom bombs, radiation poisoning, computerized bureaucracies, oil spills, electronic snooping had not yet
come. It was not menacing—it was fun—to watch the electromagnets pull the hammer against the bell above the kitchen
cabinets when your little brother completed the circuit by

pressing the doorbell button on the front porch. How else can we use those magnets? Let's fiddle around in Dad's workshop and see.

With the incredible advances in electronics and technology, much of that early fascination has given way to incomprehension, even insecurity. The maze of wiring inside the circuit box of something as (relatively) simple as an elevator now seems almost inhuman to some, beyond the scope of the individual mind. Many admit to a certain fear of modern technology; claim it makes them feel at the mercy of forces beyond their control.

But is a wholesale condemnation of electric power and technology appropriate? Does a high level of sophistication always indicate that something has become "inhuman"? Were Michelangelo and Leonardo da Vinci "inhuman" when they moved art to new plateaus beyond the reach of the common artist? Are science and technology to be condemned when their practitioners excel, whereas art is not?

Well, there is a difference; there is no denying it. Refinements and advancements in artistic insights and techniques are not likely to blow up the world. But even too much good, healthy food, even wheat germ, can put us in the hospital. Does that make food a bad thing? Look at it another way. Is not our fear of science and technology more a fear of their misuse than of the curiosity and inventiveness of men like Edison? Certainly, if someone is harshly critical of machines and electronics *only* because he does not understand them, he is taking a less-than-admirable view of things. The man who "hates" cars, for example, *only* because he is unable to keep one going without high costs and much inconvenience, and because the guy from the service station makes him feel stupid when he explains what the needed repairs entail, is no deep thinker. He is, in fact, very much like a yahoo who makes fun of the "eggheads" who like to visit art museums. Both are trying to hide their ignorance and incompetence with an air of false superiority. It is not difficult to understand that someone might have had to spend so much time studying to become a psychologist or a journalist that he was unable to learn how to fix a toaster or clean a spark plug. But only someone who has never taken the time actually to look at the precise and inventive engineering that goes into something as commonplace as the internal combustion engine could dismiss those who have mastered its intricacies as "dumb greasers."

178

The point? The degree of human inventiveness evident in modern machinery and technology, from a lawnmower to a space shuttle, is an unmistakable reflection of the nature of man. It is no more "unnatural" to use electromagnets to open a heavy door than it was for some primitive forefather of ours to hang a cover over the opening of his cave. That ability to think out a better way to work with the material of the planet is one of the key distinctions between man and animal. Beavers build their dams and robins build their nests in our time as they did in the Paleolithic Age, when men lived in the crudest of shelters. They do these things by mere instinct. Only man has been endowed with the capacity to share with the Creator in the "making" of the universe. Reason—that attribute of man which the ancient Greek and Roman philosophers used to call the "spark of the divine"—enables us not only to do things, but to understand *why* we do them the way we do; to see the purpose, the *end*, of our actions; and to adjust, adapt, and revise our methods in order to do the things we do in a more effective and efficient way. We cannot deny or disparage that process without disparaging—even dehumanizing—ourselves.

Most of the critics of technology and industry know that. Or they will if they think about it long enough. The most committed "back to earth" advocates invariably make an exception or two to their rejection of the modern world. They will move to a commune in the back woods and sew their own clothes. But they want a stereo nearby. They want birth-control devices. And they want a Greyhound bus to get them to a concert once in a while to hear rock bands that depend upon some pretty sophisticated electronics.

All of us, in some way, want the benefits of modern science. There are aspects we fear. How can we enjoy the benefits and minimize the risks? That is the question modern man is asking. Those who suggest a passive withdrawal, rather than an energetic application of human reason to our world—what we call science—cannot answer that question. We need some more Tom Edisons for that.

Walter Reed

7

Walter Reed
Doctor in Uniform

Most Americans have heard of the Walter Reed Army Hospital in Washington, D.C. It is, of course, the huge medical complex that breaks into the news every so often when a famous politician or general is rushed there for emergency treatment. There are few, still living, however, who remember the tall, straight, mustachioed Army doctor, Major Walter Reed, after whom it is named. Those who remember him, though, remember him well. In the early 1900s he achieved the kind of public acclaim rarely given medical men and research scientists. Those who excel in these pursuits usually must resign themselves to the quiet praise of colleagues able to appreciate their determination and genius. Reed was different. Not that the members of the medical profession did not hold him in high esteem. He was given a standing ovation by the delegates to the Pan-American Medical Congress on February 6, 1900, when he announced his findings to the world. But Reed's name was on the lips of the rest of the country, too, not long afterwards. Everyone was talking about the man who located the cause of one of the world's most mysterious and dreaded diseases: "yellow Jack," or

181

"yellow fever." In the years that followed his discovery, a bronze bust of Reed was placed at the entrance of the Army Medical Museum, where it sits to this day; a commemorative postage stamp was issued in his honor; his name was placed at the head of the list of the Army Register's Roll of Honor; the Congress of the United States ordered struck a commemorative gold medal bearing his likeness; and that beautiful hospital in Washington was dedicated to his memory.

Why such acclaim? Well, first of all because the disease he helped cure was such a deadly killer. In the nineteenth century, people who had to live or work, temporarily or permanently, in tropical areas played a kind of Russian roulette: you might live to a ripe old age—maybe—if yellow fever did not get you first. Reed's breakthrough brought a collective sigh of relief. The killer was no longer on the loose. But there was an added element in Reed's work, as we shall see—something that injected excitement and drama. Reed was not regarded by his fellow-citizens as a scrubbed-hands research specialist bending over a microscope in an antiseptic hospital laboratory. His search for the cure to yellow fever took him into steamy Caribbean swamps after a deadly killer that had sent home more than a few other pursuers—in pine boxes. If Reed did not conquer yellow fever, the odds were that he would get it himself. Those were the stakes.

Burning the Midnight Oil

The familiar pattern continues. America's favorites seem to come from the common folk. Rich men prove talented and successful, certainly. But the special affection that makes an American a beloved hero rather than an admired fellow-citizen seems reserved for the poor kid who makes good.

Reed's childhood was a deprived one—but only materially. His father was a Methodist minister who "rode the circuit"— preaching—to parishes from Murfreesboro, North Carolina to Belroi in Gloucester County, Virginia. Walter was one of five children. Some of his earliest memories were of encounters with Union troops crossing through the hills near his home in the last years of the Civil War, after the Confederate forces had retreated further south.

We have no IQ scores to confirm that Reed was an extremely

bright young man. But he must have been. Standardized testing as we know it was not introduced into American schools until much later. (Which leads to an interesting and provocative question: are we better off for having a way to speculate on an individual's talents apart from his actual accomplishments? The point that many have made is that a standardized test ought not to determine our fate). Whether it was more from innate ability than from hard work—or, more likely, a combination of both— Reed was an outstanding student. He entered the University of Virginia in 1867, at the age of 16. He left less than a year later with a degree that entitled him to practice medicine—at 17.

It was an accomplishment—obviously. However, it would be highly unfair to modern students to chide them for their failure to match it. It would be impossible nowadays. The American Medical Association has set standards that require young men and women to complete four years of medical school and a year's internship at a hospital before they begin to practice medicine. And medical schools require for admission the successful completion of four years of premedical training at an accredited college. Reed would have had to start college when he was eight to begin his practice at 17 if he had lived in our time. And he was not *that* bright.

But medical schools in the 1870s granted degrees to anyone who simply passed a certifying examination. For most students at the University of Virginia that meant attendance for two years or more. The trustees of the university, determined to establish a reputation for their school and the medical profession, had devised a test that few dared attempt without lengthy classroom preparation. Other medical schools were not as conscientious. The term "sawbones," used derisively for doctors in the nineteenth century, was not entirely inappropriate. There were individuals with a medical degree who were likely to do more harm than good if you went to them for anything more serious than a headache. And the only reason they were not dangerous if you went to them for headaches was that the bizarre concoctions they gave you usually did no harm. No good either—but at least the miracle elixir usually did not prevent Mother Nature from effecting her own cure.

Many young people of college age today complain that it has become unreasonably difficult to get into medical school; that unfair admission standards deny many qualified young people the right to study medicine. There is something to that. The

American Medical Association is on record in the 1970s as being opposed to building more medical schools than are "needed." Would it be unfair to say that they fear a surplus of doctors in the near future, which would force down doctors' incomes? It can be argued, in other words, that some doctors are more concerned about their bankrolls than about medical standards when they warn of the dangers of "too many" people in their profession. Nevertheless, the American Medical Association has served us well by making sure that there will be demanding standards for doctor training—so that we will not have any more "sawbones."

Reed decided to take a shot at the medical examination at such an early age for two reasons. First, he was impatient. He wanted to get out on his own, see the world, and enter upon life's adventure. But there was another reason. He was pressed for money. The longer he stayed in school, the longer it would be before he brought home a paycheck. His father had managed to get a parish near Charlottesville so that Walter could live at home, rather than pay room and board, while he attended the university. The situation was that tight.

The test was no breeze for him. He was at a double disadvantage. Not only had he skipped the years in medical school that most students who took the test had completed, but he had skipped much of high school and college as well. He had to make up on his own for what he had missed, if he expected to do well. He found himself especially weak in certain advanced mathematics and chemistry. He spent long and painful hours at his desk, poring over piles of medical books and his class notes. It got to the point where his father felt compelled to forbid him to continue his all-night sessions. He came into Walter's room one night after three A.M. The oil lamp was flickering low.

"I'm worried about you, Walter. I don't think you've had more than four or five hours sleep a night for weeks," he said.

"I'm trying to do two years' work in one, Pa," Walter responded. "I'm not brilliant, so I can't learn without working. But I can work hard."

His father was not unsympathetic. He must have admired his son's grit. (Most modern parents would give their eye teeth to get such a response from their children.) But he stressed that a man needs a good night's sleep to keep alert and physically fit, and Walter obeyed. He extinguished his lamp and went to sleep. He would arrange his day more efficiently so that he would not have to cram his study into the late-night hours.

The hard work paid off—as it usually does. Walter passed the test and, not long afterwards, found himself at the train station in Culpeper, Virginia waiting for the northbound train. He was heading for New York City and his first medical appointment, at New York's Bellevue Hospital Medical College. His brother Chris was with him. Chris was also going to New York, to study law.

It was a trying moment. The boys were Southerners, with vivid memories of the Civil War. The tracks leaving Culpeper, reaching off into the distance, would take them to a tempo and a way of life dramatically unlike the one they knew. Culpeper was "home"—friendly stationmasters with a Southern drawl; suntanned teamsters; towhead farmboys lounging on the wooden platform, waiting to see the train pull out, while whistling porters loaded the baggage; black nannies escorting rich young ladies in hoop skirts on their way to a vacation. Up ahead, at the end of the tracks, was the city they had read so much about. The tall buildings; newly arrived immigrants of many races and many tongues; hordes hustling and bustling through crowded streets; restaurants, saloons, the theater, the docks, universities, museums, gangsters, libraries; and hospitals. A doctor did not have to go to the city. He could stay in a small town in the South and build a respectable practice. But the kind of research that Reed wanted to be part of his education was done in city hospitals. Like most who leave home for the first time, he had fears. He had to force his attention on the adventure and the new experiences awaiting him, rather than dwell on the comforts of home he was leaving behind. The boys boarded the train and set out on the journey to New York.

Reed found the city as exciting as he had hoped. But he was disappointed too, especially with the medical profession. All too many of the doctors he encountered in the course of his duties as a health inspector appeared to be concerned only with amassing private wealth. The sickness-plagued, disease-infested tenements were a bothersome nuisance they preferred to ignore. Reed, who took his doctor's oath seriously, was appalled by their indifference—even more by their ignorance. Many of the doctors he met spent no time at all keeping up with advances in medicine. Medicine was just a job to them, not a profession. The last thing on their minds was sacrificing some time to seek out a cure for the lethal diseases of the time.

Cholera? Typhoid? Diphtheria? Yellow Fever? Polio? Tuberculosis? It was not their problem. But whose was it?

So complete was Reed's disillusionment, at first, that he considered resigning—leaving the practice of medicine altogether. But he overcame his disappointment. He stayed in medicine—fortunately for us.

Still, he was unhappy in New York. He was a young man with a streak of wanderlust. So in 1874, after hearing of the opportunities in the U.S. Army's Medical Corps, he decided to give the armed forces a try—maybe three or four years. A little travel, some interesting work, probably—it could be a pleasant interlude in his career. Little did he know, when he sat down to prepare for the test given by the Army's Examining Board, that the change of pace would last a lifetime.

This test gave him problems, too. It contained questions on Latin, Greek, mathematics, and history, as well as on medicine. "Imagine me," he wrote to Emily Laurence, the future Mrs. Reed (whom he had recently met), "conjugating an irregular verb, or telling what x plus y equals, or what year Rome was founded, or the battle of Marathon fought. Why the thing is impossible, I shall utterly fail."

Needless to say, he did not fail. He hit the books once again, this time without a worried father looking over his shoulder. In June of 1875 he was appointed an assistant surgeon in the Medical Corps with the rank of first lieutenant. The rebel kid who had watched in anger as the Union troops poured into his hometown was now an officer in that same army.

For the next few years, Reed traveled from post to post on the still-wild frontier of the American Southwest. The Cavalry had been assigned the job of keeping peace and containing the Indian raids against the new settlements. The medical work was not very novel or challenging, but there was plenty of it. His new bride joined him not long after his first assignment, and traveled with him to the storied outpost of Camp Apache.

Life on an army outpost was rugged, with few of the amenities of life, but seldom dull or routine. Reed recalled fondly, later in life, the post chaplain who kept a poisonous Gila monster as a pet; the Indians, grateful for his medical care, who would break into his cabin while he and his wife were away and hang freshly killed game from the ceiling rafters (it made good eating but could throw quite a scare into you when you returned to the darkened house); the hunting and fishing trips in

186

the virgin hills and deserts of the Arizona frontier; the intra-squad football and baseball games; the San Diego-El Paso stage roaring into the center of the post in a cloud of dust. And the occasional Indian uprising.

Geronimo, the legendary leader of a band of renegade Apaches who refused to sign a peace treaty with the Army, was still alive and active during Reed's stay in Arizona. Consequently, anti-Indian sentiment was strong among the settlers, and Reed may have shared it. But he was a healer, a doctor, above all else. He never refused his services. In fact, one of the incidents he remembered most fondly was the night he saved the life of a deserted Indian infant.

The soldiers from the fort had pursued a band of Apache marauders deep into the hills. Although they were never able to catch up with the Apaches, they did come across a camp the Indians had abandoned the night before, where they had left a badly burned infant to die. The soldiers wrapped the little girl in coarse bandages, swaddled her in a rough wool blanket, and carried her back to Camp Apache.

It was not yet dawn when two of the troopers knocked at Reed's cabin. As one might expect, Reed was not in the best of humor when he answered the door.

"What's this?" he demanded, half-asleep.

The soldiers were taken aback, until they realized that Reed had no way of knowing that two dusty and unshaven cavalrymen would be carrying an infant with them in the darkness.

"It's a child, sir," they explained. "Indians left her to die."

Reed ordered the men to carry her to the base hospital. Then he dressed quickly and followed. The only available space was a thick wooden operating table between cots occupied by sleeping wounded soldiers. Reed deftly snipped away the bandages the soldiers had wrapped around the child. For the next few hours he struggled to save the young life. One soldier with a broken leg tells how he awoke to see Reed busily at work, then fell back to sleep; and awoke again later, in the daylight, to find him still bent solicitously over the child. The girl was asleep now, under a sedative. Reed began to stroke the fine strands of dark hair back across her forehead. He looked up and said to an assistant:

"She'll come through."

Reed later named the child Suzie and raised her in his own household until she was in her teens. She returned to her tribe

187

and became a teacher of English to the Indians.

But Reed's claim to fame was not as a frontier doctor—as interesting as his life in Arizona is to us when we read of it. Life on the frontier had its rewards, but when Reed learned of the developments taking place in the field of preventive medicine he felt he was missing out on something important. There had been tremendous breakthroughs in the years since he left medical school. Each new discovery led to others. Robert Koch had outlined the life cycle of the bacillus that caused anthrax, a dreaded cattle disease. He identified, as well, the bacillus that caused tuberculosis in human beings. Louis Pasteur, the Frenchman, was still setting ablaze the medical journals of Europe and America: immunization for rabies, "pasteurization" of milk, among other things. Others had identified the germs that caused cholera, leprosy, pneumonia, tetanus, typhoid, malaria, and diphtheria. Reed did not know how to take a sample of diseased tissue, much less diagnose a bacillus. It simply had not been part of his training. But he was determined to remedy that. He applied to his superiors for a tour of duty that would allow him to study at Johns Hopkins University. It was 1890; Reed was near 40, just beginning his career.

Back to the Lab

At Johns Hopkins, Reed studied under Dr. William Henry Welch. A plump and bearded man with a shining bald head and a taste for cigars and cut-away dress coats, Welch headed a research laboratory called the Pathological that was blazing new trails in medicine. A bright and innovative group of doctors had been attracted to his side and Reed became one of the most promising. It was not long, in fact, before he was slicing away at cadavers on his own, searching for the tiny nodules that appeared as lumps in the lymph glands of typhoid fever victims. He never found the cure for that disease, but he did develop the research skills of a "bacteriologist"—a new breed of doctor. His eyes were opened to the idea that disease could be prevented as well as cured by a doctor. It was a new frontier, his life's work: to seek out the causes of the major diseases of mankind.

He became a lecturer at Johns Hopkins. "You can accomplish so much more good for so many more people by training other men in modern medicine," he explained to those who asked him why he had stopped practicing medicine in order to teach it. "That's what counts with me. I might be able to save ten children strangling with diphtheria, but if I teach ten men to use antitoxin, they can save a hundred."

Reed was inspired in this conviction by the success of men like the French scientist Roux, who had found a way to immunize horses to diphtheria and develop an antitoxin that would both prevent and cure the disease in humans. The organization of scientists and physicians at the International Congress on Hygiene at Budapest in 1894 literally jumped to their feet, shouting out their admiration, when Roux reported his successful experiments.

Reed became one of the leading supporters and defenders of Roux's vaccines in the United States. There were a large number of doctors who wanted to go slow, be cautious, experiment longer before administering the antitoxin. But delay would cost lives, Reed was convinced. He rose to his feet at the District of Columbia Medical Society meeting in December of 1894. The critics of the antitoxin were speaking in ignorance, fearful of what they did not understand. Their job was to acquire the knowledge they lacked, Reed insisted, not criticize the findings of those who had expanded medical horizons.

"You are theorizing," he asserted in strong tones. "We are dealing with facts. If another friend of antitoxin arises and deals it such a blow, the antitoxin will be murdered in the house of its friends. I almost feel like saying that the failure to use it in a case of human diphtheria is criminal; and I beg you that if you have not yet done so, when you stand by the bedside of your patient afflicted with this disease, you do not withhold this invaluable remedy."

Yellow Jack

It is thought that yellow fever was carried to the North and South American continents on the slave ships from Africa. The first reports of it come from Barbados in the Caribbean in 1648 when thousands were killed. It raged through neighboring West Indies islands, jumped to the Yucatan peninsula and then across the sea to Havana, Cuba in the summer of 1649, killing thousands in Cuba too.

During the next two centuries it hit periodically as if it were some deadly curse sent by angry gods to punish men for their evil ways. There seemed to be no logical, scientifically observable pattern. Some called it Barbados distemper, others *coup de barre* ("blow of a rod," in French), American distemper, yellow jack, or yellow fever. The first signs of its coming were chills and headache, then severe pains in the back and arms and legs (hence *coup de barre*), followed by high fever, nausea, and vomiting. The fever stage could last a few hours or several days and was usually accompanied by the yellow pallor that gave the disease its name. Next came the "calm"—the fever lapsed and the pains and vomiting ceased. If the attack was mild this would be the first step on the road to recovery. If it was a severe case, however, it would be only an interlude before the "febrile reaction" set in. The fever, pains, and jaundice would return—intensely—accompanied by bleeding in the kidneys and gums. Blood vessels often broke near the stomach, too, and ejected dark blood into the stomach cavity. This caused the most dreaded symptom of all: black vomit. Few would recover when the disease reached this point.

The disease rampaged across the continent. Reports tell of as many as 90 epidemics within the borders of the United States, mostly in southern port areas. One of the worst plagues, however, hit the Philadelphia area in the summer of 1793. The scenes were typical: roads crowded with the panic-stricken fleeing the city, entire families dead or dying with no one to claim their bodies, shallow graves dug dozens at a time, vacated buildings condemned by the authorities, the "dead wagons" rattling through the streets in search of corpses strewn along the roads. That was Philadelphia; and who could tell when your city's number would come up?

Memphis was hit in 1878. More than half the population fled the city in terror. Those who remained died faster than the gravediggers could dispose of them. The police force dropped from 47 to seven members. Thieves roamed the city like vultures, waiting for the next vacated building. Memphis was no better able to handle the onslaught in 1878 than Philadelphia in 1793.

Something had to be done. But what? Courageous individuals had given it their best shot. That was not the problem. Stubbins Ffirth, a medical student at the University of Pennsylvania, went so far as to swallow pills made from fresh "blood vomit" in an attempt to discover if vomit was the medium through which the disease was spread. Most experts at the time were convinced that vomit-soaked bedding, clothes, and furniture (so-called *fomites*) were the villain. But Ffirth did not contract the disease. Other researchers noticed, as well, that many friends and relatives of victims, people who had in some cases slept in sheets and bedding that had been soaked in the deceased's black vomit, often did not contract the disease. But if the vomit did not spread the disease, what did? No one had a better answer. Ffirth had swallowed his vomit pills in 1804. Many were still convinced in the 1890s that *fomites*—porous substances like cloth and wood that absorb fluids—carried the disease. But there were those who argued otherwise.

Dr. J. C. Nott of Mobile, Alabama suggested in 1848 that insects might be the carriers, but he was ridiculed by most of the medical profession for making such an outlandish suggestion. The authorities continued to burn the supposedly contaminated bedding, clothes, and furniture of yellow-fever victims.

In Havana, in the 1860s and 1870s, Dr. Carlos Finlay after long and painstaking research come to the conclusion that Nott was on the right track. His observations led him to conclude that a mosquito, the female of *Culex fasciatus,* now called *Aedes aegypti,* was the carrier. But he too was dismissed as a crank.

Then an Italian scientist, Giuseppe Sanorelli, announced in 1897 that he had identified a bacillus that caused the fever. But it remained to be demonstrated if, and how, Finlay's mosquito carried Sanorelli's germ. This was where Reed came in.

The Surgeon General of the United States assigned Reed to supervise a research team known as the Yellow Fever Commission, and sent him to Havana where the disease was a recurring problem. Cuba had just come under American control after the Spanish-American war.

Reed and his associates arrived in Cuba in June of 1900. It was an exotic setting for the North American doctors. White stucco homes of Spanish design, narrow balcony-lined streets, lush verandas reaching to the water's edge from the estates of wealthy plantation owners, dark and steamy jungles covering the hills beyond the city, palm trees and wide silver-sand beaches—Reed had never seen anything like it.

Research headquarters had been established on a nearby Army base. The first night Reed and the team assigned to him sat on the small patio of the officers' quarters, watching the night come across the bay, basking in a warm tropical breeze. "I think we're going to solve it, gentlemen," he said confidently. "Everything is in our favor: we're well equipped, well trained, and a congenial working unit. And our accomplishments, whatever they may be, will be the result of cooperative effort; the credit for them will belong to the entire board." It was a medical "pep talk" for the next morning's work.

One of Reed's first impressions confirmed the theories of those who doubted that *fomites* and blood vomit were the culprits. The base hospital was filled with yellow-fever victims, some recovering, others dead or dying. But the nurses who worked in that vomit-soaked inferno for hours at a time, for days on end, seemed no more likely to contract the disease than anyone else in Cuba. Maybe old Doctor Finlay was right, Reed thought. If *fomites* were the carrier, those nurses should be falling like tenpins.

Reed arranged a meeting between Finlay and his board. Finlay was an elderly man now, but still energetic in presenting his much-ridiculed case. He explained the feeding and breeding habits of the *Culex fasciatus*. Reed listened attentively. There certainly were mosquitos enough in Cuba. And the disease did hit most often in the American South's damp areas, or during the muggy summer months in the northern cities—when mosquitos were in abundance. Reed's mind was drawn into the drift of Finlay's arguments. He became convinced that it was worth a try. He had no alternative starting point. Those who laughed at Finlay had not been able to prove him wrong.

Reed convened his board, and after some discussion announced: "We're all agreed to make the first experiments on ourselves, then?" They were, unanimously.

Proving Finlay right was not as easy as one might think. You could not just find a yellow-fever victim, sic a mosquito on him, and then get the mosquito to bite someone else. It had to be determined, first of all, exactly when a yellow-fever victim's blood was contagious. When the fever was at its peak? Just before the victim came down with the disease? How long before? And what about the mosquito? Could it spread the contagion from one person to another within seconds after the first bite? Only within seconds? For weeks after the first bite? Only after many weeks?

It had been observed in earlier research that it took two or three weeks for the second and following cases of yellow fever to develop after the first case was spotted. Apparently the first victim was powerless to spread the disease for two or three weeks. It was this lull, among other things, that led Finlay to suspect that an insect was involved. He theorized that the insect became an "intermediate host." After feeding on a yellow-fever victim, it would take the diseased blood into its own body, where the bacilli developed. When the insect bit another victim, it would deposit the matured germs—if the germs had in fact matured. That was the question: how long did it take for the germs to ripen inside the mosquito host? It had been demonstrated that malaria was spread in this way. What was the time span for yellow fever?

In Reed's laboratories each mosquito was carried in a test tube plugged with gauze. The tube was turned upside down and, as the mosquito flew upward, the doctors would pull out the gauze and press the open end against the abdomen of a yellow-fever victim. After the mosquito fed and drew blood, the tube would be tapped, causing the mosquito to fly upward. Then the gauze was plugged back into place. (The volunteers at this stage were already yellow-fever victims, so it took little to convince them to participate in the experiments.)

In the days following, the tubes with the infected mosquitos were placed on the arms of volunteers who had never been afflicted with yellow fever. Dr. Carroll, one of Reed's colleagues, was one of the first. The small insect nestled among the hairs of his forearm, drew up its legs, and stung. Three days later, Carroll was stricken with the first symptoms. Dr. Jesse Lazear, who placed the test tube against Carroll's arm, had a mixed reaction—as one would expect. He might be the first man to induce yellow fever, but his success could spell his friend's death warrant. He quickly placed the same mosquito on the arm of a volunteer cavalryman, as well as—secretly—on his own. (He did not want to worry his wife, but felt compelled to share the risks he was inflicting on others.)

Carroll pulled through with a mild case of the fever. So did the volunteer cavalryman. Dr. Lazear did not. He died of yellow fever not long afterwards.

Reed had been called back to Washington on Army business just before Lazear started his work. He rushed back when he heard the news. He was, of course, distressed and deeply hurt by Lazear's death. But to stop now in fear and sorrow would be to allow the death to go for naught. He pored over Lazear's charts. Lazear had recorded the time of the original and secondary bites. By carefully charting the days, Reed came up with his hypothesis. The disease circulated in a contagious state in the blood of a yellow-fever victim for only the first two or three days of his illness. After that, even if he were delirious and on his deathbed, he could not pass it on. And twelve days had to elapse between the time the insect bit the yellow-fever victim and the time it could pass the disease on. That was the hypothesis—now to prove it.

The records kept by Lazear showed that when the mosquito bit a victim who had been afflicted with yellow fever for five or more days, it did not pass on the illness. Moreover, even if it bit a victim in the first two or three days of his sickness, it did not spread the disease to anyone it bit *within* twelve days after biting the original victim. Carroll, Lazear, and the cavalryman were stricken, but other volunteers were not, even though they were bitten by a mosquito that had bitten a victim in the second day of the illness, because the mosquito had bitten them twelve days or more after taking the first bite.

Now, Reed had to duplicate Lazear's results—match those time spans. He set up a three-stage experiment in an isolated area on a large farm not far from the military base. Volunteers would be bitten by mosquitos that had fed on yellow-fever victims in the early stages of the disease; others would be exposed to *fomites* for long periods of time; others injected with blood taken directly from yellow-fever victims. Thus it could be proven that *fomites* did not cause the disease; that mosquitos did; and that the blood of a victim was the source of the bacilli. If a volunteer contracted yellow fever after being bitten by a mosquito that had bitten a victim, that would prove little if the volunteer *also* had been exposed to *fomites* in some way. Likewise, it would not be conclusive evidence that a mosquito bite spread the disease if that mosquito might have settled on, say, a pile of black vomit before it nestled on a volunteer. Was the mosquito spreading a bacillus from a victim's blood, or from *fomites* it had landed on somewhere? Hence, the experiments had to be tightly and precisely controlled.

Time was of the essence. Once it became public knowledge that Reed and his associates were deliberately inflicting a potentially deadly disease, the outcry against the project would be great. Reed was not unaware of the dangers, of course. He knew he was risking lives, but was convinced that the objective was worth it. Like Lazear, he resolved to allow a mosquito to feed on himself: to endure the dangers he was asking others to accept. But that would have to come later, after he was no longer needed to supervise the experiment.

Reed's crew carefully gathered mosquito eggs and watched them hatch. (They had to be certain that the mosquitos could not have picked up the disease from some other source than a victim's blood before they put them in the test tubes.) The first two volunteers were young soldiers: John R. Kissinger and John J. Moran. Reed explained the deal. They would get $100 for agreeing to let an infected mosquito bite them; another $200 if they contracted yellow fever. Moran stepped forward and spoke for both men:

"We're not interested in being paid. The money isn't the point—it's the opportunity."

Reed sat silently in admiration of the young men: "Greater love hath no man than this, that a man lay down his life for his friends" (John XV, 13).

The experiments began on November 20. At 10:30 in the morning the test tube was pressed to Kissinger's arm. The tiny creature a man could crush with his little finger had the power to kill a man with as little effort—just a leisurely bite. Three days later he was bitten again. Then on the 26th and 29th he was given the same treatment.

But nothing happened. Why? Reed surmised that in colder weather it might take longer for the germs to ripen within the mosquito. Winter was approaching, and although it does not bring snow storms to Cuba, it does pull down the temperatures. But by the end of the month Kissinger still had not contracted the fever.

All the while experiments with the *fomites* were going on in a separate cottage. The volunteers for this part of the experiment were not taking as much risk as Kissinger and Moran. They were *not* supposed to come down with the disease. But their sacrifice was hardly trivial. They had to sleep and live for 19 days and nights in a small room with blankets soaked in black vomit of five deceased yellow fever-victims. They came out of their isolation at the end of the 19 days without a trace of the fever. (Their room had been tightly screened to guarantee no mosquitos could enter.)

Then the fireworks started. Kissinger came down with his first symptoms on December 9. Reed raced to his bedside. He noted to his associates as they stood over the aching cavalry-man: "In my opinion this exhibition of moral courage has never been surpassed in the annals of the Army of the United States." To put the icing on the cake, Kissinger pulled through after a mild bout.

In exhilaration, Reed wrote to his wife:

> Rejoice with me . . . aside from the antitoxin of diphtheria and Koch's discovery of the tubercle bacillus, it will be regarded as the most important piece of work, scientifically, during the 19th century. I do not exaggerate, and I could shout for very joy that heaven has permitted me to establish this wonderful way of propagating yellow fever.

Reed tested with three more volunteers in exactly the same way as he had infected Kissinger; all three were stricken. None of these men died, either. Reed was pulling aces.

Then, the next step:

"Now we want to show that the difference between an infected and an uninfected house is due only to the presence of loaded mosquitos. This is the experiment I've been saving you for, Moran."

"Good." Moran, like Kissinger, had signed on to *get* yellow fever. He was ready.

He moved into another of the experimental cottages. It had been cleaned meticulously. A screen had been constructed, dividing it in two. On one side, Moran's side, were released 15 mosquitos that had bitten yellow-fever victims in the early stages of the disease. On the other, a group of volunteers moved in. The living conditions were identical—scrupulously antiseptic—except for the mosquitos in Moran's half.

On Christmas day, Moran was stricken. None of the others was hit. His case was a serious one. For a few days there were doubts that he would pull through, but he did.

On New Year's Eve, Reed sat looking over his notes in the glow of a small lamp. He was alone in the quiet of his room on the Caribbean island, far from home. It had been the most important year in his life. He left his reading and picked up his pen to write to his wife:

"The prayer that has been mine for twenty years—that I might be permitted in some way or at some time to do something to alleviate human suffering has been granted! A thousand Happy New Years!"

From the far end of the camp 24 bugles were blown in unison; they cut through the tropical night—reveille for a new year and a new century, which would be healthier and happier and more secure for mankind because of Reed's just-completed mission. The scourge of yellow fever would soon be no more than a bad memory.

The research grew so intense and hectic in the weeks that followed that Reed never got around to taking a bite himself. (For instance, they propagated the disease by injecting the blood of a victim into a volunteer.) Reed's colleagues convinced him that he was far more valuable in the laboratory than in the sickbed or the grave. But it took some effort—he was determined to share the dangers as a point of honor.

In February, Reed delivered the paper presenting his findings to the Pan-American Medical Congress in Havana:

> The mosquito *Culex fasciatus* serves as the intermediate host for the parasite of yellow fever.
>
> Yellow fever is transmitted to the non-immune individual by means of the bite of the mosquito that has previously fed on the blood of those sick of the disease.
>
> An interval of about twelve days or more after contamination appears to be necessary before the mosquito is capable of conveying the disease.
>
> Yellow fever can also be experimentally produced by the subcutaneous injection of blood taken from the general circulation during the first and second days of this disease.
>
> Yellow fever is not conveyed by *fomites,* and hence disinfection of articles of clothing, bedding or merchandise, supposedly contaminated by contact with those sick of the disease, is unnecessary.
>
> A house may be said to be infected with yellow fever only when there are present within its walls contaminated mosquitos capable of conveying the parasite of this disease.
>
> The spread of yellow fever can be most effectually controlled by measures directed to the destruction of mosquitos and the protection of the sick against the bites of these insects.

These are some of the most important words in medical history. There was a thunderous burst of sustained applause. The newspapers took it from there. Pictures of Reed, strong and dignified, appeared from Maine to California—in his formal Army uniform; with his sleeves rolled up in his lab, leaning over his test tubes of mosquitos. Upon his return to the States the medical associations and the civic groups lined up for the honor of having him as a guest speaker.

Once he was back in his stateside laboratories, Reed geared himself up for an attack on the rest of mankind's most dreaded diseases. He had no intention of resting on his laurels. Perhaps —who knows—he could even unlock the secrets of polio and cancer, as he had done with yellow fever.

But ironically, Reed, one of medicine's wonder men, died on November 2, 1902 of a ruptured appendix—appendicitis. Today it can be treated by a relatively simple medical operation.

Reed did not find the *cure* for yellow fever—the antitoxin. That was done a few years later by another American, William Crawford Gorgas, in Panama, making it possible for America to complete the canal when the French could not because of the intolerably high yellow-fever death rate. But Gorgas, as great as his work was, built on Reed's foundation. He knew that. He warned those who were singing his praises to remember that he was "not a great man, merely one who is trying to follow in the footsteps of a great man, Walter Reed."

Charles Lindbergh

8

Charles Lindbergh
The Spirit of St. Louis

The Roaring Twenties

The sale and consumption of alcoholic beverages had been outlawed, but thousands of Americans knew the secret knocks that would get them admitted to the "speakeasies." These were the secret (some truly so, some not) saloons and nightclubs where politicians, high-society gay blades, and respectable businessmen sat cheek to jowl with gangsters and their molls, drinking smuggled booze and listening to the hypnotic, wailing strains of that wild new music "smuggled" up from New Orleans—jazz.

Al Capone, a brash young street punk from lower Manhattan, took Horace Greeley's advice and went west to Chicago (but not for the kind of objectives Greeley suggested, of course). Capone clawed and shotgunned his way to the top of Chicago's gangland hierarchy. Before he was finished he controlled a network of gambling joints, speakeasies, protection rackets, prosti-

201

tution rings, and rum-running enterprises with an efficiency that would make the executives at General Motors jealous. More than 700 of his hit men executed rival gang members, bombed the establishments of businessmen who would not purchase "protection," and roughed up uncooperative private citizens in broad daylight on some of Chicago's busiest streets— while Capone had private dinners with politicians and judges he controlled with his ever-growing bankroll.

"Colonel" Jacob Ruppert took his ballclub and its new "pheenom" George Herman "Babe" Ruth into the wilds of the South Bronx, clear across the Harlem River from their old home in Manhattan's Polo Grounds, betting that Ruth would reach the short right-field fence in the new Yankee Stadium often enough to pull in the crowds. Jack Dempsey, the "Manassa Mauler," and Gene Tunney met in a prize fight in Chicago, with a gate passing the two-million-dollar mark, while blow-by-blow accounts were carried by the marvel of the time, the wireless radio, to 40 million listeners. Five Americans were said to have dropped dead at their radios of the excitement.

World War I was over and America was the victor. Rudolf Valentino was setting aflame the hearts of millions of women. The automobile, railroad, telephone, telegraph—all the displays of American ingenuity and drive seemed signs of a coming American age, and a period of prosperity for the common man unparalleled in history. The world was ours. Every man saw himself as a potential investor in the greatest get-rich-quick scheme of all—the stock market. Jump on the wagon, boy. The world is your oyster. Life was good and it was going to get better. Flaming youth—hip flasks, convertible roadsters, rumble seats, the Charleston—23 Skidoo!

But in the midst of all the hoopla, the ballyhoo, superheroes and spectacle, one man more than any other became America's unchallenged darling—her fair-haired boy. And he did it in one daring two-day adventure, through which he became, in many ways, the embodiment of everything America wanted and wished for herself in those confident-yet-naive, brash-yet-innocent years. His name was Charles A. Lindbergh, a slim, blue-eyed, blonde giant of a boy-man who rode solo a 4000-pound winged metal cylinder from New York to Paris in May of 1927.

Riding in a modern commercial jet airliner makes one nearly immune to the wonder of the Lindbergh moment in history. We find it difficult to "feel" what it was all about. We enter a chrome and plastic corridor just a short walk from an airport cafeteria and souvenir stand. From there we step onto the carpeted surface of what could be a comfortable hospital waiting room, clean and scrubbed and antiseptic. Not a gearbox or propeller in sight. Greeted by smiling stewardesses, we sit down to a meal, a movie, maybe a brief nap. Before we know it we are escorted to another plastic corridor, walk to another cafeteria, a mirror image of the one we left, and we are there. That's it. Europe, Hawaii, the Middle East, wherever . . . you get there the same way. If we happen to have a window seat or are especially curious, we might see a cloud—maybe. That's flying.

Well, that wasn't flying to Charles Lindbergh, or to the American people in 1927. No sooner had Lindbergh's plane taken to the air than all of America and much of the world became an enormous and attentive rooting section, hoping and praying in unison for the Flying Fool, the Lone Eagle, Lucky Lindy, out there somewhere—God knows where—over the Atlantic. Butcher, baker, doctor, lawyer, farmer, and taxi driver held their breaths in anticipation. Lucky Lindy was at center stage. At a prize fight at Yankee Stadium on the night of the twentieth, 40,000 tough-nut New York boxing fans stood, heads bowed, for a moment of silent prayer. Radio reports that his silver plane, *The Spirit of St. Louis,* had been sighted over the southern coast of Ireland were greeted with an outburst of excitement, joy, and relief. When the news photos came back to America of the Paris mobs milling about the long, lean American, Lindbergh became an instant hero in a way no other man in America has been in the last 50 years—perhaps ever.

Portraits of him, with his handsome face, light-eyed smile, and neatly cropped curling hair, were hung everywhere—in barber shops, schools, post offices, office buildings, and in the rooms of small boys and girls all over the country. Standing before *The Spirit of St. Louis* in his leather flyer's jacket and shining knee-high boots, he looked like a character from a Hollywood casting service. But when Americans got the chance to know the man as well as the image, they learned that he was more than a dashing facade. He was not only a brave, but a good man: honest, decent, hard-working, uninterested in the fame and fortune promised him by the hucksters and tub-thumpers who would have turned him into a traveling circus in the style of Buffalo Bill. He turned down the movie contracts. He spurned the ad men who would have had him selling every-

203

thing from hair cream to foot powder. He hadn't done it for money—really. He was a man with a highminded dream, a desire to escape the commonplace—the bonds of mediocrity— and to drag his country with him, one step further in the quest for the stars.

To get to know Lindbergh the man, there is only one place to go: to *The Spirit of St. Louis,* the autobiographical account of his flight over the Atlantic and the events leading up to it. It is a unique and beautiful book that every young person owes it to himself to experience. Save it for a quiet week in the summer when you can afford to lose yourself in the upper levels of the imagination. It should be read on those quiet afternoons when the sun, high in a cloud-flecked blue sky, forces your eyes to the heavens, and a cooling breeze rustles through the tops of the highest trees. Its mysteries should envelop you when an adulthood filled with excitement and adventure still seems possible, before the workaday chores of earning a living force you to resign yourself to stiff chairs in stuffy offices and give your all to humdrum matters in collaboration with people whose company you would not endure if a paycheck were not waiting at the end of the week; when a career still seems possible in broad sunlit uplands of life with the wind at your back and the smell of excitement in your nostrils, a life where honor and daring and solitary courage count more than cunning and a good line, a life that hardens and enlivens the body and sharpens the senses rather than leaving you quivering and breathless after a twenty-yard dash to a commuter train. Of course, one need not be a teenager to feel the call to such a life. But it is, I am afraid, easier for youth. Adults usually have to live a lifetime on the memories of such childhood dreams. Lindbergh lived that life, a boy's dream come true.

To fly—to be as a god, to leave the bonds of our earthly existence, the dust and mud and slime that our religious traditions tell is the stuff of our being. To leave it behind and to soar in the clear, cool currents of the heavens. We all feel the longing at some time in our lives, usually in childhood. Lindbergh was no exception:

> When I was a child on our Minnesota farm, I spent hours lying on my back in high timothy and redtop hidden from passersby, watching white cumulus clouds drift overhead, staring into the sky . . . How wonderful it would be, I'd thought, if I had an air-

204

plane—wings with which I could fly up to the clouds and explore their caves and canyons—wings like that hawk circling above me. Then I would ride on the wind and be part of the sky.

While boys and girls in ancient Greece and Rome and the Norse countries could only dream that age-old dream, and taste its excitement through their myths and legends of winged messengers of the gods, Lindbergh found himself a member of the first generation of human beings who could—with enough initiative and daring—make the dream come true. The Wright Brothers, Orville and Wilbur, had lofted their multibraced contraption over the dunes at Kitty Hawk, and others followed in their wake. A young boy in the early years of the second decade of the twentieth century—believe it or not—could hear stories from his playmates of soaring sky-vehicles called "aeroplanes." If a boy was careful enough, he might even see one pass over his farm in Minnesota, with a giant of a pilot in white scarf, leather flap-ear cap, and goggles. He might even land in a cornfield and a boy might shake his hand, maybe sit in the cockpit. It could happen . . .

One day I was playing in our house on the riverbank. The sound of a distant engine drifted in through an open window . . . Suddenly I sat up straight and listened. No automobile engine made that noise. It was approaching too fast. It was on the wrong side of the house! . . . I ran to the window and climbed out onto the tarry roof. It was an airplane!

The young boy stood in wonder, seeing for the first time in his life a manned vehicle in the skies. He made up his mind at once, and irrevocably. He too would fly, no matter the cost, no matter the danger. It was dangerous—sure. But he knew even then as a farm boy that the things a man enjoyed in life often came with danger. It was the price you had to pay. He would be a pilot.

"It was dangerous to climb a tree, to swim down rapids in the river, to go hunting with a gun, to ride a horse, to drive my father's automobile."

After a brief, and not entirely productive, stint at the University of Wisconsin as an engineering student, Lindbergh found the road he had been looking for. He heard of a school for flying at the Nebraska Aircraft Corporation. His parents and friends at first tried to discourage him from pursuing a career in such

205

a new and unproven field, but to little avail. He wanted to be a pilot.

I'd never been near enough to a plane to touch it before entering the doors of the Nebraska Aircraft Corporation's factory. I can still smell the odor of dope that permeated each breath, like ether in a hospital's corridor. I can still see the brightly painted fuselages on the floor, still marvel at the compactness of the Hispano-Suiza engine which turned the force of a hundred and fifty horses through its little shaft of steel.

There he became a model student, able at last to discipline himself to the long hours with book and slide rule now that he was in pursuit of his life's dream. A pilot had to be able to maintain and make routine repairs on his engine, judge distance and fuel supplies, read weather conditions, chart his course on the road maps of the time (yes, *road* maps), as well as steer the primitive flying machines. Lindbergh mastered them all—a model student.

And, then, finally, the day came. He left the earth and reached for the skies on his first flight. CONTACT!

"There's a deep cough . . . vicious sputtering . . . I am bedded down in the front cockpit, goggles and leather helmet strapped tight on my head."

And then that sensation, never felt before by the young Lindbergh, that thrilled him then and every time afterwards. The propeller fires a stream of air past the fabric-covered wings with such a force that, as the plane rolls forward, a slight tremor is felt through the body of the plane. "Lift"—the physical property of air under a body in motion, makes its presence felt intensely enough. The wing-supported cylinder is moving forward—and up!

Now! . . . the roar becomes deafening . . . the plane lurches forward through a hollow in the ground . . . the tail rises . . . the axle clatters over bumps . . . trees rush toward us . . . the clatter stops . . . the ground recedes . . . we are resting on the air . . . Up, past riggers and mechanics . . . over treetops . . . across a ravine, like a hawk . . . The ground unfolds . . .

In flight! Lindbergh takes firm possession of his dream. He is still an earthman, but no longer possessed by the earth, bound to its physical surface. Yet he is still a man in control of a relatively simple and understandable machine, a machine he can service himself. It is not as if something were happening *to* him, the way it happens to us (even most modern pilots) when we fly. There is no advanced technological equipment, no radar charts, computer print-out flight patterns, radio directives from ground control. He is in control of his vehicle, his machine—a man in flight.

> Trees become bushes; barns, toys; cows into rabbits, as we climb. I lose all conscious connection with the past. I live only in the moment in this strange, unmortal space, crowded with beauty, pierced with danger. The horizon retreats, and veils itself in haze. The great, squared fields of Nebraska become patchwork on a planet's disk. All the country around Lincoln lies like a relief map below.

There were no doubts after that: he had made the only career choice compatible with his heart's desire. He knew that he would be a trail blazer in a new field that, he was confident, would change man's way of life for the better. Goods and people could be transported, he was sure, at speeds incomprehensible for those worried at the time about the dangerous excesses of the automobile. The people of the world would be drawn closer together, and if man seized the opportunity with suitable energy and moral imagination, a new era of peace and cooperation, together with material prosperity, could be on the horizon. (He did, however, have prescient doubts about whether it would ever come to pass, and fears for the way the awesomely destructive power of the plane might be used. He wondered if others would approach this power with awe and wonder and piety approximate to his own. Perhaps some would not.)

But it was not just what aviation could do to and for the world that thrilled Lindbergh. It satisfied a personal longing in the man, too. He made no bones about that:

> Science, freedom, beauty, adventure: what more could you ask of life? Aviation combined all three elements I loved. There was science in each curve of an airfoil, in each angle between strut and wire, in the gap of a sparkplug, as in the color of the exhaust flame. There was freedom in the unlimited horizon, in the open fields where one landed. A pilot was surrounded by beauty of earth and sky. He brushed

tree tops with the birds, leapt valleys and rivers, explored the cloud canyons he had gazed as a child. Adventure lay on each puff of wind.

I began to feel that I lived on a higher plane than the skeptics on the ground; one that was richer because of its very association with the element of danger they dreaded . . . In flying, I tasted a wine of the gods of which they could know nothing. Who valued life more highly, the aviators who spend it on the art they loved, or these misers who doled it out like pennies through their antlike days. I decided that if I could fly for ten years before I was killed in a crash, it would be a worthwhile trade for an ordinary lifetime.

Lindbergh was forced temporarily to leave his air training when the Nebraska company folded, but he managed to sign on with a tour of airplane daredevils barnstorming the American heartland—as a wing-walker and parachutist. It wasn't the life he wanted for himself, of course, but at least he was working close to planes and occasionally flying with these carnival performers. (He does admit to enjoying the adulation of the crowds in the towns they toured, the hushed comments that followed him when he walked through a crowd.) His days as a daredevil ended with suddenness, however, when he heard of an opening for air cadets in the Army Air Service Reserve.

Flying the Mail

After finishing his tour of active duty, Lindbergh, with his service hours of flying under his belt, was able to secure the position as chief pilot in charge of operations with the Robertson Aircraft Corporation of St. Louis, a firm that had just won a contract to fly air mail from its home base to Chicago. The year was 1924.

Flying those mail routes gave him the kind of adventures that would have satisfied most men for ten lifetimes. He flew night and day, through windstorms, fog, and rain, often going for days on end without sleep to demonstrate to the public that his employers (and the infant airline industry itself) could offer a valuable service. There were critics enough to go around who thought the idea of delivering the mail in those confounded flying coffins was an absurdity.

It must be noted, if only in passing, that Lindbergh, as an employe, showed attributes sorely missing from the American worker of today. Perhaps it is more the fault of American employers than employes, but it is clear that the economic superiority built by Americans in the middle years of the twentieth century, and apparently on the decline now, was at least partially a result of the attitudes of employes like Lindbergh. He showed a complete dedication to his job, continually speaking of "our" problems, and of how "we" managed to solve them. He worried about keeping costs low; understood the need to sacrifice salary gains until the air service was making a clear profit. He worked overtime as a matter of course, and for no extra pay. It was his job to get things done, not to "punch out" at a given minute. He kept his eye out for new ideas. He viewed the company's success as his own, its failure as his. For this workingman, a salary was not a "right" but a reward for an honest day's contribution to a successful business enterprise. His employer was not a competitor to be drained of the most money possible for the least amount of work. One gets the impression, reading the early pages of *The Spirit of St. Louis,* that Lindbergh was one of the owners of the mail service, so intensely concerned was he about the company's well-being. But, in all honesty, it must be noted that he was fortunate to be doing a job that he loved. One gets the feeling that he was more at play than at work:

> The last tint of pink disappears from the western sky leaving to the moon complete mastery of night. The light floods through woods and fields; reflects up from bends of rivers; shines on the silver wings of my biplane, turning them a greenish hue. It makes the earth seem more like a planet; and me part of the heavens above it, as though I too had a right to orbit in the sky . . . I feel aloof and unattached, in the solitude of space. Why return to that mass . . . I can fly on forever through space, past the mail field at Chicago, beyond the state of Illinois, over mountains, over oceans, independent of the world below.

His experiences were not always so serene and spiritual. Once, while testing a new plane, an OXX-6 powered biplane, he discovered that he had lost control. His hand controls could do nothing to bring the plane out of a sudden tailspin. The rudder and stick had no effect on the plummeting mass of metal and taut fabric. A quick glance over the side of the cockpit revealed the spinning earth rushing up to meet the plane. It was either parachute or meet a flaming death in the open fields below. Lindbergh rolled out over the brim and pulled his rip-cord the moment he dropped beneath the body of the plane. He reports that the "trees and houses looked tremendous . . . scarcely enough room for a parachute to string out."

But it did, and that should have been the end of it . . . a smooth, steady ride to the ground below exactly like those he had practiced dozens of times before. Except that the plane, out of control, was straight ahead and coming toward him, its pro-peller pointed directly at his chest!

Usually the stroke of death either passes before you're aware of it, or your senses are occupied with the fight for life, or there's good reason to hope you'll escape. That time I saw it coming. I was helpless. No movement I could make would have effect . . . I braced my body for the impact—propeller, wing, or whatever death's instrument might be. Every mus-cle, every nerve, was tensed for the tearing blow on flesh . . .

If the hand of death ever cracks the door that lets life's senses peek beyond life's walls, it should have cracked then. But the door stayed shut. The para-chute's shroud lines had gotten twisted in the jump, and they swung around awkwardly. In the fraction of time it took to turn my head from right to left, the plane passed and somehow missed my body and my chute.

Lindbergh's close calls lead him to speculate on the experi-ence of death. Will there be any consciousness at all? Or only nothingness?

"You couldn't come much closer to death than that. And yet I've known times when the nearness of death has seemed to crack the door—times when I've felt the presence of another realm beyond—a realm my mind has tried to penetrate since childhood."

There were other occasions when death came as close, but in

different settings. Once, while he was flying the mail to Peoria, Illinois, a curtain of fog surrounded his plane like a dark and deadly shroud. And, indeed, for a pilot of that time, working for the most part from ground markings, a thick fog could be a literal death garment. Landing fields could be lost from view entirely; mountains and trees met head on. For a few torment- ing minutes Lindbergh hung in a dimensionless void; no skies above or lights below, just a sea of moist gray reflected back upon him by his searchlight beams. His compass read 185 de- grees, approximately the direction of the landing field. But "ap- proximately" was not good enough: he might hit a tree or build- ing near the airfield.

Lindbergh peered over the edge of his cockpit, squinting for some familiar object in the thick sludge. A bright light could be seen between his right wings, but what was it? Then he remem- bered. A young boy had written to him some months back. "Your mail planes fly over my house every day so I have fixed up an electric light in our yard. Maybe it will help you when the weather is bad this winter. I will keep it lit every night."

With that backyard beacon a guide, Lindbergh was able to shift course just enough to descend until the five lanterns the mail drivers always hung on the fence next to the landing strip could be seen in a diffuse, but unmistakable, glow. He made a rough but safe landing, bumping wildly off the running strip and just missing some large objects in the dark. He could just as easily have ended up in a gnarled and smoking wreck. But fate had other things in store for him.

There were many similar occurrences during his mail-carry- ing years. More parachute jumps, forced landings, days when his engines would sputter and die in mid-air. But instead of quieting his lust for air travel, they only quickened it. Especially on those days when he allowed himself to dream a bit about the pilot's dream, the hangar gossip of all flyers of the time—the Orteig prize. $25,000 to fly the Atlantic—it had been a standing offer for more than six years now. The owner of the Brevoort and Lafayette hotels in New York, Raymond Orteig, had put up the money. All you had to do was take a flying machine nonstop from New York to Paris. That's all.

New York to Paris

Was it worth it? The money wasn't. It probably would cost as much, if not more, to make the flight. In his typically methodical and thorough way, Lindbergh spent his spare time in his sparsely furnished bachelor's quarters near the airport going over the pros and cons. The first and most obvious "con" of course was that the pilot stood a good chance of ending up as fishbait in the middle of the frigid waters of the North Atlantic. But there were advantages, too. He listed them as if he were planning a routine business investment:

1. A revival of interest in aviation in St. Louis.

2. Publicity for the St. Louis airports as centers of serious air travel for the rest of the country.

3. Aid in making America a country with a dedication to promote and develop air travel.

4. The flight would demonstrate the degree of sophistication that had been reached by the aircraft industry.

5. The cash prize would cover the expenses—financial backers could be offered a return on their money.

Getting those financial backers was the first problem. Lindbergh had about a thousand dollars of his own, but that was a drop in the bucket. A friend offered another two thousand. But they needed big investors. Where would they find them?

Harry Knight, president of the St. Louis Flying Club, provided the answer. He used his connections and good name in St. Louis with banks and the Chamber of Commerce to sell the idea. The plane would be called *The Spirit of St. Louis.* The sight of a plane emblazoned with those words flying across the Atlantic and landing in Paris should be worth far more in publicity, they reasoned, than it would cost.

But who would build it? Getting a manufacturer was not as easy as it seems. Those early manufacturers in the aircraft industry did not relish the possibility that their plane would end up sinking into the Atlantic. A reputation would be damaged immeasurably. They were trying to achieve respectability as a solid business venture. A successful flight across the Atlantic would enhance their image, surely. But what were the odds of success? Not very good. It had never been done.

Lindbergh bought a suit (he did not own one at the time) and the clothing accessories he felt he would need to make a favorable impression on the Wright Corporation, one of the pioneers in the field: overcoat, gray felt hat, fur-lined gloves, silk scarf, leather suitcase for his drawings and diagrams. He chided himself on spending much-needed money just to make an impression: "They won't add a penny's worth to my ability as a flyer." But making the right impression on the directors of the Wright Corporation was as important right then to his plans as all his years of pilot training. The flight could not be made without the right plane.

All his concern for appearances failed to carry the day, however. The Wright Corporation found the stunt too risky. His second choice, the Columbia Aircraft Corporation, was more tempted. They offered to build the plane—but insisted that the flight be made with a crew hand-picked by them. Lindbergh could coordinate and oversee all other preparations.

That, needless to say, was not Lindbergh's cup of tea. He was a pilot, not a public relations man. Moreover, he was convinced that the best chance for a successful flight depended upon keeping flying weight to an absolute minimum. It had to be a one-man job—his.

Finally, after much searching and despair, he found a company that would build the kind of plane he wanted, for the kind of flight he would make: The Ryan Airlines Co. of San Diego. It would be what the Ryan Co. calls its M2 model, equipped with a Wright Whirlwind J-5C 220 HP engine. The cost: $10,580.

After some initial groundwork with questions of design— where to place the fuel tanks, for example—the plane was completed. The fuel tanks were positioned in front of the plane, directly in front of the pilot. Lindbergh had no forward vision whatsoever. He faced a wall of controls, primitive as they were. This was done because the flight would be made by compass, not land sightings (there would be none over the ocean); but, more importantly, for safety reasons. Years of experience had taught Lindbergh that pilots sandwiched between engine and fuel tanks seldom survived a crash. There was no parachute. They could carry an extra 20 pounds of fuel instead, and a parachute would be of little use over the ocean anyway. The fuel capacity was enough for 4,000 miles. There was no radio. Every ounce of luxury and every unessential accessory was stripped.

Lindbergh then secured navigational maps of the Atlantic

from the supply houses that cater to ocean-going ships. With great care and precision he plotted his course from Mitchell Field on Long Island north to New England, across Nova Scotia, out across the Atlantic to the southern coast of Ireland, then south to Paris, France. A clean polygonic arc across the surface of the map.

I drew a straight line between New York and Paris on the gnomic projection. Then I transferred points from that line, at hundred mile intervals, to the Mercator projection, and connected these points with straight lines. At each point, I marked down the distance from New York and the magnetic course to the next change in angle. I chose hundred mile intervals as convenient distances to work with because, wind and cruising speed considered, it seems likely that *The Spirit of St. Louis* will cover about that distance each hour . . . The distance scales at exactly 3,610 miles.

Easy—a snap—most schoolboys could have plotted the course on a classroom wall map. Any boy scout—no problem. But fly it?

Takeoff

The day finally arrived, May 20, 1927. The skies were cloudy on Long Island but the forecasts called for clear skies over the Atlantic for the next few days. He could wait for the perfect day, but there were two other crews ready to make the flight—one led by the famous explorer-adventurer Admiral Richard Byrd, the first man to fly over the North Pole. Time was of the essence, so Lindbergh decided to go. If the skies did not clear up he could turn back—anywhere between Mitchell Field and the middle of the Atlantic for that matter. He would leave at daybreak and, if things went as planned, reach his first landfall, the coast of Ireland, at dusk of the following day, and Paris sometime during the middle of the following night. A total of 40 hours without sleep—tiredness would be a problem. But he had gone without sleep for as much as three days in a row and was confident that he could handle the long hours at the wheel this time.

Takeoff was rougher than expected. Apparently the heavy load of fuel was an inhibiting factor. But soon *The Spirit of St. Louis* was in flight across the sparkling, yacht-dotted waters of Long Island Sound and the finely manicured lawns of Long Island's North Shore waterfront estates.

> I'm in the air with full tanks and a following wind. The engine has withstood its test of power. It's throttled down, turning smoothly and easily. *The Spirit of St. Louis* is no longer an unruly mechanical device, as it was during takeoff; it's no longer balanced on a pinpoint . . . rather it forms an extension of my own body, ready to follow my wish as the hand follows the mind's desire.

The waters of Long Island Sound held his attention. He had flown along the shore line before, but never across the 35-mile strip of sea between Long Island and the coast of Connecticut. The Sound was suddenly a symbol to him of the flight to come:

> The Sound comes as an advanced messenger, welcoming and at the same time warning me of the empire that lies ahead—of the trackless wastes, the great solitude, the desertlike beauty of the ocean.
>
> Haze thickens behind me until the coast line becomes lost. There's not a boat in sight. Only a few spiraling gulls and dark bits of refuse on the water show that land is near. I'm the center point in a circle of haze moving along with me over the glossy water —gray haze over gray water, the one mirrored in the other until I can't tell where sea ends and the sky begins.

He soared along behind his engine's steady, rumbling growl, through the skies along the New England Coast—Connecticut, Rhode Island, Massachusetts. He worked to develop a feel for the plane. *The Spirit of St. Louis* was still a stranger to him. Before he could really know a plane, Lindbergh believed, he must feel as familiar with it as a man would with the home where he had spent most of his lifetime. The pilot must know the controls and be able to reach for them the way a homeowner would reach for a light switch in a dark hallway in the middle of the night. The hum of the engine—he must be able to hear and identify every irregular sputter and surge, the way we assure ourselves in the darkest hours of the night that the strange sounds in the house are only creaking timbers and the wind rushing through the flue in our fireplace, and not an intruder.

He thought again of his decision to fly solo against all the advice of the experts:

> What advantages there are in flying alone! I know now what my father meant when he warned me, years ago, of depending too heavily on others. He used to quote a saying of old settlers in Minnesota: "One boy's a boy. Two boys are half a boy. Three boys are no boy at all." That had to do with hunting, trapping, and scouting days when Indians were hostile. But how well it applies to modern life, and to this flight I'm making. By flying alone I've gained in range, in time, in flexibility; and above all I've gained my freedom. I haven't had to keep a crew member acquainted with my plans. My decisions aren't weighted by responsibility for another's life . . . I've not been enmeshed in petty quarreling and heavy organizational problems. Now, I can go on or turn back according to the unhampered dictates of my mind and senses. According to that saying of my father's I'm a full boy—independent—alone.

This was a large part of the American dream—he knew and held it before us in action. To do it "our way," taking the credit and blame for our fortunes. The lone cowboy riding off into the sunset after a job well done. Owning one's own business, calling the shots the way we see them as professional men, without bowing to mass opinion. Standing alone against and above the mob at *High Noon*. Leading the charge. Lindbergh was all that for two splendid days.

Soon the horizon broke. It was no longer the small stream-fed valleys, the stone-walled fields flecked with cattle and boulders, fresh with the light-green carpet of spring. Ahead was the ocean itself, stolid, massive, dark blue, flat and endless before his eyes.

There were important calculations to make as he approached Nova Scotia. According to his compass readings he should strike the coast of Nova Scotia and arc from there across the Atlantic. If he was not on course now it would indicate some serious mistakes in navigation, mistakes that could spell disaster. Ten miles off course at Nova Scotia would mean 80 miles off at Ireland.

There are neither whitecaps nor wind streaks on the water . . . just hold the compass course; no need to compensate for drift. I nose down to the low, rolling waves . . . a hundred feet . . . fifty feet . . . twenty feet above their shifting surface. I come down to the ocean, asking its favor . . . the right to pass for thousands of miles across its realm. The earth released me on Long Island, now I need approval from the sea.

He thought back to the butterflies he used to watch as a boy, dipping and bobbing across the surface of the Mississippi. They would skim the tops of the river swells in their irregular spiral maneuverings, free and agile. But if just one wing touched the surface of the water they would go down forever. He remembered seeing their beautiful bodies drifting dead and broken in the eddying river currents. "Why, I used to wonder, did they ever leave the safety of the land? But why have I? How similar my position has become."

He flew on, sensitive to every change in air pressure and every gust of wind. He sat in the cockpit with windows open at the sides. Fog, sleet, and rain were not just atmospheric disturbances on this flight, displays of nature to be observed through the thick and permanently sealed windows of an airtight flying capsule. The wind buffeted his face, the ice that formed on the wings of his craft chilled his fingertips, the clammy fog condensed in damp patches on his chin and forehead.

Soon the archvillain made its appearance. It was a worthy foe, an intriguing and sly enemy. He could not fly over it or around it. All his planning and dedication could not face it down. His exemplary courage and daring had little effect. It was still early in the first day of flight—but the temptation was strong to sleep, to close his eyes and slip into the warm folds of sleep; sleep. Even though he knew it would mean sure death he longed to let his head drop, the way it wanted to, toward his chest; to let himself go; to take the easy route. But struggling with his body's yearning for comfort and ease was nothing new to Lindbergh. He had lived a life of sacrifice and self-discipline, had struggled against his body's call for self-indulgence, in order to achieve a future reward. He had not lived by the rule of immediate self-gratification—of taking whatever he wanted whenever he wanted it, of looking out for "number one" first and foremost. He had learned that it was impossible for a man who lived by a self-centered code of conduct to accomplish things of lasting value, and now the lesson served him well. Neither an individual nor a civilization can rise above a squalid mediocrity when it just "lets itself go." Great accomplishments follow when a man or a society rises above base instincts. To earn glory, praise, and honor, to make lasting contributions to the betterment of mankind, requires a triumph of the spirit—the opposite of "letting it all hang out," to use a popular phrase.

Although at this stage in his life he was more a man of action than a deep, contemplative thinker (cruel experiences later in life, especially the kidnap-killing of his son, changed him somewhat), Lindbergh pondered the conflict between his body's call to sleep and the "something else" in him that fought to keep him awake. Just when the urge to sleep nearly won out, he discovered an inner reserve of strength that he never realized he had:

> My mind strays from the cockpit and returns. My eyes close, and open, and close again. But I'm beginning to understand vaguely a new factor which has come to my assistance. It seems I'm made up of three personalities, three elements, each partly dependent and partly independent of the others. There's my body, which knows definitely that what it wants most in the world is sleep. There's my mind, constantly making decisions that my body refuses to comply with, but which itself is weakening in resolution. And there's something else, which seems to become stronger instead of weaker with fatigue, an element of spirit, a directive force that has stepped out from the background and taken control over both mind and body. It seems to guard them as a wise father guards his children; letting them venture to the point of danger, then calling them back, guiding with a firm but tolerant hand.
>
> When my body cries out that it *must* sleep, this third element replies that it may get what rest it can from relaxation, but that sleep is not to be had . . .

Time and again during the flight, Lindbergh was forced to fight off the temptation to sleep. He stomped his feet, shook his head violently, bent his neck and diverted the air rushing past his cockpit up against his tired eyes. The call to sleep became strongest and deadliest during the hour just before daybreak on the second morning of the flight. If he could only make it until

218

dawn he was sure that the morning sun would revive him. But now, in the gray chill hours of dawn, with the sun only a faint red glow in the skies before him—those moments we all know when the alarm clock calls us from the delicious depths of sleep —he was not sure that he would make it. At times his head actually dropped and for a second or two he dozed. In fact, he was never sure how long it was before he awoke with a start to find the plane drifting off course. He was thankful for the decision he had made not to spend the extra time and money to build greater stability into the plane. The rougher, bumpier ride kept him alert and made slight deviations from the flight pattern more noticeable. Moreover the very difficulty of keeping the plane on its correct course forced him to stay attentive at the controls. There was less chance that the quiet lulls of a smooth flight would bring on a relaxing quiet in the body, and sleep—and death.

While leaning out to allow the air rushing past the cockpit— the slipstream, as aviators call it—to buffet his face, Lindbergh's mind turned, as it often did, to the marvel of flight. Why? How? The magic of flight was real, almost tangible, in that air pounding against his face.

> One of the miracles of flying is that when you look out at your wings you see neither movement nor support. As you clasp your hand in the cockpit, there's nothing tangible to air . . . nothing to carry a finger's weight. There seems no reason whatever to keep you from plummeting earthward like a rock. It's not until you put your arm outside, and press hard against the slipstream, that you sense the power and speed of flight. Then air takes on the quality of weight and substance; and you begin to understand the invisible element which makes it possible for man to fly.

Not surprisingly, the ocean below became a source of wonder to this perceptive and sensitive young man; not surprisingly, since this was the first time any man had traversed its breadth, alone and nonstop, in an airplane. The different colors of the ocean's surface—the greens and grays and blues, depending on position and atmospheric conditions; the dazzling panorama of jeweled sheets of polar ice floating like islands in the northern waters between Newfoundland and Greenland, vast unbroken plains of white that appeared and then ended suddenly in a hem of white mist, to be followed by the glassy pea-green surface of the sea.

He flew through dense concentrations of clouds, losing sight of the ocean below. Then, irregularly and briefly, he would catch a glimpse of it, as if he were viewing a river cutting along the bottom of a canyon. We can get a hint of the sensation if we look up at the cool lakes and streams of blue sky that often pierce through a mass of cumulus clouds on an overcast day. Lindbergh was looking down through those clouds, and the water he saw was real, not just blue sky.

> I've been tunneling by instruments through a tremendous cumulus mass. As I break out, a glaring valley lies across my path, miles in width, extending north and south for as far as I can see. The sky is blue-white above, and the blinding fire of the sun itself has burnt over the ridge ahead. I nose *The Spirit of St. Louis* down, losing altitude slowly, two hundred feet or so a minute. At eight thousand feet, I level out, plumbing with my eyes to the depth of each chasm I pass over. In the bottom of one of them, I see it, like a rare stone perceived among countless pebbles at your feet—a darker, deeper shade, a different texture—the ocean!

Far over the Atlantic, with Paris still more than a day away, Lindbergh began to think about the possibility that he might die on that flight. Not that he had had any serious trouble. His careful planning and the dedicated labors of his mechanics and engineers at the Ryan Aircraft Corporation had paid off. The plane was functioning beautifully. And yet . . . the water was still below him. If he lapsed into sleep, it would take only seconds for him to find himself trapped in a floating coffin, or adrift in a small rubber raft thousands of miles from help. Yes, he could die that very day:

> Is there a God? Is there an existence after life? Is there something within one's body that doesn't age with years? . . .

> It's hard to be an agnostic up here in *The Spirit of St. Louis,* aware of the frailty of man's devices, a part of the universe between its earth and stars. If one dies, all this goes on existing in a plan so perfectly balanced, so wonderfully simple, so incredibly complex that it's far beyond our comprehension . . .

worlds and moons revolving; planets orbiting on suns; suns flung with apparent recklessness through space. There's the infinite magnitude of the universe; there's the infinite detail of its matter . . . the outer star, the inner atom. And man conscious of it all—a worldly audience to what if not to God?

Surprisingly (or perhaps not, when you think of it), the solitude of the flight began to take its toll on even a mind as rational, as analytically precise, and as far beyond fearful fantasy as Lindbergh's. Twice, at least, he saw islands in the middle of the Atlantic that were on no map. He blinked and stared in amazement. Was he off course? Was it a mirage? Could he have discovered Atlantis, the fabled island lost in the Atlantic? No, it must be a mirage. But the land masses were so clear. Stark weathered cliffs, ocean-battered boulders, ribbons of rough white sandy beaches, hills and green valleys beyond. Could he have reached Ireland already? Had he miscalculated? But it couldn't be. The European coast was still nearly a full day and night away from his present location. He couldn't have miscalculated by that wide a margin. He banked *The Spirit of St. Louis* and moved in closer to the island. But the slate cliffs and boulders melted into fog and scattered puffs of mist and haze; the green hills and trees into irregular patches on the ocean surface. A mirage . . . gone!

Later he saw a boat, a small fishing boat. Not a strange sight in itself—but he was still hundreds of miles from the Irish coast. Fishing vessels do not travel that far to sea. Could it be a group of curiosity seekers out to wish him well on his journey and report his position over their radio to the thousands of others following his flight from the shore? Perhaps if he flew low enough he could wave to them briefly. It would be good to see a human being again, he admitted, and he wouldn't mind their admiring gestures of good will. It wouldn't take much fuel to circle them a couple of times.

He circled low. But the ship was deserted; not a trace of crew or passenger on deck. And it drifted strangely on the ocean swells as if out of control. Then from a cabin window he saw a face, silent and motionless, without expression. It stared impassively like a jack-o'-lantern in a window. He circled again and waved—but again, just that silent stare. He could not afford to stay any longer, so he tilted the nose upward and settled back into his course. He never found out about that ship. Was it another mirage? There were no reports of ships in distress. What of the face in the window? Was it alive? Had he met one of the ghost ships that are found in many tall tales of the sea?

The Home Stretch

Later, flying close to the tops of the waves, Lindbergh glanced out the side of his cockpit and caught a glimpse of another strange sight: something smooth and sleek and black sluicing through the surface of the water between his wings. After the mirages and phantom ships, Lindbergh was momentarily afraid to look again. It was as if childhood fears of strange shapes and dark places had returned to haunt him. What he saw, however, evoked another wonderfully poetic insight:

... there it is again, slightly behind me now, a porpoise—the first living thing I've seen since Newfoundland. Fin and sleek, black body curve gracefully above the surface and slip down out of sight.

The ocean is as desolate as ever. Yet a complete change has taken place. I feel that I've safely recrossed the bridge to life—broken the strands which have been tugging me toward the universe beyond. Why do I find such joy, such encouragement in the sight of a porpoise? What possible bond can I have with a porpoise hundreds of miles at sea, with a strange creature I've never seen before and will never see again? What is there in that flashing glimpse of hide that means so much to me, that even makes it seem a different ocean? Is it simply that I've been looking so long, and seeing nothing? Is it an omen of land ahead? Or is there some common tie between living things that surmounts even the barrier of species?

This ocean, which for me marks the borderland of death, is filled with life; life that's foreign, yet in some strange way akin; life which welcomes me back from the universe of spirits and makes me part of the earth again. What a kingdom lies under that tossing surface! Numberless animals must be there, hidden from my sight. It's a kingdom closed to man, one he can fly above all day and never recognize. How blind our normal senses are. We look at a star and see a pinpoint of light; a forest is a green carpet to a flyer's eye; the ocean, a tossing mass of water. Inner vision requires a night alone above the clouds, the sight of deer in a clearing, the leap of a porpoise far from land.

And then . . .

LINDBERGH LANDS IN PARIS *(Chicago Sunday Tribune)*

LINDBERGH DOES IT; TO PARIS IN 33½ HOURS; CHEERING FRENCH CARRY HIM OFF FIELD *(New York Times)*

DE NEW YORK AU BOURGET EN AVION AYANT TRAVERSE L'AT-LANTIQUE . . . LINDBERGH A ATTERRI HIER SOIR A 10 HEURES 22 *(Le Figaro*—Paris)

DELIRIOUS PARIS ACCLAIMS LINDBERGH (The *Times Pica-yune*—New Orleans)

This is only a sampling of the headlines that broke all over the world. Probably a greater percentage of the world's population looked at the pictures of this man and his plane on that day than at any other image at any other time in history. He became a household word; everybody's hero. He returned home to a tumultuous welcome, a ticker-tape parade in New York, audiences with the President and world statesmen. On tours of foreign countries, he was greeted with even more enthusiasm, surging crowds pressing together to get a sight of the Lone Eagle, the Flying Fool, the young American.

Why? Well it was not just for being a daredevil. Circus pilots, Lindbergh himself as a parachutist and wing-walker on the barnstorming circuit, often came closer to death. The fact that he did it alone made him the focal point of all the excitement. That was true; there was no one to share the spotlight. But there was more, an indefinable aura of promise about the man and his accomplishment. He captured the imagination of that era because to those who honored him he was a trailblazer into a new and glorious future that all mankind seemed destined to share. He was the pioneer of a life of unparalleled achievement that was to come: flight; high-speed travel; networks of air traffic uniting the globe, ferrying goods and services to and from the far corners of the planet, natural resources that would bring a life of abundance for everyday people everywhere. New jobs, new industries, new advances in science—perhaps space itself —now seemed a likelihood. The promise of the experiments of Edison and the Wright Brothers and Marconi now seemed nearer to an application to the human condition. Life was going to be different from now on—different and immeasurably better. The sky, even, was no longer the limit. (Imagine for a moment what would be our reaction to the space voyages if the pictures from the moon and Mars had revealed planets blessed with fertile plains and teeming with animal life, and you will get a hint of the awe and joyous adulation the people of the 1920s felt at Lindbergh's feat. We would see glimpses of a new land of plenty and opportunity, waiting to be developed and exploited for the benefit of those willing to take on the challenge. And everyone, at least for a moment, would imagine himself to be willing. Of course, space exploration still only reveals a cold and barren wasteland, but Lindbergh seemed to point the way to a Golden Age.)

Lindbergh certainly did not fade into obscurity after his flight. He remained a public figure of sorts and made a modest fortune for himself as an advisor to the developing airline industry in the United States. But he never again achieved the degree of brilliance of his days in the sun. That was a unique moment, perhaps one that will never be repeated in history. His life quieted down once the hoopla died away. He married a beautiful daughter of one of America's oldest and wealthiest families.

Not long after his marriage he was in the headlines again. But it was an unwelcome sort of publicity. He experienced the wound parents fear more than any other: the loss of a child. And his loss came in a particularly fiendish and despicable way. His firstborn son was kidnapped from a bedroom crib by a vicious and desperate man who later killed the child. The public horror was so great that kidnapping was shortly thereafter declared a federal crime punishable by death. It was one of the strange quirks of fate that so often seem to accompany great success, like some terrible curse. Lindbergh seldom expressed emotion, but the pictures of the man after the terrifying ordeal show a different face, etched with sorrow and even a trace of despair. The light in the blue eyes seems faded; the smile perfunctory; every gesture painful. It was as if he knew he had to live on, but without joy or exuberance.

But for those two glorious days and the months immediately following, he was everything that Americans envisioned for themselves in the first half of the twentieth century: daring, energetic, indomitable, confident, eager, ready to take the lead

224

in constructing the new world of the future—the American Century.

Many say that the American drive exemplified by Lindbergh has died. That could be. The late 1960s and 70s seem to indicate at least a dip in the line graph that stretched upward from Edison, through the Wright Brothers, Lindbergh, atomic energy, and manned voyages to the moon. There certainly is a difference between the generation of Americans that lionized Lindbergh and the one that seems more enthralled with the escapades of narcotics-addicted rock musicians. There are some, it is true, who insist that the more passive and self-indulgent anti-heroes of our time are a good sign, an indication of a healthy conversion from an assertive and acquisitive way of life likely to lead to world-wide warfare and disruption of the ecological balance. Only time will tell. But the America that loved Lucky Lindy loved itself as well. More important, so did the rest of the world. Even now, when many of the countries of the world are highly critical of America's way of life, they continue to strive to achieve it for their own people. They imitate it, which is the sincerest form of flattery. The implications of that cannot be dismissed out of hand.

Will Rogers

9

Will Rogers
Cowboy Philosopher

You would not think it was the kind of act that would make it big. A lean and angular cowboy in wrinkled jeans, chaps, and an old battered hat saunters out onto the vaudeville stage, chewing gum and fiddling with the looped end of his lariat. He does a few rope tricks—whirls it up and down in front, framing his face, and the size of the loop increases until he can step out through it. Pretty good. Spins it flat out alongside his leg, switches hands, raises it overhead and lets the loop slide down over his head and shoulders, and then shoots it up again. Nossir —not bad at all. But that was not what they came to see. They used to, when he was newer to the business. He started out with traveling Wild West shows and circuses. But he found out soon enough that the crowds seemed to like the little comments he would make between tricks or when he missed. At first he didn't like it—thought they were laughing at him, him a serious trick roper. But he caught on. They were laughing with him, enjoying his hometown commonsense observations about life in these here United States in the 1920s. So Will Rogers, the trick roper, became Will Rogers the humorist, social critic, political observer, and even philosopher (philosopher in a quite serious way, some thought. Will Durant, famous for his widely read histories of philosophy, sought Rogers' comments on the issues of the day and published them alongside those of Eugene O'Neill and George Bernard Shaw.)

By the mid-1920s Rogers' fame as a humorous raconteur reached the point where Hollywood began to come around with fat contracts, and newspaper chains opened their pages to his words of wisdom. Nearly everyone in the country was listening now, not just those lucky enough to catch his act in the big cities or at state fairs. He became a steady diet for the great masses of Americans. Laced with sly innuendo, his wisecracks about Presidents, movie stars, politicians, and rich businessmen were told and retold by men on the job, women at tea parties, students, even preachers looking for an anecdote to wake up their sleepy parishioners on Sundays. Everyone had his favorite. No matter who you were or how you made your living, Rogers would eventually come up with a corker that would say it all for you, just as you wanted it said.

But it was not only entertainment. The cowboy had a way of capturing the thoughts of the average man and woman about the increasingly complex political problems of the day. He poked fun, but not carelessly or without purpose. His wisecracks exposed the self-serving hypocrisy, and scored the pretense and sham of those in American life who were looking out for themselves and lining their own pockets while parading under the banners of "patriotism" and "the public interest." His was the sharp wit of the common man who might not have much formal education but who knows a horse thief when he sees one, who refuses to be taken in by the fast talkers and hand-wringing "servants of mankind" that are out to save the world—for a price. He was the voice of the average guy.

Rogers had a style of quick-hitting sarcasm that could be heard in less clever and polished form on farms and ranches and in small-town shops and big-city factories all over America in the 1920s and into the 1930s. It was a humor bred by angry feelings of powerlessness—powerlessness bordering on despair in some cases—in those who felt they were at the mercy of big business and big government. Mammoth corporations, sprawling government bureaucracies, Wall Street, international financiers—they all seemed to say that life in America was moving beyond the control of the people. The average guy felt himself overpowered by impersonal social forces. He doubted whether he could still survive on his own talent and effort. For him to do well, the "system" had to treat him well. And the system seemed under the control of an upper-class elite, separate and distinct from him: the managers, the financiers, the tycoons, the directors, who seemed to do quite well for themselves even in those years when he found himself out of work.

The responses varied. Some Americans were tempted by movements for a revolutionary socialism that promised to return "power to the people." Most, however, accepted the logic of men like William Jennings Bryan, and saw in socialism a remedy worse than the disease. They feared that the socialist rulers would handle power no better than the industrial and banking magnates; and in fact, because their control would be so total, a socialist elite would present an even greater threat to freedom. Some dreamed of returning to the simpler days of old, to an agrarian society where every individual would be so busy tending to the chores around his own homestead that he would have neither the time nor the interest to build commercial or government empires large enough and powerful enough to threaten anyone else.

Poking fun at the pretenders who got rich on their "sacrificial" efforts to help society and improve the lot of mankind might not cure any social evils, but it was good for the soul; a way to stay sane. It helped an individual to prove to himself and his neighbors or co-workers that he had not been taken in by the hucksters; that he knew full well that the factory owner suddenly ablaze with concern for plant safety never worried about the loose drill press until his insurance rates went up; that the politician quivering with impassioned pleas to help the farmer get his crops to distant markets had most of his money invested in the railroad that he hoped would bring civilization west of the Pecos; that the arms manufacturers financing the advertising campaign to help friendly democratic nations abroad would be less interested in those struggling democracies if they were looking for wheat harvesters instead of machine guns; that bankers who warned of the dangers of an inflationary economy just when were raising their interest rates to slow it down might not be telling the whole truth and nothing but the truth.

A leg-larruping horselaugh could make things sit better. The hypocrites might still be there in the morning, gathering in the

229

praises of their colleagues, but the cackles and snickers from the back of the hall would make it clear that they had been found out in spite of all their pious bombast. Will Rogers was making sure that they would hear the laughter.

During the ten or so years that Rogers plied his craft (he died prematurely in a plane crash near Point Barrow, Alaska in 1935), few segments of society escaped his wit. That's what made him lovable—even for those being taken down. Sooner or later everyone would get the barb. The only people who bore a grudge were those he chided for the really serious offenses, rather than for something on the usual grocery list of human cantankerousness. Even most of them eventually cooled down, since Rogers tended to skip around in his observations. If he showed folks where the cards were marked, he would not bore or irritate them by doing it over and over again. He did not take himself seriously enough for that. His most famous line—"I never met a man I didn't like"—probably could be applied with a reverse spin. Few who read him regularly disliked him. Quite the contrary. For a decade he was America's most beloved humorist.

What was his style? There is no way to describe it that does it justice. It has to be quoted at length. And while you read his words you have to keep a picture of him in mind: cowboy hat tilted back, eyes twinkling mischieviously, chewing gum being given a workout. And away he would go. Blustering, pompous politicians; self-righteous educators and religious leaders; platitudinizing corporate executives—they all would get it, with both barrels. But always with a laugh. Crooked oilmen who conspired with corrupt politicians to bilk the taxpayers out of federal petroleum reserves? Radical groups in New York City, threatening to turn America Communist? Russian dictators demanding recognition for their "workers' paradise"? He made you laugh at it, see the fraud for what it was—but never to forget that politics is not all of life. That might have been his greatest gift: his ability to remind us, through humor, that we cannot count on politics or government social schemes to make us happy in life; that there is more to America than government; that there will in all likelihood be as many snake-oil salesmen and shell-game artists in Washington, D.C. and on Wall Street as at a Medicine Bow, Wyoming county fair. Let's not take it all too serious, folks. You can't take politics with you, either, when you go.

Rogers reflected another side of the Americans of the first quarter of this century who turned to William Jennings Bryan. He was at the peak of his career when Bryan was near the end of his, but their appeal was similar. People turned to Bryan when angered and outraged; to Rogers in their more mellow moods. The enemy was the same—those who were seeking to use the intricacies of modern life to exploit the working man, but in a way clever and secretive enough to escape criminal prosecution. The crisis was felt with less urgency by the time Rogers came along. In the 20 years since Bryan took on the "gold bugs," there had been enough reforms to convince people that it was possible to bring about change in a peaceful manner. The abusers of power could be stopped and put in their place, sooner or later. We could afford to laugh, we thought. They couldn't fool us. Will Rogers had his finger on them.

His pitch was deceptively simple. He would read a wide variety of newspapers and news magazines and then comment on what he had read in a manner easily understood by the common man. He even forbade newspaper editors to correct his grammatical errors and mistakes in spelling. He wanted his writing to have the common touch. As he once said: "All I know is what I read in the newspapers." He would take a political problem, domestic or international, note the comments of the experts who claimed to have answers to the problem; make a comparison to a similar problem people face on the farm or on the job every day; then apply the common-sense solution to the national problem in question. Wars became neighborhood squabbles over property rights; national debts were the family budget; foreign aid was to be treated like the church poor box; criminals like an unruly child. People know how to handle these problems with a little bit of horse sense—why not the politicians? Why is it so different in Washington?

Such an approach is, of course, a bit simplistic. Two countries feuding over the sea lanes to Africa cannot be separated and told to shake hands and share things as easily as two boys rolling in the dust over a sack of marbles. There is a special expertise required in high-level government and business operations. There is no denying that. We could not really allow a vote on how to conduct the day-by-day workings of, say, the Internal Revenue Service. But Rogers' homespun wisdom pointed out other aspects of this question—aspects we overlook at our peril in a democracy: that the people in power who claim they have some special fund of information that better equips them to make decisions just might be using that "classified" information to protect their own interests rather than the public's; that the complicated machinery of government can be used as a screen behind which the unscrupulous direct public policy for their own dishonest profit; that they might be telling us that things are "too complex" for common sense to untangle because an application of common sense would end their racket; that, perhaps, a system should not be allowed to grow so intricate— whether it be a political or an economic system—that the people of a democracy cannot understand what is going on; that such systems cannot be made socially responsible.

Sound confusing? Well it wasn't when Will Rogers began to crack his gum and spin his lariat. That was his genius. Everything became clear. Who had whose hand in whose pocket? Who was selling whom a pig in a poke? Who was watering the corn whiskey? Who was the fox? In whose hen house? Too simplistic now? Maybe. But let's talk about things on that level for a while and see. That was Will Rogers' invitation. He did not have all the answers. He knew that:

> I am like everybody else. I could sit down by the hour and tell of plans that has been tried in the last couple of years that haven't worked, that have maby not only looked foolish, but were foolish, but darn it all that criticism wouldent do any good. It would just add to the yell of the pack. It would be just another howl in the wilderness. I could sit down from now till morning and tell you what he should not have done, but if you give me five minutes continuous time, I couldent tell you what he should have done, and neither can any of the rest of em.

But we do not have to know how to fix the carburetor on our friend's car to be able to tell him that pouring in sand as a cleaning agent is not too bright an idea. It takes a talent to see *why* a bad situation is bad—where the errors lie. And Will Rogers was a genius at that. It is not enough just to grumble and complain that things are rotten. You have to locate the source of the problem.

There were no set categories to which Rogers limited himself. Everything in the newspapers was fair game. Looking back on his columns, books, and articles, however, it becomes noticeable that there were a few favorite themes: he attacked upper-class snobbery; the abuse of power by those in high office in business or government; stupidity in those same high offices; the shortsighted and materialistic faith that many Americans had in the 1920s in get-rich-quick schemes and stock-market speculation, and the accompanying loss of the work ethic; hypocrisy and self-aggrandizement in general.

Many of the specific issues he discussed were of concern only to his contemporaries. But if you change the names of the phonies and hucksters, and switch the locales a bit, the general principles he was defending—and his description of the abuse of them—will strike a familiar note in our time. They probably will bring on a knowing nod of agreement, together with the usual chuckle, from Americans a hundred years from now.

"Going a Long Way for an Enemy"

In the years right after World War I many Americans had second thoughts about our involvement in that conflict. It was not a war where the enemy had threatened us directly. True, the Germans had torpedoed American merchant vessels, but only, they insisted, because those ships were carrying arms to England—arms that would be used by the English against German soldiers on the Continent. The Germans argued, in other words, that they were defending themselves against a deliberate American intervention in favor of England. Whether this was the case or not, many Americans, after the war was over, began to entertain doubts about whether America really had fought to "make the world safe for democracy"—as the old war slogan had us believe. The argument that German domination of Europe would have endangered American interests— whereas French and English domination would not—seemed less and less sturdy as time went by. Why did we fight in that war? Who benefited? The average American? How? A feeling began to develop, both in scholarly circles and on front porches and over backyard fences, that the war had been fought mainly to protect the monied interests of wealthy manufacturers; that the foot soldier was used as cannon fodder in a struggle that made a difference only to a small number of upper-class investors.

It is a theory that is hotly debated in academic circles to this

233

day. Many colleges offer courses with titles something like: "The Origins of World War I." It is not necessary here to rehash all the conflicting positions. Were the Germans more guilty than the French? Vice versa? What about the Russians? The English? The point is only that Americans were determined never again to become embroiled in a foreign war unless the stakes were clearer than in 1917 when we entered World War I. A wave of isolationism swept the country. The United States Senate, reflecting the mood of its constituents, even voted to keep America out of the League of Nations, the international peace-keeping organization fathered by the American President, Woodrow Wilson. The fear was that participation in such an international body would keep us involved in "foreign"— i.e., European—disputes, and lead us into war again over matters that were not really our concern.

Will Rogers caught the new mood perfectly. He never claimed to have figured out what World War I was all about. Humility was usually one of his strong points. But unless someone could show him a recognizable menace to American interests his message was George Washington's—keep out of foreign disputes. Do not assume the mantle of policeman of the world:

This patriotic business is always the Big Brother is helping the Weak Sister. But I don't care how poor and inefficient little Weak Sister is, they like to run their own business. Sure, Japan and America and England can run Countries perhaps better than China, or Korea, or India, or the Phillipines, but that don't mean they ought too. I know men that would make my Wife a better Husband than I am, but, darn it, I am not going to give her to 'em. There is a million things that other people and other Nations can do better than us, but that don't mean they should handle it.

I doubt if there is a thing in the world as wrong or unreliable as History. History ain't what it is; It's what some Writer wanted it to be, and I just happened to think I remember ours is as Cock-eyed as the rest. I bet we have started just as much devilment as was ever started against us—maybe more. So far as facts are concerned, the better educated you are the less you know.

I may be all wet, and probably I am, but when an

American starts telling a Chinese "How to live," why its like a new dude telling an old cowman how to run his ranch . . . If my son is educated at Oxford, I still dont think he can come back home and tell me how to play a hog raiser in the movies. Now you can imagine what a conglomeration of ideas a Columbia Chinese student would go back home with.

China is the only Country in the world that no Nation has to worry about. All the Missionaries in the world cant make China Presbyterian, and all the return students from foreign countries cant keep it from being Chinese. My theory of the whole Missionary business could be summed up in a sentence. If you send somebody to teach somebody, be sure that the system you are teaching is better than the system they are practicing. Some think it is, some think it aint. A difference of opinion is what makes horse racing and Missionaries.

My motto is "Save America First, then when you get it all saved, save the Portugese, for the Chinese dont need saving."

By the early 1930s it was more difficult to be as carefree about how the rest of the world was conducting its business and politics. The situation in Europe had grown grimmer. Mussolini was in control of Italy and Hitler had established himself as Führer in Germany, and both were starting to display more than a bit of aggressive intent toward surrounding nations. We know now how that story turned out. Rogers did not. He could not see into the future. Common sense didn't carry him that far. So his advice remained the same. The Europeans look like they are going to go at it again. Well, if they do, let's not get our boys killed trying to determine the outcome; not unless someone threatens us directly.

Lots of headlines today. "Mussolini's troops camped on the Austrian border," "Hitler says nothing," which means he is too busy moving troops, "England lends more support," yes and two battleships, "France backs Austrian government," and sends a few hundred planes over to deliver the message. "Japan almost on verge of prostration in fear Russia wont get into this European war." Mr. Franklyn D. [Franklin Delano Roosevelt, then President] shut

235

your front door to all foreign ambassadors running to
you with news. Just send 'em these words, "boys, its
your cats thats fighting, you pull 'em apart."

He shared a feeling with many other Americans in situations
such as these. Maybe we aren't better than the rest of the world,
and maybe it shows some poor taste to say it out loud, but this
is the best country in the world to live in, for all its problems.
There is something unique and good about life in America,
something we could lose by getting involved in the squabbles
of Europe. After returning from a trip abroad Rogers tried to
express the danger:

Oh, boy, I was glad to set my old big feet on American soil even if it has got a second mortgage on it.
Had the greatest trip I ever had in my life and believe if everybody made it they might come back a
little poorer, but better off in the feeling toward our
country. I know business is off, they say 60 percent.
Well, that still leaves us 30 percent ahead of anywhere I have seen, if we can just let other people
alone and do their own fighting. When you get into
trouble 5000 miles away from home you've got to
have been looking for it.

There was nothing to be gained in joining the fight for colonies and foreign markets, he insisted. We were a country
blessed with natural resources. If we would just keep our noses
clean and out of everyone else's business, and put them to the
grindstone for an honest day's work at home, we could build a
good life for all our people. Don't be tempted by the vainglori-
ous dream of becoming another Italy under Mussolini, who had
attacked the African nation of Ethiopia in search of a colony, so
that Italy could be like the rest of Europe:

We heard of all kinds of likely wars between nations, but this one that Mussolini dug up is a new one.
Italy versus Ethiopia. Thats going a long way for an
enemy.

The memory of our experience in World War I was too fresh in
his mind for him to consider the advantages of another American Expeditionary Force:

'Course, in the Historys, War always starts "for patriotism's sake," but you read on then down to the
Peace Conference and you find that the historian has
to write pretty fast and veil things over very cleverly,

236

or the reader is apt to discover what changed hands at the finish besides a mere satisfying of honor. You look at all Wars and you will find that there is more new deeds for land signed at these Peace Conferences than there is good will. Did you ever look on a map and see the Colonies that Germany lost at Versailles? All these Nations that are crying Debt Cancellations, you never hear 'em mention a word about returning Colonies to Germany so she would have a chance to kinder use 'em to help dig up this Reparations. So, you see, in Wars the Slogan is Honor, but the object is Land. They are always fighting for Independence, but at the finish they always seem to be able to use quite a snatch of the defeated opponent's land to be Independent on.

It would be too easy to make the World War I mistake all over again, he warned; to assume that some distant struggle for land and markets had taken on crucial moral dimensions:

When some nation wants us to help 'em out they use the same old "gag" that we should exert our "moral leadership" and we, like a yap, believe it, when as a matter of truth no nation wants any other nation exerting a "Moral leadership" over 'em even if they had one. If we ever pass out as a great nation we ought to put on our tombstone "America died from a delusion that she had moral leadership."

Obviously, then, Rogers' "mind our own business" recommendations were not based on a trustful sentimentality about the rest of the world. He advised against involvement in foreign affairs not because he was confident that no other country would ever threaten our national interests, but because he saw no feud in Europe or Asia *in his time* that truly involved us. He died in 1935, six years before America entered World War II, so it is difficult to project confidently what his attitude would have been in 1939 and 1940. Would he have continued to preach noninvolvement after Hitler marched into Paris, for example? The only certain thing is that he would have offered his advice based on what he saw as the degree of danger to America. When, and only when, there was an appreciable threat would he suggest American military intervention— which is the view most Americans held then, and hold now. But he knew that such a situation *could* develop. Repeatedly during his career he warned of the dangers of allowing American military preparedness to slip; of overconfidence, of trusting dictators:

We are the only Nation in the world that waits till we get into a war before we start getting ready for it. Pacifists say that, "If you are ready for war, you will have one." I bet there has not been a man insulted Jack Dempsey since he has been champion.

Well lots of war news in the papers today. I knew it was coming when I saw that we had cut down on our army and navy. If you want to know when a war is coming, just watch the U.S. and see when they start cutting down on their defense. Its the surest barometer in the world.

We better start doing something about our defense. We are not going to be lucky enough to fight Nicaragua forever. Build all we can, and we will never have to use it. If you think preparedness don't give you prestige, look at Japan. We are afraid to look at them cross eyed now for fear we will hurt their "Honor." Before they got a Navy neither them, nor us, knew they had any honor. Japan or England either would have just as much honor without any Navy at all, but the Navy helps to remind you of it.

All we got to go by is History, and History don't record that "Economy" ever won a war. So I believe I would save my money somewhere else even if I had to work a little shorter handed, around the Capitol there.

"Something for Nothing"

As early as the mid-1920s, just a few years after the Communists had taken over in Russia, Rogers sensed a danger to America in that dictatorship. Many American and European intellectuals disagreed. They saw in the Communist regime the wave of the future, a government of the workingman that would eliminate class and economic differences and work for human equality. Lincoln Steffens, an American writer who visited Communist Russia, echoed the feelings of many intellectuals—

among them Englishmen George Bernard Shaw and H.G. Wells, who also were guests of the Communist dictators—when he reported to his American readers upon his return that "I have seen the future, and it works." But Rogers and the great mass of Americans he represented smelled something fishy; and that included the working class whom the Communists claimed they would help the most when they established their dictatorship. The Communists talk of equality—they knew that. But what does it look like in action? Rogers visited Russia in 1926 on assignment for the then widely read *Saturday Evening Post.* His articles were later collected into one of his most perceptive books, *Not a Bathing Suit in Russia.* Not his funniest, but probably his most important. What does Communism look like under the searching rays of front-porch, barbershop, American common sense? Did Will Rogers discover something the intellectuals often missed?

This guy Marx, why, he was like one of these efficiency experts. He could explain to you how you could save a million dollars and he couldent save enough himself to eat on . . . He never did a tap of work only write propaganda . . . he wrote for the dissatisfied, and the dissatisfied is the fellow who don't want to do any manual labor. He always wants to figure out where he and his friends can get something for nothing.

That was the Communists' big problem in Russia—following through on the promise of getting something for nothing for everybody. They were in power now and the people were expecting them to pay up:

You know a Communist's whole life work is based on complaint of how everything is being done. Well, when they are running everything themselves, why, that takes away their chief industry. They have nobody to blame it on. Even if he is satisfied with it, why, he is miserable because he has nothing to complain about. Same way with strikes and Revolutions. They would rather stir up a strike than eat. So, naturally, in Russia with themselves, they feel rather restrained, for they are totally unable to indulge in their old favorite sport of going out on strike and jumping on a box and inviting all the boys out with

239

them. You make one satisfied and he is no longer a Communist. So if they ever get their country running good they will defeat their own cause.

Not that Rogers was unaware of the intellectuals who were trumpeting Communism as mankind's best hope:

> The funny part about it among those American ones [Communists] you meet over their visiting, they are all so nice and friendly and enthusiastic about it, and believe in it way above our form of government; but they all go back over home. It just looks to me like Communism is such a happy-family affair that a Communist would want to stay where it is practiced. It's the only thing they want you to have but keep none themselves . . .

But isn't it true that the lower classes were finally being given a chance in Russia; that the new Red government may not have been perfect, but the lower classes no longer had to accept the domination of the old aristocracy? Rogers had heard that idea before. But he didn't find it true during his visit:

> . . . instead of one Czar, why, there is at least a thousand now. Any of the big men in the Party holds practically Czaristic powers (to those down). Siberia is still working. It's just as cold on you to be sent there under the Soviets as it was under the Czar. The only way you can tell a Member of the Party from an ordinary Russian is the Soviet man will be in a car . . .

> There is as much class distinction in Russia today as there is in Charleston, South Carolina. Why, I went to the races there, and the grand stand had all the men of the Party, and over there in the center field stood the mob in the sun. Well, there was Bourgeois and Proletariat distinction for you . . .

> What has all these millions of innocent, peace-loving people done that through no fault of their own they should be thrown into a mess like this, with no immediate hope of relief?

Rogers never fancied himself a deep thinker, but he went on to explore the nature of political revolution, which even some moderns who consider themselves politically educated and sophisticated fail to understand. He fielded a question that many in our time consider tough to handle—and he did it easily: "But how can we condemn these Russian revolutionaries when our country was founded by revolution? Isn't Lenin just a Russian George Washington?" His answer:

> Mind you, you can't condemn everybody just because they started a Revolution. We grabbed what little batch of liberty *we used to have* through a revolution, and other Nations have revolutions to thank today. But I don't think anyone that just made a business of proposing them for a steady diet would be the one to pray to and try to live by.
>
> We all know a lot of things that would be good for our Country, but we wouldn't want to go so far as to propose that everybody start shooting each other till we get them. A fellow shouldent have to kill anybody just to prove they are right.

"Tell the Loafers Where to Meet"

Obviously, if it need be said, Rogers had little use for Communism. His remarks probably did more than anyone else's to deaden any potential appeal Communism might have had for American workers. Not because his quips were so much more brilliant than scholarly studies, but because they were more widely read, and understood. But he was hardly a tub-thumper for laissez-faire capitalism either. The words stressed in the last quotation—"what little batch of liberty *we used to have*"—indicate that he saw other threats to American liberties besides Communism. Especially after the coming of the Depression, he never let wealthy industrialists forget that they, too, had some questions to answer. He captured poignantly a deep-rooted American resentment against economic arrangements that favor the privileged few at the expense of the working man.

His family (which was part Indian) was an Oklahoma farming and ranching family. Rogers, from childhood, knew the meaning of a life of toil. He never forgot the "working stiffs" of the country even when his writing and acting career had brought him considerable personal wealth. (At least this was his public image. Rogers, like everyone else, had his detractors, those who insisted his concern for the little guy was a front behind which he did exactly what he accused the hypocrites in business and government of doing—lining his pockets. His attackers were

241

not numerous, however. And, besides, our concern is with what the American people knew, and liked, about him, why he was a hero, not with what they didn't know.) Rogers never let America forget that the working men and women are the backbone of the country, the producers. He once spent a few days on a friend's ranch (a friend he identifies only as "Mr. Lane") while the Prince of Wales was staying there. He liked the Prince, the heir to England's throne; called him "the Duke" in fact:

> When the Prince was up there before, he went out to Lane's Ranch where they were rounding up a big Herd and was riding around on a Horse. Finally Lane yelled at him. "Hey, Prince, get out of there. You are getting in the way of my Cowboys working."
>
> This Prince seems to be a mighty fine kind of Guy and it is a shame that he should have been handicapped by birth, for there is a Boy who would have made something out of himself.

Rogers would have liked him better if he had achieved success by himself, through his own efforts. But the Prince could not help that. Rogers' anger was saved for Americans who were, apparently, determined to build for themselves as much rank and privilege as the nobility of Europe:

> He [millionaire J.P. Morgan] said he was just going to Scotland for the Grouse shooting season. Can you imagine what would happen if some one told him he was trespassing during his hunting over there. He would just say to his valet, "Boy, buy this lower end of Scotland for me and send my Secretary the bill; and by the way, Boy, purchase a couple of more million Grouse and turn them loose here. Fix it so that no matter which way I shoot I will at least hit one."

His main concern, however, was not with the life of ease the very wealthy were able to enjoy for themselves through big business. It was the damage he felt they were doing to everyone else in the pursuit of their millions; the disruption of the economy:

> Put a tax on the New York stock exchange, so they say they are going to move to New Jersey. There is no industry that could move easier. All they have to do is change their telephone number, pick up the

blackboard, and tell the loafers where to meet tomorrow.

It offended Rogers that the worth of a man's labor or his crops was determined by the fluctuations of the commodities market or stock exchange; that the ups and downs of a system conducted by speculators could determine if the man toiling all year long in the sun in Nebraska had produced anything worthwhile. In simpler times, it seemed, if a man produced something of value, it *was* of value. Now it *might* be. But the people who made the big money were the speculators who acted as brokers for the grain purchases—when there was big money to be made. When the price of grain suddenly went sky high, those who had purchased large amounts from the farmers at low prices made a bundle. But when there was a glut the farmer made nothing at all. Suddenly there were no buyers, even though the farmer heard people were going to bed hungry in places around the country:

It's all right to let Wall Street bet each other millions of Dollars every day but why make these bets effect the fellow who is plowing a field out in Claremore, Oklahoma? Mind you, I am not going to remedy it right now. I will allow Wall Street to run on a few days. Maybe their conscience will hurt them. (What's that you said would hurt them?) But, on the level, it does seem funny these guys can sit here, produce nothing, ride in Fisher Bodies, and yet put a price on your whole year's labor.

You mean to tell me that in a Country that was run really on the level, 200 of their National commodities could jump their value millions of Dollars in two days? Where is this sudden demand coming from all at once.

I am supposed to be a Comedian, but I don't have to use any of my humor to get a laugh out of that.

Rogers would almost stop being a "Comedian" when social reforms were proposed to alleviate the plight of the poor, but knocked down because they were too "expensive" or "dangerous to the economy." There were those, for example, who argued that laws to protect child labor would increase production costs, raise prices, and make it difficult for American companies to compete with foreign countries that used child labor exten-

243

sively. Rogers more than hinted that those who fretted over these things were probably just a bit more concerned about lower profits:

> If Congress would just pass one law, as follows, they wouldn't need any [Child Labor] Amendment: *"Every child, regardless of age, shall receive the same wage as a grown person."* That will stop your child labor. They only hire them because they pay them less for the same work that they would have to pay a man. If Children don't do more for less money, why is it that they want to use them? No Factory or Farmer or anybody else hires a Child because he is so big hearted he wants to do something for the Child. He hires him because he wants to save a man's salary. It's become a habit and a custom that if a Child does something for us, no matter how good and prompt they do it, to not give them as much as we would a grown person, because, I suppose, people think they would just spend it foolishly if they had too much.

He came out swinging, too, during the debate on the veteran's bonus. World War I veterans had been promised money at the end of the war to be paid to them at a future date. Because of the depression, certain veterans organized to get the money earlier than promised, to help them get over the hump of the economic difficulties. The questions at issue? Would it be too much for the Treasury to pay them in the midst of the depression difficulties? Would such payments make it look as if these men had fought for money rather than for patriotic duty and set a bad example for young men called upon to fight in future wars? Rogers spotted some crocodile tears on those worried about the effect on the nation of giving the reward a little bit earlier than promised to these men who served their country:

> My opinion on the bonus is based on what I heard uttered to soldiers in the days when we needed them, when they were looked on not as Political organization with a few votes to cast, but as the pick of One Hundred Million People, the Saviors of Civilization.
>
> You promised them everything but the Kitchen Stove if they would go to War. We promised them

244

everything, and all they got was $1.25 a day and some knitted Sweaters and Sox.

They got a Dollar and a quarter a day. Out of the millions of bullets fired by the Germans every day, statistics have proven that an average of 25 Bullets were fired at each Man each day. That figures out at the rate of 5 cents a Bullet. Now, the boys in this Bonus want the Salary at least doubled. And I don't think that 10 cents a Bullet is an exorbitant price.

Now the only way to arrive at the worth of anything is by comparison. Take Shipbuilding. Wooden ones, for instance. Statistics show that the Men working on them got, at the lowest, $12.50 per day, and, by an odd coincidence, Statistics also show that each Workman drove at the rate of 25 Nails a day—the same number of Nails as Bullets stopped or evaded by each Soldier per day. That makes 50 cents a Nail.

Now I don't think that there is 45 cents per Piece difference. I know that Bullet stopping comes under the heading of Unskilled Labor, and that Ship Building by us during the War was an Art. But I don't think that there is that much difference between skilled and unskilled . . .

Now, as I say, while the Soldiers got no overtime, the Nail Experts got Time and a Half for overtime, up to a certain time, then Double Time after that. Of course, he lost some time in the morning selecting which Silk Shirt he should Nail in that day. And it was always a source of annoyance as to what Car to go to work in.

Now I may be wrong, for these Rich Men who are telling you that the Nail is 10 times harder to handle than the Bullet know, for they made and sold both of them to the Government . . . Tax Exempt Securities will drive us to the Poor House, not Soldiers' Bonuses . . . Now if a Man is against it why don't he at least come out and tell the real truth. "I don't want to spare the Money to pay you Boys." I think the best Insurance in the World against another War is to take care of the Boys who fought in the last one. *You may want to use them again.*

245

In fact, he had a plan to avoid all these squabbles. Next time there was a war, why draft just young men and ask them to be willing to give their all? The manufacturers who stand to make a great deal of money supplying the war effort should be "drafted" too:

When that Wall Street Millionaire knows that you are not only going to come into his office and take his Secretary and Clerks, but, that you come in to get his dough, say Boy, there wouldn't be any war. You will hear the question, "Yes, but how could you do it?"

Say, you take a Boy's life, don't you? When you take Boys away you take everything they have in the World, that is, their life. You send them to war and part of that life you don't lose you let him come back with it. Perhaps you may use all of it. Well, that's the way to do with wealth. Take all he has, give him a bare living the same as you do the Soldier. Give him the same allowance as the Soldier—all of us that stay home. The Government should own everything we have, use what it needs to conduct the whole expenses of the war and give back what is left, if there is any, the same as you give back to the Boy what he has left.

There can be no Profiteering. The Government owns everything till the war is over. Every Man, Woman and child, from Henry Ford and John D. down, get their Dollar and a Quarter a day the same as the Soldier . . . But, no, it will never get anywhere. The rich will say it ain't practical, and the poor will never get a chance to find out if it is or not.

The rich were not the only ones who felt the cutting edge of his humor, though. Rogers warned that the speculator's mentality—a get-rich-quick mentality based on the hope of getting something without having to work for it—was beginning to take over the minds of the average American. He argued—and before the financial collapse of 1929—that there was something fundamentally unsound about an entire country living on the installment plan—whether you were stretching out payments on the National Debt or payments on a new refrigerator. He warned that you cannot forever enjoy more material wealth than you produce. The sight of a financier putting down $5,000 on the stock market one day and selling out at $15,000 the next was causing people to forget that, he feared. "Found" wealth was beginning to look normal. Live it up, spend—the money will come from somewhere. Where? Who knows? It just comes —look at the stock market.

Rogers never claimed to be an economist. But as he looked at the installment-plan way of life, he wondered what it would mean in the long run; not just to the financial structure of the country—to its heart and soul. What kind of people would we become? What would happen to our regard for the value of work—the work ethic?

We don't have to worry about anything. No nation in the history of the world was ever sitting as pretty. If we want anything, all we have to do is go an buy it on credit. So that leaves us without any economic problem whatever, except perhaps some day to have to pay for them. But we are certainly not thinking about that this early.

This would be a great world to dance in if we didn't have to pay the fiddler.

We never will have any prosperity that is free from speculation till we pass a law that every time a broker or person sells something, he has got to have it setting there in a bucket, or a bag, or a jug, or a cage, or a rat trap or something. We are continually buying something that we never get from a man that never had it.

We are going at top speed, because we are using all our natural resources as fast as we can. If we want to build something out of wood, all we got to do is cut down a tree and build it. We dident have to plant the tree. Nature did that before we come. Suppose we couldent build something out of wood till we found a tree that we had purposely planted for that use. Say, we never would get it built. If we want anything made from Steam, all we do is go dig up the coal and make the steam. Suppose we dident have any coal and had to ship it in. If we need any more Gold or Silver, we go out and dig it; want any oil, bore a well and get some. We are certainly setting pretty right now. But when our resources run out, if we can still be ahead of other nations then will be the time to

247

brag; then we can show whether we are really superior.

You see in the old days there was mighty few things bought on credit, your taste had to be in harmony with your income, for it had never been any other way. I think buying Autos on credit has driven more folks to see the Revolver as a regular means of livelihood than any other contributing cause . . . Even our old Shack has got more junk in it that has never been used, or looked at than a storage place. Most everybody has got more than they used to have, but they havent got as much as they thought they ought to have.

But we must admit that other things being equal the Nation that works and saves and dont let the profits go into the hands of a few thousand or million men, They are going to be dangerous competitors. We cant just laugh it off. We prospered for years on nothing but our natural resources.

In fact, Rogers spotted an anti-work frame of mind developing in the minds of educators—a contempt for manual labor; a promise that higher education would free us from the need to work for a living, get us a "good" job where we would not have to dirty our hands. College would do that for us—and everybody should go to college:

. . . can any of you parents get head or tail of what they are doing, what they are taking, what they are learning? This modern education gag has sure got me licked, I cant tell from talking to em what its all about.

Our schools teach us what the other fellow knows, but it dont teach us anything new for ourselves. Everybody is learning just one thing, not because they will know more, but because they have been taught that they wont have to work if they are educated. Well we got so many educated people now, that there is not enough jobs for educated people. Most of our work is skilled and requires practice, and not education.

But none of these big professors will come out and tell you that our education might be lacking, that it might be shortened, that it might be improved. They know as it is now that its a "Racket" and they are in on it. You couldent get me to admit that making movies was the bunk either. None of us will talk against our own graft. We all got us our "Rackets" nowadays. There is just about as much "Hooey" in everything as there is merit.

He wrote that more than 40 years ago.

Of course we all know that the Great Depression did hit in 1929. And Rogers was entitled to gloat a bit. The practice of buying on the installment plan did bring about a collapse. They called it buying "on margin" on Wall Street. Buy $5,000 worth of stock with, say, $500 down on credit; the rest will be payable in the near future. Then sell a few weeks later when the stock's value has risen considerably; pay off the money you owe and keep the rest as a quick profit. Then invest that in an even higher-priced stock—and on, and on. A big pyramid, resting on nothing. Money being made with no money—a house of cards that collapsed in 1929, carrying the entire economy with it, as everyone tried to sell out in a hurry, but found there was no *real* money around with which to buy.

The unemployment and soup lines formed; the apple sellers hit the streets; hoboes who had never been hoboes before jumped on the trains. Every kind of scheme imaginable was proposed as an answer to the mess: socialism, Communism, fascism. But Rogers continued to drawl and quip away at his old themes. They made even more sense now. People had to be put to work, he agreed. But let's not allow panic to cloud our judgement. Let's use some common sense:

I will never forget in one of the Arkansaw towns that I visited with Frank Hawkes last year on our tour. They had been feeding something over three hundred in their Soup kitchen, and one night they announced that they had arranged so that everyone would be given work the next morning at about (I think it was $1.50 a day). You could get a real meal in town for 25 cents, and after three meals that would have left you 75 cents. Well the next morning there was less than seventy five out of the hundred showed up.

You just cant give people something for nothing, you got to do something for what you get.

No—hardly anyone was spared. Rich and poor, tycoon and radical social reformer, small-town merchant and those on home relief—they all got it sooner or later. Rogers might annoy you one day a month, but the rest of the time he would be giving it to the other guy—the one who deserved it!

It is this inconsistency that made it difficult to take Rogers too seriously as a social critic. He was a humorist first and foremost. He did not have to be systematic in his analysis of society's ills. He did not have a program, a specific ideological cure for the problems of the time the way Marx did, for example, or George Bernard Shaw. They are remembered as serious social critics even if their proposals have never proven effective. As long as it was a systematic ideological solution, it could be studied and remembered. It could be applied to life the way you would a yardstick to a piece of fabric. The guy who just shakes his head and tells us that mankind can be pretty ornery, and that all of us are a little to blame for our society's plight—well, he is just a commentator. He might be more correct. But he cannot be pinned down, put in a pigeonhole. That was Rogers' problem.

It must be stressed once again—as he often did—that he also lacked the background he would have needed to come up with a program to right society's wrongs. He threatened to run off his ranch with a shotgun anyone who came around trying to get him into politics: "I not only don't 'choose to run' but I don't even want to leave a loophole in case I am drafted so I won't 'choose.' I will say 'won't run' no matter how bad the country will need a comedian by that time." Not that he thought he would stand a chance, of course: "More men have been elected between Sundown and Sunup than ever were elected between Sunup and Sundown."

But Rogers made Americans think in a quite serious way; made us examine ourselves while we laughed. We would begin by laughing at "those phonies" and "those hypocrites"—and end up troubled about ourselves. He was a healthy reading experience—the kind this country could profit from immensely today. Why?

Are there any of us who play the game Rogers could spot so well? Any of us who hypocritically work to line our own pockets while we pretend to be working for the good of our fellow man? Any of us who could use a shot of sarcasm? When labor leaders assure us that their primary objective is to promote social justice and protect the legitimate rights of working men, are they not

250

also guaranteeing high-paying positions for themselves? When heads of big businesses tell us that their main concern about high wages is the inflationary effect they have on the American economy, are they not also worried about lower profit margins? What about teacher and social-worker associations that demand more funds be allotted to education and welfare for "the good of the children"? Aren't they looking out for their salaries? How many oil company executives are willing to speak out against the Arabs? Blacks willing to criticize welfare cheats? Whites willing to defend a family's right to live in whatever neighborhood it can afford? How many farmers oppose wheat sales to Russia? Are there workers near retirement who agree that some government-sponsored pensions are too generous? Are there taxpayers who want to pay more so that senior citizens can live decently? Americans, in other words, who are willing to sacrifice their personal interests for the good of their fellow man? Who will do more than talk a good fight? Or are all of us in one of Will Rogers' "rackets" and determined to protect its domain? Do we disguise our "racket" with high-sounding talk about "the public interest"? Could we use a Will Rogers to knock us off our high horse?

Babe Ruth

10

George Herman Ruth
The Babe

In Greek and Roman mythology there were certain gods revered for reasons we find curious: not for their nobility and willing spirit of sacrifice, but for a near-exhaustive pursuit of pleasure and excitement in life. Bacchus and Dionysus are the most obvious examples—gods of wine and sensual pleasure. Such gods seem off-key to Americans who worship a God who demands that we harness, not indulge, our carnal appetites in the name of a higher spiritual good. But Americans often display a tendency similar to that of the Greeks and Romans—although for motives that aren't kept out in the open. We seem to have, in spite of ourselves, a reservoir of affection for the hell-raiser, the good old boy, the devil-may-care adventurer, especially if his riotous living is accompanied by feats of physical prowess and strength. In recent years football stars—Joe Namath and Paul Hornung, among others—have tapped that reservoir. People smile and nod admiringly and applaud their exploits even though they would not want themselves or their children to behave like these "greats" in their private lives. We seem willing to wink and forgive all after a comeback victory, a spirited attack, a smile. Forgive? It would be more accurate to say that we admire their rip-roaring night life, all the wine, women, and song, as long as the hero can achieve a great and dramatic victory on the athletic field. They could almost be called the Babe Ruths of our time. Almost. No other athlete has ever come close to the mass adulation given the Babe, the Bambino, the Sultan of Swat, George Herman Ruth.

To this day his name is a synonym for excellence, and not only in athletics. We have heard Willie Sutton called "the Babe Ruth of bank robbers"; we hear of "the Babe Ruth of opera tenors," the "Babe Ruth of racing," the "Babe Ruth of sky diving," the "Babe Ruth of ballet," and every few years, in spring training, some young outfielder is heralded as "the new Babe Ruth." But always inaccurately.

Perhaps Ruth wasn't the best baseball player ever to play the game. Perhaps. Many baseball fans would vote for Ty Cobb, Tris Speaker, Joe DiMaggio, Willie Mays, Hank Aaron, Ted Williams, Joe Morgan. But the partisans of those others would have to admit that they would not bet that the man-in-the-street in Topeka, Manhattan, or Hong Kong would be as likely to recognize their man's name. The Babe is in a category unto himself. Even children who were born 20 years after his death know the name; and the figure: the bulky giant of a man, in Yankee pinstripes, with the swollen stomach and (by comparison) spindly legs, the broad-nosed face carved into a boisterous and mischievious grin, the unmistakable stance—feet close together, shoulders slightly hunched, bat flicking effortlessly while he waits for the pitch. And the swing—the swing! The violent full sweep that carried the barrel-chested torso into a near-complete 180-degree turn, legs crossed, left knee almost touching the ground. Looking at the films, you can't help but think that the people in the box seats really could "feel the breeze" when he missed. There would be no exaggeration in that old baseball knock in his case. Films, though, can't capture for us what the old-timers tell us was the most spectacular sight of all: the soaring trajectory of one of his home runs in flight. (But after all, any home run is only the second most glorious sight in baseball; second to the play when a fast baserunner tries to make it from first to third on a sharp single to right against a strong-armed rightfielder). Those who witnessed his home runs, even those without the gift of words, help us imagine what they were like. The ball would crash off his bat and then soar

—soar, up and out, and out, over fences, rooftops, parking lots, and trees in the streets outside ballparks, all over the country. No one ever hit them like the Babe, they tell us. His home runs would leap off the bat, but they climbed so high that the crowds had time to gasp and cheer and stand with craned necks to follow the flight. And with the "dead ball." They always add that, the old-timers. Always.

There are no tests that can accurately measure if today's baseballs travel farther than those in Ruth's time. Or, for that matter, whether those of Ruth's time traveled farther than those of the generation of hitters before him. "Home Run" Baker, the epitome of home run hitters before Ruth, never hit more than 12 in a season. Ruth once hit 60. Old-timers will tell you, though, without a trace of doubt, that today's tightly bound, tightly covered ball jumps like a golfball in comparison with the ball of Ruth's time.

But it really doesn't matter. Ruth hit more home runs and farther than anyone who ever lived, anyway. Henry Aaron, it is true, hit more over a lifetime. And it is hardly demeaning to be second to a hitter like Aaron. But it must be noted that Aaron took many more seasons, many more times at bat to reach his total. Aaron never hit as many as 50 in a single season. Ruth scored 50 or more for six years straight, from 1926 through 1931, as well as hitting the 50 mark in 1920 (54) and 1921 (59). His career total was 714.

Ruth's reputation depended on the home runs—of course. But it was embellished by his off-the-field antics. That is the point. The home runs were being hit by a laughing big-eater-and-drinker; a big-time spender and gambler; a womanizer; a fast-driving, flashy-dressing son of a gun. That kind of thing was expected of the Babe. Why?

One thing must be remembered. The most sordid and seamy details of his private life (and there were some) were not known to the average man of Ruth's time. Ruth, and the sportswriters who followed him, went to great pains not to ruin his image by "telling it all." Many of his escapades are just now making their way into print. Everyone knew that he was an enormous eater and drinker, with a roving eye for the ladies. But such character traits can exist on many levels, some more offensive than others. Ordering a second steak and washing it down with a second quart of beer is not the same, for most people, as eating and drinking yourself into an unconscious mess; and flirting with and dating many different women is not the same as openly insulting a dutiful wife by parading around town in the company of prostitutes. It is likely that Ruth's legions of admirers pictured him as leading a much more temperate night life than he did. But that just evades the point. Everyone knew that the Babe was living it up. But he was beloved, not criticized, for it. To millions he was a "hell raiser"—not a notorious sinner; a "rogue"—not a cheat; a "trencherman"—not a glutton; a "bonvivant"—not a drunk. Why?

Ruth's boyhood was spent in a school for orphans and delinquent boys. He was one of the delinquents. The school was St. Mary's Industrial School for Boys, in Baltimore. He was committed in 1902 when he was eight years old, listed as an "incorrigible" with a record of drinking, chewing tobacco, and petty theft already well established.

At St. Mary's the discipline was strict, and religious training was considered an important part of the curriculum. Judging from his later life, Ruth did not absorb much of the education or religion (although he did convert to Catholicism and served as an altar boy while at the school). But under the influence of a man Ruth always remembered fondly, a Brother Matthias, he did go from street punk to respected member of the school community. He was liked and admired by the other boys.

There was one thing, however, that Ruth did learn at St. Mary's: baseball. That he did. At that time baseball was just coming into its own as the national pastime. There were two major leagues in the country where men could make double and triple what they could earn in a factory or mine, and minor leagues and semiprofessional teams by the hundreds where even those who never made the majors could become hometown celebrities. In converted cowfields and city lots, crowds gathered on weekends and on lazy, balmy summer evenings with their picnic baskets to relax for a few hours and "see a game."

Some argue that football has replaced baseball as the country's favorite sport. It could be—although baseball is still the game children almost invariably are drawn to first in life, and the one that almost all Americans have played—not just watched—somewhere along the line. But in the early 1920s— no competition. No one complained then about the length of a game, the time it took a pitcher to reach the mound from the bull pen. The longer the better. Out there in the sun with a soda or a beer, watching the heroes of the day—why there *was* no better place to be. Of course there were no traffic jams to contend with on the way home. Probably only a pleasant evening walk, or a trolley ride. There was no rush.

It was the perfect sport. Brawny hitters smacking that round ball with a resounding crack deep and high into the cloudless sky; lanky pitchers wheeling to whip the ball to the plate so fast that all you could see was a white blur; perky infielders darting and leaping like bobcats to make the double play; gazelles in the outfield racing long distances, straining and lunging to turn potential extra-base hits into long outs and then gunning the ball with pinpoint accuracy to catch a sliding runner trying to take an extra base. Bunts, stolen bases, trick pitches, hit-and-run —the possibilities seemed endless, a chess game in motion. There was drama—no swarming team rushes or heaps of bodies. Always one on one. The batter striding alone to the plate amidst the booming cheers and jeers of the crowd; the pitcher staring him down, making him guess the next pitch. You needed no instant replay in this game to tell the hero from the goat. In every village and hamlet in the country there was a legend: the guy who could hit the ball all the way to the river, break a catcher's hand with his fastball, steal a base at will—who would make it to the majors some day—or who would have if he hadn't broken his leg against Artie's Bakery or Leo's Plumbing and Heating.

By the time Ruth was in his late teens he became one of those legends in the Baltimore area. But not, surprisingly, as a hitter. Ruth was a left-handed pitcher with a fastball that was the talk of the town. Not that he was a powder-puff hitter. He had a stroke, even as a boy, that was good for an average of one home run per game in the high school league.

He caught the eye of the owner of the Baltimore Orioles, then a minor league team, and was signed to his first pro contract: $600 for the season. He was 20. With the job offer, Ruth was released from St. Mary's. He was on his own in the world for the first time since his years as a roughneck on the Baltimore streets.

The change was enormous: from the regimented life at school to a life in the city and on the road with a baseball team. He had $100 a month in his pocket. There was a world of new experiences to contend with, and his teamates, the typical roughhouse ballplayers of the time, were not exactly helpful. On his first

257

train trip he inquired about the low-slung hammock that stretched along the side of his upper berth. Rather than telling him its true purpose—to hold his clothes—they told him it was a sling for pitchers to rest their arms on during the night. Ruth tried it for a good while.

He was a great success for the Orioles. In marvelous shape at this stage of his career, with a belly as flat as a washboard, broad shoulders, and long arms, he could whip his fastball towards the plate at impressive speeds. No one thought he would make it big in the majors as an outfielder and hitter. He could hit all right. But there were more good hitters around than pitchers with his kind of fastball. Were they home run hitters like Ruth? Well, that is the point. There was no such thing as a home run hitter like Ruth before Ruth. No one could even imagine it. He revolutionized hitting. You might compare him to a high jumper who suddenly started clearing record distances in the pole vault; an end in football who leaped so high that he *never* missed a pass; a basketball player who began to hit 80 percent of his shots from the top of the key; a runner breaking a three-minute mile.

It was with the Orioles that Ruth got the nickname "Babe." The older players and sportswriters called him "Dunnie's Baby" or "Dunnie's Babe" (Dunn was the owner of the Orioles), and the name stuck.

Most baseball players of that time were a poorly educated and unsophisticated bunch. But even they found Ruth something out of the ordinary, an overgrown child. One day he almost crashed into the owner and the captain of the team while speeding around a street corner on a bicycle he had borrowed from a bunch of kids. Ruth always seemed most comfortable in the company of kids. On another occasion he almost "lost his head" while riding up and down the elevators in the team's hotel. He was looking out the door as the elevator started to rise. Only the shouts of some of his teammates got him to jerk in his head before it slammed against the ceiling.

In 1914 the Orioles, in spite of Ruth's fine play, were in severe financial trouble and about to fold. Players were sold to the highest bidder. But Ruth was one of the lucky ones. He was sold to the Boston Red Sox, along with two of his teammates, for about $30,000.

It was not until the 1915 season, however, that he really began to make his mark. In 1914 he was actually sent down to the Red Sox minor league affiliate to get some seasoning. But 1915—that was a different story.

He was 21 in 1915, legally free from the reform school for the first time. (Until then he could have been forced to return for any objectionable behavior.) He was earning more than $3,000 a year. He met a young waitress who caught his fancy, and he was starting to win games for the Red Sox. But the fans were watching something else. The kid swung the bat like nobody in the game. He didn't always hit the ball. He broke all the rules, in fact. But could he swing the bat!

At that time a good hitter was a "slapper." More likely than not he choked up high on the bat, and held his hands close to his chest. The object was to get a piece of the ball, take a short, neat stroke, and "hit 'em where they ain't," between the infielders or, on a soft bloop, between the outfielders and the infielders. The good teams were the ones that played "the inside game"—get a man on base with a single, sacrifice him to second, and then hope for another single to drive him home. Games, consequently, were usually low-scoring, with the stress on baserunning and strategy. Home runs happened so infrequently that they were considered unimportant; almost accidents, freaks. You did not win games with them, that was for sure.

And a strikeout was a serious failure for a hitter. With that short, choked-up stroke, anyone who was worthy of being a major leaguer should be able to get a piece of the ball. Because Ruth was a pitcher, he was freed from this expectation. He did not have to worry about strikeouts. Pitchers are not expected to be good hitters. Their skill is in throwing the ball; that is what they practice—their specialty. So Ruth could swing from the heels with the bat held behind his ear, getting his whole body behind the flow of his long, thick-barreled bat. And he struck out a lot. If he had not been a pitcher he would have been benched. But he was a pitcher and he could go on swinging for the seats those first few years—and every so often he would connect. His heavy lumber would slam into the horsehide sphere and send it where it had never been before. And the fans loved it. He did not hit one regularly, only every so often, but you never knew when it would happen. You sat on the edge of your seat when this kid came to the plate. You could go for a hot dog when ordinary mortals were up, but not when the Babe was in action. You might miss the fireworks.

It wasn't long before Ruth learned to control that mighty swing and cut down on the strikeouts. He ended the 1915 season hitting .322—the only .300 hitter on the team. He had four home runs—not much, except when you consider that the league leader that year had seven. His win-loss record as a pitcher was 18 and 8. The Red Sox won the pennant and the World Series, and everyone admitted that the newcomer from Baltimore had much to do with it. Ruth used his World Series money to buy a bar and restaurant in Baltimore for his father (whom he had seldom seen since he had been committed to the reform school). It was that kind of spontaneous generosity that made people willing to forgive a great deal of his personal misbehavior.

Ruth's love affair with the fans really developed after the 1915 season. He became a celebrity of sorts around the league. He kidded with the crowd before the game, especially within the intimate confines of Boston's Fenway Park; sometimes he signed autographs for kids for hours after the game. More important, he showed his flair for the dramatic and flamboyant gesture on the playing field.

Once a group of newly inducted servicemen had been invited to see a game between the Red Sox and the Yankees at the Polo Grounds in New York. It was to be a going-away present from the management before they were sent overseas. Ruth was pitching for the Red Sox that day. The soldiers wanted to see one of his home runs. They stood and cheered boisterously whenever he appeared at the plate. In the sixth inning he gave them a whiff of what they wanted. They came to their feet when he lofted a foul—up and over the rightfield roof and out into the street. It had all the distance they had come to see, but it was still just a long strike. They had to settle for a single.

In the ninth inning, though, he made his amends. He crashed a legitimate home run into the right-centerfield bleachers. The crowd roared its approval as Ruth circled the bases, a beaming grin on his face. In the last of the ninth, with the Red Sox now leading 8–0, Ruth decided to give them a little more of the hitting they enjoyed so much. He could not do it himself from the pitcher's mound. But he could see to it that the Yankees did some booming. He had been mowing them down with ease all afternoon; now their bats suddenly came alive. He was grooving his pitches—straight and slow, right where they liked them. Everyone in the ballpark knew what he was doing. If they

260

didn't know enough about baseball, they could tell from Ruth's ear-to-ear grin. One Yankee after another stroked the ball for a hit, while Ruth laughed and waved to the uproariously delighted servicemen who were standing and begging for more. He gave it to them—until the score was 8–3. Then he set down the Yankees in order, to end the inning. He walked from the field tipping his hat to the cheering throng. Ruth ended that season with 24 wins, and batted .325, better than anyone in the league except Ty Cobb, George Sisler, and Tris Speaker. Not bad company for a young hitter. No one has ever excelled him in *both* pitching and hitting, before or since.

It became clear to Ruth's managers, though, that sooner or later he would have to settle down—become one or the other, hitter or pitcher. He would tire himself out doing both, perhaps so much so that he would lose his edge and do well in neither. The crowd appeal that he generated as a hitter largely determined their choice. Baseball is a business as well as a sport; gate receipts are the bottom line. In May of 1918 he first tried a position other than pitcher. On the days he wasn't pitching he would play first base or the outfield. But after a while that ended; his pitching career was over. By midseason Ruth was batting an incredible .484. He was the sensation of major league baseball. The crowds would boo when an opposing pitcher walked him, and jeer with enthusiasm as opposing outfielders moved far back toward the fences when he came to bat.

But as everyone knows, when you think of Babe Ruth you think of the New York Yankees. It was with that team that the legend came to life. In 1920 the Red Sox sold Ruth to the new owner of the Yankees, "Colonel" Jacob Ruppert, the heir to a successful brewing empire. The Red Sox were in deep money trouble, and the new owner of the Yankees wanted to make a winner of his perennial second-division team, whatever the cost. It was marriage made in heaven. The deal was complicated, but Ruth became the highest-priced—over $400,000—and highest-paid—approximately $20,000 per year—player in the game. But he truly was in a separate class. By his third season in the majors he had become the leading home run hitter of all time. His total after three years, in other words, surpassed the *career* total of anyone else who ever played the game. In one game in spring training before the 1919 season, he hit a ball that people to this day consider the longest ever hit. It cleared the fence in the Tampa, Florida ballpark and rolled across the railroad track beyond. No one ever hit a ball like that. The spot where it landed was measured: 597 feet from home plate. During that season, he hit four home runs with the bases loaded; and seven in one twelve-day span. He finished the season with twenty-nine, having hit at least one home run in every city in the league. Certainly impressive—but not nearly as impressive as what he would eventually do with the Yankees. With them, he led the league in homers twelve times; averaged more than forty homers per year over a span of 17 years. When he hit his last, his 714th, he had more than twice as many as the man who was second on the list.

Ruth was the most impressive of Ruppert's ballplayers, but there were others who were hardly second-rate: "Home Run" Baker, Wally Pipp, Bob Meusel, Carl Mays, among others. The team played at that time in the home of the New York Giants: the legendary Polo Grounds. With Ruth, the batting order became known as "Murderer's Row." In 1920 the team hit 115 home runs—with Ruth getting an absolutely unheard of 54! There was a new dimension to baseball. This Yankee team became the first team in history to draw more than one million paying customers to a ballpark in one season. The lines would stretch for hundreds of yards as the fans lined up to see their heroes in key games. Often they could have more than doubled the attendance at the Polo Grounds in those years—38,000— had there been greater capacity.

New York City in the 1920s and 30s was made for the Babe. The city was growing in population at an enormous rate from the flood of immigration. It was a city of opportunity and advancement. There was money to be made, even during the depression. And there was money to be spent, even by the newest of the immigrants, the Italians—who gave Ruth the nickname "Bambino" (the little babe in Italian). What better place to spend some of that pocket money than in the sun-drenched oasis of clipped green grass in the middle of the teeming gray tenement city—an island of fresh breezes where men in clean, vanilla-ice-cream-colored uniforms and bright caps slammed baseballs with what seemed like a freight train's impact against the short left- and right-field fences or chased booming fly balls far up the centerfield canyons. On summer nights in the later years, the bright overhead lights carved a halo out of the darkness of the city. The roar of the crowd seemed to rise and reverberate visibly high above the stadium.

Radios in tenement windows carried the game without intermission for those strolling the city streets. Men sat on front stoops arguing about their favorite players. Who was the best—after the Babe? If a kid were lucky enough, he might even get to the ballpark a few times a year. Maybe get there early enough and see the players pull up in their flashy cars, all-white collars, and deep tans. Newspapers—more than ten of them in New York at the time—tried to outdo each other with pictures and in-depth stories. Young boys hawked them on the streets. "Extra! Extra! The Babe Hits Another One!"

Ruth loved the city. He ravaged it, took all it had to offer. One writer said Ruth would always live in his memory as a "bulky figure in an expensive camel-hair coat and cap, standing before his hotel, his nostrils sniffing in anticipation the promise of excitement in the night air." The nightclubs, the bars, the restaurants, and less savory palaces of nighttime pleasure were his beat. He drank high-priced booze before, during, and after Prohibition, sometimes in the company of jazz cornetist Bix Beiderbecke. He roared through the streets in his expensive cream-colored convertible. His stomach ballooned. But so did his batting average, home run production, and incomparable heroics. The Babe could be out all night, get home for a cup of coffee and a shower and maybe a couple of hours of sleep, be at the ballpark ten minutes before game time—and go three for four with two homers. Everyone knew that. Even when he had been in bed by ten the night before (there were occasionally such nights), the crowd believed he had been out living it up in all the hot spots. The Babe's life was one rip-roaring party. All the time. Everyone had a favorite Ruth story. He ate three hot dogs and drank a bicarbonate of soda before every game—which was true for a good part of his career. He once promised to hit a home run for a boy he met who was dying in a local hospital. The boy was so overjoyed when the Babe came through for him that he made a miraculous recovery—a story true only in a vague way.

Then there was the time Ruth was speeding to the ball game. He was stopped by a policeman who was not a baseball fan. (There probably were a few such strange birds.) Ruth was taken before the judge, whose superior training in the law enabled him to spot the enormity of the error; especially since it was only a few minutes before game time. Ruth put on his uniform in a jail cell while the judge ordered up a motorcycle escort and put through a fine to satisfy the legal technicalities for the speeding violation. Ruth's gleaming roadster, surrounded by a phalanx of motorcycle police with flashing lights and sirens, sped up Harlem River Drive. The Babe stepped from his car in full uniform and trotted through the centerfield gate. The game was already in progress—the Yankees were losing 3–2. When the crowd spotted the familiar figure, they rose and greeted him with a standing ovation. The Yankees, inspired by his presence (or so the story goes), went on to win 4–3.

Ruth's statistics for his first year with the Yankees? He batted .376, hit 54 home runs, nine triples (as heavy as he was, he was not slow), 36 doubles, scored 158 runs, batted in 137, stole 14 bases. His slugging average was .847, a record that stands to this day. It was the best season any baseball player ever enjoyed. Only one other team in 1920 hit more than 44 home runs *as a team*. Ruth hit 54 by himself. But the Yankees did not win the pennant. That did not come until the next year: unforgettable 1921.

In 1921 Ruth hit 59 home runs. He batted .378; he had 119 extra-base hits; he scored 177 runs and batted in 170; he slugging average was .846; 457 total bases; 204 base hits; 144 walks. Perhaps the best way to put the season in perspective is to note that when Ruth came to bat the odds were 50–50 that he would reach base in some way.

Often the point is made that player statistics were higher in the early days of baseball, and that Ruth would not be able to perform at the same level if he played today. There might be something to that. Night baseball and the arduous airline trips from coast to coast during season, plus the longer schedule, undoubtedly have combined to cut down on the performance of hitters. The difficulty of applying this logic to Ruth is plain, however, when you compare his statistics with the level of other players of his day. The statistics of the players second and third to Ruth in his time were better than those of the modern major-league leaders—but not that much better: ten or so home runs in some years; maybe ten points higher in batting average. Ruth was in a category by himself. And chances are that he would be if he played today. He was the kind of hitter who comes along once in an era, an incredible hitting machine with a combination of power and hand-eye coordination never equaled. It boggles the mind to try to imagine what his performance would have been if he had gone to greater pains to keep his marvelous body in tiptop shape. (Although the suspicion arises that his exuberance for life, when carried over to hitting, was the key to his success.) Moreover he was an excellent fielder, with a fine and accurate throwing arm; he ran the bases well, knew how to slide to avoid the tag. If he had been just a great hitter, instead of a superhuman one, he might be remembered more for these other aspects of the game.

The 1921 World Series was the New Yorker's dream—a "subway series." The Giants had won the National League pennant; the Yankees the American. The Giants won the Series; but the Yankees were on their way. Baseball had never seen anything like what was to come: year after year of Yankee pennants and World Series victories—a dynasty.

The next year Ruth held out for a salary increase, eventually signing for $52,000. He had been offered $50,000 by the Yankee negotiator—for each of the coming five years. With typical Ruthian logic, Babe responded: "Make it $52,000 and its a deal." Why make such a fuss over a "mere" $2,000? "Well," said Ruth, "there are 52 weeks in a year, and I've always wanted to make a grand a week."

"Home Run" Baker, a legendary hitter in his own right, was the next-highest-paid Yankee—$16,000. Wally Pipp, who twice led the league in home runs: $6,500. In 1957, T. Coleman Andrews, the Director of Internal Revenue, was asked what Ted Williams, the highest-paid player in baseball at that time, would have to make to equal Ruth's $52,000. His answer: over a million dollars per year. And this contract would not be Ruth's best. After the 1927 season, when he hit his record 60 home runs, his salary climbed to $80,000 per year, $5,000 more than Herbert Hoover, the President of the United States. Many were scandalized that a baseball player should make more than the President. A group of sportswriters is supposed to have asked Ruth to comment.

"Why not?" he shrugged. "I had a better year then he did."

Of course, the drinking and carousing continued all during the glory years. Before the 1925 season he actually collapsed and had to be hospitalized after a month-long binge in Florida. He was carried from the ball park on a stretcher. The newspapers covered the story—and then some. He had stuffed himself with dozens of hot dogs. He was carrying a hip flask in his uniform pocket. He had not gone to sleep in over a week. He was going to die. He would never be the same. Some of it was true.

But Ruth returned. He stayed away from the liquor for a while; got himself back in shape and returned to his home run pace of old. Not that he became a teetotaler by any means. He continued to live high on the hog, but never enough to require hospitalization again for any length of time. Once a roommate was asked what it was like rooming with Ruth. "How should I know. I didn't room with Ruth. I roomed with his suitcase," was the answer.

Why did Ruth not discipline himself—for his own good, if for no other reason? It is probably safe to say that he never even thought about it. If it had not been for the agent he eventually hired he might have died broke. He lived and spent by emotion, instinct, impulse, without planning or foresight; "like an animal," was the way someone who knew him once put it. If he hurt himself or others by his actions, it was not because he planned it that way. He just wanted to have some fun, that's all. That was what made his excesses forgivable for so many who knew him. He could be cruel and inconsiderate to his wife and teammates, but the next morning he would be found at a veterans' or children's hospital. He never bore a grudge. He was like a big child in so many ways—carefree, hurtful, irresponsible, mischievous, self-indulgent, even bad, but never mean-spirited or deliberately vindictive. His fight with Wally Pipp is a case in point.

Ruth, like most ballplayers of the time, had a liking for rough and often vulgar ribbing of opposing players and even teammates. "Bench jockeying"—getting on, or riding, the other players they call it in baseball. Ruth had been making digs at Pipp, who was committing more than his share of errors one July. After booting a ball at first base one inning, Pipp stormed angrily into the dugout and motioned over his shoulder at Ruth trotting in from the outfield.

"If that ape says one word, I'm going to belt him," said Pipp.

Ruth stepped down into the dugout, his face set in mock seriousness and woe.

"For God's sake, Pipp," he groaned.

Pipp, a strong, rangy man with quick hands, popped Ruth's face with several open-handed slaps. Ruth swung wildly and furiously, barreling in at Pipp until they were separated by teammates.

"We'll settle this after the game!" Ruth shouted in consuming anger, while other Yankees gripped his powerful arms.

"That's all right with me!" Pipp shot back.

It would be some fight. They could fill the stadium if they wanted to sell tickets.

The game went on, with Pipp and Ruth conscientiously avoiding each other. Ruth hit a home run to give the Yanks a 2–1 lead. But the St. Louis Browns, their opponents, scored five runs in the last of the seventh to pass the Yankees and take the lead 6–3. In the eighth Ruth lashed out with a double to right, driving in a run, making the score 6–4. And then he homered again in the ninth to tie up a Yankee victory.

The Yankees rushed from the field, shouting and jumping for joy at their comeback win. Ruth, naturally, was at the head of the pack. Pipp came over and faced him.

"I'm ready," said Pipp.

Ruth, still shouting and laughing, stared at him in utter bewilderment. What could Wally want now? He had completely forgotten. Then he remembered.

"Wally," he smiled, "come on. Heck, forget it." He walked away to rejoin the merrymaking.

Entire books have been written retelling Ruth's best days at the plate. There were so many exceptional days that often the humorous ones stand out even more. One cannot help but wonder if the people of Ruth's time talked more about the three home runs he hit in a World Series game against the Cardinals in 1926, or the time someone threw him a straw hat from the stands? The Babe picked it up, put it on his head, and walked to the plate to the cheers and laughter of the crowd. Or did they remember more the times he came so close to the Triple Crown —only one category away in 1921, 1928, 1924, 1926, 1931? Or the time he sent a wrapped package to one of his teammates as he stepped to the plate in the first inning before a packed stadium? Such presentations from fans were not unusual at the time. The player stepped back to open his gift. It was an honor for a player to be given this kind of fan recognition. That's what *he* thought. When he opened the box he found a brown derby —a humorous symbol of incompetence and blundering at the time because of a bumbling character who wore such a hat in a popular comic strip. The crowd nearly fell from their chairs with laughter.

The greatest Yankee teams ever were the ones that played with Ruth in their new home, Yankee Stadium, in the late 1920s. They still call that ballpark the "House That Ruth Built." It was constructed in the South Bronx, just across the Harlem River from the old Polo Grounds. The bleacher seats in right-center field are still called "Ruthville." Both terms are quite appropriate. Without the money that Ruth brought through the turnstiles, the Yankees might never have been able to build the grand new ballpark. And Ruth would slam home runs into those bleacher seats at a record rate. The ballpark was designed for him. The rightfield fences, straight down the foul line, were less than 300 feet from home (in the remodeled Yankee Stadium they are slightly farther out), a nice short and inviting porch for Ruth to loop some pop-fly home runs onto. But the old-timers will tell you, Ruth's homers were more often hit toward right-center. And even if he got a few cheapies over the short fence, he lost far more in the depths of straightaway center field—480 feet away.

The Yankee lineup in 1927 included such stars as Tony Lazzeri, King Kong Koenig, and Earle Combs, as well as Bob Meusel, a holdover from the earlier days. Plus a young hitter of German-American parentage named Lou Gehrig. Gehrig and Ruth went on to become the best one-two punch in baseball. In 1927 the Yankee batting averages were phenomenal. Lazzeri, .305; Combs, .356; Meusel, .337; Gehrig, .373; Ruth, .356. Ruth hit 60 homeruns. Gehrig hit 47. Year after year it went on like that. In some years Gehrig even surpassed Ruth. The short fence in right field probably had something to do with the number of home runs hit by these two powerful lefty hitters. But it should not be overestimated. Out of all the Yankee greats down through the years, only three others ever hit more than 40 home runs while playing in the ballpark. Mickey Mantle did it four times, Joe DiMaggio once, Roger Maris once. Gehrig did it five times. Ruth hit 40 or more 11 times; 50 or more four times.

So devastating was this "Murderers' Row," with Gehrig and Ruth at the heart of it, that there continues to this day the story of how they completely demoralized the Pittsburgh Pirates *before* the 1927 World Series. The Pirates had taken their batting practice before the first game, hitting a ball here and there over the home run fence at Forbes Field in Pittsburgh, and were sitting on the dugout steps to get a view of the Yankees in operation. Ruth, Gehrig, Meusel and the rest stepped to the plate. Everyone who saw it says it was awesome. Ball after ball crashed into the seats or pounded off the distant outfield walls. It was an exceptional batting practice even for this team. The display of unbridled raw power was hard to believe. "They're beaten already," said Wilbert Robinson, the manager of the Brooklyn Dodgers, who was a spectator himself that day, as he watched the benumbed expressions on the faces of the Pirates.

Of all Ruth's exploits, though, the most mentioned are the times he would call his home runs, much as Muhammed Ali would call the round of his knockouts. Sports' historians now tend to doubt many of the accounts. It is easy to see why. Getting some of the bat on a small round ball thrown at speeds in excess of 90 mph is a feat perhaps as difficult as any other in sports. Ted Williams, who did it as well as anyone, including Ruth, always argued that. Hitting it solidly as it dips and curves is harder still. Getting the right angle of impact so that the ball will be lofted over the outfield fences rather than slammed in a line drive at eye level—it sounds almost impossible. To do it at all is a remarkable achievement. To call the time and place? Never. But the stories persist, and they come from eyewitnesses. One such account appeared in *Sports Illustrated* after the magazine had published a story in which the author cast severe doubts on the idea that Ruth ever called a home run:

> A friend and I skipped school and took a street car at 4 A.M. to get bleacher seats to the fourth game of the 1928 World Series. We sat in the leftfield bleachers behind Ruth. He took a lot of good-natured booing. About the middle of the game, as he took his position in left field, he held up the number of fingers for the next inning and pointed to the right field bleachers. And the next inning he hit a homerun. As I recall, he did this twice during the game.

But the called shot that everyone talks about was not that one —if he did indeed call it. It came in the 1932 World Series against the Chicago Cubs. The Cubs had been needling Ruth mercilessly and obscenely. And Ruth, as one might expect, was giving more than his share in return, especially when he heard that the Cub players had voted to award only one-half a World Series bonus to one of their key players in the drive for the pennant—he had only come up from the minors in midseason. It was Ruth's old teammate Mark Koenig.

The fans at Wrigley Field hooted and shouted at Ruth from the stands for berating their beloved Cubs, and they gathered in the street near his hotel to continue their jeering. One woman spat on Ruth's wife as she was entering a cab.

Ruth complained that the press had brought on the wrath of the fans by publishing his comments: "They wrote about me riding the Cubs for being tight and about me calling them cheapskates," he said angrily.

"Well, didn't you?" a reporter asked.

"Well, weren't they?" Ruth answered. He smiled. "I wish I had known that they only voted that kid Demaree a quarter-share. Would I have burned them on that one."

During the third game the baiting continued at a fever pitch. The Cubs' trainer got in on the act: "If I had you, I'd hitch you to a wagon, you potbelly." That was too much for Ruth. Nobility has its privileges. It was different when other ballplayers got on you. But not the trainer! Didn't this Chicago team have *any* class? From his position in the on-deck circle, Ruth, with a big grin on his face, pointed to the rightfield bleachers.

There were runners on first and second as Ruth ambled to the plate. No one out. The pitcher tried to set Ruth up: fastball outside—ball one; fastball inside—ball two. Then a fast one on the outside corner. That was what he wanted. It was a good pitch. It would have been a strike. Except that Ruth pulverized it, sending it in a high arc into the rightfield bleachers where he had pointed.

He came up again in the fifth, and this time, the story goes, he took his bravado a step further. The Cubs pitcher got two quick strikes on him. The crowd and the Cubs bench howled and jeered. They would get the big blowhard this time. Then Ruth lifted his bat and pointed with it to the same spot in the rightfield bleachers. And on the next pitch he blasted the longest home run ever hit in Wrigley field, deep into the right-centerfield bleachers. To put the icing on the cake, Gehrig hit another one right after Ruth's—although the drama was considerably less.

Did Ruth point? Did he make any gesture at all? Paul Gallico, the famous sportswriter for the *New York Daily News*, was there and wrote: "He pointed like a duellist to the spot where he expected to send his rapier home." Another writer noted to

270

Ruth after the game that he would have looked like a fool if he had not come through with the homer. He said that Ruth responded: "I never thought of that." However, the pitcher, Charlie Root, has always denied that Ruth ever pointed, as do many others who were there that day. In fact, Root has said that he would have knocked down with his next pitch any batter who made a grandstand play like that. The papers covering the game were not unanimous on the incident. Not all of them reported it; and they would have covered such an extraordinary occurrence if they had seen it. What does seem certain, at the very least, is that Ruth did dare the pitcher to give him his best pitch, and taunted the Cub bench that he was going to hit another home run, the second of the day. Whether he pointed or not . . .

When Ruth was asked later in his life by then baseball commissioner Ford Frick, his answer was deliberately noncommittal.

"Did you really point to the bleachers? Frick asked.

"It's in the papers, isn't it?" was Ruth's answer.

"Yeah, it's in the papers," Frick persisted, "but did you really point?"

"Why don't you read the papers? It's all right there in the papers."

Ruth played longer than he should have. By the late 1930s he was even more overweight than usual, and playing with the Boston Braves. He had lost that something extra in his swing and his hand-eye coordination. He was, after all, in his forties by that time. He never got the major league managing offer that he wanted—much to his disappointment. A whispered remark was circulating among the owners of the teams in both leagues. The newspapers picked it up, and it was no longer whispered. It might have been an unfair remark, but it was based on some hard evidence. His reckless life was catching up with him. "If he can't manage himself, how can he manage others?" was the baseball wisdom of the time.

Ruth's retirement was mostly spent playing golf. He and his wife put on some weight, living the good life on the investments his agent had made for him. Then, in the late 1940s, the doctors gave him the bad news. He had cancer.

He returned to Yankee Stadium for the last time in June of 1948. A packed, standing-room-only crowd came to see an Old Timer's game. A frail and stooped Ruth put on his old pinstripes

271

with the number "3" on the back for the last time. The sickness had turned him into a shadow of his former size. He sat in the dugout until they called his name over the loudspeaker. He stepped out of the dugout into a wall of thunderous cheers and applause. He used a bat as a cane and walked slowly toward home plate to take his bow and make a feeble wave. He was too weak to play the two-inning game. He walked down the dugout steps and the fans saw his back with the big "3" for the last time. It was the last time anyone ever appeared in a Yankee uniform with that number. He walked through the runway into the club house. Later Jumping Joe Dugan came in after finishing his one-inning stint with the Old Timers.

"Hiya Babe," said Dugan.

"Hello, Joe."

"Can you use a drink?"

"Just a beer."

Dugan got the drink from the small bar that had been set up for the Old Timers. He sat down next to Ruth.

"How are things, Jidge?"

"Joe, I'm gone," said Ruth. "I'm gone, Joe."

Both men started to cry. Ruth died on August 16, just eight weeks later.

One must be careful when trying to evaluate the Babe's career. There is no doubt that Ruth was a hero to Americans. We have seen the reasons why. But should he have been? Should Americans be criticized for their admiration of self-indulgent men? How many home runs make up for the pain and suffering and mental anguish such a life can cause? It is said that Ruth never cheated a man nor took advantage of an innocent girl— which was probably true; that we must remember his early life was spent in poverty in an orphanage, and he just could not handle the change to big money and easy pleasures—which makes *some* sense. But not too much. Many other men and women have risen from worse disadvantages without such excesses.

But these things were not what Americans saw in the man. Indeed they chose to ignore them. Certainly fathers did when they took their sons to the ballpark and pointed out the legendary Babe. For all those countless millions he was something *good*—a representative of a part of American life that was desirable even if it could be carried to unhealthy extremes. Ruth was the poor boy who made good; the natural and unaffected small-town hero who put the city slickers in their place; the uncomplicated man of the people who loved life and simple, earthy pleasures. He took them with gusto in an age when psychiatrists were analyzing life with Freudian categories of guilt and assorted other human neuroses. Ruth was the hero who won on God-given talent alone, in an arena where connections in high places help not at all in the end; the boy-man, unimpressed by bank presidents and even Presidents of the United States, who was more comfortable in the company of orphans and the "little guys" even when "fancy" people sought his company. He was the man of strength who "shows 'em all," who cannot be denied his place in the sun. But most of all he was the man who showed us that life in America can be good for the common man, and fun; that taking the rewards offered to a man of talent in America brings no shame, except when you go overboard (and Ruth showed us what that looked like too). No king on the planet lived better than the Babe—not by the standards of the common man. The Babe knew how to live: that life was to be lived, not analyzed and brooded away. A teammate was asked why he liked the Babe, in spite of his sometimes cruel behavior.

"Aw, heck—he's fun to be around. He don't mean all the other stuff."

For the rest of America, too, he was "fun to be around," and there are far worse things you can say about a man.

Eddie Rickenbacker

11

Eddie Rickenbacker
The Ace

I f you pick up *Rickenbacker* at a local library, Eddie Rickenbacker's action-packed, lavishly illustrated, fun-filled autobiography, the chances are good that you will find on the inside
cover a letter of introduction from an organization called America's Future. This organization, together with other admirers of
Rickenbacker, raised the money to donate the book to more
than 30,000 public and private high school and college, as well
as community, libraries all across America. They liked the book
that much. As they state: "This book is the authentic personal
story of one of America's greatest heroes . . . a man who per-
sonifies, not merely the old Horatio Alger* tradition, but also
those traits of character—duty, faith, daring, honesty, fearless-
ness, self-reliance, and abiding patriotism—those sterling values
that have traditionally been the hallmark of every great American and America itself." It is almost as if they are seeking to

*A nineteenth-century author who wrote stories about young Americans who
made financial successes of themselves by working hard, saving money, and
developing their skills as businessmen. They were stories with a moral: that
individuals in America could climb the ladder of success.

demonstrate the premise of *this* book: that certain Americans have reached the status of the ancient mythological gods and heroes.

Eddie Rickenbacker is remembered first and foremost, of course, for his career as a flier of fighter planes in World War I. He was America's Ace of Aces, commander of the legendary Hat-in-the-Ring Squadron, and was awarded the Congressional Medal of Honor for his daring exploits in that conflict. Rickenbacker caught the attention of the American public with his incredible bravery and imaginative air combat. There is no doubt about that. But he held it for more than 40 years because of additional qualities of character. There were other war heroes comparably brave, but most of their names have been forgotten. How many Americans can name even three other Medal of Honor winners?

How do you explain Rickenbacker's appeal? Perhaps the words of one average American who read the book *Rickenbacker* summarize it best: "That's the kind of life I wish my sons could live." It is likely the men and women who raised the money to donate the book to so many libraries would put their stamp of approval on that sentiment. Rickenbacker lived the American dream. He was proof that the dream can be realized. He was not only a dashing Ace of Aces (the flier with the most victories in air combat) but a hard-working, honest businessman who turned just about every business venture he touched into gold. He started by sweeping floors and ended up behind the president's desk in more than one company. And when he became chief executive, he proved time and again that employers and employes do not have to be constantly at each other's throats in labor-management disputes. For those workers who put in an honest day's work, and performed with a sense of loyalty to the company, he would do his best to get them every penny possible in salary and benefits. He believed—and acted as if he believed—that a good worker should be regarded as a participant in a well-run company's financial success. But he would fire shirkers and laggards on the spot. Hard work should be rewarded, laziness discouraged—he practiced what many of us only preach. He ran a business the way we all say one should be run—except of course when such discipline affects *us* adversely.

Rickenbacker was a devoted husband and father who always

276

tried, by his good example, to defend the family in American life.

He was a God-fearing man who understood that a country without a spiritual foundation is unlikely to remain free. He never let Americans forget that our republic depends upon a self-disciplined citizenry, devoted to God and country. Our fellow Americans must know there is such a thing as virtue, and strive to achieve it. His life and words are testimony to that faith.

He was an "uneducated man"—if by that you mean that his resume never showed he had been to college. But he demonstrated that wisdom and human worth are not acquired simply by putting in time in a classroom. He showed us why a healthy society ought to respect genuine accomplishment rather than mere certificates of learning. It should reward those who engage successfully in the task of providing for society's needs, both spiritual and material. And he warned us that a society will founder when its members forget that truth and assume, instead, that society "owes" them a living.

More than anything else, Rickenbacker's life gives hope. For those Americans who retain faith in the American "system"— our religious, political, and economic institutions—Rickenbacker's life reassures us. America is not perfect. But Rickenbacker is proof that our way of life—representative democracy, free enterprise, and belief in God—offers genuine opportunity not only for a happy and prosperous life, but for a decent and honorable one. America "worked" for Rickenbacker. And it can work for future generations if our young people develop the character traits of an Eddie Rickenbacker. That, in any event, is the thought that inspired the donation of 30,000 copies of his autobiography to places where young Americans are likely to come across them.

Admittedly, only those who find life in America happy and fulfilling, the way Rickenbacker did, react with such pleasure to "Captain Eddie's" experiences. But that was the great mass of Americans, who continued to admire him right through a depression and two World Wars. Nearly everyone knew Rickenbacker's flashing smile and rugged good looks, the dashing Hat-in-the-Ring insignia that adorned his World War I fighter planes, and the popular comic strip and movie serial, "Ace Drummond," a fictionalized account of his wartime adventures.

The white scarf blowing in the wind, the flier's goggles, leather jacket, and high boots, were part of a uniform that generations of young Americans yearned to wear. If his life story no longer appeals to young Americans, it indicates a deep and dramatic change—a sea change, as the saying goes—in our national character that has to be pondered, and probably worried about.

"Where Else But in America"

From his childhood (he was born in 1890), life in America seemed to suit Rickenbacker to a "T." Not that it was easy. There was no silver spoon in this baby's mouth. His father and mother were both Swiss immigrants. His father worked as a laborer on the railroads in the Midwest—until he saved enough money to go out on his own as a mason and builder, and handyman. It was a risk, leaving a steady job and a steady paycheck, but Rickenbacker senior had the same ambition and drive that characterized the son. He took the chance—went out on his own in an attempt to better himself; to get the little bit more from life that comes to those willing to do a little bit more. That's the American dream. William Rickenbacher (yes Rickenbacher—we'll explain why later) never became rich in his little business. He died a workingman. But he was able to make ends meet, to feed and house his family. His greatest gift to his children cannot be measured in dollars and cents. He taught them to value an honest day's work. He taught them innovativeness, frugality, and a sense of responsibility. And he made sure that his children understood the unique blessing of life in America: that even the most recent of immigrants, if they work hard and save diligently, can make a good life for themselves here. As Rickenbacker states it: "America was truly the land of opportunity. His own strength and knowledge and energy constituted all the security he needed." "Where else, my parents would say, could a man begin with nothing and feed his children apple pie for dessert."

Apple pie for dessert? It does not sound like much to us (thanks to our being accustomed to an *American* standard of living), but for much of the population of the globe in the beginning of the twentieth century such feasting was reserved for rare occasions, if then. And things have not changed too much even today. Eddie learned these lessons well: "Above all, our parents taught us to love America. I have always loved this land of ours, and I shall never stop loving it." America! The immigrants' dream—the land of opportunity. We read much of late in popular literature about the painful experiences of the nineteenth-century immigrants to America. There is a conscious and determined effort—for a variety of reasons—to downgrade the image of America as the land of the Golden Door. And there is no doubt that America did not "work" for many. For the Rickenbacker family it did. Who is to be given credit? Blame? Let us go on with those questions in mind.

It was not money and the promise of a life of comfort, however, that made a man like Rickenbacker love America. The abundances of nature mean little in a country with a population unable to reap the bounty. Some of the most impoverished countries in the world today are richest in natural resources. Ironically, a population interested only in comfort never achieves it. One of the most attractive forms of comfort is indolence—laziness, the pleasure of just sitting back and letting the world go by. There have to be other reasons why individuals approach life with inventiveness and drive. Hard work and achievement have to be seen as *good* things, worthy of honor and emulation even if they do not bring immediate financial reward:

"What a wonderful childhood we had!" says Rickenbacker. "Of far greater value than mere riches was the opportunity to work together, play together, learn together, and produce together, all under the loving yet strict Old World guidance of our parents."

Rickenbacker's view on parental discipline should be noted, too, if only in passing. He was able to intuit (whether he did so as a child as well he does not say) a truth our society seems to have lost. He *appreciated* the fact that his parents disciplined him. For him, discipline was not the blind, angry use of force by one person against another in order to coerce him to act against his will. He understood that a healthy family, or society, disciplines out of love. Discipline is an attempt to share with others—truth, virtue, happiness. In a healthy society, those who have been disciplined usually come to appreciate, in time, the penalties that were handed out to help them "see the light" and "get back on the right path"—once they understand the "error of their ways" (these are, of course, the time-worn phrases used by those who have been kept from straying into *serious* error

279

by a stern application of discipline). It can be said confidently: Those who hesitate to discipline hesitate because they have doubts about the values or beliefs they are supposed to uphold and teach. A refusal to discipline is a sign of loss of will and confidence, not a sign of charitable concern for the rights of others. No parent frets about taking away his child's "right" to play with the daisies on the side of a cliff.

The fact that discipline has broken down in so many families and schools and even prisons and military installations is an indication that America's traditional values are under attack— that we have lost our commitment to our way of life; that we no longer are truly confident that we have something *good* to defend. Does the prisoner really *deserve* his jail sentence? Is *he* to blame? Does the student *deserve* expulsion? By *whose* standards has he misbehaved? These are the questions that haunt modern authorities. Rickenbacker was never seriously troubled by such self-doubt. He loved his father for keeping him on "the straight and narrow." (Let us once again stress that it might be good for America to be rethinking its values. A Christian in a Communist country or in Nazi Germany would want to instill as many doubts as possible about the legitimacy of the powers that be in those places. If the values and kind of life lived by Rickenbacker no longer appeal to our people, we will obviously want to encourage doubts about the beliefs that made him the man he was. If, on the other hand, we want the best of Eddie Rickenbacker's America to survive, our authorities are not serving us well when they stand for tolerance and leniency *above all else,* when they excuse violators of our laws too readily, rather than enforce the law with vigor. It is not really a question of whether discipline should be administered, but for what ends.)

Rickenbacker moved into the work force at an early age. His father died when Eddie was in grade school. To help hold the family together, Rickenbacker quit school and went to work in a glass factory, working 12 hours per day, six days a week, from six in the evening until six in the morning. It was a long and arduous grind for a 13-year-old boy (he had told the plant owners he was 14 in order to get the job), and he admits he was tired much of the time. But he found another experience on the job —the genuine pleasure of doing a job well, of learning new skills, of making himself valuable to an employer. Rickenbacker never questioned his employer's right to an honest day's work.

280

His concern, he tells us, was not with defining his duties as narrowly as possible in order to get away with as little work as possible, but to make himself needed. He did not think a hard day's work was an unfair imposition. His employer deserved it and was entitled to demand it of him.

But that does not mean that he resigned himself to work for the same employer until the end of time. He would give his best, but expected to be rewarded for it. He wanted to climb the ladder of success—to be all he was capable of becoming. His goal was to improve himself, develop his skills, make himself worth more; not to ask for more money for performing the same service. (This outlook got him into some difficulty with labor unions later in his life when he had achieved the status of chief executive—when he became an employer himself.) A healthy economy, for Rickenbacker, was one in which people bettered themselves financially by bettering themselves as individual workers. The worker ought to have that drive to excel. It was needed to fuel the economy—to make all of us participants in the search for better ways of doing things. Employers, in turn, ought to construct their businesses to provide genuine opportunity for the workers, a chance for genuine advancement. It makes no sense to tell a worker to give his all and improve his skills if he will be kept at the level of floor sweeper after he does. Whether the contrasting labor union mentality seen in some quarters today—demanding more for doing less—is more the fault of "greedy" employers or "lazy" employees is an important and perplexing question. But whichever, it is a sign that the American economy no longer works the way it did in its period of greatest growth and expansion. The last quarter of the twentieth century will show us what the changes in attitude mean; whether the labor unions have won for their membership important worker "rights," or killed the drive for accomplishment needed for the economy's survival.

Young Eddie Rickenbacker, in any event, got the raises he wanted. He changed jobs three times in his first year as a worker, looking for the new challenge and better opportunity:

"When I heard of a job capping bottles in a brewery . . . I quit without hesitation. No worries, no fretting, no indecision. If I didn't like what I was doing or if another pursuit offered greater challenges or more advantages, I acted immediately, without fear of the future. I have never been afraid to quit."

His was an attitude vastly different from so many modern

workers who, while still in their twenties, pore over their union contracts to find out their retirement benefits; who work only so that they can stop working as soon as possible. Certainly there is a chance that an individual can become too wrapped up in his job and forget that there are other things in life—home, family, and God, for example. But an impartial observer would have to agree that a country is in danger if its labor force does not see work as an *opportunity* to do things, to create things of value for themselves and others. An impartial observer would have to wonder about a society whose members aspire to old age and retirement, to a withdrawal from productive work.

It was not long before the young Rickenbacker was able to save up enough money to spend some of it on "luxury" items. He planted a new lawn in front of the family home, one of the sloping, raised lawns that were popular at the time. He labored long hours carrying topsoil and fill from a vacant lot to his front yard. Then he built a neat white picket fence. "It all meant a lot of work," he admits, "but it did beautify our property so much that the accomplishment would have been its own reward, even without Mother's happiness and pride."

Rickenbacker was fortunate. He was able to stop working just for money early in life. He found a career—a love, a calling of beauty. He saw an automobile with the hood up.

> I have always accepted without question the affinity between art and mechanics. People who have not been exposed to both do not see the similarity. To take a piece of rough steel and transform it on the lathe into a polished object that is not only shiny and beautiful but also a functional part of an apparatus serving a useful purpose became, in my mind, even more fulfilling than the creation of a painting or sculpture.

After a brief stint in the machine shop of the Pennsylvania Railroad, he took a position in an automobile repair garage. He took a cut in pay, but he was convinced it was worth it. He was getting in on the ground floor of an industry with the potential to transform American life: our transportation, travel, housing patterns, industrial centers. He pictured, in the early 1900s, a network of roads connecting distant urban centers, roads that would carry food and manufactured goods, as well as passengers, over their smooth surfaces in large vehicles powered by the internal combustion engine. One of his biggest thrills was taking home a Waverly electric convertible and driving his mother around the neighborhood at the incredible speed of ten miles per hour.

Rickenbacker's approach to being a mechanic was no different from his approach to everything else. He wanted to be a mechanic, the best possible mechanic, to learn all there was to learn in the greasy pits of that small garage; but not to stay down there. He was confident that those noisy, hand-cranked, oil-burning roadsters that demanded so much maintenance and repair could be improved—turned into sleek and smooth passenger cars that anyone could drive. He applied for a correspondence course and spent more long hours, after the long hours on the job, studying attentively the finer points of automotive engineering: gear ratios, piston stroke and bore, valve-lifter clearance, bearing sizes. He found this kind of educational experience invigorating—and "relevant" (that quality so many teachers and students seek with little success nowadays). Rickenbacker's experience has much to teach us. "Relevance" is not something easily built into a curriculum or given to a student in a redesigned textbook. It is something that depends, for the most part, upon the student's determination to develop in himself the skills and understanding needed for success in life:

> I had to teach myself to think. I did not realize then, as I laboriously worked away at the lessons all alone, that I was receiving a greater benefit from them than I would have received from the same courses in a classroom. As there was no teacher of whom I could ask an explanation, I had to work out the answers myself. Once I reached the answer through my individual reasoning, my understanding was permanent and unforgettable.

Whether this correspondence-school approach to learning would work for everyone is a question. But it did for Rickenbacker. Soon, he notes, the engines "talked to me." He went from his job in the repair shop to a position with the Frayer-Miller automobile company, one of the pioneers in the automotive industry. He was put in charge of research and testing, although he was only 17 years old. Some of the 15 to 20 men under him resented being in the charge of such a young whippersnapper—at first; until they saw him in operation. The boy knew engines. They learned that, as did Charles D. Firestone, the founder of the Firestone tire companies. Firestone had bought a car from the Frayer-Miller company and was pleased with the product. He became a valued customer. So it is not surprising that Rickenbacker was sent to his aid when the car broke down one day in 1907 in the countryside around Columbus. Firestone was sure that he had no choice but to have his horseless carriage towed home; perhaps by a horse-drawn wagon driven by a teamster with a smug "get a horse" smile lining his face. He was even surer when he saw the skinny 17-year-old mechanic sent out by the Frayer company. It took Rickenbacker less than five minutes to locate and fix the problem, a small misplaced spring in the intake valve. The valve was stuck in the open position; the cylinder had no compression. When Rickenbacker returned to the garage, his boss called him in:

"Say, what did you do for the old man?" he asked. "He thinks you're the seventh wonder of the world."

It was not long before Firestone bought into the company, turning out one of the most distinctive early cars: the Firestone Columbus. And Rickenbacker became the official "ambassador" of the new company, roaming the country, helping dealers set up efficient sales and service departments. He came up with solutions for quite a few big problems in the early days of the automobile. He designed new clutches as well as a system for distributing factory-manufactured replacement parts, and straightened out a mechanical kink that threatened to end Firestone's automobile sales south of Ohio.

One of the most successful Firestone franchises was in the oil-rich Dallas, Texas area. There were enough people with money in "the Big D" to sell large numbers of a well-made car. But the Firestone was boiling over in the southern heat. The pistons would lock solid in the cylinder. The cooling system that worked well in the Midwest could not handle Texas heat. Rickenbacker discovered the cure, quite by accident, one day while testing the car. He was driving the car under the conditions that customers said led to the boilover—over a Texas backroad. Sure enough, the car grew sluggish and then just stopped. It was what he wanted to see happen; but not that day, in those boondocks! He had met one of those dazzling Texas girls and had a date for that evening. What to do? The car was overheated, but he could not pour cold water into the radiator while it was hot. The quick change in temperature would crack the radiator. But he wanted to make that date. He found some cool water in a lonely waterhole and carried it in his hat to the car; then poured it in, slowly. To his surprise not only did the radiator not crack, but the car started up like a dream and got him back to town for his date with time to spare.

He tried the same thing the next day; and got the same results. The car overheated, but the water from the pond did the trick. Could it be something in the water? He took a sample and had its chemical content analyzed. Just rain water. What was the magic? Then it came to him. Rickenbacker was not a chemist or a metallurgist (that is to say, he did not have a college degree in these fields). But he had a feel for machinery. The cool water, he deduced, was microscopically shrinking the size of the pistons, allowing them to move freely inside the cylinders. The engineers, designing the engine up north, tested the car in cold climates, where it performed well. But the clearance between cylinder and piston was too small for the hotter climates. A slight reduction in the diameter of the pistons would make the engine suitable for the South. The car went from being a problem to a success.

The Big Teuton

Not long afterward, Rickenbacker became fascinated by the world of automobile racing. It was not just the excitement and thrills of barreling around a dirt track with the likes of Barney Oldfield and Louis Chevrolet, the daring Frenchman, that got to him, although that was of considerable interest to the adventure-loving young man. The thrill of high speeds had lured him since his childhood (he once rode a coal-carrier down a track with the pitch of a roller coaster when he was a boy—almost killing himself). He was certain that automobile racing could be more than just a thrilling spectator sport. New engineering theories could be put to the test, performance adjustments tried and checked at conditions of maximum stress, engine adjustments watched in the heat of competition. What worked well for long hours on hairpin turns at breakneck speeds should work, too, on the main streets of America. Automotive experts could learn from each other and from their own mistakes—and make those mistakes in a controlled environment rather than waiting for their customers to tell them about the problems from a hospital bed. Sure, it was risky. But the drivers were a breed of men who reveled in the danger.

Rickenbacker signed on with one of the bright young stars in the racing fraternity—Fred Duesenberg, who was experimenting at the time with a chain-driven, two-cylinder model called the Mason. Rickenbacker became his chief mechanic and driver. He took the Mason to first place in more than one competition in the next two years, including the Sioux City 300, one of the top races of the decade. With that victory under his belt, he was able to sign on with the French Peugeot team, a three-man team of drivers. The other drivers were Barney Oldfield and Bill Carlson—an all-star lineup if there ever was one. Rickenbacker's name and picture started to pop up in the sports pages. He became known to hundreds of thousands of the avid followers of the new American sport as the "Speedy Swiss," the "Baron," the "Big Teuton," and the "Dutch Demon." It was a wild and wonderful few years for him—making the circuit, touring the cities and tracks from the Canadian border to southern California. But Rickenbacker did not become the boozing and brawling racing-car driver of Hollywood fame. He was in an exciting and death-defying profession, but that did not mean he should be irresponsible. He wrote a booklet for the men who worked under him during those years. He instructed his drivers and mechanics: "Always conduct yourself as a gentleman. If you do not, you not only discredit yourself, but also automobile racing, the means by which you earn a livelihood."

Some call it the "work ethic," or the "Protestant ethic." Call it what you will. It is the vision of life that made America the prosperous nation it is today, a country with a higher standard of living, shared by a greater percentage of the population, than any other nation in history. A job well done is an accomplishment worthy of great praise, a *good* thing, a virtuous thing—and a good man does a good job. Not only Protestants in America buy that.

Rickenbacker tells us:

> The trouble with a lot of people, is that they are not willing to begin anywhere in order to get a fighting chance. My advice is: throw away that false pride. No honest work is beneath you. Jump in and demonstrate your superiority. Once you get on the pay roll, make up your mind to master everything about your own job, and get ready for the job at the top. Your

particular task is merely one end of a trail that leads
to the driver's seat.

How different from the scorn many modern workers express, and often are encouraged to express by some of their leaders— their disdain for "company men" and "eager beavers" and "suckers" who "butter up" the bosses. It is undoubtedly true that there are employers who would demand too much from their workers if they were not limited by contractual stipulations and union militancy. Yet the question begs to be asked: Can a country survive with a work force determined to define its duties as narrowly as possible? Rickenbacker probably would have considered the answer self-evident: No. Rather than ask whether labor or management is more responsible for this sad state of affairs, it makes more sense to ask which of the two is going to rescue us from it.

Work was not everything to Rickenbacker. We have noted that. He believed in God. Spiritual values were important, not just profit margins. He prayed—even during his years as a "wild" racing car driver—and to a personal God. He maintained a sound mind in a sound body—he did not believe in looking for ulcers, nor did he wear the sickly pallor of a man who never looks up from his accountant's reports. Nevertheless, he showed by words and example that an honorable man knows he has a role to play during his stay on earth, a creative and productive role in his society's commonweal: work.

Looking for the Red Baron

The Flying Circus, the Red Baron, Spads, Sopwith Camels, Fokker triplanes, the Nieuport, the Albatross, the Hat-in-the-Ring Squadron—they all saw air combat over France in World War I. The daring young men in their flying machines brought a new romance to warfare—a return to the spirit of the courtly jousts of the Middle Ages. The infantry was slugging it out in the muddy trenches below, breathing in the fumes of poison gas and coughing to a bloody death. But in the clear blue skies over the Western Front a new breed of war was taking place. Dogfights—planes diving and climbing at unheard-of speeds, machine guns blazing through their propeller blades, in search of the foe. The cream of a generation of fighting men volunteered to put their lives on the line (at very unfavorable odds, too), driven by the dream of becoming an "Ace," a pilot with five or more victories over the enemy. Newsreels carried the flickering images to darkened movie theaters on Saturday afternoons and millions of young men thrilled to the sights: hand-cranked propellers bursting into a whirl; young men lifting themselves over the props and into the cockpits as if they were mounting a charger, lowering and adjusting their goggles and then smiling while they signaled "thumbs-up"; and then taking off, perhaps never to return. Smiling—they went to their deaths smiling. And even that death seemed somehow different. Americans never went as far as the World War II Japanese kamikaze pilots, who spoke of death as a beautiful thing—"as sharp and as clean as the shattering of crystal." But they did see something, well, "different" about it, more glorious than the agonizing death of the infantryman.

Rickenbacker was the Ace of Aces, commander of the elite Hat-in-the-Ring Squadron. He finished the war with 134 air battles under his belt; 26 victories. Winner of the esteemed French war decoration, the Croix de Guerre. And—the award he prized above all others—the United States Congressional Medal of Honor, for service above and beyond the call of duty. All that was Captain Eddie.

It started inconspicuously enough. He saw an airplane. He was taken for his first ride while he was in Riverside, California for an automobile race in 1916. Glenn Martin, one of the trail-blazers in aviation—a student of the Wright Brothers, in fact—took him up. Rickenbacker sensed immediately the wonder and potential of flight. The plane could do for the globe what the automobile would do for the United States. A fire was lit in his imagination, one that burned so fiercely that Rickenbacker put aside his first love, the automobile. There was a new frontier to explore. He was determined to fly, especially when World War I broke out. He volunteered for the Army and offered to form a squadron of fighter pilots to be made up of racing car drivers. His scheme was to bring to the war effort a group of men familiar with machinery who had demonstrated superior coordination, reflexes, and daring, and had compiled a record of good judgement under stress. He was turned down, however. The Army higher-ups thought he was too old—they thought he was 25; he was 27 in fact—and had set a policy of commissioning only college graduates for the aviation corps. Rickenbacker pleaded that his men would have practical experience more

288

valuable than an academic degree, but the Army brass were firm in their opposition. If it had not been for Rickenbacker's persistence, and some good luck, the Ace of Aces might have spent World War I as a mechanic in a hangar somewhere in France.

Rickenbacker got his break when he ran into an old friend from his racing days who was in charge of organizing a flying school in France. He wanted Rickenbacker as his chief engineer.

Rickenbacker accepted, of course, but noted to his new boss that "I think an engineering officer for a flying school ought to know how to fly himself." He was determined. If he could not become a fighter pilot through the front door maybe he could find a rear door somewhere.

Not that he allowed his dream of flying to distract him from his responsibility to set up the fliers' school. He organized an efficient parts-and-repair shop, recruited a crew of top-notch mechanics, constructed new hangars and classrooms—and also trained an assistant capable of handling all of his responsibilities. The assistant would be helpful in the event that Rickenbacker had to go off somewhere unexpectedly, in an "emergency"—maybe as a pilot.

Rickenbacker got his pilot's training on the sly. He would pop in on ground-school classrooms whenever he got a chance— which was regularly. When everyone else had gone home for the day he would sneak out an airplane for an unsupervised training session. Rickenbacker got his first lessons on his own! Most pilots solo only after many hours of serving as copilot. Rickenbacker's first flights were solo. He started with a 23-meter Nieuport, then worked his way up to an 18-meter job that was faster and more maneuverable, and then a 15-meter, the smallest and fastest of the breed. He even tried his first tailspin on his own:

> I overheard the instructors and young pilots talking about one particularly difficult maneuver, the tailspin. It was a good stunt to know, as in combat a plane in a tailspin is hard to hit. To go into a tailspin, the pilot stalls the plane, then kicks the rudder hard. The nose drops, the tail starts swinging around, building up centrifugal force. . . . By constant practice far from the field all by myself, I finally mastered the tailspin. I could flutter down almost to the

289

ground. The other students were bragging about how many revolutions they could make before pulling out, but I kept my mouth shut.

Every Sunday afternoon at Issoudun, the college boys put on a football game. The big brass in Paris would make special trips to see the game. One Sunday I had to fly over to Tours, and I returned while the football game was in progress. Players were running up and down the field, and spectators were crowding in on the sidelines. It was an excellent opportunity to demonstrate a real tailspin. I came down low over the field at about five hundred feet, stalled and threw the plane into a spin. Down it went, closer and closer and closer, right over the players. Frankly, it scared the pants off me too. Everybody beneath me, players and spectators alike, scattered for cover. Only then did I pull out of the spin—and just in time too. I sure broke up that ball game. Major Spaatz called me on the carpet as soon as I landed, gave me a blistering lecture and grounded me . . . But it was worth it.

Soon everyone became aware that Rickenbacker could fly with the best of them. When the first crew of trainee pilots was sent on to gunnery training at Cazeau in southern France, he was with them. His persistence paid off. A man who went to the lengths he did to get a chance to fly in combat would not have his heart in his work elsewhere—and would be "no d—n good to me around here," as his immediate supervisor put it with a faked frown.

The gunnery training at Cazeau was not what Rickenbacker expected at first. The trainees sat in a small boat in the middle of a lake with a .30-caliber rifle. They would stand in the bobbing boat and fire as a target was pulled past them by another boat. Only after this drill was mastered did they take up a plane and fire—at a huge "sock" about ten feet long and three feet in diameter that was pulled by an old Caudron aircraft. "After burning up a few tons of ammunition, I got so that I could hit that target," Rickenbacker notes, although once he shot the tow rope in two instead, much to the annoyance of the French Caudron pilots.

Finally, in March of 1918, his training completed, Rickenbacker joined the 94th Aero Pursuit Squadron and went into

290

action. His first combat flight could have come from a story-book. He went up under the lead of the then Ace of Aces, Raoul Lufbery, a native of France who had come to the United States as a child. Lufbery had returned as a volunteer to fight for France even before the United States entered the war. He was not the only American to do this—an entire regiment known as the Lafayette Escadrille was formed from volunteer Americans —but he might have been the best known. By the time Ricken-backer arrived at the air base, Lufbery had already downed 17 German planes.

They cruised out over the battle lines between Rheims and Verdun. "Below us was a scene that was appalling. Armies had been fighting over that once beautiful farmland for more than three years, and what was left was wasteland. Not a house, not a farm, not a tree was left standing."

Before long German anti-aircraft picked up the American planes. Puffs of black smoke marked Rickenbacker's path. The pilots called the deadly anti-aircraft fire from the 18-pound shells "Archie," or "ack-ack," or just "flak." But by flying what Lufbery called a "corkscrew" pattern—weaving back and forth irregularly, from right to left and back—they were able to get through unscratched. As long as you swerved right when the ground gunner swerved left, and vice versa, you were okay, flying on through the explosions around you. They circled back and returned to base. Apparently no German pilots were look-ing to dogfight that afternoon.

Back in the hangar, Rickenbacker told the mechanics that there was not another plane in the sky. Lufbery smiled and chuckled.

"Sure there weren't any other planes around, Rick?" he asked.

"Not a one!" Rickenbacker answered confidently.

"Listen," Lufbery said patiently, "one formation of five Spads crossed under us before we passed the lines. Another flight of four Spads went by about fifteen minutes later, five-hundred yards away. D—n good thing they weren't Boches [the French nickname for Germans during the war]. And there were four German Albatrosses ahead of us when we turned back and another enemy two-seater closer to us than that. You must learn to look around."

Rickenbacker excelled at the tasks he undertook because he was talented. But not just because of that. He sought out the

291

best of advice and took it to heart; he learned from his mistakes. He became the Ace of Aces, surpassing his teacher Lufbery in time, because from that day forward he never again was careless about what was going on in the sky around him.

That lesson served him well not long afterwards. While flying over Saint-Mihiel, Rickenbacker caught a glint of sunlight shining off a lone German Pfalz. His moment of truth had arrived. He had come to France to be a fighter pilot and now he was going to have to fight. Two planes—enemies—were facing each other in a quiet sea of air high above the fields of France.

"My heart started pounding. The image of a Liberty Bond poster popped into my mind. It was a beautiful girl with outstretched arms. In big black letters were the words 'Fight or Buy Bonds.' Well, I did not have much choice."

The German pilot climbed first, but then—seeing that there were other American planes behind Rickenbacker—banked into a dive and headed for the safety of his lines. Rickenbacker pounced on him like a lynx on the tail of a hare. He roared at full speed until the Pfalz was in his sights. He pulled both triggers.

Every fourth shell was a tracer; Rickenbacker knew he was on target. He describes it as "two ropes of fire"—going from his guns into the enemy. He could direct the fire "like raising a garden hose." Suddenly the German plane swerved out of control. It spiraled wildly, leaving a long trail of smoke until it crashed in a burst of flames on the ground below.

Rickenbacker's first victory received more than the usual amount of attention. His racing days had made him a celebrity of sorts before the war, and the public was interested in how the "Big Teuton" would make out against the Germans. Newspapers carried the story and his picture. Telegrams of congratulation poured in. But Rickenbacker was pleased more by the way he was received by the other pilots—a group he considered the most exclusive fraternity in the world. It was not long before the rest of the country thought so too.

Reports of American victories began to pile up. The insignia of Rickenbacker's squadron—the Hat-in-the-Ring; literally, a star-spangled Uncle Sam hat in a bold circle—became known to nearly everyone on the home front. It was a style of warfare that the public could follow, with high drama, unlike the massive, impersonal (only to the spectator, of course, not to the soldier) infantry charges. It was flier against flier, Ace against Ace—our

292

"boys" against the feared and respected German "Flying Circus" led by the legendary German Ace, Manfred von Richthofen, the Red Baron. People checked the papers daily and eagerly, as if they were following the batting averages in a close and heated pennant race.

Month after month the reports came across the wire services from France. RICKENBACHER SCORES . . . RICKENBACHER—VICTORY AGAIN . . . RICKENBACHER GOES AFTER THE FLYING CIRCUS . . . RICKENBACHER AWARDED THE CROIX DE GUERRE. It truly was as if the knights of old had returned. Even the combatants regarded each other with a courtly and chivalrous respect. Says Rickenbacker:

> Frequently two pilots of equal skill would spend an hour or more fencing in the sky, each seeking to obtain the superior position over the other. When one or both ran low on gas, they would simply give each other a wave and fly back to their respective aerodromes. Though we were out to shoot down planes and the best way to shoot down a plane was to put a burst of bullets in the pilot's back, there was never, at least in my case, any personal animosity. I would have been delighted to learn that the pilot of the Pfalz or any other pilot I shot down had escaped with his life.

But, make no mistake about it, it was a fearful business. Being riddled by machine-gun bullets or burned to a crisp in a flying inferno or slamming violently into a cow pasture after a 3,000-foot fall—there are more pleasant ways to spend a war. Pilots would force themselves not to think of these things. Of course, not everyone could. One pilot in the squadron simply refused to go up one day. He lost his nerve. "If you think I'm going to get shot down myself, you're mistaken," he said.

Rickenbacker was not critical of the man. Not everyone could be a fighter pilot. The man transferred.

"None of us felt any rancor. It was obvious that he was not emotionally qualified to be a fighter pilot, and driving him into combat would be tantamount to killing him."

The newspaper stories of Rickenbacker's exploits continued. But there was a new name in the papers that year. Until then Rickenbacker had spelled his name the way his family had done all along: Rickenbac*h*er. In a letter to a friend, Eddie, on impulse, spelled it the way we all know it now: Rickenbac*k*er. He placed a bracket around the "k." He was "taking the Hun out of his name"—that was the way the papers carried the story, no longer using the clearly German spelling of his name now that he was fighting the Flying Circus. It caught on, and he spelled it that way from then on.

It would be difficult, if not impossible, to choose the most exciting of Rickenbacker's flights. After all, he was in combat 134 times. Each was spine-tingling drama. (Read Rickenbacker's *Fighting the Flying Circus,* available even now, to get a first-hand account of many of them.) But if one had to choose, he might pick the day Rickenbacker met four Fokkers—Fokkers with their noses painted red—the insignia of the dreaded Flying Circus. Von Richthofen was no longer around; Rickenbacker never did get the chance to meet him in combat. He had been killed a few months earlier, although some thought it would never happen. But there was a pack of younger German pilots struggling to earn the right to don the Red Baron's mantle. The Flying Circus was no less effective without him—not much less, anyway.

Guns began barking behind me, and sizzling tracers zipped by my head. I was taken completely by surprise. At least two planes were on my tail. They had me cold. They had probably been watching me for several minutes and planning this whole thing.

They would expect me to dive. Instead I twisted upward in a corkscrew path called a "chandelle." I guessed right. As I went up, my two attackers came down, near enough for me to see their faces. I also saw the red noses on those Fokkers. I was up against the Flying Circus again. I had outwitted them. Two more red noses were sitting above me on the chance that I might just do the unexpected . . . I zigzagged and sideslipped, but the two planes on top of me hung on, and the two underneath remained there. They were daring me to attack, in which case the two above would be on my tail in seconds. They were blocking me from making a dash for home. I was easy meat sandwiched between two pairs of experts. Sooner or later one would spot an opening and close in.

For a split second one of the Fokkers beneath me became vulnerable. I instantly tipped over, pulled

294

back the throttle and dived on him. As my nose came down I fired a burst ahead of him. Perhaps he did not see the string of bullets. At any rate, he flew right into them. Several must have passed through his body. An incendiary hit his gas tank, and in seconds a flaming Fokker was earthbound. If I had been either of the two Fokkers above me in such a situation, I would have been on my tail at that very moment. I pulled the stick back in a loop and came over in a reversement, and there they were. Before I could come close enough to shoot, they turned and fled. I suppose that the sight of that blazing plane took some of the fight out of them.

It did not take any fight out of me. I started chasing all three of them back into Germany . . .

My Spad was faster. One Fokker began to fall behind. He tried a shallow dive to gain speed, but I continued to close in. We were only about a thousand feet up. He began stunting, but I stuck with him and fired a burst of about two hundred shots. He nosed over and crashed. I watched him hit.

All around the crashed plane, I saw flashes of fire and smoke. I was only about five hundred feet above the deck, and the Germans on the ground were shooting at me with all the weapons they had. I could see their white faces above the flashes. The air around me must have been full of flying objects. I got out of there fast and went home to report that I had blundered into a trap and had come out of it with two victories.

A Car Worthy of Its Name

After the war Rickenbacker returned to months of parades, testimonial dinners, barbecues, picnics put on by veterans' organizations, and speaking engagements. He agreed to provide the background information for the Ace Drummond comic strip, but held back on many other showbiz-type offers even though great amounts of money were involved. He was determined not to cheapen the image of war hero that was his; he never consented to the offers for Rickenbacker bubble gum, cigarettes, scarfs, etc., nor allowed exaggerated versions of his adventures to be produced. He later wrote the first-hand account of the air war as he experienced it, *Fighting the Flying Circus*. (It became one of the favorite books of teen-age boys at the time, and met with much success when it was re-issued in 1965.)

Not that Rickenbacker refused to use his name. He wanted to take advantage of his fame—but for something worthwhile. His love for automobiles helped him decide how. He set off on a venture; one that seems a failure when we look back on it. He put all his money, as well as large amounts of borrowed capital, into the production of what he hoped would become the finest example of American automotive workmanship. He wanted to make the American dream car: a high-quality, precisely engineered, medium-priced car that would become the model for the industry—the Rickenbacker. The company folded after about two years of operation, leaving Rickenbacker in debt to the tune of $250,000, a considerable sum, especially by the standards of the 1920s. It sounds like an early Edsel.

But the failure was not due to the poor quality of the car. Car aficionados consider the Rickenbacker one of America's automotive milestones. Pictures of the "Super Sport" coupe, the "Vertical-8 Superfire," and the "Phaeton" brougham and convertible make those who know cars drool. They have the box-like design of all cars of the era, but there is a sleek yet sturdy look to them that places them far ahead of their time. And they were more than "no-go showboats." Rickenbacker was a stickler for engineering and performance detail. He introduced four-wheel brakes, for example—taking the ridicule of competitors who thought that such equipment would never work. One company actually took out full-page ads arguing that four-wheel brakes were dangerous because they would stop a car too quickly, throwing the passengers up against the dashboard!

Why did he go broke, then? For one thing, the country went into an economic slump in the years he brought out his first models. No car company was selling its products very well. Furthermore, few new products do well their first few years on the market; they have to earn a name first. Big car companies can live on their past profits through a few bad years. Rickenbacker could not. America lost what would, in all likelihood, have become one of its best cars, put out by an owner who was going to take a personal hand in guaranteeing the buying public the best possible product at the lowest possible price. Judging from the pictures of the Rickenbackers of old, a 1970s model would have been something to see!

Rickenbacker's biggest problem now was to pay back the loans. He could have declared bankruptcy and washed his hands of the whole mess. But that was not his style. He did not succeed (and become a rich man) by making light of his obligations to others. He resolved to pay back every penny to his creditors. Not that Rickenbacker had to be *encouraged* to think big—but you don't pay back $250,000 in a reasonable length of time by "taking a job" somewhere. He needed an opportunity, not a job.

He found it in the Indianapolis Speedway. While already in debt for that $250,000, Rickenbacker raised $700,000 more to buy the old track. And then he borrowed substantially more to rebuild the old walls with steel supports, improve the pitch of the track bank, resurface the roadbed in Kentucky rock asphalt, and install an 18-hole golf course. He later had to persuade the city of Indianapolis to build a four-lane highway to handle the miles of paying customers who lined up to enjoy a day of auto racing at the comfortable, refurbished track. He made back his money—and then some.

Rickenbacker liked being the boss of the dream track:

> I exulted in the color and competition of the Speedway right along with all the other thousands of spectators . . . When the starter drops the green flag, it's like pulling a trigger. The drivers jam the accelerators to the floor. They barrel down the straightaway into the first turn.

But there was more to it than the color and excitement:

> The real gratification in operating the Speedway came from the realization that we were enabling the automotive and allied industries to make great strides in their art. Those grueling five hundred miles on Memorial Day are equal to one hundred thousand or more miles of ordinary driving on the highways and byways of America. It would require ten years, perhaps even fifteen, of routine testing to equal the job done on the Speedway in one day . . .

> Imagine driving an automobile over today's superhighways with two-wheel brakes. Well, four-wheel brakes were tested and proved on the speedways of

297

the world. So was the expanding type of brake in use on most cars today and the newer disc brake. Hydraulic shock absorbers were developed on the Speedway. So was the low-slung frame . . .

. . . countless improvements have come about under the hood. I remember the 12-cylinder Packard and the 16-cylinder Cadillac: today automotive engineers receive more power from lighter, smaller 4-cylinder engines than both those heavy old motors could produce, thanks to design and materials tested in competition . . .

The tire industry has benefited greatly from racing . . . I remember reading, as a teenager, a tire advertisement guaranteeing three thousand miles. Today's motorist expects thirty thousand miles . . .

Fuels have been improved on the speedways . . .

. . . petroleum engineers developed new oils and fuels that would give more mileage . . . engineers [have provided] better pistons, better cylinder walls and better valve operation . . . These benefits have not accrued solely to the automotive industry. The fuel-injection system, perfected on the Speedway, became standard on all aircraft piston engines. The low-pressure tires developed on the Speedway have also been adapted for use on airplanes. I could name a hundred improvements brought about in the automotive world alone by racing.

While still operating the Speedway, Rickenbacker branched out into aviation. When the opportunity came up to buy a foundering airline, he made his move. He took over Eastern Air Lines and turned it into a money-making operation, defying all the pessimists who said it could not be done without large amounts of federal subsidy. He accomplished this turnaround by living up to the letter and spirit of what he called his "Constitution." It is a creed honest businessmen will applaud; and buyers will wish they could promote. It seems safe to say that only the most bigoted of Marxists would be able to find fault with American capitalism if all American businessmen approached their responsibilities in the Rickenbacker spirit:

MY CONSTITUTION
APRIL 1938

(1) My goal will be to do a good job and sell, sell, sell Eastern Air Lines at all times.

(2) I will plan my work and work my plan each day arranging details in advance as far as possible.

(3) I will make a business of arriving on duty on time and then think of nothing but doing my best to help make Eastern Air Lines the best airline in the world.

(4) I will spend my time just the same as I would spend my money, as it is the only capital I have to invest, and I will keep a strict accounting of every hour.

(5) I will try to do nothing at any time which will undermine my health, as clear thinking and effective action depend on feeling fit.

(6) I will [take] stress as well as I can and keep my mental attitude right, never allowing myself to think of my work as a "grind" but rather as a pleasure and a privilege.

(7) I will endeavor to give careful thought as to the needs of our company and its customers.

(8) I will avoid misrepresentation as dishonest and poor policy.

(9) I will be fair competition but be firm, using diplomacy, remembering "a knocker never wins, a winner never knocks."

(10) I will always keep in mind that I am in the greatest business in the world, as well as working for the greatest company in the world, and I can serve humanity more completely in my line of endeavor than in any other.

(11) I will become an expert by continuing to study and learn.

(12) I realize that most of salesmanship is "MAN," and that success depends on the superiority of Eastern Air Lines' service.

"A winner never quits and a quitter never wins."

Eastern Air Lines went on to become a huge success—one of the giants of American industry.

Rickenbacker was proud of that success. Not just the profits. (Not that he was displeased by the profits. To him, profit was the sign that a businessman was effectively satisfying people's needs and wants.) He was pleased that the cash registers were chiming at Eastern, but especially that it was done without large amounts of taxpayers' money in the form of government subsidies. Many other airlines were arguing that they were entitled to government aid since the country as a whole stood to benefit from air travel. It was not an argument without merit. But Rickenbacker's success with the free-enterprise system convinced him that the system worked best when the government stayed as far away as possible and let innovative businessmen pursue an honest profit. That was how to get efficiency, he argued; that was how to get the people what they wanted and needed at the lowest possible price. Moreover, government involvement smelled too much of something he feared would one day fool Americans: socialism. Rickenbacker knew that its supporters said socialism would benefit the common man. But he also knew that where it was tried it did nothing of the kind, and that it was almost always accompanied by a dictatorship of some sort. Americans did not need that. The system of private property and free enterprise that built America made us the envy of the world; it could solve the problems of the twentieth century, he was convinced.

After retiring from the active management of businesses, Rickenbacker spent much of his time writing and lecturing, trying to prove this to Americans. He saw the last half of the twentieth century as a proving ground, as a contest between Communism and free enterprise, with men's minds as the prize. The world would turn to one of the two systems. America must demonstrate to the world that mankind's material needs could be satisfied without turning to Communist dictators who would enslave men's minds and reduce us all to bleak, subsistence-level living.

> Opportunities? They are stored in abundance wherever we look. They are waiting to be tapped by anyone with imagination, imagination backed by faith in our freedom of enterprise and fortified by the courage to try.

> To give the world the leadership it needs, to lead the world out of the current chaos and confusion, the United States does not need any new world-shaking discoveries in political science. We need to follow only one course, and it is so clearly marked that our

300

failure to recognize it is frightening. To create harmony among nations and restore dignity to man, we need only to rediscover for ourselves the principles of the American way of life that have been tried and proved over nearly two tumultuous centuries. Rediscover them first, practice them at home and then preach them to all of our friends and associates throughout the world. We have the greatest opportunity ever afforded mankind to sell this concept of freedom to the world. I'm convinced that, if each and every one of us would renew his faith in the principles of our freedom . . . no power for evil could ever prevail against us. Freedom, once more would be the hope instead of the despair of mankind . . .

It is not old fashioned to wave and love the flag of our country or to worship God in heaven. Let us acknowledge and be grateful for the blessings of freedom that God has given us. Let us dedicate our lives to the perpetuation of the American principles of freedom and confidence. Let us stop and analyze ourselves to find out what life means to us . . . Let us therefore pray every night for the strength and guidance to inspire in others the gratitude, the love, the dedication that we owe our beloved country for the sake of our posterity.

There is so much more that could be said about this remarkable man. The strength and leadership he showed when a group of men were stranded with him in a lifeboat after their plane crashed into the Pacific; the years he spent trying to wake up America to the likelihood that there would be a World War II and that we had better build a military capacity second to none to be ready for it; his role as a diplomat during World War II and the years just after; his loyalty as a husband and father; his work for veterans' and charitable organizations. The best advice is just to recommend to you his wonderful autobiography: *Rickenbacker.* Teen-agers with spirit are bound to love it, read it in a gallop, and then go back over their favorite parts—which will be many—and reread them slowly.

If young Americans can be inspired by Captain Eddie's life and accomplishments—inspired to emulate them—there is still hope that America's free-enterprise system will solve the economic problems our country is facing. A generation of young

Rickenbackers would be able to handle all the unemployment, oil shortages, poor workmanship, pollution, rising prices, labor strife, and corporate corruption that ten countries could turn out. But if they don't step forward, the bleak and dreary socialism he feared—and the accompanying loss of freedom—just might inherit the earth.

Walt Disney

12

Walt Disney
Something Wonderful

In an installment of *All in the Family*, Archie Bunker, network television's 1970s caricature of the average American guy, tells a drinking buddy in hushed tones and with heartfelt sincerity: "Disneyworld . . . You wouldn't believe Disneyworld. Jeez . . . I tell ya, it's so beautiful. I want to be buried at Disneyworld."

The line drew some hearty laughter, as intended.

Most of the laughter on shows like *All in the Family* comes from political sarcasm. It does not always flow spontaneously. It comes deliberately often, and on call, like applause, to register a level of derision and contempt for those in society who hold the views being satirized; it also serves as a self-identifying ritual, to permit the person laughing to assure himself and inform others that he is not like the stupid and contemptible people being ridiculed. A conservative might break out laughing when someone who spends most of his time professing love for mankind and a yearning for racial justice proves unwilling to inconvenience himself even for his own family. A liberal will guffaw when a well-meaning but tactless Christian patriot tells

305

his neighbors that God always sides with America.

The laughs at Archie's reverence for Disneyworld fit within this framework. Some might have laughed at Bunker's buffoonery, his childishness. But the heartiest laughter, one can safely conclude, came from those who sought to make the point that Bunker and Walt Disney belong together; that Disney's "unfortunate" popularity is stimulated by the distressingly large numbers of uncultured and brutish Bunker types in America; that Disney is a symptom of a loathesome middle-class disease of the mind and imagination.

There is no better indication of the size of Disney's audience and the impact of his work on the American mind than the stridency of his critics. Those who say things like "no child in America can escape his baleful influence," and "he has ruined some of the most precious childhood experiences for generations of Americans," and he is guilty of the "debasement of the traditional literature of childhood"—those who say such things obviously feel that Disney is a cultural force to be reckoned with (in their view, *attacked*) in a most serious and thoughtful way. Disney's defenders agree on his impact, but applaud it.

There is no denying that his influence has been great. But if it has been harmful, the great mass of Americans do not see it that way. Parents and grandparents, who thrilled as children to Disney's *Pinocchio, Snow White,* and *Fantasia,* and countless other films, watch the papers intently to spot the next Disney revival so that their loved ones "won't miss" the Disney classics. It is as if it were a serious parental obligation, comparable to church and Sunday school.

Whether Disney's work is of high enough quality—whether it will endure long enough—ever to be considered myth is doubtful, but Americans in the middle years of the twentieth century did use the Disney movies *as myths,* as teachers of virtue. The Greeks wanted their children to thrill to (and emulate) the bravery of Hercules; the Norsemen, the daring of Thor; twentieth-century Americans, the indomitable spirit of Disney's Jim Hawkins *(Treasure Island), Robin Hood,* and the conscience-quickened *Pinocchio.* In fact, and unfortunately, a substantial percentage of Americans born since 1930 probably have had few childhood literary experiences other than those encountered in a Disney children's book.

"Unfortunately," however, not because of the unhealthy in-

306

fluence of a Disney book or movie. No matter how beloved or good Disney's work is, there is a vast and wonderful world of childhood literature in addition to his creations. A child whose fantasy world was limited to Disney experienced a vision of life most Americans approved, but he was deprived of a wealth of other enriching experiences. There is a brand of silly humor and cutey-pie sentimentality in some of Disney's work, and occasionally it lacks the deeper expressions of humor, courage, tragedy, and the mystery of life that are found in the classics of children's literature: C.S. Lewis, the brothers Grimm, Hans Christian Andersen, Tolkien, A.A. Milne in the original, Robert Louis Stevenson, Jack London, and Mark Twain, for example.

Yet it is a curious criticism to *blame* Disney for the failure of those parents who limited their children to his work. It implies that the children who saw *Snow White* and never heard of C.S. Lewis' *Voyage of the Dawn Treader* never heard of Lewis *because of* Disney—which makes little sense. It is more logical to argue that if they had not seen Disney they would have encountered no tall tales at all, except perhaps on some loud and trashy television show. (Television complicates our judgement of Disney's impact. His influence on America was obviously greater before the days of television, even though Disney has had a successful series of television shows. Since the coming of home television, Disney has had more competition for the leisure time of America's young. He is not the dominant force in the 1970s that he was in the 1940s.) Often, it was not a case of Disney *or* Lewis and Stevenson, but Disney or nothing—or *The Munsters.*

It was never Disney's goal to drive the rest of children's literature out of existence. His field was popular entertainment. He did not claim more. He grew so immensely popular, it is true, that he dwarfed other authors of children's stories. ("Dwarfed?"—no pun intended.) But there is no reason why a child taken to see *Peter Pan* in the afternoon could not have *A Child's Garden of Verses* read to him that evening. Added to a healthy balance of the children's classics it is difficult to see why one would be critical of the Disney presence in America, unless . . .

Unless you see in Disney's work something not only lacking in artistic refinement, but also morally and politically offensive.

Which is the case with some. The truly serious criticism of

307

Disney comes from those who find the content of his work unhealthy—who see him as the moral guide of the Archie Bunkers of America.

What is it that these critics dislike? Many things, but they share a common denominator: Disney's obvious affection for the traditional values of small-town America. In Disney's world, the well-scrubbed, clean-cut, apple-cheeked, self-disciplined, honest, open, brave, and kind are the heroes and heroines. Knights, fair damsels, cowboys, schoolmarms, football players, girl scouts, boy scientists and backyard tinkerers, upstanding farmers and frontiersmen, fill Disney's films. The women are always homespun and pure, the children open-faced and smiling, with no hints of dark neuroses and inner compulsions. And the villains are villainous. They are not driven to crime by "the system" or "society's injustices." They steal and kill because they are—well—greedy and cruel. The Disney films defend and seek to preserve our way of life, not expose its failings.

There are no hints that life in America, lived in compliance with the norms and values of our forefathers—representative democracy, private property, and belief in a personal God—need be dishonorable, shallow, or base. Quite the contrary. As one of Disney's critics puts it, he raised small-town, rural America into a cultural ideal, a magical land of material well-being and spiritual contentment for those who lived by its rules. In Disney's world, a boy called Wart could become a King Arthur, and fair maidens who are truly fair could sing with confidence "Someday My Prince Will Come." Honor does not require a dramatic alteration of the system, a revolution, the breakdown of "middle-class narrowmindedness"—that lesson permeates Disney presentations. Decent and hard-working Geppetto, the deep and understanding motherly love of Mrs. Darling in *Peter Pan,* any of the characters Fred MacMurray and Dean Jones play, Robin Hood's patriotic reverence for King Richard the Lion-Hearted, Davy Crockett's frontier wisdom, Uncle Remus' acceptance of Christian gentleness and compassion, Zorro's defense of the downtrodden. . . . A child reared in this Disney land would end up, according to Disney's critics, proud and pleased with his and Walt Disney's American way of life. Not the best way to encourage an angry radicalism in search of social change.

Making the rounds in the late 1960s and early 1970s was a full-length cartoon feature, *Fritz the Cat,* that makes the point

308

well. The creator of this proudly X-rated movie captured a style and thrust that pleased many of those who complain about Disney. The animator shows the "real America"—an X-rated world of hate-filled, pig-faced policemen; sex maniacs, pimps, prostitutes, hustlers; scheming, lecherous politicians and merchants; hatchet-faced racist clergymen; dope-fiend teen-agers. Better to be filled with such images than to dwell in Disney's idyllic land of noble Christians, say Disney's critics; better to shake up middle-class complacency and encourage impatience with American society. Drive out the illusions; tell it "like it is."

Moreover, say the critics, Disney's smiling and uncomplicated heroes and heroines are cardboard characters. They give no hint of the deep psychological drives that motivate human behavior. Disney acts as if Freud never put pen to page. He never indicates that infantile sexual urges and childhood bathroom habits have more to do with how we behave as adults than our loyalty to God and country and our free choice to do the right thing in difficult situations. Disney showed no grasp of the major intellectual developments of the twentieth century, they tell us. Praise and blame cannot be distributed as easily as he would have us believe. There are reasons why people do things (as with J. Worthington Foulfellow and Captain Hook), and children should be taught that. Villains are not *really* villains. Society is usually to blame. But Disney? He almost makes his audience think it was the most natural thing in the world for Pinocchio's nose to grow, just because he told a lie!

One of Disney's severest critics, after ridiculing and attacking Disney's failure to deal with psychological realities, showed his readers that he himself is not so unenlightened. He "understood" Disney's problem:

> One must suspect that Disney found in this story [*Pinocchio*] elements of autobiography, since he had himself been a child denied the normal prerogatives of boyhood. It is certainly possible that at least some portion of his drive for success was a compensation for his failure to find the father who had, in psychological sense, been lost to him since childhood . . . In any case, such an interpretation suggests why *Pinocchio* is the darkest in hue of all Disney's pictures and the one which, despite its humor, is the most consistently terrifying. The menacing whips that crack over the heads of the boys who are turned into

309

donkeys after their taste of the sybaritic life may
have had their origin in his recurrent nightmare of
punishment for failure to deliver his newspapers.
And, of course, one suspects the dream of winning
the neglectful father's approval by a heroic act—such
as rescuing him from a living death in the whale's
maw—must have occurred to Disney at some point
in his unhappy youth. [For the record, Disney admits
to having a difficult youth, but not an unhappy one.]
(Richard Schickel, *The Disney Version*, p. 232.)

The fact that Disney rode so high on the popularity charts
apparently means that Americans preferred Disney's simpler,
Biblical understanding of human behavior: that man was
created with free will in the image and likeness of God, and
therefore with responsibility for his actions. Disney's tales took
Americans (and people round the world—some of his biggest
successes were scored at European and Asian box offices) to a
high, cool, sunlit land; and to an enchanted world of broad
plains, deep forests, and swelling seas, where the brave are
brave, and the virtuous are virtuous, and evildoers are worthy
of blame; they are not morally neuter lumps of clay molded by
social and psychological pressures. Americans turned to Disney
for their children's entertainment, sensing—if not expressing it
in so many words—that without blameworthy villains there can
be no praiseworthy heroes. They showed no signs of being
eager to purchase a weary moral indifference for their children.
We all might not become King Arthurs, but there is no reason
why we should not dream of it as children. As Dr. Max Rafferty,
an admirer of Disney, phrased it:

Disney was the greatest educator of this century—
greater than John Dewey or James Conant or all the
rest of us put together . . . he launched into something unprecedented on this or any other continent
—compensatory education for a whole generation of
America's children. The classics written by the tow-
ering geniuses out of the past who had loved children
enough to write immortal stories for them began to
live and breathe again in the midst of a cynical, sin-
seeking society which had allowed them to pass almost completely into the limbo of the forgotten
. . . lone sanctuaries of decency and health in the
jungle of sex and sadism created by the Hollywood

310

producers of pornography . . . Many, many years from now—decades, I hope—when this magical Pied Piper of our time wanders from this imperfect world which he has done so much to brighten and adorn, millions of laughing, shouting little ghosts will follow his train—the children you and I once were, so long ago, when first a gentle magician showed us wonderland.

A bit overstated? Perhaps. But millions of Americans must have found something like "celluloid sanctuaries" in Disney's films. He was a private man; it would be inaccurate to say that he was a personal hero to Americans. But he did something people appreciated even more. He created heroes, heroes who have lived on now for three generations of Americans. They probably will endure for many generations yet to come. (There might never again be animated films in the same league as *Pinocchio* and *Snow White*. They might *never* become outdated.) But even if they fail to endure, the popularity they have enjoyed for nearly half a century is a high tribute to their creator.

A Man and a Mouse

Disney was born in Chicago in 1901. Even as a boy he was fascinated by the magic of drawing. A few deft strokes of a brush or pen could bring a blank page to life. Much of his boyhood was spent on the family farm. The barnyard antics of the pigs, chickens, ducks, and cows became, and remained, his favorite subjects.

He was not a great artist. He never became one. But after his family moved to Chicago, where Disney was able to take some formal art classes, he became confident he could make a living as an illustrator. He knew he would never paint a *Mona Lisa*, but he did think he could find work with an advertising company or a newspaper.

His job hunting was interrupted by a brief stint as an ambulance attendant in France during World War I (he decorated the inside walls of his ambulance with his cartoon figures.) Upon his return, after some legwork, he found the opening he wanted —with a Kansas City advertising firm, drawing cement blocks, tools, and farm equipment for sales brochures. From there he went to a Kansas City newspaper where he met another illustrator, Ub Iwerks. The two young men formed a friendship and later a partnership that was to endure from Kansas City to the heights of fame in Hollywood. Iwerks collaborated with Disney on many of the Disney classics.

Disney and Iwerks left the newspaper to form an animation service. Operating out of a small Kansas City garage in the early 1920s, they provided animated shorts for local movie theaters —ads for local merchants and novelty cartoons to fill the gap between the feature films. One version of *Little Red Riding Hood* was successful enough to catch the eye of a New York City distributor. He signed a contract for a number of cartoon versions of famous fairy tales. Disney and Iwerks would draw the cartoons and he would act as agent to theaters across the country. Disney and Iwerks had high hopes, but the distributor went broke and never was able to pay for the films the two young animators had completed. So Disney went broke too; he had pinned his hopes on the scheme and had borrowed money to expand his operation.

Rather than sit around feeling sorry for himself, Disney set out for Hollywood. He no longer had a cartoon company, and he had no money, but he had a suitcase full of drawings and a mind bursting with ideas. He spent some frustrating weeks making the rounds of the movie studios, but eventually was able to sell an idea to a Hollywood distributor. He called them the *Alice Comedies*, a series of cartoon shorts in which a real-life child actress moved through a string of adventures in a cartoon land of animated trees and animals.

These *Alice Comedies* were not in the same league as *Snow White*. In fact there was little to distinguish them from the other cartoons of the era. Flat, simply drawn characters moved about in a flickering sequence of gimmicky scenes. But it opened the door. Disney was able to set up a studio, purchase his basic equipment, and hire some assistants with the money that came in. It was not long before he came up with another character, *Oswald, the Lucky Rabbit*. Oswald, too, was a moderate success.

A business dispute, however, forced Disney to give up on Oswald. Oswald was selling well. Disney thought the profits should be poured back into production in order to refine the cartoon. More elaborate backdrops could be drawn, a smoother movement could be given to the cartoon characters with more

312

artists at work. It is doubtful that even Disney at this time envisioned the herky-jerky cartoons of the time being transformed into the wonderland of *Pinocchio,* but he did want to make improvements. He went to the distributor with his ideas, but was turned down. The cartoons were doing well enough, he was told. Furthermore, Disney was informed, if he didn't like the way the profits were being split, there were hundreds of other cartoonists in the country who would jump at the chance to draw Oswald under the existing contract. He found out, in other words, that he did not *own* Oswald. The contract he had signed passed ownership rights to the distributor. He could go out on his own, but not with the character he created. (Disney left anyway. Oswald was taken over by Stu Lantz and endured for many years afterward, but not with as many fans as the future Disney characters.)

Disney never made that mistake again. The rights to Disney films and cartoons since then have never been taken from the control of Walt Disney Productions. No Disney creation appears on television, for example, except on a Disney-controlled show. No other film in Hollywood is in this category. (*Gone with the Wind* was, until 1976.)

And who was the character Disney created to take Oswald's place? Does anyone in America have to be told? Disney dreamed up a squeaky but pleasant little mouse, first called Mortimer Mouse, then Mickey Mouse. Mickey came center stage for the first time in 1928 in a short called *Plane Crazy.* It is hard to believe, but the cartoon was a flop and Disney lost money. (Although the cartoon has made a bundle in re-releases since then.)

Audiences did not like Mickey Mouse? Impossible? Yet, it was true. The moviegoing public in 1929 had found a new love— the "talkies." Al Jolson's *The Jazz Singer* was the "talk" of the town. Disney decided then and there his mouse would have to talk, too. So *Steamboat Willie* was produced with Mickey gamboling in a sea captain's hat on the deck of a rattling river boat. The rest, as they say, is history. England's King George V refused to go to a movie unless a Mickey Mouse cartoon was playing. Franklin D. Roosevelt held private showings of Mickey Mouse films at the White House. The Encyclopaedia Britannica devoted an article to Mickey Mouse. A figure of him was placed in Madame Tussaud's Wax Museum. Africans and Asians lined up to see Mickey Mouse; by 1937, thirty-eight nations of the

313

world showed Mickey Mouse cartoons: Miki Kuchi in Japan; Miguel Ratoncito in Spain; Topolino in Italy; Musse Pigg in Sweden; Mikel Mus in Greece; Camondongo Mickey in Brazil.

The Mickey Mouse shorts became the vehicle with which other Disney favorites were introduced to the public. He got a girl friend, Minnie; a dog—the rambunctious and lovable Pluto; a sidekick—the affectionately bumbling, buck-toothed Goofy. And in one memorable feature, *The Band Concert,* a maniacal and abrasive duck was seen selling popcorn to the crowd while Mickey, in an oversized coat, struggled hopelessly to lead the band. Donald Duck, of course. In time, in fact, these characters all surpassed Mickey in box office appeal.

In the late 1920s Disney made the first of what were to be his many innovations in animation. He developed a method to fit the musical score to the flow of action in his films, to make music an integral part of the cartoon. Movie music was not new. The potential of a musical setting for cinema action was recognized even by the makers of silent films. Local theaters in the smallest of small towns hired piano players who ran through a score that came on lease with the movie print from the distributor.

Disney's problem was greater though. He wanted a score that would be *part of* the animation, not just set the mood. He wanted the violins to intone menacingly when a witch peeps from behind a tree, the tubas to boom when Dumbo plops on his backside, the trumpets to skitter as Mickey leaps back and forth across the enemy pirate's blade. The answer was simple, but enormously effective. It made sound almost as important to the impact of a Disney film as sight. Imagine Monstro swallowing Pinocchio without that hurricane-like symphonic accompaniment.

After standardizing sound speed at 90 feet of film per minute, or 24 frames per second, the musical tempo could be set as well —two beats per second, or one every 12 frames. Disney then had his artists make a thin slash of India ink at every twelfth frame, which caused a white flash to appear on the screen every half second when the film was projected—a flash on every beat. So a conductor assigned to orchestrate a Disney film could key his beats to the flashes and end his score precisely as the film came to its end.

Throughout the 1930s Disney piled success upon success. Between 1932 and 1942 he failed to win the Academy Award for best animated feature only twice. The innovative *Silly Sym-*

314

phonies, The Three Little Pigs, Pied Piper, Spider and the Fly, Old King Cole, and *Mickey's Polo Team* were remembered long after the feature films they accompanied faded away. Nine-minute Disney escapes into lands of wonder and straightforward laughter; magical potions, haunted houses, merry ranches, fairy tale kingdoms of old—Disney's world, a place where moviegoers were happy and secure even if only for a brief interlude in a world of depression and war. It might not have been very realistic, but it was life the way people *wanted it to be.* Tolkien and A.A. Milne do the same thing more poignantly, perhaps. But they are touching the same nerve endings. Animals do not know this level of aspiration, only humans. This is not the place to dip deeply into the Judeo-Christian understanding of man's eternal destiny and spiritual nature. But the longing in man that is satisfied only by the imagination's projections of something gentle and good and wonderful hints at man's identity. Animals have no fairy tales.

At the height of his success with his animated shorts, Disney proposed to his studio associates—his studio was growing by leaps and bounds—a scheme that staggered many of them and most of the experts who learned of the idea. Disney wanted to make a *feature-length cartoon.*

Snow White and the Seven Dwarfs took five years to complete. More than 700 workers were employed to finish the task. It cost nearly $2 million—two million uninflated Depression dollars. The cost today might well be five times that figure, if anyone in Hollywood still had the talent, interest, and creative energy to tackle something like it.

The critics were near-unanimous in praise. Disney's detractors did not come until later. The film was so unlike anything anyone had ever seen before, everyone was too stunned to look for flaws. We have become accustomed to the Disney magic, but imagine the reaction of a world that thought of "Felix the Cat" when it heard the word "cartoon"! Howard Barnes, the film critic for the *New York Herald-Tribune,* hardly a man who gave praise freely and easily, had the following to say after viewing the film:

> After seeing *Snow White and the Seven Dwarfs* for the third time, I am more certain than ever that it belongs with the few great masterpieces of the screen. It is one of those rare works of inspired artistry that weaves an irresistible spell around the be-

holder. Walt Disney has created worlds of sheer enchantment before with his animated cartoons, but never has he taken us so completely within their magic bounds. *Snow White and the Seven Dwarfs* is more than a completely satisfying entertainment, more than a perfect moving picture, in the full sense of that term. It offers one a memorable and deeply enriching experience.

A later critic of the Disney films added that
most of all the film exudes a feeling of joy, a radiant glow of happiness that is so persuasive that, at the end of the film, you're ready to believe that somewhere in the world there must be happy endings such as this—they've just got to be real. [True—but, as we hinted above, a Christian might add that these happy endings *will* be real in a kingdom not of this world.]*

As incredible a production as was *Snow White,* Disney was convinced that there was still another step that could be taken —an added dimension. No matter how talented the cartoonist, there seemed to be no way to capture the feeling of *depth* in a cartoon, the visual impression of moving *into* a scene. In real-life films we take this effect for granted. A camera placed in a canoe can capture the feel of gliding across a northern lake; positioned in an airplane, it can give an accurate visual representation of what it is like to face an oncoming fighter; clamped aboard a rampaging stagecoach it can make us feel the terror of watching a horde of Indians on horseback racing closer and closer.

But an animator works on a flat surface, in two dimensions. He can draw his objects in perspective—but how does he create the feeling that the viewer is moving *forward,* deeper *into* his picture? It seemed impossible.

Disney and his engineers refused to buy that. They came up with an answer that revolutionized animated-movie making: the multiplane camera. It was a camera with the capacity to shoot through separate layers of drawings spaced according to perspective. The process is complicated, but basically, the camera could move not only up and down and across the pictures being photographed, but backward and forward, *into* them in

*Leonard Maltin, *The Disney Films,* p. 31.

effect. It was as if the drawings and characters were standing freely in space, rather than on a film surface, and the camera was able to move between and around them. Sound complex? It is, but one need not be an optics expert to appreciate the results. Think back to the opening sequence of *Pinocchio*—as you descend from the sky, down into the snow-crusted mountain village in the Italian Alps, bathed in blue starlight; as you pass solemn church steeples, over winding cobblestone streets, until you spot the warm amber glow from the fireplace of the toymaker's cottage in the distance, and then drop onto the curtained and mullioned windowsill. That shot was not taken from an airplane somewhere in Europe. You have descended into a drawing! That is what the multiplane camera was all about.

The feature-length films, of course, were a smashing success. During the 1940s and 1950s came *Pinocchio*, the unbelievable *Fantasia, Dumbo, Bambi, Song of the South, So Dear to My Heart, Cinderella, Alice in Wonderland, Peter Pan.*

Disney branched off into real-life adventure films, too: children's classics *(Treasure Island, The Story of Robin Hood, 20,-000 Leagues under the Sea, Kidnapped);* historical adventures; nature films; light comedies *(The Absent-Minded Professor, Son of Flubber)*—and, just when many of the experts felt he had run out of steam, his Oscar-winning *Mary Poppins* in 1964. He also moved into television with his *Wonderful World of Disney* and *The Mickey Mouse Club.*

Not all of these productions were in the same league as *Snow White* and *Pinocchio* of course. Few of them were meant to be. Disney admitted freely that many of his productions were turned out mainly to accumulate the money needed to finance the more ambitious undertakings. But then not all of Shakespeare is comparable to *Hamlet* nor all of Beethoven in the same category as *Eroica.*

Disney died in 1966 after a brief illness. His company continues in his spirit—although most old-timers admit that it is difficult to maintain the same level of expertise and enthusiasm without the master around.

But the films made after Disney's death—even re-issues of some of the clinkers—do well. American parents prefer films with the Disney name on them to just about anything else on the market. They trust Walt Disney. He will never drag down

317

their children's minds or senses or spirit. At worst, he will provide an afternoon or evening of silly laughter. At his best—well, he will give us a tantalizing taste of, a brief glimpse into, that noble world of the spirit and moral imagination where we feel most at home.

Douglas MacArthur

13

Douglas MacArthur
Duty, Honor, Country

Does America have a Thor, an Odin, a hero comparable to the Nordic gods of war and plunder? A case could be made that we do: General George S. Patton, perhaps. There is, however, a noticeable reluctance in America to come out openly for love of war, war for its own sake, as Patton did. Instead, we seem to prefer men who fight—fight willingly, proudly, and enthusiastically—when they have to, and because they have to; men who fight for Duty, Honor, and Country. We prefer a Christian knight, a Sir Galahad or a Lohengrin, to a pagan warrior like Thor. Douglas MacArthur fills this bill for many. Far more in his lifetime than now, it is true. But at the peak of his popularity, when he was removed from his command in Korea, for example, even his enemies conceded that about 70 percent of the American people were solidly behind him.

What we have said should not be taken as a criticism of General Patton. George Patton's severest critics will admit—grudgingly, perhaps—that when the cannons roll and the war planes fly, he is the kind of man you need: the kind who wins wars. And there are some who hold Patton in the highest esteem. But usually these unreserved admirers are reluctant to tell their fellow countrymen exactly why. They might love war like a Patton—even be willing to echo his words: "Compared to war all other human activity shrinks to insignificance"—but they understand the rest of America does not agree; that most people, after all, are not like them, not cut out to be warriors. And that is a good thing—a sign of the Christian conquest of primal pagan bloodlust. Patton's admirers, in fact, most often will take refuge in a self-conscious grimace and an admission that: "Sure, I know, in peace a guy like that can be hard to take. He was kind of strange in a lot of ways." In their heart of hearts they might cherish the fact (or illusion) that they too are "strange" in those ways; that they are of that special breed of man—warrior, knight, cavalier, soldier. Still, they usually concede that it would not be desirable for a civilized country to be filled with men eager to take up arms, like the Vikings who pictured heaven as a place where they would spend their days splattering foemen's skulls with crushing blows from their broadswords.

In many ways Douglas MacArthur was like Patton. He too dressed and spoke flamboyantly—more so, in fact. No one ever mistook MacArthur for anyone else. His fine, expensive leather jackets, "scrambled egg" caps, wire-rimmed sunglasses, riding crop, and famous corn-cob pipe were known by all. Tall and erect, he carried himself with an aristocratic bearing, determined to serve as a living example of the high station in life he felt rightly reserved for the nation's defender—the soldier. (A noble, remember, was called "noble" in feudal Europe because he had accepted the solemn responsibility of putting his life on the line—being willing to die—to defend his fellow man.)

The difference between the two men lies in MacArthur's ability to put into words the reason *why* he was fighting. He might have thrilled to combat as much as Patton. He probably did (although often he was physically sick at the sight of soldiers killed under his command, whereas Patton is reported to have whispered to an aide, as they viewed the carnage on a battlefield in Europe: "God help me, but I love it!"). But MacArthur seemed more aware of, or better able to articulate, the nature of the cause, the mission, the noble goal of the American war effort.

And the thousands of American fighting men in those wars, and their loved ones at home, revered him for it. He provided inspiration for the heavy blood sacrifice; reassured and comforted, especially when the enemy became the expanding and aggressive Communist powers after World War II. He put into lofty language the nature of the threat to America posed by Communism.

If his words appear excessive and inflammatory with the passing of time—as they do to many in our day—it can mean only one of three things: either a) he was wrong in his understanding of the inevitability of an ambitious Communist drive toward world domination; or, b) the Communist powers have changed their stripes and no longer pose the threat MacArthur feared; or, c) America has changed, and become so much like the Communist "enemy" that we no longer see them as the enemy (something else MacArthur warned would happen). Let us examine these possibilities one at a time.

Communist Drive for World Conquest

It makes a tough row to hoe to argue that MacArthur was in error in his analysis of the global ambitions of the Communists. The Communist Party holds a Party Congress every few years in Moscow. It has done so since the Bolsheviks under Lenin took control of Russia through revolution in the fall of 1917. At every one of these Congresses—every one—Communists from countries around the globe, including the United States, have met to discuss *how* to spread Communism to those countries not yet in the fold. There have been differences of opinion over the best methods for doing so, but never over whether to try. In the 1920s, for example, a fierce quarrel developed between the supporters of Josef Stalin and those of Leon Trotsky, the two Communist leaders who were in the best position to take control of the Communist Party in Russia after the death of Lenin. Stalin wanted to build Russia into a powerful state, bristling with the best of modern weaponry and industrial might, and then use Russian military strength to carry Communism to the rest of the world. Communism would come to other countries "on the backs" of the occupying Russian armies. Trotsky argued, in opposition, that it was shortsighted and counterproductive in the long run to spend large amounts of time, money, and energy on Russia; that Stalin was excessively concerned about Russia's position in the world, and not concerned enough about Communism itself. Trotsky reminded Stalin's followers that a Communist is not to have a special affection for the country of his birth. He is a Communist first, not a Russian, or Frenchman, or American, or whatever. A Communist's loyalty ought to be to the "working classes of the world"—to use Karl Marx's words. Better to use all the time and energy, Trotsky argued, to help Communist groups in other countries succeed at a revolution like the one carried out by the Bolsheviks in Russia.

The dispute was eventually settled in Stalin's favor. Trotsky was forced into exile; Stalin assumed control of Russia. Trotsky was found dead not long afterwards in a Mexican hotel room with a mountain climber's axe buried in his head—at the hands of an agent of Stalin, most experts agree. Under Stalin's leadership the Russian state was launched on the road toward the superpower status it holds today.

But the point is that such disputes, and modern variations on the same theme, center on *how* to spread Communism. Even the oft-discussed "peaceful coexistence" and "detente" of today come within this framework. Those Communists who sincerely intend to give detente a try argue that it will be possible to demonstrate to the rest of the world the superiority of Communism during a period of peace with America; that without the worry of conflict with America, Communists in Russia will be able to build a workers' paradise that, by its example, will convert non-Communist countries, including America, without the need for armed conflict. Other Communists (the vast majority) support detente only as a smokescreen, as a ruse, a way of lulling the capitalist countries to sleep while Russia builds superior military strength. On Christmas Eve, 1975, *Izvestia,* the Communist-controlled newspaper in Russia, said directly: "Detente does not mean and cannot mean a freezing of the social status quo . . . Supporting of national liberation movements is one of the most important principles of Soviet foreign policy." Put it another way: the effort to build Communist subversive groups within the borders of non-Communist countries must not slacken during the time when the Russian state finds itself compelled—for whatever reasons—to let up on its efforts to spread Communism by *direct* military action. Detente, then, as Communist Party Chairman Leonid Brezhnev remarked, is merely another "form of struggle," to be used when open warfare has become an unacceptable risk. *Pravda,* the official organ of the

Soviet Communist Party, elaborated: "Peaceful coexistence does not mean the end of struggle . . . the struggle between world socialism and imperialism will be waged right up to the complete and final victory of Communism on a world-wide scale" (August 22, 1973). One can only speculate on the face Soviet Communism will show to the world when the massive military buildup going on in Russia reaches its goal—when open warfare will no longer be such an unacceptable risk, *for them*.

It would be impossible for Communists to renounce this dream of a world united under the principles of Marx and still remain Communists. Disagree about the best method to effect the conversion—yes. Surrender the hope for an ultimate world-wide victory—never.

Why? It must be remembered that the Communist countries of the world today do not claim to be truly Communist—yet. They assert that they are in a preparation stage: the "dictatorship of the proletariat," a government entrusted with the responsibility for training people to behave, and to *think,* as Communists. A "real" Communist, say the Communists, is one who has lost his self-interest, his desire to rise above his neighbors through the accumulation of personal, private wealth. A Communist ought not to think of himself as an "I"—an individual. His goal is to become part of a "we"—the human community —a fulfilled member of the perfected human community: a "comrade."

Obviously, a change like this in human behavior as we know it will not come easily. If most people are reluctant even to clean up their own blood-brothers' and sisters' rooms without some great extra reward, how will men and women work their hardest for a comrade halfway across town? Or halfway across the country? That is why the dictatorship of the proletariat must be so powerful and total. Communist theoreticians admit that the task awaiting this dictatorship is one that might very well take hundreds of years.

But for a Communist, it can be done. Human nature can be bent and molded to such a degree. Non-Communists, at least those who hold the Judeo-Christian understanding of man's fallen nature—original sin, man's inclination toward evil—think otherwise. The Christian belief is that men will behave as virtuously as in the Communist dream, but through God's grace and only in a paradise not of this world. (This is why many consider

325

Communism a distortion of Christianity—a heresy. Communism appeals to many who lose their religious faith, by offering an alternative idealism.)

For the Communist, on the other hand, the only heaven we will ever know will be on this earth. Communists are atheists—on high principle. They believe in no God or life after death. Once men have been trained to think as Communists—to become true comrades in the human family—an unprecedented flowering of the human potential will take place, which will be "heaven." The world will be filled with love and brotherhood and intense activity by one and all for the good of all; the whole world working together in the spirit of friendship seen among frontier families at a barn raising in a 1940s Hollywood movie. Arabs will work their hardest to provide oil for their Israeli comrades. American farmers will toil in the sun to feed their Pakistani and Russian brothers. African miners will go deep into the earth in search of the mineral treasures needed in England and France. It will take time, they admit. But it can be done. The job is to start changing man now, to point him in the direction of the Marxist utopia.

Now the fulcrum; the key. In this world of the future, the spirit of human cooperation will be so genuine and so all-pervasive that the state, the government as we know it, will *disappear:* "wither away," to quote Marx. Mankind will not need police forces or armies or jails or courts, or arsenals of destructive weapons. These things were needed to preserve the peace between competing individuals who wanted more than their fellow man. In a world of self-sacrificing comrades who want to advance themselves only *as members of the community,* they will become unnecessary. But there is the problem! If not all of the countries in the world have taken this step; if there are are some who have remained "greedy" and "selfish," who still seek after personal profit; if there are some who still have their armies and navies and bombs, they will move in and conquer the peaceful Communist brothers whose armies have "withered away." Thus, all the world must turn Communist before any one country can turn Communist (move beyond the dictatorship of the proletariat). The Communists *have* to be in favor of a world-wide communism—by their own definition.

326

The New Breed of Communist

But perhaps MacArthur did not understand that the Communists have given up on this world-wide ambition. Perhaps they do not really intend to do what they say. Perhaps it is mere rhetoric. Perhaps they are not intent upon following every one of Marx's principles. One might be able to argue this point intelligently in our time. But the point is that during MacArthur's public career the Russians *had* lowered the Iron Curtain around the ancient and Christian countries of Eastern Europe, bringing them by force into the Communist "brotherhood." (They got their foothold in those countries when their troops marched through in 1944 and 1945 on their way into Hitler's Germany, as the English and American troops moved in from the west in the pincers movement that crushed the Nazi state.) Later, in 1949, Communists aided by Russia took control of China through a bloody civil war. Russian and Chinese Communists then supplied the Communist dictator Kim Il Sung in North Korea, helping him launch an attack on non-Communist South Korea. MacArthur's reaction? They all along have been saying that they want to expand Communism everywhere, including the United States. They are starting that expansion. If we do not want to make the same mistake we made with Hitler (allowing an aggressive dictator to take territory without opposition, in order to save the peace, thereby encouraging him to expand until he had to be stopped with an earth-shaking world war), we had better stop them.

America never did respond to Communist expansion as vigorously as MacArthur wanted. But we did put up opposition in Korea. We did form organizations such as NATO and SEATO that promised United States assistance to any country faced with Communist aggression. President Truman did draw the line in the sand, so to speak, and threaten Russia with war if she continued to press into Greece and Turkey. President Kennedy did intercept Russian nuclear missiles being transported to Cuba, threatening to fire upon Russian ships bearing the missiles, even if that should mean war with Russia.

And the Russians calmed down—at least on the surface. Expressions like "detente" and "peaceful co-existence" were coined. There was an easing of tensions. But it must be noted that this relaxation *followed* the MacArthur-style threats. The Russians did not surrender their commitment to the words and predictions of Marx until they found out the words were not going to come true without a war effort costly to themselves. And Marx's predictions were not coming true because they were being met with a threat of American force. Would the Russians have abandoned their deeply held ideological beliefs if they were racking up success after success in country after country? Not likely. Why should they have? If they are Marxists, and Marx calls for world-wide Communism, and Communist expansion is taking place with a little help from Russia—why give up on it? Must it not be admitted, simply, that any changes in Communist aggressiveness we see in our time are a result of the American challenge to their ambitions? A result of the United States taking a stance halfway similar to that urged by MacArthur? If so, then MacArthur was not wrong in his evaluation of the Communist threat in his time.

Perhaps, after reading MacArthur's ideas on how to meet the Communists in Asia, a reader will agree with MacArthur's critics: that he was too belligerent, too willing to risk a major war with the Communist Chinese and the Russians; that Communist takeovers can be stopped without his "extremism." This can be argued intelligently. What cannot be argued is that there was not a Communist thrust outward from Russia and China in the late 1940s and early 1950s that all Americans who are anti-Communist would want contained; a thrust that was softened only by *some* American resistance.

Has America Changed?

Of course, if you do *not* see Communism as an enemy system, an evil, atheistic ideology that advocates a way of life hostile to our own, you will not want America to take great pains and to make the sacrifices required to check Communist expansion. MacArthur's willingness to go to war, if necessary, to stop Communism seems irrational to many in our time because they do not see Communism as "all that bad." We hear much praise of late from newspapermen, journalists, and television commentators concerning the valuable "reforms" brought about in China, Russia, Cuba, etc., since the Communists came to power.

MacArthur understood that just such an attitude was devel-

328

oping in America, and he believed that many were hostile to him because they did not want Communism fought energetically. These, he thought, were broadly sympathetic to Marxism itself. He died convinced of that. Others, he argued, were simply "appeasers"—those who championed slogans like "Better Red Than Dead." They would be willing to live under any political system as long as they were not called upon to take up arms. It was not that they loved Communism; just that they did not have an affection for anything else—our way of life, for example—fervent enough for them to die in its defense. Throughout his career MacArthur warned that these two influences—pro-Communism and peace-at-any-price defeatism—would drain Americans of their will to resist expanding and dynamic Communist Russia and China.

Whether he was right has not been settled once and for all. MacArthur's modern critics point to the period of cooperation and negotiation between America and the Communist world that is evident today; they shake their heads in disbelief, and even in contempt, at the man who might have brought on a major war with Russia and China. His defenders warn that the current detente is merely the lull before the storm, a cover behind which the Communists arm themselves for a future war that America might not be able to win; while we could have won any war that might have broken out during MacArthur's command in Asia. Some of his other defenders stress instead that we will not be *willing* to fight the war that is coming; that we will surrender because we have succumbed to the twin devils of Marxism and defeatism that he warned us about. Only time will tell if America is changing that much.

Army Brat

MacArthur was born in the Army. His father, General Arthur MacArthur, was an officer who served in the Civil War, in the Indian wars, and in the Philippines after the United States took possession there at the close of the Spanish-American War. As far back as MacArthur could remember his goal was always the same: to follow in his father's footsteps as a soldier.

On June 13, 1899, he enrolled in the United States Military Academy at West Point. During his stay at the Academy, MacArthur won a letter for varsity baseball, became First Captain of the Corps, achieved the highest academic record in 25 years, and graduated in 1903 with the rank of second lieutenant of Engineers.

His first assignment after graduation was in the Philippines. It was the beginning of a long and deep involvement with the land and its people:

> The Philippines charmed me. The delightful hospitality, the respect and affection expressed for my father, the amazingly attractive result of a Spanish culture and American industry, the languorous laze that seemed to glamorize even the most routine chores of life, the fun-loving men, the moonbeam delicacy of its lovely women, fastened me with a grip that has never relaxed.

His engineering assignments were challenging and plentiful. But, typically, high adventure came his way as well. While supervising the cutting of timber for a dock he was constructing deep in the jungles of Guimaris Island, which is located at the mouth of Iloilo Harbor, he was waylaid by two armed desperadoes. He was riding on horseback along a narrow trail in a dense rain forest when they sprang from the brush armed with old but deadly looking rifles. "Like all frontiersmen," reports MacArthur, "I was expert with a pistol. I dropped them both dead in their tracks, but not before one had blazed away at me with his antiquated rifle. The slug tore through the top of my campaign hat and almost cut the sapling tree immediately behind me." An aide to MacArthur, after surveying the bullet hole, so close to MacArthur's scalp, rolled a wad of tobacco from one side of his mouth to the other and drawled in a full Irish brogue, "Begging the Lieutenant's pardon, but all the rest of the Lieutenant's life is pure velvut." It was only the first of many close calls with death.

The dock was completed. It was used by MacArthur's forces when they landed to drive out the Japanese in the final months of World War II.

MacArthur remained proud to the end of the role he played in the Philippines, both during this early tour of duty as a young officer and later as commander of the United States forces in the Southwest Pacific. He was confident that the United States had something to offer the undeveloped areas of Asia; that the American success story could be duplicated, with some changes, in what is now called the Third World. He pictured a future in which Asian nations would be joined in friendship with the United States for the betterment of all. If representative government could replace rule by tribal chieftains; if industriousness, and pride in an honest day's work, could supplant a primitive contentment with subsistence-level agricultural life; if modern science and education could take the place of ancient pagan superstitions; if hospitals, roads, docks, and libraries could be constructed, a whole new civilization could be built in the Orient. And with American help, friendship, and investment these things could be done. It was MacArthur's dream:

"Here was western civilization's last earth frontier. It was crystal clear to me that the future, and, indeed, the very existence of America, were irrevocably entwined with Asia and its island outposts."

The modern tendency is to scorn, deride, or chastise such sentiments. We are told they are all too representative of an "ethnocentric" and "imperialist" mentality, a white-American drive to dominate the world; a mentality that must be eradicated from our consciousness. Indeed, the message in the late 1960s and early 1970s, found in many books, movies, and television shows, is that it is the American and European vision of life that is most in need of uplift and conversion. The biggest laughs in movies and television shows like *M*A*S*H* are supposed to come when some pretentious and pompous military type (usually a none-too-subtle caricature of Douglas MacArthur, in fact) begins to spout off about the duty to bring civilization and Christian values or the American way of life to the rest of the world. The Third World characters are almost always depicted with a quiet dignity and decency missing in the narrowminded American superpatriot.

It is a revealing tendency. The new mood indicates that Americans have lost confidence in their religious, political, and cultural values; that grave doubts have arisen about the worth of our civilization. MacArthur was eager to involve America in the development of Asia because he was confident we had something *good* to offer. Nowadays we are reluctant to "interfere" because we are unsure that what we offer is any better than what the rest of the world already has.

But it is not a question of "minding our own business," or of letting the Third World countries develop in their own way, or of respecting their cultural values. "Nature abhors a vacuum," as the science books put it. If a nation as strong as the United

331

States does not play a role in the world arena, a power vacuum will be created into which the Communist superpowers inevitably will be drawn. An American refusal to act to shape the world's development in the way we think best (for the world and ourselves) implies that such assertiveness is wrong for us, yet somehow permissible and praiseworthy for the Communists; that they have good things to offer, while we do not. Nowadays we notice a curious phenomenon: the same groups, newspapers, and magazines that attacked MacArthur for his "imperialism" are writing stories in praise of Chinese Communist attempts to build hydroelectric facilities in new African nations.

Over There

World War I gave the first opportunity for MacArthur to display the military daring and ingenuity for which he became world famous. In the muddy trenches of France he piled up military honor after honor: two Distinguished Service Crosses, the French Croix de Guerre, five Silver Stars, a nomination for the Congressional Medal of Honor (he did not receive the Medal of Honor this time, but did in World War II for his valiant action "above and beyond the call of duty" in the Philippines.) He was made an Honorary Corporal of the 8th Regiment of the Line, with the Légion d'Honneur Fourragère, and Honorary First Class Private of the *Bataillon de Chasseurs Alpins*, with the Médaille Militaire Fourragère—to list a few awards.

MacArthur commanded troops at some of the biggest and bloodiest battles of the war. Time and again, at Chalons, Chateau-Thierry, Sergy, Saint-Mihiel, Metz, the Meuse-Argonne, against the famed Hindenburg Line, MacArthur hurled his troops "over the top," often taking the lead across the open "no-man's land" toward the German installations. Riding crop pointing the way, the young officer, not yet 40 years of age, became a legend on the firing lines. Veteran commanders and battle-hardened troops agreed: they were in the company of a military man who was a cut above the ordinary. Before the war was over, MacArthur was promoted to the rank of division commander of the famous Rainbow Division—the 42nd. He was now General MacArthur, as he would be known to the world from then on. The letters of praise, the honors, citations, and medals came in a deluge.

General Pershing: "MacArthur is the greatest leader of troops we have."

General Gouraud: "The most remarkable officer I have ever known."

General Menoher: "MacArthur is the bloodiest fighting man in this army. I'm afraid we're going to lose him sometime, for there's no risk of battle that any soldier is called upon to take that he is not liable to look up and see MacArthur at his side. At every advance MacArthur, with just his cap and his riding crop, will go forward with the first line. He is the source of the greatest possible inspiration to the men of this division, who are devoted to him."

A veteran enlisted man: "If I were a regimental commander and wanted a divisional general I could depend upon to map my plan of attack, that man would be MacArthur. If I were a father and had my choice of the man to lead my sons, that man would be MacArthur."

A noncommissioned officer in the 166th Ohio Regiment: "He's a hell-to-breakfast baby, long and lean, kind to us and tough on the enemy. He can spit nickel cigars and chase Germans as well as any doughboy in the Rainbow."

After the war MacArthur was assigned as Superintendent at West Point. It was an interlude in his combat career he was to remember fondly. The sprawling campus, with its massive stone buildings rising from the woodlands high on the cliffs overlooking the Hudson River, always held a special place in his heart. MacArthur was too much the fighting man to stay content with an academic setting for long, but his years at the Point allowed him the time and opportunity to tackle a chore he was convinced was badly in need of doing.

We Americans display a curious quirk in our character. In time of war our fighting men are placed high on a pedestal. (The war in Vietnam was an exception, for reasons that become clearer when we look at it from the perspective of MacArthur's career. The American soldier in Vietnam fought as valiantly as his predecessors in earlier wars, and in conditions as difficult. But Vietnam veterans received few of the honors and fanfare, parades and rallies given to the returning heroes of earlier wars.) But once the enemy is beaten and "normalcy" returns, we tend to forget the military. The image of the soldier drops. We no longer honor him as a gallant knight-errant, a defender of civilization. The military man is disdained as a leech, seeking ever more funds from the hard-pressed taxpayer who creates the "productive" wealth of the country. We behave as if we think that each war will be the last, that all the bad guys have been beaten.

In the years after World War I, the tax dollars that were needed to support adequately the military academies were cut back in an economy move. MacArthur feared it would become impossible to provide a reservoir of high-quality soldiers to defend the country. He badgered the press and the Congress with the zeal of a missionary. He appealed to the Congress in formal presentations and drew up detailed reports and programs for reform of the curriculum at the Academy.

He was convincing. More money was allocated. The curriculum was expanded and improved to a level comparable to that of the best colleges and universities in the country; modern science courses were made mandatory, as were courses in history and the classics to insure that the cadets would be made familiar with the world's cultural development and divisions; advanced science and engineering courses were added—chemistry, electricity, aerodynamics, mechanics; language courses were stressed; physical training and participation in varsity athletics were required of all. As MacArthur stated, his goal was to insure "a course of physical, mental, and moral training which we believed was unexcelled by any institution in the world." It was a lofty goal, but when MacArthur was transferred to the Philippines in 1922, he was entitled to say with confidence that he had succeeded. The Corps had increased in size from 1,334 cadets to approximately 2,500. The roster of graduates who trained under his superintendency reads like an honor roll of the American military: two future chairmen of the Joint Chiefs of Staff, Lyman Lemnitzer and Maxwell Taylor; two Chiefs of Staff of the Air Force, Hoyt Vandenberg and Thomas White, head the list.

Canker in the Body Politic

MacArthur returned from the Philippines in 1925. He was stationed in the Baltimore area, where one of his duties was to organize the United States team for the 1928 Olympics. Another tour in the Philippines followed. When he returned stateside the next time, in 1929, it was as Army Chief of Staff.

During the years following MacArthur made an enemy. He placed himself squarely in opposition to groups within American society that he was convinced were inimical to our national well-being. On June 8, 1932, he delivered a speech at the University of Pittsburgh, in which he pinpointed those forces:

> Pacifism and its bedfellow, Communism, are all about us. In the theaters, newspapers, and magazines, pulpits and lecture halls, schools and colleges, it hangs like a mist before the face of America, organizing the forces of unrest and undermining the morals of the working man.
>
> Day by day this canker eats deeper into the body politic. For this sentimentalism and emotionalism which have infested our country, we should substitute hard common sense. Pacific habits do not insure peace or immunity from national insult and aggression. Any nation that would keep its self-respect must be prepared to defend itself. Every reasonable man knows that war is cruel and destructive, and yet very little of the fever of war will melt the veneer of our civilization. History has proved that nations once great that neglected their national defense are dust and ashes. Where are Rome and Carthage? Where Byzantium? Where Egypt, once so great a state? Where Korea, whose death cries were unheard by the world?

The reaction from the American left wing and its sympathizers was instant and clamorous. MacArthur was pinned with the labels that stayed with him all through his career: "militarist" . . . "racist" . . . "superpatriot" . . . "right-wing extremist" . . . "a man dangerous to American democracy." The criticism grew even more intense after the confrontation between troops under MacArthur and the Bonus Marchers in 1932.

In this explosive encounter MacArthur had to deal with a time-worn tactic of the Communist Party in America: the skillful use of sympathy for the plight of a group with a legitimate problem in order to stir up a potentially revolutionary anger against the American government. He did not back down an inch. As a result, MacArthur became a serious obstacle for the

Communists. He was one of the hardnoses who could not be won over, or frightened or shamed into letting the Communists get their way. He could not be circumvented; he had to be beaten. This point can be made clearer by looking closely at the Bonus March controversy and its implications.

As mentioned earlier (in the chapter on Will Rogers) it can be argued that the Bonus Marchers deserved their money. Will Rogers thought so, and no one called *him* a Communist. The marchers' basic demand was that as veterans of World War I, they deserved to be helped through the depression; that the government ought to give them, then and there, 1932, when they needed it, the money promised them at a future date: approximately $1,000 in bonus awards for their service in the European war. MacArthur, one of America's most vigorous pro-soldier advocates ever, was not opposed to the idea on principle.

But when a march on Washington was planned by a group of veterans with the intention of parading around the Capitol and the White House and camping out on the open lawn areas of Washington in order to pressure the legislators—that was something else again. Especially when MacArthur learned that Communist Party organizers had worked their way into the veterans' leadership. By June of 1932 a crowd estimated at near 17,000 had made its way to Washington. The men camped out in vacant lots throughout the city. As MacArthur states the problem:

> For two fruitless months they lived in abject squalor, making their daily marches to the Capitol, to the White House, and to all of the other sacrosanct federal buildings where they hoped to loosen the pursestrings of government. In the end, their frustration, combined with careful needling by the Communists, turned them into a sullen riotous mob . . .
>
> At night, morose men squatted by burning campfires listening silently to the endless speeches, always tinged with the increasing violence of Communist propaganda.

Finally rioting and violence broke out. The Washington police were attacked. A mob of more than 5,000 moved up Pennsylvania Avenue toward the White House and engaged in pitched battle with the police, who were outnumbered five to one. Gunfire echoed through the streets of Washington.

Immediately, in desperation, the Washington police called for Federal troops. The situation was beyond their control. Either the Congress of the United States would be forced to pass a law to satisfy the anger of a mob (a situation that could not be tolerated in a representative democracy); or the mob must be disbanded so that government by the elected representatives of the people could continue.

The Bonus Marchers were ordered to leave Washington and promised carfare home when they did. Those who remained were to be disbanded, and arrested if they resisted. MacArthur, with the assistance of two younger officers, Major Dwight D. Eisenhower and Major George S. Patton, was assigned that task.

What followed was an unpleasant scene. MacArthur's troops, with clubs and tear gas, moved in against American civilians armed with sticks, clubs, and stones. And the civilians were veterans of World War I, the brave doughboys who had come home to unemployment and poverty. MacArthur was described in some papers as riding in on a fiery white charger, bloody sword in the air, in full dress uniform, leading a trigger-happy band of cavalrymen—a would-be dictator mowing down innocent Americans.

The facts were otherwise. Not a shot was fired by a soldier under MacArthur's command. There were no serious injuries on either side. MacArthur had no sword with him. He had no white horse. There was no cavalry charge. Among those arrested that day were James Ford, the American Communist Party candidate for Vice-President; Emmanuel Levin, a leading New York Communist; and John Pace, an admitted former Communist. FBI examination of 4,723 Bonus Marchers indicated that 1,009 had criminal records, including rape and murder. MacArthur states that "not more than one in ten of those who stayed was a veteran . . . the Communists had gained control."

The Communists agreed.

A spokesman for the Communist Party at their headquarters in New York, three days after the riot, stated: "We agitated for the bonus and led the demonstrations of the veterans in Washington . . . We stand ready to go to Washington again and fight for the workingmen. We started the march from here for Washington and we will lead the way again."

Benjamin Gitlow, an admitted Communist, wrote in his book, *The Whole of Their Lives:*

337

General Douglas MacArthur, Chief of Staff of the United States Army, stepped in to prevent serious bloodshed after a fight between Communist-led veterans and police resulting in the death of one veteran and the shooting of an innocent bystander. It was just what the Communists wanted. It is what they had conspired to bring about. Now they could brand Hoover as a murderer of hungry unemployed veterans. They could charge that the United States Army was Wall Street's tool with which to crush the unemployed and that the government and the Congress of the United States were bloody Fascist butchers of unarmed American workmen.

John T. Pace testified under oath before a Congressional committee:

I led the left-wing or Communist section of the bonus march. I was ordered by my Red superiors to provoke riots. I was told to use every trick to bring about bloodshed in the hopes that President Hoover would be forced to call out the army . . . Moscow had ordered riots and bloodshed in the hopes that this might set off the revolution . . . General MacArthur put down a Moscow directed revolution without bloodshed, and that's why the Communists hate him.

MacArthur understood the motive for Communist-generated demonstrations, marches, and protests in a way many modern leaders do not. He knew that Communists do not protest in order to cure a social ill. Communists do not want social ills to be cured—not by a capitalist government. Their goal is to embarrass the American government, to make it impossible for it to function. Or, as a Communist might phrase it, to reveal the corruption and upper-class domination inevitable in a capitalist country. They seek to alienate the population of the non-Communist countries, especially the lower classes; to achieve a "polarizing"—a division into opposing camps—of the people; to make as many Americans as possible see the government as an illegitimate and tyrannical elite opposed to their interests—a tool of the upper classes, the enemy; to set the stage for revolutionary upheaval. The last thing the Communists want, in other words—whether on the Bonus March or in a campus demonstration against a local ROTC—is for the American system to work to satisfy a genuine complaint in a just and effective manner. The Communists organize a protest not to satisfy the needs of the poor, the oppressed, the unemployed, antiwar college students, but to promote the overthrow of the government. This is not a groundless accusation. Communists the world over are Communists precisely because they favor the overthrow of the governments in what they call the "bourgeois democracies." They admit as much. They take pride in it. It is their life's mission. Real justice cannot be obtained, for a Communist, until the coming of *his* revolution.

MacArthur was sensitive to this "role playing" of the radicals. He knew the long-range goal. Rather than sit down and discuss the "justifiable demands" of the radical leaders of the Bonus March as if they were concerned fellow-citizens, he treated them as the revolutionaries they admitted they were; as subversives in a plot to overthrow our way of life and establish a Communist dictatorship. He would not give to their revolutionary strategies an appearance of respectability. Compromise was out of the question. Little wonder he became the great villain for the radical left. He allowed it no room to maneuver. A country run by people with a MacArthur-type view of Communism would drive Communist groups from the center stage of political activity and paint them in the role of enemies of the public, where the campaign to win converts to their cause would be much more difficult.

The left wing's hatred for MacArthur abated, however, during World War II. Once Communist Russia became more concerned with the threat of conquest at the hands of Germany than with encouraging revolution abroad, those American "superpatriot" generals leading the assault against the Nazis and their Japanese allies were given a period of grace. First things first. The MacArthur who led the bloody American assault against the Japanese in defense of American interests in the Pacific was seldom ridiculed or vilified; whereas, as we shall see, the MacArthur who proposed military action against the Korean and Chinese Communists in 1951 was called a warmonger.

A most interesting parallel, by the way, can be seen in the ups and downs of J. Edgar Hoover's reputation. Shame and abuse have been heaped on his memory in the 1970s. Exposé movies and books pull out all the stops in an attempt to demonstrate that the head of the Federal Bureau of Investigation—the fabled "G-man" of the 1930s and 1940s—was an unbalanced bully who used his power to intimidate unfairly Americans using their democratic right to work for social change. Hoover was, by this view, a menace—sending agents to infiltrate groups of idealistic campus radical groups and civil-rights organizations; snooping on Americans connected with left-wing organizations (by tapping their telephones and opening their mail, for example); building a record-keeping system so complete that its very existence threatened every American's sacred right to privacy (he might have a file on *you,* we are warned). The picture we get, in short, is of a man who died none too soon; who might have established a police state in America if he had his way. It has been suggested, quite seriously, that his picture and name be removed from the new FBI headquarters in Washington.

But in the 1930s and 1940s? Hoover was a storybook hero. Boys shining their Junior G-men badges wondered if they could make it as agents, G-men, gangbusters. They listened religiously to *The FBI in Peace and War* on their radios. They knew their chances were not good. Only the cream of the crop could get to serve under "The Chief." But a boy can dream, can't he? Those agents—brave, sure; but, more important, they were smart—crafty, ingenious, sly. The best minds of the hoods and the Nazis could not beat *them.* They had the equipment and the know-how. Bootleggers? Ku Klux Klanners? Spies? Traitors? Kidnappers? The FBI would get them all. Death-defying agents would infiltrate these groups. With sophisticated electronics the FBI could find out their plans *before* a crime could take place. What could be better than that? Preventive crime-fighting. Fingerprint records and extensive dossiers allowed the FBI to keep track of the dangerous elements in society. Movies were made about it. Give the perky secretary a name and she scampers into this cavernous room where the files are kept. In the time it takes to say Jack Robinson, she's back with the information. That's crime-fighting for you. The FBI. Pictures of the most wanted criminals were published regularly in the papers and on post office walls. The radio shows, *Gangbusters* and *The FBI in Peace and War,* read descriptions every week of one of the ten-most-wanted so that the whole country could lend a hand to the professional crime fighters.

Hoover's agency—if the point is not obvious enough—was once praised and glorified for doing the things it is criticized for now. The same kind of investigation and surveillance that we are told should shock high-minded Americans won the audi-

340

ence's applause in the 1940s spy thrillers from Hollywood. It is undeniable. Watch the old potboilers on the late-night and weekend television movies. James Cagney, Alan Ladd, and Lloyd Nolan spent a good part of their film careers snooping, making supposedly illegal entries, and violating the right to privacy of the "enemies of American democracy."

The point? Hoover, like MacArthur, was pictured as a menace when he expended his energies against certain people and certain people only. It is the objective, *not* the methods, that draws the fire of his attackers. Those who are sympathetic to the goals and programs of the groups MacArthur and Hoover moved against were the critics of Hoover and MacArthur.

Exhibit A: In the late 1960s a radical student group at the University of Wisconsin bombed a research center where work was being done for the United States military. A young research assistant, with a wife and young child, was killed in the blast. These days Hoover is criticized for the actions the FBI took against such radical groups. After years of hiding, "Buzzy" Fine, one of the young men accused of the bombing, surfaced in the mid-1970s. Left-wing groups at the university and across the country helped raise the funds for Buzzy's defense. They excused Buzzy, even though he took a human life, because of his "idealism." At the same time, these left-liberals deplore J. Edgar Hoover's vigilance as a national disgrace. A man is a hero only when he chases the "really bad guys"—not Marxist revolutionaries.

"I Shall Return"

MacArthur found himself in combat against the Japanese earlier in the war than other American commanders. He was in the Philippines as commander of American forces in the Southwest Pacific when the Japanese struck the American naval base at Pearl Harbor, on the island of Oahu, Hawaii, December 7, 1941. Within days of the Japanese bombardment of the American fleet at Pearl Harbor, the Japanese moved land and sea forces against the Philippines. It was another step in the Japanese plan to complete a ring of Japanese-controlled territory from Japan up through Manchuria, down through coastal China, Southeast Asia, the Philippines, and up again through a planned network of island bases in the Pacific (Wake, Guam, Midway, Iwo Jima,

341

etc.), and back to Japan. If this blockhouse ring could be forged, the Japanese were confident that America would agree in short order to a compromise peace that would allow Japan a free hand in the Orient. Preoccupied in Europe with the war against Germany, the United States would be unable to spare troops and ships for a war against Japan—or so the Japanese thought.

MacArthur was driven from the Philippines early in 1942. A Japanese fleet sailed to the northern rim of the islands and landed assault forces that pressed down against MacArthur's American and Filipino armies. Outnumbered, MacArthur stood little chance of holding off the surging Japanese tide, but he resolved to fight to the last, retreating as slowly as possible, taking a heavy toll of Japanese soldiers as he went. Then, when his men were cornered on Bataan, a peninsula across the bay from Manila, and defeat seemed imminent, he could disband his armies into smaller groups and escape into nearby hills to wage a guerrilla war, pinning down large numbers of Japanese troops. That was the plan.

Washington, however, did not want its best general in the Pacific fighting in his shirtsleeves in a tropical rain forest. When the time for an American counterattack came—and it was already being planned—MacArthur would play a leading role. He was ordered to vacate the islands, escape to Australia, and organize the American and Australian troops being gathered there for the offensive. Before leaving he uttered three of the most famous words of World War II. He told the troops he was leaving behind, and the Filipinos who would bear the brunt of the Japanese conquest, that "I shall return."

MacArthur left his forces under the command of General Jonathan Wainwright. When the Japanese moved forward into Bataan, and Corregidor, a small island off the coast of the Bataan peninsula, United States troops suffered two of the worst and most demoralizing defeats of the war. Thousands were killed, trapped with their backs to the sea against the deadly Japanese steamroller. Others, including Wainwright, were captured and forced to march long and hard miles to Japanese prisons. The march became known as the "Death March." Twenty-five thousand Americans and Filipinos dropped from either Japanese guns, heat prostration, hunger, or thirst. In one of the last battles in the Pacific before the Japanese surrender, MacArthur personally led the siege against the Japanese soldiers of the 16th

Division, who conducted this Death March. As he remembered that day:

"The enemy's losses in the . . . campaign were terrific. . . . Their dead numbered 80,557 . . . there were no survivors from the Japanese 16th Division."

From Australia, MacArthur directed the famed "leapfrog" attack, the triphibious (land, sea, and air) assaults against the Japanese-held territories in the Pacific. The objective was to break the Japanese stranglehold over the Pacific sea lanes; to cut off their transport routes and to open up the seas around Japan for American battleships, troop transports, and aircraft carriers. The names are legendary in United States military annals: the Solomons, Guadalcanal, Wake, Midway, the Coral Sea, Iwo Jima, Bougainville, and Leyte Gulf. MacArthur did return, in 1944. One of the most famous pictures of the war, taken by *Life* photographer Carl Mydans, shows the dramatic moment as MacArthur waded boldly through the surf from his personnel carrier at Lindayen.

The whole story of the war in the Pacific theater is long and complex, but makes fascinating reading for those interested in the intricacies and drama of twentieth-century warfare. MacArthur did not always find the conduct of the war to his liking. There were clashes with other generals and with the authorities in Washington—over certain invasions, troop priorities, the division of the command, allocation of resources. He made some enemies in high places.

Still, when the time came for the Japanese to sign the surrender, it was MacArthur who was chosen to represent the United States forces at the signing on the battleship *Missouri* in 1945.

At the conclusion of the war MacArthur was one of America's most famous and beloved generals—a household word. The medals and military honors and letters of commendation rolled in once more. But MacArthur did not return to the states to bask in glory. He accepted, instead, one of the most serious responsibilities in the postwar world, supervising the peace in Japan. His job was to construct a peacetime Japanese government with which the United States could live in friendship and which the Japanese people could accept without dishonor.

Historians generally agree that he handled this enormously sensitive and difficult responsibility wisely and well. That judgement can be confirmed best not by a detailed examination of his

343

actions in the years from 1945 to 1950, but by the fact that to this day, Japan, the country upon which the United States inflicted atomic warfare, remains our close friend and working ally in the Pacific. Instead of seeking revenge, the Japanese today, living by the constitution drawn up under MacArthur's direction, seek constantly to improve relations with us. By diligently striving to incorporate basic American ideals of representative democracy and free enterprise into a political order acceptable to the Japanese mind, MacArthur was able to set the stage for the stunning national redevelopment that has made once-war-torn Japan the most prosperous nation in the Pacific; indeed, one of the most prosperous in the world.

More to the point: this American-assisted development was achieved without any significant Japanese resentment of American "domination." MacArthur proved that it was possible for an Asian country to work in partnership with America without being a "stooge" for American capitalism; to prosper in friendship with the United States while retaining a cultural heritage distinctly Asian. This was MacArthur's "imperialism" —American-assisted growth toward representative democracy and a free-market economy; Americans offering our political and economic achievements to the rest of the world. Arrogant? Proud? Pompous? Ethnocentric presumption?

But he saw it work in Japan! And the Japanese agreed. They never (except for their Communists) complained that they would have been better off if MacArthur had been less "assertive." If he had, it would have allowed the Russians to play the dominant role instead. Would that have been better? A Communist would think so. Who else would agree?

Crossing the Yalu

It was this dream for an American-Asian friendship that made MacArthur so uncompromising when the North Koreans launched their attack against South Korea in 1950.

North Korea? South Korea? Where did they come from?

In the months before the United States dropped the atomic bombs on Hiroshima and Nagasaki, the United States "persuaded" Soviet Russia to enter the war against Japan. This was a Washington decision that greatly puzzled and disturbed MacArthur. Why get Russia into the act in Asia? Early in the war he had pleaded with Washington to demand that the Russians open a second front against Japan along the Russian-Manchurian border. Russia refused, and State Department officials in Washington seemed not to mind at all. Maybe there were good reasons; the Russians were rather busy with the Germans at the time. Okay. But why invite them in now that they were *not needed,* now that the Japanese were near surrender? Why allow them to enter the last stages of a war *already won by American fighting men,* and secure for themselves a position of power and influence in China? (Actually, we needed the Russians even less than MacArthur suspected. We had the A-bomb, but even as highly placed a general as MacArthur did not know it until shortly before the bomb was dropped.)

Students of Asian history ask those same questions to this day. MacArthur suspected the answer had something to do with Communist sympathizers in high places in Washington. Or, at the very least, it had something to do with a "Russophile" mentality that made certain American statesmen eager to cooperate with Russia in administering a world peace after the war. MacArthur was troubled by this extravagant faith in the Communists. It led to a "giveaway mentality." If you believed the Russians were not really interested in world domination (or if you saw nothing *wrong* with that), you would want to invite them into positions of power after the Germans and Japanese were defeated. If you were convinced that the Russians were interested in guaranteeing free choice to the countries liberated from their Japanese and German conquerors—if you were convinced that the United States could work with them—why not? It was this mind-set that permitted the Russians to take what we now call the Eastern European "satellites"—Poland, Hungary, Czechoslovakia, etc.

MacArthur took the Communist belief in Communism too seriously to accept a benign view of Russian intentions. He was confident that the Russian and American partnership would break up as soon as the common enemies, Germany and Japan, were defeated; that the Communists would attempt to use their positions of power to bring Communism to as many countries as possible.

But his advice was ignored. The Russians were invited in against Japan, and given the victor's right to administer certain territories. North Korea was one of these; Korea was divided into two sections at the 38th Parallel. Russia occupied north of that line of demarcation; the United States to the south. The two wartime partners were to work together to reunite the countries eventually under a government acceptable to the Korean people. It never happened. A U.S.-Soviet feud developed—the Cold War. The 38th Parallel became the boundary line between two separate Koreas—one allied to Russia, the other to the United States (so it stands to this day).

In 1950 the North Koreans invaded the South. MacArthur was called up from Japan to command the U.S. troops stationed in Korea and reinforcements being transported from the United States. The United Nations, friendlier then to the United States' interests than now, requested troops from other member-nations as well to oppose this flagrant violation of the peace, an act of aggression. (Russia was boycotting the U.N. in a dispute over whether Communist China should be admitted to the world body, and so was unable to veto the decision.) In fact, the troops MacArthur commanded, including American, actually fought under the flag of the United Nations in this so-called "police action" to prevent the aggression against South Korea.

When MacArthur arrived the position was precarious. The North Koreans, equipped by the Russians and the Communist Chinese (the Russians had used their position in Asia to aid a Communist takeover in China in 1949), were sweeping down into South Korea, driving the South Korean army toward the sea. "For a time," said MacArthur, "it was touch and go. The Cassandras of the world gloomily speculated on a vast Asiatic Dunkirk"—U.S. and South Korean troops with their backs to the sea, being rescued in desperation by a fleet of American ships and planes.

MacArthur reacted with a stroke of military genius. Rather than organize his forces to meet the advancing enemy in a Custer-like last stand, he counterattacked. He planned and executed an amphibious landing *in the rear* of the advancing North Koreans, cutting off their supply lines from the North and, more importantly, surrounding them. He chose as his landing point the Inchon Peninsula, which juts out into the Yellow Sea just south of the city of Seoul, then in Communist hands. (It is most helpful to consult a map of Korea in order to appreciate this bold and ingenious troop movement.)

MacArthur selected the 7th Army Division and the 1st Marine Division to make the landing. He was criticized severely by more cautious military leaders. He would never make it, they told him. His troops would get bogged down in thick mud flats off the coast of Inchon and be picked off by the North Korean gunners like fish in a barrel. His transport ships sailed quietly and secretly from their bases, and in the darkness of night assembled off Inchon. MacArthur watched intently:

> That evening I stood at the rail of the Mount McKinley and watched the sun go down beyond China over the horizon. I had made many landings before, but this was the most intricately complicated amphibious operation I had ever attempted. Next morning we would have to thread our way over the shifting bars of "Flying Fish Channel," under the guns of Walmi-do, and skirt the edges of the deadly mud banks that stretched for 2 miles across the harbor. All over the ship the tension that had been slowly building up since our departure was now approaching its climax. Even the Yellow Sea rushing past the ship's sides seemed to bespeak the urgency of our mission. That night, about half past two, I took a turn around the deck. The ship was blacked out from stern to stern. At their posts and battle stations the crew members were alert and silent, no longer exchanging the customary banter. At the bow I stood listening to the rush of the sea and watched the fiery sparklets of phosphorescence as the dark ship plowed toward the target, the armada of other craft converging on the same area, all now past the point of no return. Within five hours, 40,000 men would act boldly, in the hope that 100,000 others manning the thin defense lines in South Korea would not die. I alone was responsible for tomorrow, and if I failed, the dreadful results would rest on judgement day against my soul.

The military judgement, in any event, was favorable. He took the chance and won. His troops moved in, driving the North Koreans before them. MacArthur put his objective succinctly:

> I directed the prompt seizure of Seoul to be followed by an advance toward the south. This would place the bulk of the enemy's army between the two giant prongs of my forces—the X Corps from the north, the 8th Army from the south. This would form the pincers, both the anvil and the hammer for the

stroke of complete annihilation of the North Korean armies.

As he predicted, the North Korean army broke under that blow. A demoralized and disorganized retreat ensued as ragtag bands of North Koreans fled as best they could back across the 38th Parallel. Trucks, tanks, jeeps, artillery were abandoned in the hasty retreat. Thousands were killed; the total captured was near 130,000.

Now, MacArthur thought, time for the mop-up. Move his troops north of the 38th and destroy the enemy's ability to reorganize; seize the North Korean capital of Pyongyang and force a surrender—the way you would in any war. But this war was not like any other war, he soon found out.

Newspapers, journals of opinion, members of Congress back in the United States began to stir up a hornet's nest. MacArthur wanted to go too far, they insisted. He should not cross the 38th Parallel. His mission was only to drive the Communists from the South, not defeat them militarily. (The same logic governed the conduct of the war effort in Vietnam.) A meeting was held between MacArthur and President Truman to clear the air. MacArthur records that he was satisfied by the meeting; Truman did not forbid him to take Pyongyang. The 8th Army moved in.

The occupation of the North Korean capital was important militarily, certainly; but also psychologically and symbolically. It signaled the fall of the Communist government; an American victory. The tide was not going to roll in favor of the Communists any longer. America had the will and the power to stop them; maybe even start the water flowing the other way. With a pro-American government in control of Korea, an attack against the Communists in China by the Chinese Nationalists from Taiwan was not out of the question.

The Communist Chinese sensed this as well. They moved massive troop concentrations across the Manchurian-Korean border. They supplied the North Koreans, moving their trucks across bridges over the Yalu river, which forms the boundary between Chinese-held Manchuria and Korea. North Korean planes were given refuge across the Chinese border as well. They would strike against American troops and installations and then flee for the nearby safety of the border.

In order to bring the North Koreans (and their Chinese allies) to a surrender, MacArthur decided it was imperative to do what

—in military terms—was the logical thing. Bomb the bridges across the Yalu, thus cutting off the supplies to the North Koreans, cutting off the guns and ammunition that were earmarked for use against American soldiers. Then pursue the North Korean planes striking at the American forces—wherever necessary—to destroy them. Bomb the North Korean hydroelectric plants on the Yalu to cut off the source of their power, even if, in doing so, a plane might accidentally cross the winding river into Chinese air space; even if a bomb might fall on the wrong side of the river, the Chinese side. The Chinese had chosen to aid the North Koreans in their war effort. If they did not want military action on their border, all they had to do was cease giving that aid.

But the orders came from Washington: "Do not bomb within five miles of the Chinese border." MacArthur was perplexed. Washington, concerned about the *possibility* of an accidental violation of the Chinese border, was going to prevent him from using the military tactics needed to defeat the North Koreans; even though the Chinese were *openly and intentionally* aiding the North Koreans. His troops would have to fight longer and suffer greater losses to ensure that the United States would not violate the territorial integrity of a country aiding our enemy. When else in history had we fought a war like that—hampered by an apparently deliberate "no win" policy set in the highest councils of government?

We were not allowed to violate Manchurian territory, and by violation of the territory I mean we were not allowed to fly over an inch of it. For instance, like most rivers, the Yalu has several pronounced bends before getting to the town of Antung, and the main bridges at Antung we had to attack in only one manner—in order not to violate Manchurian territory, and that was a course tangential to the southernmost bend of the river . . . These people on the other side of the river knew that and put up their batteries right along the line, and they peppered us right down the line all the way. We had to take it, of course, and couldn't fight back. In addition to that, they had their fighters come up alongside and join our formation about two miles to the lee and fly along at the same speed on the other side of the river while we were making our approach. And just before we got to bomb-away position, they would veer off to the north and climb up to about 30,000 feet and then make a frontal quarter attack on the bombers just about the time of bomb-away in a turn. So they would be coming from Manchuria in a turn, swoop down, fire their cannons at the formation and continue to turn back to sanctuary . . . One of those bomber pilots, wounded unto death, the stump of an arm dangling by his side, gasped at me through the bubbles of blood he spat out, "General, which side are Washington and the United Nations on?" It seared my very soul.

Why were the Communists to be treated with kid gloves? Some say that America feared a major war with the millions of Chinese and their Russian allies, a most unattractive possibility so soon after the end of World War II. It would have meant World War III, maybe an atomic war. Our leaders might have thought so, at any rate. In actuality, the Russians and the Chinese had no supply of atomic weaponry capable of inflicting substantial damage on United States forces. MacArthur saw another reason: defeatism—either a deliberate attempt to help the Communists win or a fear of warfare so intense that it amounted to the same thing.

He wrote privately to a member of the U.S. Congress, Joe Martin, Minority Leader of the House of Representatives, describing his fears and explaining the need for a more vigorous war effort along the Manchurian border. Martin, acting on his own, and without MacArthur's foreknowledge, released the letter to the press in the spring of 1951.

In that letter MacArthur was critical of President Truman's policies, for all the reasons outlined above. There is no doubt about that. And military men in our democracy are supposed to carry out war policies, not make them. Foreign policy is the prerogative of the elected representatives of the people. MacArthur always insisted that he did not intend the letter to become a public attack on President Truman; that he was merely replying to a letter from a member of the Congress of the United States, a branch of our Federal government (something that should be considered acceptable by modern critics of the "Imperial Presidency," by the way).

President Truman, of course, saw things otherwise. He un-

350

ceremoniously and angrily removed MacArthur from his command in Korea. He fired him, to be exact.

A Hero's Return

MacArthur returned to the United States to tumultuous acclaim. America had not held parades and rallies for any other individual since Charles Lindbergh like the ones organized in MacArthur's honor. This undisguised and enthusiastic affection led some of his enemies to envision the beginning of a military takeover of our government, led by MacArthur; that he would use his enormous popularity to stage a coup, making himself dictator. (The book and movie *Seven Days in May* feature a MacArthur-like Air Force general attempting just that.)

But MacArthur never even hinted at such a thing. He always embraced the American principle of civilian control of the military. He did not argue that Truman did not have the right to fire him, only that he was firing him for dangerously short-sighted reasons. He outlined those reasons in a speech before a joint session of the Congress not long after his return from Korea. It is a speech that should be studied—not just read, but studied—by all who are concerned about America's role in the modern world, especially our dealings with the Communist powers. He speaks specifically of Korea and the Pacific, but the logic can be applied to any theater in the world:

Mr. President, Mr. Speaker, and distinguished Members of the Congress:

I stand on this rostrum with a sense of deep humility and great pride—humility in the wake of those great American architects of our history who have stood here before me, pride in the reflection that this forum of legislative debate represents human liberty in the purest form yet devised. Here are centered the hopes and aspirations and faith of the entire human race.

I do not stand here as advocate for any partisan cause, for the issues are fundamental and reach quite beyond the realm of partisan consideration. They must be resolved on the highest plane of national interest if our course is to prove sound and our future protected. I trust, therefore, that you will do me the justice of receiving that which I have to say as solely expressing the considered viewpoint of a fellow American. I address you with neither rancor nor bitterness in the fading twilight of life with but one purpose in mind—to serve my country.

The issues are global and so interlocked that to consider the problems of one sector, oblivious to those of another, is but to court disaster for the whole.

While Asia is commonly referred to as the gateway to Europe, it is no less true that Europe is the gateway to Asia, and the broad influence of the one cannot fail to have its impact upon the other.

There are those who claim our strength is inadequate to protect on both fronts—that we cannot divide our efforts. I can think of no greater expression of defeatism. If a potential enemy can divide his strength on two fronts, it is for us to counter his effort.

The Communist threat is a global one. Its successful advance in one sector threatens the destruction of every other sector. You cannot appease or otherwise surrender to Communism in Asia without simultaneously undermining our efforts to halt its advance in Europe.

Beyond pointing out these simple truisms, I shall confine my discussion to the general area of Asia. Before one may objectively assess the situation now existing there, he must comprehend something of Asia's past and the revolutionary changes which have marked her course up to the present. Long exploited by the so-called colonial powers, with little opportunity to achieve any degree of social justice, individual dignity, or a higher standard of life such as guided our own noble administration of the Philippines, the peoples of Asia found their opportunity in the war just past to throw off the shackles of colonialism and now see the dawn of new opportunity, a heretofore unfelt dignity, and the self-respect of political freedom.

Mustering half of the earth's population and 60 percent of its natural resources, these peoples are

352

rapidly consolidating a new force, both moral and material, with which to raise the living standard and erect adaptations of the design of modern progress to their own distinct cultural environments. Whether one adheres to the concept of colonization or not, this is the direction of Asian progress and it may not be stopped. It is a corollary to the shift of the world economic frontiers, as the whole epicenter of world affairs rotates back toward the area whence it started. In this situation it becomes vital that our country orient its policies in consonance with this basic evolutionary condition rather than pursue a course blind to the reality that the colonial era is now past and the Asian peoples covet the right to shape their own free destiny. What they seek now is friendly guidance, understanding, and support, not imperious direction; the dignity of equality, not the shame of subjugation. Their prewar standard of life, pitifully low, is infinitely lower now in the devastation left in war's wake. World ideologies play little part in Asian thinking and are little understood. What the peoples strive for is the opportunity for a little more food in their stomachs, a little better clothing on their backs, a little firmer roof over their heads, and the realization of the normal nationalist urge for political freedom. These political-social conditions have but an indirect bearing upon our own national security, but form a backdrop to contemporary planning which must be thoughtfully considered if we are to avoid the pitfalls of unrealism.

Of more direct and immediate bearing upon our national security are the changes wrought in the strategic potential of the Pacific Ocean in the course of the past war. Prior thereto, the western strategic frontier of the United States lay on the littoral line of the Americas with an exposed island salient extending out through Hawaii, Midway, and Guam to the Philippines. That salient proved not an outpost of strength but an avenue of weakness along which the enemy could and did attack. The Pacific was a potential area of advance for any predatory force intent upon striking at the bordering land areas.

353

All this was changed by our Pacific victory. Our strategic frontier then shifted to embrace the entire Pacific Ocean which became a vast moat to protect us as long as we hold it. Indeed, it acts as a protective shield for all of the Americas and all free lands of the Pacific Ocean area. We control it to the shores of Asia by a chain of islands extending in an arc from the Aleutians to the Marianas held by us and our free allies. From this island chain we can dominate with sea and air power every Asiatic port from Vladivostok to Singapore and prevent any hostile movement into the Pacific. Any predatory attack from Asia must be an amphibious effort. No amphibious force can be successful without control of the sea lanes and the air over those lanes in its avenue of advance. With naval and air supremacy and modest ground elements to defend bases, any major attack from continental Asia toward us or our friends of the Pacific would be doomed to failure. Under such conditions the Pacific no longer represents menacing avenues of approach for a prospective invader—it assumes instead the friendly aspect of a peaceful lake. Our line of defense is a natural one and can be maintained with a minimum of military effort and expense. It envisions no attack against anyone nor does it provide the bastions essential for offensive operations, but properly maintained would be an invincible defense against aggression.

The holding of this littoral defense line in the western Pacific is entirely dependent upon holding all segments thereof, for any major breach of that line by an unfriendly power would render vulnerable to determined attack every other major segment. This is a military estimate as to which I have yet to find a military leader who will take exception. For that reason I have strongly recommended in the past as a matter of military urgency that under no circumstances must Formosa fall under Communist control. Such an eventuality would at once threaten the freedom of the Philippines and the loss of Japan, and might well force our western frontier back to the coasts of California, Oregon, and Washington.

To understand the changes which now appear upon the Chinese mainland, one must understand the changes in Chinese character and culture over the past fifty years. China up to fifty years ago was completely nonhomogeneous, being compartmented into groups divided against each other. The warmaking tendency was almost nonexistent, as they still followed the tenets of the Confucian ideal of pacifist culture. At the turn of the century, under the regime of Chan So Lin, efforts toward greater homogeneity produced the start of a nationalist urge. This was further and more successfully developed under the leadership of Chiang Kai-shek, but has been brought to its greatest fruition under the present regime, to the point that it has now taken on the character of a united nationalism of increasingly dominant aggressive tendencies. Through these past fifty years, the Chinese people have thus become militarized in their concepts and in their ideals. They now constitute excellent soldiers with competent staffs and commanders. This has produced a new and dominant power in Asia which for its own purposes is allied with Soviet Russia, but which in its own concepts and methods has become aggressively imperialistic with a lust for expansion and increased power normal to this type of imperialism. There is little of the ideological concept either one way or another in the Chinese makeup. The standard of living is so low and the capital accumulation has been so thoroughly dissipated by war that the masses are desperate and avid to follow any leadership which seems to promise the alleviation of local stringencies. I have from the beginning believed that the Chinese Communists' support of the North Koreans was the dominant one. Their interests are at present parallel to those of the Soviet, but I believe that the aggressiveness recently displayed not only in Korea, but also in Indochina and Tibet, and pointing potentially toward the south reflects predominantly the same lust for the expansion of power which has animated every would-be conqueror since the beginning of time.

The Japanese people since the war have undergone the greatest reformation recorded in modern history. With a commendable will, eagerness to learn, and marked capacity to understand, they have, from the ashes left in war's wake, erected in Japan an edifice dedicated to the primacy of individual liberty and personal dignity, and in the ensuing process there has been created a truly representative government committed to the advance of political morality, freedom of economic enterprise, and social justice. Politically, economically, and socially, Japan is now abreast of many free nations of the earth and will not again fail the universal trust. That it may be counted upon to wield a profoundly beneficial influence over the course of events in Asia is attested by the magnificent manner in which the Japanese people have met the recent challenge of war, unrest, and confusion surrounding them from the outside, and checked Communism within their own frontiers without the slightest slackening in their forward progress. I sent all four of our occupation divisions to the Korean battlefront without the slightest qualms as to the effect of the resulting power vacuum upon Japan. The results fully justified my faith. I know of no nation more secure, orderly, and industrious—nor in which higher hopes can be entertained for future constructive service in the advance of the human race.

Of our former ward, the Philippines, we can look forward in confidence that the existing unrest will be corrected and a strong and healthy nation will grow in the longer aftermath of war's terrible destructiveness. We must be patient and understanding and never fail them, as in our hour of need they did not fail us. A Christian nation, the Philippines stand as a mighty bulwark of Christianity in the Far East, and its capacity for high moral leadership in Asia is unlimited.

On Formosa, the Government of the Republic of China has had the opportunity to refute by action much of the malicious gossip which so undermined the strength of its leadership on the Chinese mainland. The Formosan people are receiving a just and enlightened administration with majority representation on the organs of government, and politically, economically, and socially they appear to be advancing along sound and constructive lines.

With this brief insight into the surrounding areas I now turn to the Korean conflict. While I was not consulted prior to the President's decision to intervene in support of the Republic of Korea, that decision, from a military standpoint, proved a sound one, as we hurled back the invader and decimated his forces. Our victory was complete and our objectives within reach when Red China intervened with numerically superior ground forces. This created a new war and an entirely new situation—a situation not contemplated when our forces were committed against the North Korean invaders—a situation which called for new decisions in the diplomatic sphere to permit the realistic adjustment of military strategy. Such decisions have not been forthcoming.

While no man in his right mind would advocate sending our ground forces into continental China and such was never given a thought, the new situation did urgently demand a drastic revision of strategic planning if our political aim was to defeat this new enemy as we had defeated the old.

Apart from the military need as I saw it to neutralize the sanctuary protection given the enemy north of the Yalu, I felt that military necessity in the conduct of the war made mandatory:

1. The intensification of our economic blockade against China;

2. The imposition of a naval blockade against the China coast;

3. Removal of restrictions on air reconnaissance of China's coastal area and of Manchuria;

4. Removal of restrictions on the forces of the Republic of China on Formosa with logistic support to contribute to their effective operations against the common enemy.

For entertaining these views, all professionally designed to support our forces committed to Korea and bring hostilities to an end with the least possible

357

delay and at a saving of countless American and Allied lives, I have been severely criticized in lay circles, principally abroad, despite my understanding that from a military standpoint the above views have been fully shared in the past by practically every military leader concerned with the Korean campaign, including our own Joint Chiefs of Staff.

I called for reinforcements, but was informed that reinforcements were not available. I made clear that if not permitted to destroy the enemy buildup bases north of the Yalu; if not permitted to utilize the friendly Chinese force of some 600,000 men on Formosa; if not permitted to blockade the China coast to prevent the Chinese Reds from getting succor from without; and if there were to be no hope of major reinforcements, the position of the command from the military standpoint forbade victory. We could hold in Korea by constant maneuver and at an approximate area where our supply line advantages were in balance with the supply line disadvantages of the enemy, but we could hope at best for only an indecisive campaign, with its terrible and constant attrition upon our forces if the enemy utilized his full military potential. I have constantly called for the new political decisions essential to a solution. Efforts have been made to distort my position. It has been said that I was in effect a warmonger. Nothing could be further from the truth. I know war as few other men now living know it, and nothing to me is more revolting. I have long advocated its complete abolition as its very destructiveness on both friend and foe has rendered it useless as a means of settling international disputes. Indeed, on the 2nd of September 1945, just following the surrender of the Japanese nation on the battleship *Missouri*, I formally cautioned as follows: "Men since the beginning of time have sought peace. Various methods through the ages have been attempted to devise an international process to prevent or settle disputes between nations. From the very start, workable methods were found insofar as individual citizens were concerned; but the mechanics of an instrumentality of larger international scope have never been successful. Military alliances, balances of power, leagues of nations, all in turn failed, leaving the only path to be by way of the crucible of war. The utter destructiveness of war now blots out this alternative. We have had our last chance. If we will not devise some greater and more equitable system, Armageddon will be at the door. The problem basically is theological and involves a spiritual recrudescence and improvement of human character that will synchronize with our almost matchless advances in science, art, literature, and all material and cultural developments of the past 2,000 years. It must be of the spirit if we are to save the flesh."

But once war is forced upon us, there is no other alternative than to apply every available means to bring it to a swift end. War's very object is victory—not prolonged indecision. In war, indeed, there can be no substitute for victory.

There are some who for varying reasons would appease Red China. They are blind to history's clear lesson. For history teaches with unmistakable emphasis that appeasement but begets new and bloodier war. It points to no single instance where the end has justified that means—where appeasement has led to more than a sham peace. Like blackmail, it lays the basis for new and successively greater demands, until, as in blackmail, violence becomes the only alternative. Why, my soldiers asked of me, surrender military advantages to an enemy in the field? I could not answer. Some may say to avoid spread of the conflict into an all-out war with China; others, to avoid Soviet intervention. Neither explanation seems valid. For China is already engaging with the maximum power it can commit and the Soviet will not necessarily mesh its actions with our moves. Like a cobra, any new enemy will more likely strike whenever it feels that the relativity in military or other potential is in its favor on a world-wide basis.

The tragedy of Korea is further heightened by the fact that as military action is confined to its territorial limits, it condemns that nation, which it is our purpose to save, to suffer the devastating impact of full naval and air bombardment, while the enemy's sanctuaries are fully protected from such attack and devastation. Of the nations of the world, Korea alone, up to now, is the sole one which has risked its all against Communism. The magnificence of the courage and fortitude of the Korean people defies description. They have chosen to risk death rather than slavery. Their last words to me were, "Don't scuttle the Pacific."

I have just left your fighting sons in Korea. They have met all tests there and I can report to you without reservation they are splendid in every way. It was my constant effort to preserve them and end this savage conflict honorably and with the least loss of time and a minimum sacrifice of life. Its growing bloodshed has caused me the deepest anguish and anxiety. Those gallant men will remain often in my thoughts and in my prayers always.

I am closing my fifty-two years of military service. When I joined the Army even before the turn of the century, it was the fulfillment of all my boyish hopes and dreams. The world has turned over many times since I took the oath on the Plain at West Point, and the hopes and dreams have long since vanished. But I still remember the refrain of one of the most popular barrack ballads of that day which proclaimed most proudly that— "Old soldiers never die, they just fade away."

And like the old soldier of that ballad, I now close my military career and just fade away—an old soldier who tried to do his duty as God gave him the light to see that duty.

Good-bye.

MacArthur could have been wrong in all this, of course. If the future truly does hold for us a period of peace and cooperation with the Russians and Chinese, as the defenders of detente say it will, he will be proven dramatically wrong. If, on the other hand, there will be a future war bloodier and far more brutal than anything that could have come about during his command, or if America surrenders to Communism in a "Better Red Than Dead" mood of resignation, then Americans alive in those sad days—those who remember and still believe in the America established by our forefathers—will look back on MacArthur's career with angry bewilderment and regret: "Why didn't the fools listen? Why didn't they listen?"

His speech in the Congress was certainly memorable. But the far better way to end a discussion of his career is the speech he delivered when he received the prestigious Thayer Award at his beloved West Point on May 12, 1962, just two years before his death. It is a speech that could point America to a new dawn, or serve as a lament, a eulogy, for an America we will never see again:

> As I was leaving the hotel this morning, a doorman asked me, "Where are you headed for, General?" And when I replied, "West Point," he remarked, "Beautiful place. Have you ever been there before?"

> No human being could fail to be deeply moved by such a tribute as this. Coming from a profession I have served so long, and a people I have loved so well, it fills me with an emotion I cannot express. But this award is not intended primarily to honor a personality, but to symbolize a great moral code—*the code* of conduct and chivalry of those who guard this beloved land of culture and ancient descent. That is the meaning of this medallion. For all eyes and for all time, it is an expression of the ethics of the American soldier. That I should be integrated in this way with so noble an ideal arouses a sense of pride and yet of humility which will be with me always. . . .

> Duty–Honor–Country. Those three hallowed words reverently dictate what you ought to be, what you can be, what you will be. They are your rallying points; to build courage when courage seems to fail; to regain faith when there seems to be little cause for faith; to create hope when hope becomes forlorn. Unhappily, I possess neither that eloquence of diction, that poetry of imagination, nor that brilliance of metaphor to tell you all that they mean. The unbelievers will say they are but words, but a slogan, but a flamboyant phrase. Every pedant, every demagogue, every cynic, every hypocrite, every troublemaker, and, I am sorry to say, some others of an entirely different character, will try to downgrade

361

them even to the extent of mockery and ridicule.

But these are some of the things they do. They build your basic character; they mold you for your future roles as custodians of the nation's defense; they make you strong enough to know when you are weak, and brave enough to face yourself when you are afraid. They teach you to be proud and unbending in honest failure, but humble and gentle in success, not to substitute words for actions, not to seek the path of comfort, but to face the stress and spur of difficulty and challenge; to learn to stand up in the storm but to have compassion on those who fail; to master yourself before you seek to master others; to have a heart that is clean, a goal that is high; to learn to laugh yet never forget how to weep; to reach into the future yet never neglect the past; to be serious yet never to take yourself too seriously; to be modest so that you will remember the simplicity of true greatness, the open mind of true wisdom, the meekness of true strength. They give you a temper of the will, a quality of the imagination, a vigor of the emotions, a freshness of the deep springs of life, a temperamental predominance of courage over timidity, an appetite for adventure over love of ease. They create in your heart the sense of wonder, the unfailing hope of what next, and the joy and inspiration of life. They teach you in this way to be an officer and a gentleman.

And what sort of soldiers are those you are to lead? Are they reliable, are they brave, are they capable of victory? Their story is known to all of you; it is the story of the American man-at-arms. My estimate of him was formed on the battlefield many years ago, and has never changed. I regarded him then as I regard him now—as one of the world's noblest figures, not only as one of the finest military characters, but also as one of the most stainless. His name and fame are the birthright of every American citizen. In his youth and strength, his love and loyalty, he gave all that mortality can give. He needs no eulogy from me or from any other man. He has written his own history and written it in red on his enemy's breast. But when I think of his patience under adversity, of his courage under fire, and of his modesty in victory, I am filled with an emotion of admiration I cannot put into words. He belongs to history as furnishing one of the greatest examples of successful patriotism; he belongs to posterity as the instructor of future generations in the principles of liberty and freedom; he belongs to the present, to us, by his virtues and by his achievements. In twenty campaigns, on a hundred battlefields, around a thousand campfires, I have witnessed that enduring fortitude, that patriotic self-abnegation, and that invincible determination which have carved his status in the hearts of his people. From one end of the world to the other he has drained deep the chalice of courage.

As I listened to those songs of the glee club, in memory's eye I could see those staggering columns of the First World War, bending under soggy packs, on many a weary march from dripping dusk to drizzling dawn, slogging ankle deep through the mire of shell-shocked roads, to form grimly for the attack, blue-lipped, covered with sludge and mud, chilled by the wind and rain, driving home to their objective, and, for many, to the judgment seat of God. I do not know the dignity of their birth but I do know the glory of their death. They died unquestioning, uncomplaining, with faith in their hearts, and on their lips the hope that we would go on to victory. Always for them—Duty–Honor–Country; always their blood and sweat and tears as we sought the way and the light and the truth.

And twenty years after, on the other side of the globe, again the filth of murky foxholes, the stench of ghostly trenches, the slime of dripping dugouts; those broiling suns of relentless heat, those torrential rains of devastating storm, the loneliness and utter desolation of jungle trails, the bitterness of long separation from those they loved and cherished, the deadly pestilence of tropical disease, the horror of stricken areas of war; their resolute and determined defense, their swift and sure attack, their indomita-

363

ble purpose, their complete and decisive victory—
always victory—always through the bloody haze of
their last reverberating shot, the vision of gaunt,
ghastly men reverently following your password of
Duty–Honor–Country.

The code which those words perpetuate embraces
the highest moral laws and will stand the test of any
ethics or philosophies ever promulgated for the uplift of mankind. Its requirements are for the things
that are right, and its restraints are from the things
that are wrong. The soldier, above all other men, is
required to practice the greatest act of religious
training—sacrifice. In battle and in the face of danger and death, he discloses those divine attributes
which his Maker gave when He created man in His
own image. No physical courage and no brute instinct can take the place of the Divine Help which
alone can sustain him. However horrible the incidents of war may be, the soldier who is called upon
to offer and to give his life for his country is the
noblest development of mankind.

You now face a new world—a world of change.
The thrust into outer space of the satellites, spheres,
and missiles marked the beginning of another epoch
in the long story of mankind—the chapter of the
space age. In the five or more billions of years the
scientists tell us it has taken to form the earth, in the
three or more billion years of development of the
human race, there has never been a greater, a more
abrupt or staggering evolution. We deal now not
with things of this world alone, but with the illimita-
ble distances and as yet unfathomed mysteries of the
universe. We are reaching out for a new and bound-
less frontier. We speak in strange terms: of harnessing the cosmic energy; of making winds and tides
work for us; of creating unheard-of synthetic materials to supplement or even replace our old standard
basics; of purifying sea water for our drink; of mining
ocean floors for new fields of wealth and food; of
disease preventatives to expand life into the hundreds of years; of controlling the weather for a more
equitable distribution of heat and cold, of rain and

shine; of space ships to the moon; of the primary
target in war, no longer limited to the armed forces
of an enemy, but instead to include his civil populations; of ultimate conflict between a united human
race and the sinister forces of some other planetary
galaxy; of such dreams and fantasies as to make life
the most exciting of all time.

And through all this welter of change and development, your mission remains fixed, determined, invio-
lable—it is to win our wars. Everything else in your
professional career is but a corollary to this vital dedication. All other public purposes, all other public
projects, all other public needs, great or small, will
find others for their accomplishment; but you are the
ones who are trained to fight; yours is the profession
of arms—the will to win, the sure knowledge that in
war there is no substitute for victory; that if you lose,
the nation will be destroyed; that the very obsession
of your public service must be Duty–Honor–Country. Others will debate the controversial issues, national and international, which divide man's minds;
but serene, calm, aloof, you stand as the nation's war
guardian, as its life-guard from the raging tides of
international conflict; as its gladiator in the arena of
battle. For a century and a half, you have defended,
guarded, and protected its hallowed traditions of liberty and freedom, of right and justice. Let civilian
voices argue the merits or demerits of our processes
of government; whether our strength is being
sapped by deficit financing, indulged in too long; by
federal paternalism grown too mighty; by power
groups grown too arrogant; by politics grown too
corrupt; by crime grown too rampant; by morals
grown too low; by taxes grown too high; by extrem-
ists grown too violent; whether our personal liberties
are as thorough and complete as they should be.
These great national problems are not for your professional participation or military solution. Your
guidepost stands out like a tenfold beacon in the
night—Duty–Honor–Country.

You are the leaven which binds together the entire
fabric of our national system of defense. From your

365

ranks come the great captains who hold the nation's destiny in their hands the moment the war tocsin sounds. The Long Gray Line has never failed us. Were you to do so, a million ghosts in olive drab, in brown khaki, in blue and gray, would rise from their white crosses thundering those magic words—Duty–Honor–Country.

This does not mean that you are warmongers. On the contrary, the soldier, above all other people, prays for peace, for he must suffer and bear the deepest wounds and scars of war. But always in our ears ring the ominous words of Plato, that wisest of all philosophers, "Only the dead have seen the end of war."

The shadows are lengthening for me. The twilight is here. My days of old have vanished tone and tint; they have gone glimmering through the dreams of things that were. Their memory is one of wondrous beauty, watered by tears, and coaxed and caressed by the smiles of yesterday. I listen vainly, but with thirsty ear, for the witching melody of faint bugles blowing reveille, of far drums beating the long roll. In my dreams I hear again the crash of guns, the rattle of musketry, the strange mournful mutter of the battlefield. But in the evening of my memory, always I come back to West Point. Always there echoes and reechoes in my ears—Duty–Honor–Country.

Today marks my final roll call with you. But I want you to know that when I cross the river my last conscious thoughts will be of the Corps—and the Corps —and the Corps.

I bid you farewell.

Reading between the Lines

Chapter 1: Daniel Boone

1. In what way did the western frontier add a dimension to Daniel Boone's life often missing in the modern day and age? Is America healthier without an obvious frontier, or do we need a "new frontier"?

2. Daniel Boone—by all accounts—seemed to like the Indians and to enjoy the Indian life, often going to great pains to become fully accepted as an equal by neighboring tribes. Was it hypocritical for such a man to become the redoubtable Indian fighter of American history?

3. Explore the full implications of Boone's knowing participation in the illegal purchase of Indian lands in Kentucky. To be specific: Would you defend Boone's decision to "purchase" land from Indian tribes that did not even claim they owned it?

4. Is it possible to construct—even now, over two hundred years later, with all the advantages of hindsight—a realistic compromise that would have allowed colonial whites and their descendants to live in peace with the Indian and his way of life?

5. It could be said that Daniel Boone was not truly a "civilized man": not a man who felt at ease in the company of the more cultured, educated, and refined people of his time. Is that a serious defect in a man? What does one lose by living like a Daniel Boone? What does one lose by living the opposite way —in the urban or suburban environment of today?

Chapter 2: George Washington

1. What is it about the legends of Washington's boyhood (the cherry tree story, etc.) that seems to offend the taste and values of many modern young Americans? Why do stories that stress honesty, piety, courage, self-discipline, purity, and patriotism seem "corny" and "square" to some young people today?

2. George Washington went from being ardent supporter of his king, to revolutionary, to no-nonsense President of his country—a defender of law and order and an antirevolutionary. Is this inconsistent?

3. Discuss in general outline the reasons why Washington decided to break with the British Crown. Was he disloyal? Was he a traitor?

4. Discuss Washington's position toward the Jeffersonians and the Hamiltonians. Of what did he hope to remind those working for one or the other point of view?

5. Washington warned against "entangling alliances." Would he favor modern American military alliances such as NATO? Defend your position by referring to the goals of Washington as head of the new American nation-state.

Chapter 3: Robert E. Lee

1. It is common knowledge that Robert E. Lee opposed slavery. What was his proposal for ending slavery in America? Was it at all realistic? Could it be argued that even if his proposal would not have freed the slaves as quickly as Lincoln's approach did, it would have been preferable to the horrors of the Civil War, and more effective in the long run? Are the responses of modern blacks and modern whites bound to be different on this point?

2. When we hear the word "chivalry" we usually think of the Middle Ages and knights in armor. Yet Robert E. Lee and other military men, North and South, often used the word. What did they mean by it?

3. Contrast Lee's view of the nature of the political bond between the individual states and the federal government (a "confederacy") with that of Lincoln, and with the view of most modern Americans.

368

4. Was General Sherman's view of war a return to an ancient and primitive barbarism, or merely a more realistic view of the nature of warfare in the modern age—a healthy refusal to sentimentalize combat?

Chapter 4: Abraham Lincoln

1. Could one make a case that Lincoln's frontier boyhood gave him a view of the future of America that was irreconcilable with the Southern slaveholding view?

2. What was the "deal" that Lincoln offered the slaveholding states *before* the outbreak of the Civil War? Do the compromises offered in that deal lower a modern reader's estimate of Lincoln's character?

3. Why did Lincoln find the stakes at Sumter so crucial? Why was he willing to risk war at this time when he had tried so hard to avoid it earlier?

4. In the Gettysburg Address Lincoln adopted a new, less conciliatory attitude toward the existence of slavery in the South. How can this new view of the union between the states be explained? Was it a new idea that Lincoln dreamed up and then forced on the South? Did Lincoln see it that way? (He did not. The question is why not.)

5. What might America look like today if the Confederate understanding of the union between the States had emerged victorious after the Civil War? (It could be interesting to take both sides here—picture a thriving, free, and prosperous America living by the South's idea of a confederation of sovereign states; then project some disasters that might have befallen our country had it been organized in such a way.)

Chapter 5: William Jennings Bryan

1. Why did the gold standard seem such a crucial issue to Bryan?

2. Bryan was known as a defender of the private property rights of the American farmer. Why then was he so anxious to have the government take action against the leaders of Amer-

ica's wealthy industries—to limit *their* private property rights?

3. How was Bryan able to reconcile his belief in the accuracy of the Bible with the discoveries of modern science?

4. Was Bryan's trust in the opinions of the average American an unqualified trust in the citizens of all countries at all times in history? Or did he think there was something "special" about the average American that made him worthy of democracy?

5. Has the theory of evolution become the "official" view of the origin of man in America's public schools? Has Bryan lost this fight? Or is it still a live issue?

Chapter 6: Thomas Alva Edison

1. Can Edison's failure in grade school be attributed to his superior intellectual ability? Do most superior students find problems with a school system set up for the average student? Should all school systems have separate facilities for the gifted student?

2. Discuss why the electromagnet was of such crucial importance in the development of electric power.

3. What physical property of the spoken word was the key to the reproduction of sound by people like Bell and Edison?

4. How would a defender of Thomas Edison's contributions to the human race answer the charge that electronic technology has disrupted the "normal" and "natural" relation between humans and their environment?

5. Which of Edison's inventions has proven to be the most instrumental in changing the quality of human life?

Chapter 7: Walter Reed

1. Contrast Reed's view of the responsibilities of a doctor with the attitudes of the doctors he found so disreputable during his years as a health inspector in New York City. Are modern doctors more like Reed or like the New York doctors he criticized?

2. Outline the probable origin and early history of Yellow Jack in North and South America.

3. List the causes of Yellow Jack that were thought

most probable before Reed's experiments.

4. What led Reed to suspect that a mosquito might be the carrier of this dreaded disease?

5. Why did the time between mosquito bites become so important an issue in Reed's controlled experiment?

Chapter 8: Charles Lindbergh

1. Why did airplanes fascinate Lindbergh? What did he picture for the world once the airplane became a useable tool of man? Was he right?

2. What did Lindbergh hope to prove by his trip across the Atlantic?

3. Can Lindbergh's reaction to the experience of flight be put into words, or is it too personal and mystical? (Reading *The Spirit of St. Louis* in its entirety would be helpful here. This might end up being the most enjoyable extra schoolwork you will ever undertake.)

4. Picture yourself in the cockpit with Lindy. What would be the most frightening moment of the flight?

5. Why did Lindbergh become so popular a hero so quickly? What did Americans see in him?

Chapter 9: Will Rogers

1. Could a case be made that there was an element of ignorance and a trace of jealousy in Rogers' attacks on the rich and well-educated? Or was he a voice of the noble underdog against ruthless exploiters? Or was there some of both in him?

2. How would one describe Rogers' scorn for Communists? It is not likely that he read seriously the works of Communist theorists. His reaction was based more on personal observation. What did he notice about Communists and Communism that he disliked?

3. What was it about Wall Street investors that offended Rogers? It was not just that they were rich. Rogers himself was rich. What was it?

4. What did Rogers mean by the "installment plan" view of

371

life which he felt was draining the moral energy of the American people?

5. There is a curious mixture of advice in Rogers' foreign-policy recommendations. He seems to advocate increased military spending; at the same time he wants to avoid conflict situations abroad. Is that self-contradictory? Why the increased military spending if he does not want to use it?

Chapter 10: Babe Ruth

1. What was it about America in the 1920's and 1930's that led so many Americans to idolize Ruth? Would he be acclaimed in quite the same way today?

2. For the sports purists: Were the sportswriters right when they argued that being a pitcher actually helped Ruth develop his famous home run swing?

3. Why is Yankee Stadium called "The House That Ruth Built?"

4. Why was it that Ruth's reputation as a "high liver" did not detract from his fame?

Chapter 11: Eddie Rickenbacker

1. Why did Rickenbacker appreciate life in America even as a boy, and even though his immigrant parents never rose very far above what we would now call the poverty level?

2. Discuss Rickenbacker's view of a job as an opportunity to prove himself and better himself by doing his best for his employer at all times? What would happen to a worker today if he approached his job with such a conscientious attitude?

3. Is it possible to put into words the fascination men like Rickenbacker feel for machinery? Often men who work with their hands are not very wordy and cannot express this idea themselves. John Steinbeck was an exception. Read the sections of *The Grapes of Wrath* which tell of the trials of keeping an old pickup truck on the road between Oklahoma and California.

4. How can we account for the aura of excitement and pleas-

ure that surrounded the air combat of Captain Eddie during World War I, when in our time almost everyone seems to be greatly concerned with the horrors and inhumanity of war? Have we become more humane? Or less courageous? Or something else?

5. Re-read Rickenbacker's Code of Ethics. Then try to summarize what it was he feared about socialism.

Chapter 12: Walt Disney

1. What in Disney's films offends some modern critics? Can this criticism be answered?

2. How would a Walt Disney who accepted the criticism above change his approach to animated cartoons and historical adventures?

3. What was the multiplane camera and why was it such an important improvement in animated films?

4. It has been implied that Disney's popularity is rooted in his ability to touch a spiritual longing in people—perhaps that the fantasy world of a Disney film is attractive to us because it gives us a glimpse of the world the way we wish it would be. What do the major religions in America tell us about such a thought?

5. Choose a favorite Disney film or two, think back on it, and try to recall why your parents took you to see it. What were the ideals and principles they were trying to develop in you through the Disney film?

Chapter 13: Douglas MacArthur

1. In our time the idea of American "interference" in the development of the political and economic life of Asian and African countries is met with condemnation by many—especially in American schools. It is called imperialistic. MacArthur, on the other hand, was proud of the role he played—"interfering"—in Asian political development. Why the difference?

2. What made MacArthur oppose Communism? Why would he care about the way Russians and Chinese run their countries? And why would he not regard Communists in the United

States as just another political party working to spread its ideas?

3. How did MacArthur's opinion of the Communists active in the Bonus March differ from the way politicians view various left-wing Marxists involved in demonstrations and protests today?

4. In the Korean War MacArthur was ordered to fight very differently from the way he was expected to wage World War II against the Japanese. To be blunt, he was ordered not to win. Why the difference in President Truman's eyes? Why did MacArthur disagree?

5. After reading the speech MacArthur gave before the Congress when he was recalled from the Korean war, what position do you suppose he might take on a variety of global hot spots, e.g., the Middle East, the Berlin Wall, Korea, South Africa, Cuba. What do you think his position would have been on the war in Vietnam? (Be careful . . . the answers here are not that obvious . . . and they are conjecture.)